Advanced Research Methods in Psychology

How do you perform a MANOVA? What is grounded theory? How do you draw up a repertory grid? These, and many other questions are addressed in this wide-ranging handbook of methods and analytic techniques which uniquely covers both quantitative and qualitative methods.

Based on a broad survey of undergraduate curricula, the book takes curious readers through all of the methods that are taught on psychology courses worldwide, from advanced ANOVA statistics through regression models to test construction, qualitative research and other more unusual techniques such as Q methodology, meta-analysis and log-linear analysis. Each technique is illustrated by recent examples from the literature. There are also chapters on ethics, significance testing, and writing for publication and research proposals.

Advanced Research Methods in Psychology will provide an invaluable resource for advanced undergraduates, postgraduates and researchers who need a readable, contemporary and eclectic reference of advanced methods currently in use in psychological research.

David C. Giles is Senior Lecturer in Psychology at Coventry University with a particular interest in psychology of the media. He has published in books and journals using a mixture of quantitative and qualitative methods.

Advanced Research Methods in Psychology

David C. Giles

First published 2002 by Routledge
27 Church Road, Hove, East Sussex, BN3 2FA

Simultaneously published in the USA and Canada
by Routledge
29 West 35th Street, New York, NY 10001

Routledge is an imprint of the Taylor & Francis Group

© 2002 David Giles

Typeset in 10/12pt Times by Graphicraft Limited, Hong Kong
Printed and bound in Great Britain by Biddles Ltd,
Guildford and King's Lynn
Cover design by Lisa Dynan

British Library Cataloguing in Publication Data
A catalogue record for this book is available
from the British Library

Library of Congress Cataloging in Publication Data
Giles, David, 1964–
    Advanced research methods in psychology / David C. Giles.
        p. cm.
    Includes bibliographical references and index.
    ISBN 0-415-22771-2
    1. Psychology—Research—Methodology.   2. Psychology,
Experimental.   I. Title.
    BF76.5 G55 2002
    150'.7'2—dc21   2002190394

ISBN 0-415-22771-2

Contents

Figures

Tables

Preface

The idea for this book came from Vivien Ward, formerly psychology editor at Routledge, in response to my call for an accessible methods text that took students on from the basics of ANOVA and regression, at the point where most psychology degree courses start to diverge on the basis of staff interests and expertise. I originally envisaged the book as a kind of 'Coolican 2' that picked up where Hugh Coolican's *Research Methods and Statistics in Psychology* left off (although Hugh is continually revising his book so this point is not permanently fixed). This text is highly popular with students at A-level and at degree level, although some university teachers unfairly (in my opinion) deride it as a 'cookbook', presumably because it fails to introduce students to advanced algebra, and is actually written in English. The same cannot be said of most texts covering quantitative or qualitative methods in psychology beyond the basic level 1 material, and so I saw this as the gap that my text would fill.

Initially, the book was intended to start with one-way ANOVA and take readers all the way through to MANOVA, with the idea that psychology departments might see it as a level 2 undergraduate text. At this point I was working at Sheffield Hallam University, and many thanks go to Grace Naylor, my research assistant at the time, with whom I worked through many of the ideas, and we tried them out with level 2 students . . . only for me to bin the whole lot. This decision was taken largely because so many books already cover ANOVA, and because this book would eventually turn into a sprawling monster if I was to cover all the more advanced stuff I wanted. So I decided to kick off with ANCOVA and leave the basics to existing texts. I also thank my office colleagues during this period – Dan Ellingworth, Ronnie Moore and Iain Garner, who made many useful suggestions, and particularly John Maltby, who contributed significantly towards Chapter 9 (Factor analysis).

From these beginnings, the book grew into something of an albatross, going through several editors in the process – after Vivien left the project, Alison Dixon, Caroline Osborne, Paul Dukes and Caroline again have all taken turns to grab the reins, with Rachel Brazil and Lucy Farr helping them out. In addition to Routledge staff, many reviewers have been called on to offer their views on different sections of the book, and some of these have been very constructive and have influenced the overall structure. I would like to thank Paul Stenner and Steven Brown in particular for their positive and helpful comments.

Finally, I would like to thank friends and colleagues who have commented on the manuscript at various times, in particular Tony Cassidy, Hugh Coolican and Stephen Joseph, and the many students who have been subjected to this material in the role of guinea pigs at Sheffield Hallam University and Coventry University.

1 Introduction

For a long time now, the psychology textbook market has been flooded with books on introductory statistics and basic research methods. Most of these books repeat the same information, covering experimental design, descriptive and inferential statistics, and a smattering of other research methods that are likely to be encountered in the first year of a psychology degree. Sometimes lecturers deliver their material straight from these texts; otherwise, students are recommended the textbooks as supplementary reading.

I am sure that, with teaching quality assessment shaking up psychology departments in the last decade, the provision of teaching materials has improved dramatically, but in most cases, supplementary reading is essential for students to grasp some of the more complicated material encountered in lab classes and statistics workshops. However, there comes a point in most psychology undergraduates' education when the supply of useful supplementary information begins to dry up. This point usually arrives midway through level 2 (in English universities, at any rate), when research methods staff have the freedom to start delivering more specialised material.

The idea behind the present text was to dispense with introductory methods material and start somewhere in the middle, so that it would cover all the further statistical techniques that undergraduates can expect to encounter, along with qualitative approaches and more esoteric methods. The choice of content is based on an exhaustive trawl through the websites of British universities during 1999, when roughly half of the psychology departments posted sufficient information for me to identify the techniques covered.

However, I do not want readers to think of this book as an undergraduate text as such. Because of the variation in material covered in psychology degrees from level 2 onwards, I envisage this book being useful for psychology researchers well past undergraduate level. Indeed, I have already lent drafts of various chapters to colleagues. The increasing popularity of qualitative research in psychology is a case in point. Some qualitative psychologists have queried whether these chapters really deserve to be classified as 'advanced' methods; perhaps they are of little use to postdoctoral discourse analysts or grounded theorists. However, many experienced psychologists have received training only in quantitative methods, and freely admit that they are ill equipped to supervise qualitative projects at level 3, or even to teach these methods at levels 1 and 2.

Because I have decided to start in the middle, this book makes a lot of assumptions about the knowledge expected of a reader. I would be very surprised if any reader has failed to complete at least one year of an under-graduate degree; therefore, I am assuming that s/he will be familiar with intro-ductory methods material. Typically, the first year of a degree is spent training students to understand inferential statistics, weigh up the pros and cons of basic research design (mostly experimental), write lucid formal reports, and consider some of the wider issues involved in psychological research (ethics, reliability and validity, and so on). More specifically, I would expect the reader to have covered the following:

- Mean/median/mode
- Standard deviation/Normal distribution
- Variance
- Statistical error
- Generalising from sample to population
- Difference between parametric and nonparametric tests
- Correlation and simple linear regression
- t-tests, one-way ANOVA, repeated measures ANOVA, factorial ANOVA
- Basics of reliability and validity
- Difference between interval, nominal and ordinal scales
- Difference between independent and dependent variables
- Basics of experimental design
- Conventions of report writing

Some readers may wonder why I have neglected to cover basic ANOVA. The reason is that many departments now expect undergraduates to master ANOVA at level 1, even as far as factorial designs and interpreting inter-actions. Furthermore, there are very few introductory research methods and statistics texts that do not cover ANOVA, even as far as two-way mixed designs. Inevitably, there is great variation in the depth of this coverage. For instance, there are very few texts offering an adequate and accessible cover-age of multiple comparisons in factorial designs. However, I would argue that this is *their* problem! It would be unwise of me to attempt to patch up other textbooks' coverage of advanced issues in ANOVA without starting from the basics myself. So this book kicks off with a section that I have termed 'Beyond ANOVA', in which I introduce readers to more advanced techniques that build on the basic ANOVA model.

Occasionally, I make reference to the tension between Fisherian approaches to statistics and the Neyman-Pearson tradition. In brief, Fisherian approaches are those that centre around the null hypothesis as the key concept in infer-ential statistics, as argued by Ronald Fisher in his influential writings before the Second World War (e.g., Fisher 1935). ANOVA is the most important technique in this tradition, having been devised by Fisher as a way of directly testing null hypotheses under rigidly controlled experimental conditions. The Neyman-Pearson tradition (following Jerzy Neyman and Egon Pearson) focuses on correlation and regression as statistical techniques, arguing against the tradition of null hypothesis significance testing and in favour of more exploratory techniques examining the relationships between variables.

It has been argued that research methods training in psychology has evolved by way of an unsatisfactory hybrid of these approaches (Gigerenzer and Murray 1987). In the UK, much criticism has been levelled at A-level teaching of statistics in psychology for treating the null hypothesis as gospel, and asking students to learn by rote confusing and inaccurate interpretations of statistical significance (MacRae 1995). These issues are discussed in more detail in Chapter 21. More generally, there is increasing pressure on editors of psychology journals to supplement null hypothesis significance testing (if not abandon it altogether) with other statistics, notably effect size and confidence intervals, and to force authors to consider the *power* of their designs (a key concept in the Neyman-Pearson tradition).

I have resisted the temptation to address power concerns in the book as a whole because the jury is still out on how much they matter to psychology. To some researchers, power concerns are simply another restraint imposed by statistical purists demanding unrealistically large sample sizes; to others, they are no alternative to statistical significance, just a means of ensuring a better chance of obtaining a significant value. *A priori* power calculations are meaningful only where effect sizes can be predicted, and population norms known (as, say, with IQ); does this mean that psychological research can only be conducted on a select handful of measures and – possibly dubious – concepts? At worst, for most studies in psychology (where effect sizes tend to be small), high power requirements threaten to stifle research on interesting topics and populations. Furthermore, just how much more detail is really necessary to drive home a point in the Results section of a paper? The day when all authors are required to report confidence intervals may never arrive. Therefore, in most of the book, I have focused on the kinds of statistics you are likely to see reported in papers published in the 1990s and early 2000s.

The first two parts of the book are differentiated loosely on the Fisherian/ Neyman-Pearson distinction. Part I (Beyond ANOVA) deals with techniques which emerged on the back of the factorial ANOVA model and are primarily aimed at testing null hypotheses, typically differences between means, in an experimental context. In practice, MANOVA and discriminant analysis are used far more often to analyse data collected in survey-type studies than in true experiments. Nevertheless, they are frequently used, even in this context, as a way of testing hypotheses by comparing group means.

In contrast, Part II (Measures of relationship: regression techniques) deals with statistics which have been developed in the Neyman-Pearson tradition, building on the basic linear regression equation to explore relationships between large numbers of variables. In these techniques, significance testing is concerned largely with the 'fit' of specific models that are designed to predict a particular variable. For this reason, significance testing plays a less prominent role in these techniques than in those deriving from Fisherian principles. In Chapter 7, I introduce the reader to structural equation modelling (SEM), an advanced set of techniques which became extremely popular in psychology during the 1990s. There is not enough room in this book to cover SEM in full, though, and anyone who seriously considers using it for analysis will need to consult a more specialist text.

In Part III (Questionnaires and scales) the emphasis shifts from statistical analysis towards research design in general, as I describe the steps involved in constructing tests and scales, and techniques for measuring their reliability. There follows a chapter on factor analysis, which – in its exploratory form – shares much in common with other Neyman-Pearson type techniques; indeed, it largely dispenses with significance testing. However, the development of *confirmatory* factor analysis, along the same lines as SEM, throws a bit of a spanner in the works, since it is heralded by its supporters as a significance testing technique. This section closes with a round-up of some alternative techniques for data reduction such as cluster analysis and multidimensional scaling, methods which are popular in research but rarely covered at undergraduate level.

The following section (Part IV) represents something of a departure from traditional methods texts in that it contains a detailed look at qualitative research in psychology. More and more psychology departments throughout the world are incorporating qualitative methods into their research methods teaching at undergraduate and postgraduate level, and qualitative research is increasing rapidly in the social sciences in general. The British government has recently included qualitative methods in their 'benchmarks' for psychology degrees. However, there is still a lot of suspicion surrounding the merits of qualitative research, and teachers and researchers in the quantitative tradition sometimes still regard it as a soft option for students who can't add up. To set the record straight, I have covered two qualitative techniques (grounded theory and discourse analysis) in some depth, and suggest some ways of ensuring that qualitative research meets the rigorous demands of scientific inquiry.

Traditional quantitative psychologists often find the idea of qualitative research confusing. What counts as 'qualitative'? I have often heard content analysis referred to as a qualitative method. While qualitative content analyses *are* beginning to appear in the literature (see Chapter 14), in most cases the term content analysis is used to describe the coding of data, typically in text or transcript form, for *statistical* analysis. More confusing still is the growing tendency for statistically-oriented psychologists to speak of 'qualitative variables' when they mean category variables (see Everitt 1998 for an example). I have even seen the term 'qualitative' used as synonymous with 'interpretative' (Macdonald 1993). Such usage may make sense within the context of these specialised discussions, but it does not help those studying psychology, or even those highly qualified, to grasp the essential points of difference between quantitative and qualitative research.

At the same time, I disagree with the common portrayal of qualitative and quantitative psychologists as two warring sets of academics who cannot understand each others' perspective. There is no reason why an individual researcher should not simultaneously conduct a series of psychology experiments to test a causal hypothesis while conducting a discourse analysis to examine the social construction of the same phenomenon as part of the same research project. (Admittedly, I have yet to see such a project attempted, and would be surprised to see the conservative funding councils support it!). While different approaches may be underpinned by different epistemologies, I believe there is no need for an individual researcher to commit to a lifelong position.

Part V ('Other approaches') is something of an odds and ends section. It opens with (quantitative) content analysis, and in the same chapter I discuss log-linear analysis, a technique that is growing in popularity in psychological research, and is particularly appropriate for data derived from this type of content analysis. Statisticians may wonder why I did not cover log-linear analysis along with logistic regression (a related technique); the answer is that the organisation of the book is based more on common usage of methods rather than mathematical lines.

In this section I also cover meta-analysis (Chapter 18), which is growing increasingly popular as an alternative to the traditional literature review paper. Some would argue that the term 'meta-analysis' is merely a statistical technique for combining effect sizes. Again, from a theoretical perspective I could have placed this elsewhere, perhaps by combining this chapter with the one on statistical significance and power. However, in practice, meta-analysis is almost always conducted as a kind of quantitative literature review, and its usage provokes many questions about the way we evaluate research in the quantitative tradition. As with statistical power, I have strong reservations about how appropriate meta-analysis is when applied to psychological data, which is rarely consistent in its methods and measures, not to mention its sampling procedures.

Finally, the book ends with a section (Part VI, 'Uses and abuses of research') that contains issues of importance for budding researchers, but may also prove interesting for established psychologists. It is almost obligatory for a methods textbook to include a section on ethics; here I have tried to address the issue of what ethical clearance is actually for. Too often it is treated as a form of political correctness, and I sometimes wonder whether the idea of having separate chapters on ethics in books helps dispel this concept. Ethical concerns are at the heart of all research methods and should be design issues, not a list of spoilsport restrictions. Above all, they call into question the whole *point* of research. Chapter 21 is the aforementioned chapter on statistical significance and related issues. Here you will find details on how to calculate power and confidence intervals.

The book ends with two useful chapters on writing research papers and applying for grant money. These activities are of paramount importance in academic life today, but newly-qualified psychologists often find themselves abandoned after postgraduate study without any real guidance. The typical case is a young lecturer who, immediately on finishing a PhD, lands a lecturing post in a cash-strapped department which is desperately trying to plug a hole in its teaching timetable. Senior staff may be research-inactive, or too jaded to pass on advice; without any opportunity to build a research profile, the new lecturer has little chance of an escape route. These two chapters are dedicated to that lecturer, but postgraduates, or anyone thinking of starting a research career, may also benefit from the information.

Finally, a feature of the book is the frequent use of detailed examples from the psychological research literature. Recently, I read a meta-analysis chapter in a general psychology methods textbook which failed to give a single example, from the many available, of a meta-analysis that had been conducted by a psychologist. I fail to see how a reader unfamiliar with the technique could come away from that chapter any the wiser. Where possible I have used two examples of each technique, especially where there are variations in use, and I have tried to draw them from literature published in the five years before the book's publication. I hope in doing so I have made the book directly relevant to psychology in the twenty-first century.

Part I

Beyond ANOVA

The first part of this book is devoted to statistical procedures that have emerged from the broad concept of analysis of variance, which dates back to Ronald Fisher's work on experimental design in the 1920s. Fisher was primarily interested in the effects of different fertilisers on crop yields, which may seem rather remote from the kind of experiments you are likely to carry out in psychology. Nonetheless, from the 1930s onwards, psychologists began to adopt Fisher's techniques as gospel, and they are fundamental to the way statistics and experimental methods are taught to psychology students today.

The more advanced techniques in this chapter were developed after the Second World War, as statisticians and psychologists found the basic ANOVA model insufficient for more complex studies, where, for example, you have more than one dependent variable that you want to include in the overall design. The introduction of correlational statistics (as in ANCOVA) led to the development of the general linear model (GLM) which has evolved into a framework covering both analysis of variance and multiple regression. I have preferred to keep ANOVA-based techniques and correlational techniques apart for this book because they are rarely combined in research reports. ANOVA and its extensions tend to be used for the analysis of complex experiments, or between-group studies using multiple measures, while regression and linear modelling are more likely to be used to investigate relationships between variables in a large data set, typically the outcome of a survey, or a battery of psychometric tests.

2   Analysis of covariance (ANCOVA)

ANCOVA first appeared in the literature during the 1950s, and has since become a widely used method in psychological research. It consists of an ordinary ANOVA design in which one of the variables is adjusted according to its relationship with an extraneous variable. The extraneous variable is referred to as a *covariate*.[1]

An ordinary ANOVA assumes that all the factors in the design are truly independent. A significant F ratio for, say, the effect of age, can be interpreted as meaning that age 'explains' the variance between groups on the dependent variable (scores on a memory test, for example). But the real situation may be more complicated than that. Suppose the different age also had significant differences in a related cognitive ability, such as IQ. It might be that the difference in IQ explains the memory variance better than the difference in age. If we incorporate the factor of IQ into the ANOVA model, we can explore how much of a confounding effect it has on age.

This means that, rather than designing a 2-way ANOVA with factors of age and IQ, we design a one-way ANOVA with IQ as a covariate. The idea behind this is to 'partial out' the variance caused by IQ.

It does this by *adjusting* the means for the different age groups. For example, participant 1 has a memory score of 17 out of 20 and an IQ score of 124, while participant 2 has a memory score of 7 and an IQ score of 102. Partialling out IQ involves regressing the memory value on to the IQ value for each group, and then deriving adjusted scores from the coefficients. The adjusted memory scores are, respectively, 16 and 8.

By taking IQ into account, the means difference is slightly less. Of course this is a tiny example – but, if the same pattern was repeated over a large number of scores we might find that the differences of two sets of scores attributed to age are significantly confounded by partialling out IQ, and that a significant F ratio can be turned into a non-significant one.

ANCOVA produces a separate F ratio for the covariate as well as an F ratio for the independent variable, then adjusts the latter accordingly, so that the significance test is done on a new F statistic. Incidentally, ANCOVA does not always result in a lower level of significance for the independent variable (it may be used to tease out a confounding dependent variable). In partialling out IQ we may discover that we have *under*estimated the factor of age. It may explain more of the variance than we originally thought.

Worked example of a one-way ANOVA with a single covariate

This example is based on some actual research I carried out when working towards a PhD. I was investigating the role that visual memory plays in children's spelling[2] and I thought I had designed the perfect test of visual memory that would be able to discriminate between good and poor spellers, based on the hypothesis that poor spellers would perform less well on visual memory measures (given the need to retrieve irregular, nonphonetic spellings from memory). I collected visual memory data from a number of schools where the special needs teachers agreed to identify poor spellers for the study whose spelling difficulties could not be attributed to other factors, such as low intelligence. The mean visual memory score for the control group was considerably higher than that of the poor spellers, and a t-test showed this difference to be significant at $p < 0.05$.

My enthusiasm for this test was, however, dampened when the local education authority finally produced the IQ scores for the participants (they were held in a vault at the county council and it took a while to retrieve them[3]). The mean IQ value for the poor spelling group was 85, well below average, while the mean IQ value for the controls was 104. I re-ran the analysis, this time using IQ as a covariate, and found that the difference was no longer significant at the 0.05 level (in fact it was nowhere near). This finding changed the direction of the research as a result.

Table 2.1 displays a mock data set based on this study. If you were to enter this data into SPSS you would need to stack both groups together into 2 columns (IQ and vismem). You would then need to create a separate variable for 'group'. The visual memory test was scored out of 20.

Ignoring the IQ values, the difference in the means suggests that the controls do indeed have higher visual memory performance and that this might account for their superiority in spelling. We can run an ordinary one-way ANOVA on this data and obtain the results displayed in Table 2.2. A look in the critical value tables will tell you that this F value is significant at $p < 0.01$ for df (1, 18).

Now we need to introduce IQ into our design. In educational psychology the role of IQ is considered important because the usual way of diagnosing dyslexia is 'by exclusion' – in other words, the difficulty with reading or spelling is not attributable to other factors. If nothing in the child's background can be found that would predetermine reading/spelling problems in particular, then a diagnosis of dyslexia can be made. An 'eyeball' test of the IQ data immediately arouses suspicion that the groups are not differentiated by spelling ability alone. The mean IQ score for the controls is much higher (too high for them to be considered controls, as it happens, but we'll ignore

Table 2.1 IQ and visual memory scores for both spelling groups

Controls IQ	Visual memory	Poor spellers IQ	Visual memory
127	15	99	11
113	13	101	10
133	14	102	9
109	9	88	12
114	18	103	8
121	16	97	14
122	11	94	9
115	15	101	7
125	14	75	13
108	18	89	5
Mean = 118.7	14.3	94.9	9.8
SD = 8.2	*2.8*	*8.8*	*2.8*

Table 2.2 ANOVA table for one-way visual memory between-groups study

Source	SS	df	MS	F
Between groups (spelling)	101.25	1	101.25	12.86
Error	141.7	18	7.87	
Total	242.95	19		

that technicality for now) than that for the poor spellers. It looks as though IQ may explain the visual memory difference *as well as* the spelling difference.

To perform ANCOVA by hand we would need to calculate two further *F* ratios – one on the IQ data separately, and *F′*, which is an adjusted *F* statistic for the independent variable (IV – spelling). There are various ways of calculating *F′* by hand, and at this point it will save you hours of effort simply to stick to your preferred software package. In the SPSS program running an ANCOVA is easy because the ordinary ANOVA dialog box contains a slot for running a covariate. Entering IQ into this slot gives us the output in Figure 2.1.

In the 'Tests of Between Subjects Effects' you can find the line for GROUP and the adjusted *F* statistic. This is now down to 0.574, considerably smaller than the one-way value we obtained without the covariate, and well below the critical value needed to reject the null hypothesis. Why the huge difference? The answer lies in the table headed 'Estimates'. This displays the adjusted subgroup means after partialling out IQ (it tells you below that the adjustment was calculated by levelling IQ out at 106 for all the participants). The

Tests of Between-Subjects Effects

Dependent Variable: VISMEM

Source	Type III Sum of Squares	df	Mean Square	F	Sig.
Corrected Model	120.182[a]	2	60.091	8.321	.003
Intercept	8.232E-02	1	8.232E-02	.011	.916
IQ	18.932	1	18.932	2.622	.124
GROUP	4.145	1	4.145	.574	.459
Error	122.768	17	7.222		
Total	3147.000	20			
Corrected Total	242.950	19			

[a] R Squared = .495 (Adjusted R Squared = .435)

Estimates

Dependent Variable: VISMEM

spelling group	Mean	Std. Error	95% Confidence Interval	
			Lower Bound	Upper Bound
good	12.862[a]	1.229	10.269	15.455
poor	11.238[a]	1.229	8.645	13.831

[a] Evaluated at covariates appeared in the model: IQ = 106.80.

Figure 2.1 ANCOVA table and estimated marginal means

adjusted means for the two groups are much closer than the observed means (12.8 for controls and 11.2 for the poor spellers). Therefore it appears that the group difference in IQ scores can explain the difference in visual memory scores.

A word of caution here. In the same way that you learn not to infer causation from correlation, so we cannot necessarily say that the poor spellers' low IQ values are 'causing' them to perform badly at the visual memory task, or that low IQ causes poor spelling. It is enough to state simply that they are *related* to, or associated with, one another.

Data screening

As with all statistical techniques, you need to ensure that ANCOVA is an appropriate test for the data you have collected. You will already be familiar with the kinds of parametric assumptions that are made about ANOVA in general (if not, any basic statistical textbook covering ANOVA should cover this). However, the introduction of a covariate brings with it further potential pitfalls that need to be identified through screening of the data.

This is a feature of multivariate statistics in general, and many of the screening procedures necessary for ANCOVA are also necessary for the tests covered in later chapters.

Linearity

The most fundamental assumption for ANCOVA is that there is a *linear relationship* between the dependent variable under investigation and the covariate. In other words, the relationship between the two can be illustrated by a straight regression line. This is not a major restriction – it simply rules out curvilinear (U-shaped) relationships. The best way to check that your dependent variable (DV) and covariate(s) have a linear relationship, or display linearity, is to get your computer package to produce scatterplots for them. Figure 2.2 displays the scatterplot (with regression line) for the DV (vismem) and covariate (IQ) in the worked example from pages 10–12. The line is straight, showing a clear linear relationship between the two variables.

If the line of best fit is too bent or curved, then the covariate may not be suitable for ANCOVA, and you are better off turning it into a factor and performing a two-way factorial ANOVA. For example, we might convert

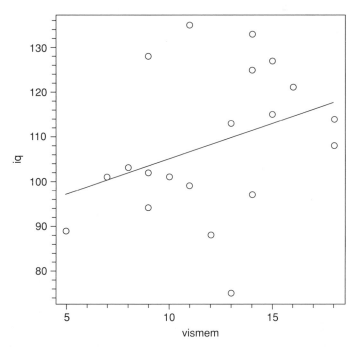

Figure 2.2 Scatterplot of visual memory scores against IQ scores with regression line

IQ into a categorical variable, with two levels – low and high.[4] The obvious question that follows from this is: how do you identify linearity in border-line cases? Alas, there is no fixed cut-off point for defining non-linearity. Ultimately the decision whether or not to use a variable as a covariate lies with the researcher. Indeed, screening for unsuitable variables by examining scatterplots has been likened to reading tea leaves (Tabachnick and Fidell 2001).

There is an additional assumption if we are using more than one covariate in a design. In our earlier example, in addition to IQ (a culturally biased measure) we might want to include another measure of general cognitive ability, such as performance on a visuo-spatial task. However, before we incorporated this measure into the ANCOVA model we would need to ensure a) linearity between visuo-spatial scores and general memory scores; and b) linearity between the visuo-spatial scores and IQ. Violations of this assumption are likely to reduce the power of the test.

Multicollinearity

While linearity is an assumption for all the measures in the ANCOVA design, we want to avoid pairs of variables that show *too* strong a linear relationship with one another. When covariates correlate with each other as highly as $r = 0.90$, we have a situation known as *multicollinearity*, which is an important phenomenon to avoid for multivariate tests in general. It is important in ANCOVA because it reduces the independence, or *orthogonality*, of the covariates. Suppose we found that, in addition to having high positive correlations with memory, IQ and visuo-spatial scores had a high correla-tion with each other (say, $r = 0.75$). This would suggest that each factor is explaining the same amount of variance in memory scores. If the correlation between IQ and visuo-spatial score is low, e.g., $r = 0.25$, they are more likely to explain discrete portions of variance in memory scores. Go back to the adjusted memory scores on the previous page, and adjust them again for a second covariate with similar values to IQ. The scores are unlikely to change much. How do you know which covariate is causing the adjustment?

Homogeneity of variance

ANCOVA, like ANOVA, makes the assumption that the variance within each cell of the data table is similar. It is also reasonably 'robust' to violations of this assumption, but only up to a point. Unequal cell sizes are OK, for example, but it is not wise to have any cell that is four times the size of the smallest cell. If this happens (because participants have dropped out, or whatever) then the variances of the cells need to be screened to ensure that no cell has a variance larger than ten times the size of the smallest.

If so, the data will need to be transformed, using either logarithms or standard (Z) scores. The latter is very easy in the SPSS program, where the

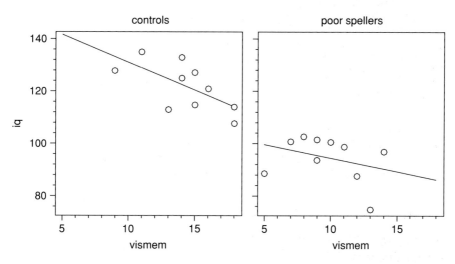

Figure 2.3 Scatterplots and regression lines separately for the poor spellers and controls

Z scores are saved as variables so that they can be entered into statistical tests like the raw scores.

Homogeneity of regression

While there is an assumption that the variables in ANCOVA display linearity in the data overall, there is also a further assumption that the regression lines for each group in the study show similarity. In our worked example, therefore, we would expect the vismem/IQ regression lines to be similar for the controls and for the poor spellers. Figure 2.3 displays the relevant scatterplots and regression lines for these two groups.

Surprisingly, for each group the relationship between vismem and IQ is negative. This is not a major problem for this study, although it demonstrates the importance of examining the separate regression lines since this negative relationship is obscured in the overall data set by the disparity in the IQ levels of the two groups. If there was heterogeneous regression – for example, a negative vismem/IQ relationship for controls, and a positive relationship for poor spellers – then ANCOVA would be unsuitable because the overall vismem/IQ relationship is inconsistent across the subgroups. In a situation like this, you would have to suspect that another factor was responsible for this strange pattern. You would probably have to rethink the study altogether.

The homogeneity of regression assumption is a key issue in ANCOVA – heterogeneity is generally regarded as the most common and serious violation. It raises the likelihood that the variables under examination *interact*, and this would make ANCOVA an inappropriate test to use. In the heterogeneous example given in the above paragraph, you might say that there was an interaction between spelling and IQ. In these circumstances a 2-way ANOVA would be more suitable. Indeed, one way to examine homogeneity of regression is to perform an ordinary factorial ANOVA on the data, treating the covariate as a *factor* rather than a covariate (and recoding it). What you would be looking for is a non-significant interaction between the IV and the covariate.

One of the reasons for the homogeneity assumption is the sensitivity of multivariate techniques to *outliers* – cases in the data which show marked deviations from the mean. These are more of a problem in MANOVA so I will discuss them in more detail in Chapter 3.

ANCOVA using more than one covariate

It may seem, from the above example, that ANCOVA is little more than a troubleshooting device for dodgy data. Indeed, ANCOVA does tend to be used only when collected data yield unforeseen problems. Few researchers would *design* a one-way ANOVA study with a single covariate in advance of collecting the data. In psychological research in general, it is probably more likely to be used to analyse individual components of a series of measures. One example from the literature is a study of bridge playing in older adults (Clarkson-Smith and Hartley 1990). Here, participants were assessed on a number of cognitive tasks related to memory and reasoning aspects of the game of bridge, and performance on these tasks was measured using a mixture of one-way ANOVAs and MANOVAs with age as a covariate in all of them.

Where more than one covariate is included in the design, certain strictures about the use of covariates need to be observed. As stated earlier, in addition to linearity with the dependent variable, we must be careful that covariates do not correlate too highly with one another because they may be 'explaining' the same variance in the dependent measure. Even if they have low correlations, there comes a point beyond which additional covariates contribute less and less to the analysis. However, if your group is small – and this may be unavoidable when using specialist populations, for example, in clinical psychology – use of more than one covariate may increase the power of the ANOVA to detect a significant result.

Huitema (1980) suggests the following procedure as a limit to the use of covariates (C = number of covariates, J = number of groups):

$$\frac{C + (J - 1)}{N} < 0.10$$

Therefore, in our previous example, if $N = 20$, we need to find a numerator of less than 2 in order to meet the < 0.10 requirement. $(J - 1) = 1$, and so C will have to be < 1. In other words, the use of *any* covariate is not recommended with such a small sample. If $N = 50$, on the other hand, we could use up to three. If the left hand side of the equation *exceeds* 0.10, it is argued, the values of the adjusted means may fluctuate across replications.

Worked example of ANCOVA with more than one covariate

For convenience's sake, we will ignore Huitema's advice and look at a fictitious study on a sample of 10 with three covariates. Let us return to the visual memory study and the original set of scores from the controls and the poor spelling group. This time we will overlook the IQ scores and administer a new set of tests to half the original participants. There are sound reasons for unpacking IQ into subskills; for various reasons, IQ is considered a biased and potentially meaningless statistic by many psychologists working in the fields of cognition and education. It is particularly important in dyslexia research, for example, to separate verbal intelligence from non-verbal intelligence – after all, if a test requires the respondent to read instructions, a dyslexic participant is likely to have a disadvantage from the start.

We might decide to focus on three distinct areas of cognitive ability which are all related to visual memory. One could be a verbal task, such as a comprehension measure; another could be a visuo-spatial task like the Corsi block-tapping task (where the participant has to reproduce a visual sequence by tapping an arrangement of wooden blocks); a third task could be a measure of non-verbal intelligence, such as the Raven's Matrices (where participants need to deploy reasoning skills to match patterns).

Incorporating these tasks into the design gives us the set of imaginary data in Table 2.3, where all three tests are scored out of 20.

Checks for linearity and homogeneity of regression give us sufficient grounds to pursue an ANCOVA. Significant positive correlations are present between visual memory and all three other variables. Scatterplots reveal linearity among the three covariates among themselves, although they do not correlate significantly with each other and multicollinearity is not a problem (see Table 2.4).

We can further examine the suitability of the covariates by performing a custom model in ANOVA and testing the interaction between all four variables. This turns out to be non-significant ($F < 1$), so we can assume that there is homogeneity of regression, although we need to look at the regression slopes for final confirmation.

Perform the ANCOVA in the same way as the previous example. The results show that each of the covariates independently discriminates between the controls and the poor spellers, and that the factor of spelling is non-significant overall. This is pretty much the same finding as when IQ was used as a single covariate. The difference this time is that we cannot be certain that each of the covariates is exerting the same influence over the factor of spelling. One way of finding out is to run a series of ANCOVAs using each variable as a single covariate.

Table 2.3 Visual memory scores and three covariates grouped by spelling ability

	Visual memory	Verbal comp	Block-tapping	Ravens
Controls	15	13	17	14
	13	10	14	19
	14	13	15	15
	9	17	12	6
	18	14	20	11
	16	13	15	12
	11	8	13	16
	15	13	12	12
	14	12	16	9
	18	11	16	20
Poor spellers	11	9	5	10
	10	10	6	12
	9	15	3	8
	12	10	10	11
	8	9	7	7
	14	11	8	15
	9	2	5	10
	7	7	8	6
	13	14	12	15
	5	2	10	3

Table 2.4 Correlation matrix for visual memory and the three covariates

	Verbal comp	Block-tapping	Ravens
Vismem	0.54*	0.72**	0.71**
Verbal comp		0.39	0.24
Block-tapping			0.42

Notes: * significant at $p < 0.05$
       ** significant at $p < 0.01$

Table 2.5 Adjusted subgroup means and *F* ratios for single ANCOVA tests

Covariate	Estimated marginal means		Adjusted F ratio
	Poor spellers	Controls	
Block-tapping	10.2	13.8	6.62*
Ravens	10.6	13.5	6.79*
Verbal comp	11.6	12.5	0.21

As you can see in Table 2.5, the block-tapping scores and Raven's matrices have an almost identical effect on the group difference. *F* remains significant when these covariates are partialled out on an individual basis (though not when the two are combined, reducing it to 3.37). However it is the verbal comprehension scores that produce the most dramatic single effect, reducing *F* to well below 1. The adjusted means show only a marginal difference between controls and poor spellers.

How can we interpret these findings? One argument is that the block-tapping and Ravens tasks are related to visual memory because there is a visuo-spatial element to them, but they do not discriminate between the subgroups sufficiently to 'explain' the significant difference in visual memory scores. Even when these covariates are combined, the adjusted *F* only just fails to reach significance. Verbal comprehension, however, seems to discriminate between the groups too severely to be a chance factor, and when the means are adjusted on this basis, the two groups' visual memory scores are relatively close. We could therefore argue that the confounding effect of IQ has been traced to a specific subskill – verbal ability – and that, despite the attempt of the experimenter to design a completely labelling-free test of visual memory we are still stuck with some verbal contribution that is disadvantaging poor spellers.

Statisticians might criticise the above example: why run an ANCOVA with three covariates if one of them is having such a profound effect by itself? This would be a fair question, but the study was designed in the first place as an attempt to unpack IQ, so the three variables were necessary (in fact, this would make it more suitable for a MANOVA). In any case, if you are using computer software to perform analysis, it really doesn't matter if you start off with a complex design and whittle it down – although you inflate the error rate by doing so. In any case, this was a purely hypothetical example. In reality the same pattern of results is highly unlikely!

Two examples of ANCOVA from the psychological literature

Gatton, DuBois and Faley (1999): occupational gender stereotyping

This study was concerned with the way that different occupations are seen as intrinsically 'masculine' or 'feminine', and how much the organisational context contributes to these stereotypes. The authors began by getting students to rate a wide variety of professions on a masculine–feminine dimension. There is remarkable concordance in male and female ratings (out of interest, secretary and receptionist received the highest (i.e., feminine) ratings, while overhead crane operator and forklift operator received the lowest ratings).

Then two descriptions of organisational settings were created; one describes a stereotypically 'feminine' organisation, with much emphasis on employee satisfaction and altruistic principles; the other describes a 'masculine' organisation, with a ruthless hiring-and-firing boss who is perpetually at loggerheads with the union.

This was a between-groups study with three groups: experimental (feminine), experimental (masculine) and control. Each group comprised a mixture

of male and female undergraduates. The feminine group read the description of the feminine organisation and then rated eight occupations on a
masculine–feminine scale. The masculine group read the masculine description and then rated the occupations, and the control group carried out the
rating task without receiving any description.

In addition to the experimental manipulation, other information was
collected from participants. Each completed a measure of social desirability,
and indicated both their 'race' (ethnicity) and the number of hours they
worked each week. It was found that these last two variables had significant
negative correlations with the occupational ratings.

As a result, a 2×3 ANCOVA (gender $\times$ group) was set up in which 'race' and
hours per week were entered as covariates. Both main effects were found
to be significant: women rated occupations as significantly more feminine
than men, and *post hoc* tests found that the feminine group rated the occupations as significantly more feminine than the controls. There was no interaction
between the factors.

This study is typical of most ANCOVA designs in that the covariates are
simply 'nuisance' variables and are not a major part of the analysis. Since
no information is presented about the analysis without the covariates, we
are unable to comment on their contribution. We can probably assume that
the authors have included them in order to deflect possible criticism.

Stroebe, Stroebe and Abakoumkin (1999): gender and bereavement

Here is another study exploring gender differences that uses an ANCOVA
design. However it is not an experimental study; it is an analysis of selected
variables from a German database relating to bereavement. Unlike the Gatton
et al. study, the covariate plays a key role in the analysis.

The dependent variables in this study comprised:

• *Depressive symptomatology* The score on a questionnaire concerning
  depressive symptoms, completed by male and female groups of widowed
  and married individuals under retirement age.
• *Loneliness* A short questionnaire measure.
• *Perceived social support* Where a number of questions are asked about
  people who they feel they can rely on for support (when necessary).

First, the interaction of gender and marital status was examined by three
2×3 ANOVAs on the DVs listed above (the marital status factor, in addition to 'married' and 'widowed' included a third level, 'refusers', who were
widowed participants who rejected the request for an interview for a separate
study).

Widowed participants scored more highly on depression and loneliness
than married participants. There was a significant gender $\times$ marital status
interaction on both these measures, with male refusers and female widowed

displaying the highest scores. For social support, married participants scored slightly higher than widowed, but this effect was stronger for men than for women.

The ANCOVA in this study is conducted as a check on the depression and loneliness scores. The 2 × 3 ANOVA on this measure was run again, with perceived social support entered as a covariate to see if it moderated the effects. Here, we can interpret the role of the covariate more clearly than in the Gatton *et al.* study because the analysis has been run with and without it. Both the main effect of marital status and the gender × marital status interaction are still significant in the ANCOVA, although the covariate has a different effect: it reduces the strength of the main effect, but boosts the interaction. With regard to loneliness, the same pattern of results is obtained.

Alternatives to ANCOVA

Rutherford (1992) lists a number of alternatives to ANCOVA. He argues that the most important requirement of ANCOVA is homogeneity of regression, and that the other assumptions described earlier, such as linearity between the DV and covariate, are not necessary to run the test. I shan't discuss all the alternatives he lists, but here are a selection of possibilities.

Convert the design into a linear regression model

Rutherford's first alternative is to turn the basic ANOVA design into a hierarchical multiple regression (see Chapter 5), where the covariates are entered first. Of course, in an experimental study, this would require you to treat the independent variable as a nominal variable, and logistic regression (Chapter 6) or structural equation modelling (Chapter 7) may be more appropriate.

Compute adjusted scores using a covariate and use as DV in normal ANOVA

This involves breaking down the ANCOVA calculation into two steps and seems like a sensible option if you have the software. In SPSS, adjusted scores can be saved as a variable in your data file through the commands for simple linear regression.

Fractional interpretation

This alternative is proposed when there is heterogeneity of regression. Rutherford describes a formal method for testing homogeneity of regression, which is preferable to the tealeaf reading which is the only way of assessing linearity, but highly complex nonetheless. Interested readers can consult the paper by Hendrix, Carter and Scott (1982). The basic idea is that you split your data into homogeneous and heterogeneous 'components' and then interpret the components separately. This is probably only worth doing if you have an enormous data set.

Stratification

This is effectively the same approach as described in the earlier section on linearity, where you convert the covariate into a separate factor using appropriate cut-off points. Rutherford suggests that you would do best allocating participants to groups (e.g., based on IQ scores) before actually running the study, although in practice these things are largely unforeseen. In the spelling/visual memory example, for instance, had I known in advance what effect IQ would have, I would have gone back to the drawing board and designed a brand new visual memory test!

Substitute the covariate for the treatment (i.e., independent) variable

This alternative is suggested under conditions of multicollinearity – that is, where the covariate and dependent variable are very highly correlated. This is probably more suited to large data sets, where you can pick and choose from a variety of variables, than to small experimental studies where the independent variable is a key part of the study.

Compute average distance between regression lines

One way of looking at homogeneous regression is to study the regression lines together on the overall scatterplot and take the 'treatment effect' as the distance between the lines. Figure 2.4 displays the regression lines from the worked example overlaid on the same scatterplot. With these homogeneous regression lines, we can see that the treatment effect (i.e., the difference in visual memory score between the two groups) is greater at low IQ levels than at high IQ levels, but not spectacularly so (bearing in mind the scale along the y-axis). However, if the poor spellers' regression line was horizontal (say, at a visual memory value of 10, demonstrating an interaction), the treatment effect at an IQ of 70 would far exceed that at an IQ of 140. In that situation, Rutherford suggests that we could compute an average distance between the lines. This does, of course, restrict the range of inferential statistics we could use to interpret our data.

Summary

This chapter has introduced the reader to the technique of ANCOVA, which involves running a standard ANOVA but introducing a covariate, an

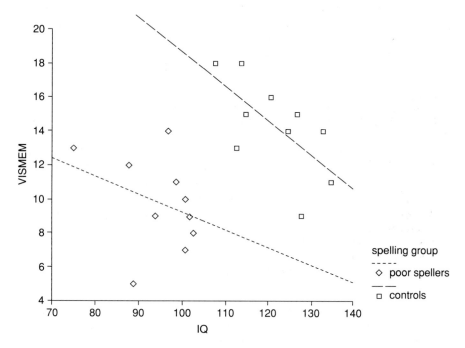

Figure 2.4 Regression lines on the same scatterplot for the spelling/visual memory
example

extraneous variable which is believed to be exerting an influence on the
others. This is not a practice that is always recommended by statisticians,
who advise the use of alternative designs, which I have discussed here. However, ANCOVA tends to be used in psychological research when our data
yield unforeseen problems, and when a re-design is not practical without
redoing the whole study, so it is a useful technique for a researcher to have
up their sleeve. It is also useful when we are working with large data sets,
and wish to perform ANOVA on selected variables which may not be
entirely independent from the influence of other variables in the same set.
While statistical purists may sometimes baulk at such practices, this is a
common situation in large-scale research projects. For an up-to-date reference concerning ANCOVA which takes an explicitly GLM approach, see
Rutherford (2000).

Notes

1 The *covariance* of two variables – the degree to which they vary together – is the
building-block of tests of correlation such as Pearson's Product-Moment. It is
calculated by multiplying the deviations of the two sets of scores and then dividing
by the population estimate.

$$\text{cov}_{xy} = \frac{(\bar{X} - X)(\bar{Y} - Y)}{N - 1}$$

2 Interested readers can consult Giles and Terrell (1997) for a report of the study as a whole. The overall conclusion was that poor spellers do not necessarily have poor visual memory but are disadvantaged when it comes to verbal labelling. My visual memory test, in reducing the possibility of labelling, had levelled out the good and poor spellers – not only when adjusted using IQ as a covariate, but also in a follow-up study where children were selected on the basis of IQ scores. Incidentally, the question of visual memory and spelling is not to everyone's liking in the world of reading and spelling research – many researchers prefer to talk about *orthographic processing* (essentially, a more abstract memory for word forms). I can't help feeling that the visual system is involved somewhere along the line; perhaps it would need a visual imaging study (using a PET scanner) to solve the puzzle . . .
3 When the study took place in the mid-1990s, most primary schools were required to test children's IQ shortly before leaving, at age 11, using the 'Cognitive Abilities Test'. These scores were then stored at the LEA headquarters.
4 One way of doing this is to use the median value as a cut-off point (referred to as a *median split*).

3 Multivariate analysis of variance (MANOVA)

Factorial analysis of variance deals with models with one dependent variable (DV) and more than one independent variable (IV). It is extremely useful for investigating the effects of different factors on a single measure, but very often a single measure fails to capture the complexity of a psychological construct. One of the examples in Chapter 2 concerned the unpacking of IQ into a number of related, but discrete components. In that example, the three components were treated as covariates in an ANOVA design with a single DV. This is an appropriate procedure when the DV is the only variable of interest. If, however, we were mostly interested in IQ, we would either have to collapse the three components into a rather artificial single value, or examine the effect on the three values simultaneously. The latter procedure is known as multivariate ANOVA, or MANOVA for short.

Many statistics textbooks treat MANOVA separately from ANOVA. In some respects it is closer to tests like multiple regression than factorial ANOVA, where our calculations are based round a single set of values. This is particularly important for by-hand calculation. Instead of adding and multiplying single values you need to work with *matrices* of numbers. Some degree programmes still require students to take a crash course in matrix algebra before they are allowed to use these techniques. However, with the universal adoption of statistical software, this hardcore number-crunching has (for most of us) become a thing of the past, like learning obscure computer languages in order to run programs.

MANOVA – and factorial ANOVA too – are often combined with multiple regression and other statistics within a *General Linear Model*. In fact, as you've no doubt noticed, later versions of SPSS include all factorial and repeated measures ANOVA calculations under this command. This practice stems from a paper written by Jacob Cohen in 1968 which suggested that we could use multiple regression techniques (see Chapter 5) to compute ANOVA and MANOVA. One example of this is the practice of entering 'group' codes as a single column in SPSS files (known as a *dummy* variable).

In this book I am including MANOVA in the analysis of variance section because the research questions it is designed to answer have more in common with ANOVA than with regression. Essentially it is a test of group *difference*, and so it is frequently used in experimental designs. Sometimes, when dealing with large data sets (the sort collected during a questionnaire-based survey, for example), it is used to compare psychometric data across groups in a quasi-experimental fashion.

Also, the interpretation of MANOVA is very similar to that of ANOVA (in terms of F statistics, and so on – in fact it doesn't need to use F statistics at all, and most MANOVA tests have to be converted to an approximate F). There is also a historical justification for including MANOVA with ANOVA, since it evolved from the same basic model. There is also a link with ANCOVA, since a MANOVA can be run with covariates – in which case it becomes a MANCOVA design.

Data screening

Like ANOVA and ANCOVA, MANOVA works on the basis of a set of assumptions – most of which will be familiar from the previous chapters. However, violations of these assumptions are more important for MANOVA, and so we have to be more careful to screen our data before performing the tests.

Linearity of dependent variables

This assumption is certainly more important in MANOVA than ANCOVA. Where, in the latter, it is the DV and covariate which ought to display linearity (i.e., they are described by a straight regression line), in MANOVA it is the DVs which should have linear relationships with each other. Again, multicollinearity between any pair of variables (correlation coefficients in excess of 0.90) should be avoided. This is best screened by examining the correlation matrix of the dependent variables. (However, it has to be added that curved regression lines are really quite unusual in psychological studies.)

Homogeneity of variance

This is the assumption of equal covariance of every pair of DVs (or levels of a within-subjects factor). Violations of this assumption pose a major problem for univariate ANOVA, and it is for this reason that many researchers advocate the use of MANOVA. With MANOVA, it is the variance–covariance *matrices* which are assumed to be equal to one another; but since this is extremely unlikely to be the case, it is only serious violations of homogeneity that cause a problem. In any case, most computer packages provide a statistic for homogeneity of variance, typically Box's M, or Bartlett's test of sphericity. If either of these is significant at $p < 0.05$, have another look and consider transforming your data (the likelihood is that you have unequal group sizes, so drop cases if you can afford to).

Normality of distributions

Another reason to screen our data before running a MANOVA is to check that the distribution of the dependent variables is relatively normal. This is also an assumption in ANOVA (or for any parametric test), but MANOVA is particularly sensitive to violations. One violation that is important to avoid is *platykurtosis*, where the distribution curve resembles a low plateau. This can be detected either by obtaining a histogram of the variable concerned, or by examining kurtosis statistics. Critical values for platykurtosis, which vary according to group sample size (*n*) can be found in a table in Stevens (1996: 255). Alternatively, if you obtain the standard error of kurtosis you can divide kurtosis by this figure to obtain a measure of normality: if this figure is over +2 or below −2, then the variable in question may require logarithmic transformation to be included in the MANOVA.

Another problem that may occur in MANOVA is the violation of normality by *outliers*. These are data points which are found well beyond the area covered by the normal distribution, representing extreme values. These are problematic in multivariate analysis in general, partly because they can be hard to detect from the raw data (if participant number 125 in a large data set has incongruous measurements on a selection of variables, the overall pattern may be hard to see at a glance).

There are two ways of screening for outliers in MANOVA, depending on your preferred software. You could simply compute *z* scores for each variable and investigate those values above +2.5 or below −2.5 (i.e., more than 2.5 standard deviations from the mean). Sometimes, however, a particular case may be an outlier because its *pattern* of values is substantially different from other cases. For example, if a participant from the visual memory example in the last chapter had a vismem score of 14, block-tapping score of 17, Ravens score of 7, and a verbal score of 14, then this case would probably be an outlier because his or her pattern of scores was unusual compared with the rest of the sample. To examine this possibility, some packages compute a statistic known as *Mahalanobis distance*, expressed as D^2, which is a measure of the distance between the combined scores of the particular case and its group *centroid* (the combined mean scores of the group that the case comes from). If D^2 is found to be significant for this case, there are two possible remedies. You could solve the problem by transforming the data. Alternatively, an easier solution might be simply to drop the offending cases. Clearly this is harder with small numbers, and, as a result, tests for violations of normality tend to be more lenient with small sample sizes.

How many variables?

There are clear limitations on the usefulness of MANOVA when it comes to piling up DVs. Adding variables may not increase the error rate like in univariate ANOVA but it decreases the power of the test, so it is worth choosing variables carefully. There is no MANOVA equivalent to Huitema's formula in ANCOVA, and it is really up to the researcher to base his or her choice of variables on the underlying concepts being explored and the relative contribution of measures to the study.

WORKED EXAMPLE OF A 3 × 2 MANOVA WITH THREE DEPENDENT VARIABLES AND THREE COVARIATES

I will demonstrate MANOVA by using a single imaginary data set which can be analysed in a number of different ways.

The following example is based on the (not entirely unreasonable) hypothesis that sophisticated modern media consumers find distressing film of real-life events more stressful than video 'nasties' and other clearly fictitious material. The experiment designed to test this involves exposing three different groups of participants to three different films, and measuring their anxiety levels before and after the session. We need a control condition, perhaps an exciting piece of film like a car chase, and two 'distressing' sequences, one real and one fictitious (clearly not *too* distressing, and we would need to screen for participants who may find the footage disturbing).

- Factor A, therefore, is FILM, with three levels.

Our participants are further organised into two age groups across each level of film. This is a *random* factor in that we have simply split the participants into two groups using age 18 as an arbitrary cut-off point.

- Factor B, therefore, is AGE, with two levels.

How might age affect the film type/anxiety relationship? It could be that younger participants, being less worldly-wise, are more affected by fictitious trauma. However the opposite effect (fear of the unknown being worse) is a plausible outcome.

The dependent variables in this experiment are a number of pre- and post-test measures of ANXIETY. First of all, a self-report measure (essentially, a series of questions asking how anxious you feel at the moment to which participants respond on some sort of rating scale) is completed before and after the screening. Because anxiety is a complex phenomenon, it is clearly not enough to rely on self-reports alone, so some physiological measures are also included, so that we have *three* variables: anxiety rating, pulse rate and breathing rate. These are organised into two batches representing 'before' and 'after' measures. The full data set is displayed in Table 3.1.

Table 3.1 Full data set for film type × anxiety study

Type of film	Age	Anxiety rating		Pulse rate		Breathing rate	
		Before	After	Before	After	Before	After
	Under 18	6	6	71	67	17	16
		3	4	64	66	14	15
Neutral	Over 18	7	6	72	65	18	17
		4	4	62	67	16	17
		2	1	68	69	14	13
	Under 18	3	3	69	69	14	16
		8	10	77	76	18	20
Fiction		2	2	66	65	13	13
	Over 18	5	4	81	80	17	16
		4	4	72	74	16	16
	Under 18	3	6	70	78	15	18
		7	8	80	88	18	19
Nonfiction		6	8	75	83	19	21
	Over 18	3	9	62	72	14	19
		5	8	64	72	17	20
		5	7	70	78	15	18

MANOVA with one IV and three DVs

We will start by performing a basic MANOVA analysis on the between-subjects factor of film type and the three 'after' DVs. This is an example of the simplest kind of MANOVA, although it would not be a good way of answering our main research question unless we had controlled for pretest differences between the groups. We are also ignoring the factor of age (for the time being).

Before we begin, we need to take a number of preliminary steps. Some form of data screening will be necessary to ensure that the MANOVA assumptions are not violated too severely. Even before this, it is always a good idea to obtain the descriptive statistics for the individual cells, since they will guide our interpretation of the data set as a whole. From the means in Table 3.2, it looks as though our initial hypothesis may be supported, with the highest anxiety ratings in the non-fiction group. But there is also the possibility that we have a linear trend for all three measures, with slightly higher anxiety in the fiction group.

Data screening

Using your preferred software, obtain histograms for the three DVs. You will find that the distributions for Rating2 and Breath2 are fairly normal,

Table 3.2 Cell means and standard deviations for film type × 'after' measures

Type of film	Rating2	Pulse2	Breath2
Neutral	4.3 (*1.1*)	66.8 (*1.8*)	15.6 (*0.9*)
Fiction	4.5 (*1.1*)	73.5 (*1.8*)	16.2 (*0.9*)
Non-fiction	7.7 (*1.0*)	78.5 (*1.6*)	19.2 (*0.8*)

although the distribution for Pulse2 is somewhat positively skewed. This shouldn't be too much of a problem, since MANOVA is fairly robust to violations of this sort. Then obtain scatterplots for each combination of variables; these clearly demonstrate linearity. Also, by running a Pearson Product-Moment, obtain the correlation matrix. Here we can see a potential problem: they are all correlated significantly with each other, but particularly Rating2 and Breath2 ($r = 0.92$). This is a very strong relationship, and suggests that the inclusion of breathing rate as an extra DV is not really adding anything to self-reported anxiety (if you're out of breath, perhaps you feel anxious anyway!). Keeping it in might lower the power of the test unnecessarily. Nevertheless, we will plough on and keep this issue in mind when we interpret the result.

Calculations

The calculations for MANOVA work in the same way as for ANOVA, except the data are in a different form so it is much harder to perform the analysis by hand. Most readers may prefer to skip the next section and rejoin again at 'Interpreting the computer output'. However, it is often useful to know what the computer is doing once we have implemented our commands; otherwise, we may as well simply call it 'magic'. So I will now try to explain what is going on in as simple a manner as possible.

Working with matrices (optional)

There are two sets of tests we need to calculate: first, we need a *multivariate* test, which combines the DVs in a single analysis that can be tested for significance; then we need *univariate* tests for each DV by itself, to examine their individual effects.

First, because we are examining the effect of combined DVs on the IV, we have to juggle several values for each case in the study. So when we set about working out sums of squares, we are no longer adding together single values, we are adding and multiplying *matrices* of values. We could start off with the scores on the DVs, and the first two participants in the neutral film group would have matrices of DV scores as below (remember, we are only interested in the 'after' scores at the moment):

$$\begin{bmatrix} 6 \\ 67 \\ 16 \end{bmatrix} \begin{bmatrix} 4 \\ 66 \\ 15 \end{bmatrix}$$

The *means* across subjects would also form a set of matrices, known as **W**, which represent the within-groups variance (composed of $\mathbf{W_1}$, $\mathbf{W_2}$ and $\mathbf{W_3}$ – the within-group variance for each 'film' group). Then we work out **B**, the matrix of between-group means, and add **W** and **B** to find **T** (matrix of total variance).

The *determinant* of a matrix is the difference in cross-products; for example, for the matrix **A** below, |**A**| is calculated by multiplying the values on the main diagonal, which represent the variance elements (5 × 2) and subtracting the values on the cross diagonal (3 × 3), which represent the covariance in the type of matrices we are dealing with. The determinant of **A** is therefore 1:

$$\mathbf{A}\begin{bmatrix} 5 & 3 \\ 3 & 2 \end{bmatrix} \Rightarrow |\mathbf{A}| = (5 \times 2) - (3 \times 3) = 1$$

Now we need to calculate a statistic which will be tested for significance. There are a number of ways of doing this in MANOVA. The most popular statistic is *Wilk's Lambda* (Λ), which is calculated by taking the determinant of **W** (|**W**|), and dividing it by the determinant of **T** (|**T**|). Values range between 0 and 1 – the lower the value, the greater the difference between the groups.

Interpreting the computer output

The variance–covariance matrices for our study are much more complicated than the above example, so from now on we can let the computer do the donkey-work. Figure 3.1 contains the kind of display you would expect after running this MANOVA design (in this case, SPSS 9.0).

Lambda (Λ) in our study comes out at 0.357. We can interpret this in two ways. We can convert Λ to an approximate *F* value, which turns out to be 2.4 (all software packages do this automatically). This actually just misses significance at the 0.05 level. Perhaps the inclusion of Breath2 has not helped.

Most software packages (including SPSS) calculate three additional measures of significance. The higher row in Figure 3.1 has a set of tests on the 'intercept'; this is a measure derived from the General Linear Model, where it performs a regression analysis on the data – you can ignore this line. The bottom row is our multivariate test. Along with Wilk's Lambda we have Pillai's Trace, Hotelling's Trace and Roy's Largest Root, all of which produce different figures. How do we know which to use?

Multivariate Tests[c]

Effect		Value	F	Hypothesis df	Error df	Sig.
Intercept	Pillai's Trace	.997	1439.245[a]	3.000	11.000	.000
	Wilk's Lambda	.003	1439.245[a]	3.000	11.000	.000
	Hotelling's Trace	392.521	1439.245[a]	3.000	11.000	.000
	Roy's Largest Root	392.521	1439.245[a]	3.000	11.000	.000
FILM	Pillai's Trace	.694	2.127	6.000	24.000	.087
	Wilk's Lambda	.357	2.469[a]	6.000	22.000	.056
	Hotelling's Trace	1.656	2.761	6.000	20.000	.040
	Roy's Largest Root	1.564	6.258[b]	3.000	12.000	.008

[a] Exact statistic

[b] The statistic is an upper bound on F that yields a lower bound on the significance level

[c] Design: Intercept+FILM

Figure 3.1 SPSS output for multivariate significance tests

Pillai's trace

Sometimes referred to as the Pillai-Bartlett trace or Pillai's criterion, this is the most conservative measure available for testing multivariate significance; if it is significant we can feel very confident in reporting our outcome! It is calculated by adding the *eigenvalues* from the **B** and **T** matrices multiplied (**BT**). (An eigenvalue may be described as the 'root' of a particular matrix; it is a figure which best represents, or accounts for, the variance in a matrix. See Chapter 9 for a more detailed explanation.) It is then converted to an *F* for significance testing. For this solution, Pillai, like Lambda, fails to reach significance at 0.05.

Hotelling's trace

Also known as the Hotelling-Lawley trace, this is the sum of the eigenvalues of **BW**, and so is a ratio of the pooled effect variance to the error variance. The *F* approximation is, for our example, significant at $p < 0.05$. When there are only two groups of the IV, this will be identical to Pillai and Lambda, so any one of them can be used.

Roy's largest root

Also known as Roy's gcr. This is clearly a biased measure, since it refers to the largest eigenvalue, or root, in the solution, rather than pooling the variance. This can be seen from our example, in that the approximate *F* is over 6, which is significant at $p = 0.008$. Ultimately, your choice of tests relies on your concerns as a researcher. Lambda is the most commonly used. In our report we would feel justified, however, in quoting the Hotelling statistic too, to demonstrate the 'borderline' nature of the finding.

Univariate tests of significance

So far, our test has shown that there is a slight, marginally significant, effect of film group, using the three DVs in combination. We can find out more by performing multiple comparisons as in ordinary ANOVA. The first thing we can do is to run tests of significance on the individual DVs, effectively unpacking the combined multivariate solution. This simply consists of running standard one-way ANOVAs on each column of data.

Univariate tests are run automatically by whichever software you are using. They can be found in SPSS immediately below the multivariate tests, in a table headed 'Between-Subjects Effects'. The row in the data table labelled GROUP gives you the F statistic for each separate DV. Individually, the effect of group is significant for all three, particularly Pulse2 ($p < 0.01$). However, if we were simply to accept these one-way ANOVAs, then we would have to apply the Bonferroni adjustment to control the error rate, so our significance level would go up to 5%/3, i.e. 0.016. Pulse2 still reaches significance with this correction and Breath2 would, but only just. Thus it looks as though Pulse2 may make the largest single contribution to the multivariate solution. It is also the measure with the highest observed power (0.86).

We could examine this possibility further, by conducting a *Roy-Bargmann Stepdown Analysis*. This is similar to stepwise multiple regression, in that it allows us to enter variables into the multivariate solution one by one, in order to see what effect each one is having by itself. On SPSS this is not an option within the Multivariate command, but you can perform the analysis by selecting a variable as a covariate and running the MANOVA with the remaining two variables as DVs.

We might, on the basis of our univariate tests, choose to partial out the Pulse2 scores. Running a MANCOVA with Pulse2 as covariate, and Rating2 and Breath2 as DVs, would give us a Lambda value of 0.72, which is nowhere near significant. In fact, whichever of these variables you decide to partial out will generally lead to the same conclusion – suggesting that, in a sample this small, the high correlations between the DVs have led to a high level of redundancy. Our composite measure shows a slight effect, but once we have started to unpack this, we find that any of the anxiety measures by itself would discriminate equally well between the film groups.

Not all statisticians agree on the use of univariate follow-up tests in MANOVA. Huberty and Morris (1989) present a powerful case against doing so, arguing that multivariate and univariate ANOVA are designed to tackle completely different research questions. This may be true of studies exploring the pattern of response across a number of discrete variables. Where the variables are closely related, however, it does little harm to investigate further. As in a multiple regression, it is interesting to see which variables are making the greatest contribution to the overall significant effect. What Huberty and Morris are warning against in particular is the use of MANOVA as a *preliminary* step in the analysis.

Post hoc **and** *a priori* **comparisons**

Having unpacked the combined effect of the dependent variables, we now need to know where the significant difference lies between the film groups. We can do this by requesting *post hoc* comparisons like the ones used in ANOVA – such as Tukey. This calculates a critical difference between the groups on each of the three measures. However, unless you can be bothered to calculate this by hand, you will find that SPSS and other programs give you little control over the error rate. A Tukey analysis finds that the neutral and fiction groups differ substantially on Pulse2 ($p = 0.006$), but the other comparisons are less reliable.

An alternative approach, depending on your initial hypothesis, is to carry out a planned comparison test by using the Contrasts subcommand in SPSS. We could test for a linear trend – and we would find this significant on all three variables. Alternatively, we could carry out a *Helmert comparison*, which selects one group (for our hypothesis, that would be group 3, non-fiction), contrasts it with the remaining groups, and then contrasts the remaining groups against one another. If we perform this test we find that non-fiction is significantly different from the other two groups, but that neutral and fiction are not significantly different from each other. This effect is consistent for all three DVs. This result would be all the information we need to reject our null hypothesis.

MANOVA with two IVs and three DVs

Now, build the factor of *age* into the design by running film group and age as fixed factors. You will find that you have a significant effect of film group, even using Wilk's Λ, but that there is no main effect of age. There is also a significant interaction between group and age – which is reason enough for adding it to the model – with an effect size of $\eta^2 = 0.42$. If we examine the univariate tests you can see that this significant interaction only holds up for the Pulse2 data, as depicted by the lineplot in Figure 3.2.

This shows quite clearly that, while adult participants experienced a faster pulse than under-18s after watching the disturbing fictitious footage, the situation was reversed for the non-fiction. You could make all kinds of inference about this finding – perhaps younger people are more desensitised to fictional trauma, perhaps they are more worried by real-life trauma. Two things need to be held in check before making too bold a statement: first, how good a measure of *anxiety* is pulse rate? It seems to correlate highly with our other measures, which is perhaps a good sign. Second, we cannot say too much about the factor of age in this study, since our groups are differentiated on the basis of a cut-off point alone (above or below 18). After all, we may have to have quite an old over-18s group before making a causal inference about desensitisation to on-screen trauma. And anyway, how *young* are our under-18s? Beware of ambiguous or misleading independent

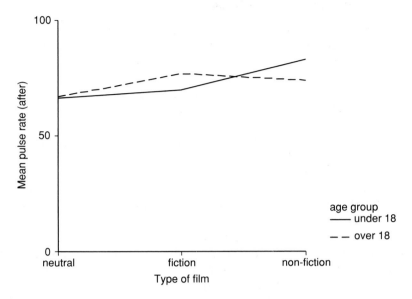

Figure 3.2 Lineplot of film type × age for Pulse2 data

variables (although for such a study to be publishable, we would need to provide descriptive statistics of the participants to assure readers that we were not making ludicrous claims!).

MANCOVA with one IV, three DVs and three covariates

Up to now, for the sake of simplicity, we have ignored the pretest measures in our data base. However, it would not be worth doing the film × anxiety study *without* the pretest measures. These could influence the sampling and design aspects of the study in advance of any data collection; for example, they could be used as baseline measures of pulse rate, breathing rate, and so on, which we use to ensure equivalence across the three groups. If we were confident that there were no pretest differences on these measures we would accept the results of the analyses conducted so far.

An alternative is to use the 'before' measures as *covariates* in our multivariate analysis. This would be a particularly useful model if we were using participants who were hard to recruit, in a clinical setting for example. We are often unable to screen 100 participants for each group in advance of testing: if our experimental group requires people with a rare psychiatric condition, we may have to make do with a sample of 20 that we have scraped together over several months!

By using Rating1, Pulse1 and Breath1 as covariates, we are partialling out the baseline data so that the 'after' measures are adjusted to account for any pretest differences between and within the film groups. If the 'non-fiction' group happened to consist of several individuals with high pulse rates to begin with, then the higher pulse rates registered in this group will be adjusted down accordingly (unless the other groups had high baseline pulse rates too).

Enter the data into the MANOVA command on your preferred software and place the three 'before' variables into the covariate slot. Select film group as the independent variable, or fixed factor (ignore age difference for this example). Run the analysis – since you have already screened the data for homogeneity of variance and regression – and you will find that the multivariate test on film group is now significant even using Pillai's trace ($F(6,18) = 5.05$, $p = 0.003$). All the univariate tests are also significant.

On the face of it, this result would seem to support our hypothesis – and we might assume that the non-fiction group's higher anxiety ratings have been bolstered by taking the pretest measures into account. However, in looking at the adjusted means in Table 3.4, the means for the non-fiction group have, if anything, been adjusted *down*! (Note that the means are adjusted according to the *combination* of covariates, not just to the related covariate – so Rating2, for example, is adjusted according to the means of Pulse1 and Breath1 as well as that of Rating1.) However, this has not affected the difference between non-fiction and the other groups – run a Helmert, or Difference, contrast on this data and you will find non-fiction to have significantly higher anxiety measures scores than fiction and neutral. The other groups now differ significantly on Rating2.

What, then, might explain why the use of the covariates has resulted in higher overall significance? There are two possible explanations. First, this is an example where the use of covariates bolsters the differences found in the post-test means when there is equivalence in the pretest means. Second, with specific reference to this study, we might consider how the use of

Table 3.3 Results of multivariate significance tests

	Hypothesis df	Error df	Value	F	Sig.
Pillai's trace	6	24	0.69	2.13	0.09
Wilk's Lambda	6	22	0.36	2.47	0.06
Hotelling's trace	6	20	1.66	2.76	0.04
Roy's largest root	3	12	1.56	6.26	0.01

Table 3.4 Adjusted cell means (distance from original means in italics) for MANCOVA example

Type of film	Rating2		Pulse2		Breath2	
Neutral	3.9	*−0.3*	69.1	*+2.3*	15.2	*−0.4*
Fiction	5.3	*+0.8*	70.5	*−3.0*	17.0	*+0.8*
Non-fiction	7.4	*−0.3*	78.5	*0.0*	18.8	*−0.4*

covariates has adjusted means on particular dependent variables. While the mean for the fiction group has increased relative to the neutral group on Rating2 and Breath2, on Pulse 2 the change has been in the opposite direction. It was clear from our original study that Pulse2 accounted for the most influence in the model as a whole (perhaps because Rating2 and Breath2 are so highly correlated). A change on Pulse2 will create a more substantial change in the overall solution than a change on the other DVs.

Therefore, we can conclude that, with pretest means adjusted to account for slightly higher baseline pulse rates in the fiction group, the post-test means show very little difference between the neutral and fiction groups. Since Pulse2 appears to be the best single measure of anxiety (in this study), we can confidently reject the null hypothesis.

Split-plot 3 × 2 MANOVA with three dependent measures

There is one final way you could analyse the data. Select a Repeated Measures command in your software program which allows you to specify a within-subjects factor. In our case, this could well be a measure of TIME (pretest vs. post-test). Enter the pretest measures as different measures of level 1 (before) and the post-test measures as the different measures of level 2 (after). Request Tukey's *post hoc* tests too. You will find that there is a significant overall (multivariate) interaction between film group and time, and that pulse and breathing rate successfully distinguish the non-fiction group from the others using Tukey's HSD.

Two examples of MANOVA from the psychological literature

Kashima et al. *(1995): culture and self-construal*

Self-construal is an area of great interest in cross-cultural psychology. Much research has focused on the apparent differences between Eastern and Western concepts of self – most notably, the extent to which significant others are incorporated into the individual self-construal. Notably, males in Western society tend to have a more individualistic self-construal than females, and Westerners in general have a more individualistic self-construal than Easterners.

Kashima *et al.* (1995) chose to investigate the two-way interaction between culture and gender on a set of 'self' measures that together made up an individual's 'self-construal'. Like IQ (see Chapter 2), it is argued that self-construal is not such a simple quality that it can be captured using a single value. Therefore multivariate measures are essential for serious research on the topic.

The authors did not stop at MANOVA. They employed two further methods – Discriminant Function Analysis (to be covered in Chapter 4) and

Multidimensional Scaling (Chapter 10) to explore between-group differences. They argued that this was necessary in order to lend their study *statistical conclusion validity* (i.e., if two or more techniques concur on a result, it strengthens the confidence of your findings).

Kashima *et al.* chose to compare standard (i.e. 18–21 years) undergraduates in five different cultures – Australia, Hawaii, Japan, Korea, and the United States. These cultures were chosen so that they could be ranked (with Australia and the US at the 'Western' end of the dimension, Korea and Japan at the 'Eastern' end, and Hawaii in the middle). Male:female ratios varied in different groups, but there was a total number of 634 females and 377 males. Self-construal measures were obtained through a combination of questionnaires, which were then factor analysed to produce seven dependent variables:

1   Collectivism (dependence on social group in decision-making)
2   Relatedness (the degree of relatedness to the social group)
3   Allocentrism (dependence on culture in decision-making)
4   Agency (independence from social group and culture in decision-making)
5   Assertiveness (independence from social group and culture in behaviour)
6   Cohesiveness (of friendship networks)
7   Self–other similarity (with others in friendship network)

These measures were standardised (transformed into Z scores) twice before testing. They were standardised first of all within each participant (i.e., using the participant's own mean and standard deviation). This was done to control for response bias (the tendency to use one end of the scale, or extreme ends). The second standardisation was within-culture – in other words, to use the mean and standard deviation for the participant's cultural group. This was intended to ensure that there was no confounding between-groups variance that would make the analysis inappropriate for MANOVA.

Multivariate tests showed significant main effects of culture ($F = 22.3$, $p < 0.05$) and gender ($F = 12.1$, $p < 0.005$), and there was a significant interaction between culture and gender ($F = 2.1$, $p < 0.005$). (Alpha, the significance level, was set at 0.005 for the study because of the large N.) Effect sizes were small, particularly for the interaction, where $\eta^2 = 0.016$. Effect size is a more important statistic in a huge study like this. $F = 2.1$ is a small F ratio and would be well below the critical value for a small study, yet here it is significant even at the corrected alpha.

Univariate tests showed a significant effect of culture on all DVs. There was a significant, though small, effect of gender for relatedness and cohesiveness. There was a significant interaction, though with a small effect size, between gender and culture for allocentrism. On inspection of the means, this proved hard to interpret, with no discernible pattern (for instance, Korean women scored more highly than Korean men, but the trend was reversed in Japan). Inspection of the means for the main effects of culture also revealed no distinct patterns, although, as predicted, Western groups tended to score higher on 'individualistic' measures such as Agency and Assertiveness.

Kashima *et al.* concluded that culture was a more important factor in this study than gender: in other words, the differences *between* cultures were more pronounced than the (gender) differences *within* cultures. However, there were unexpected differences between cultural groups on some items, and this led the researchers to wonder whether measures that had been devised in the West were not inherently biased towards the Western view of self-construal!

Brewer, Socha and Potter (1996): gender and supervisors' use of feedback

This is an example of an experimental study that uses a MANOVA design. Once again, gender is a key independent variable. Male and female undergraduates took part in an experiment where they were required to supervise both a male and a female confederate as they worked on a series of word puzzles. After each puzzle had been completed, the participant was invited to give written feedback on the confederates' performance. The feedback consisted of a controlled selection of phrases which were coded as

- General negative ('You are doing poorly. Try harder.')
- Specific negative ('You missed the goal on the last one by _____. Try harder.')
- Specific positive ('You met the goal exactly on the last one. Keep it up.')
- General positive ('Your performance is excellent.')
- Neutral ('Keep working as hard as you can'.)

A $2 \times 2 \times 2$ MANOVA was run, using these five measures as the dependent variables. The independent variables were (participant gender × confederate performance: either high or low × confederate gender). Using Wilk's Λ, no effect was found of supervisor gender, but there was a significant effect of performance (poor performers receiving more feedback), and of confederate gender (males receiving more feedback). There were also significant multivariate interactions between participant gender and confederate gender, and between performance and confederate gender.

These were investigated further using a stepdown analysis. The type of feedback that accounted for the most variance in total feedback score was specific negative, while general positive accounted for least variance. Specific negative feedback produced significant differences between male and female participants, with males giving twice as much negative feedback as females. Males also responded more quickly to poor performance than females.

The most surprising finding was the participant gender × confederate gender interaction; stepdown analysis here revealed that it was only the neutral feedback category that produced a significant effect (with specific positive, specific negative and general negative acting as covariates). There is no theoretical explanation for this finding, an example of the potential problems encountered when trying to unpack the DVs in a MANOVA.

Summary

MANOVA is a useful technique to use when we design an experiment with more than one dependent measure, such as a pretest post-test study. Because each case in the data set has more than one dependent value, matrix algebra is necessary for the calculation, but few researchers today would attempt such feats by hand. However it is still useful to know how the computer arrives at its values, particularly in order to correctly interpret the output. I have outlined the basic steps involved in calculating statistics such as Wilk's Lambda, which are converted to F ratios in order to interpret their statistical significance. I have also explained how to unpack a MANOVA calculation to conduct follow-up analyses, and the use of covariates in MANCOVA designs.

4   Discriminant function analysis

Discriminant Function Analysis (DFA), often just called discriminant analysis, is related to various multivariate techniques and could be covered just about anywhere in the first three parts of this book. However I have included it under analysis of variance since it is a logical follow-on from MANOVA. If MANOVA enables us to explore differences between groups, DFA allows us to predict group membership on the basis of the same dependent variables. In effect, it is MANOVA in reverse.

It does this by producing a limited number of 'discriminant functions' that can be used to divide up the participants, or cases, in the study. The functions in this context are the (linear) combinations of variables in a data set that best predict group membership. It is the researcher's task to identify, or label, those functions in a way that makes good theoretical sense. By requiring such interpretative analysis from the researcher, it is closer to factor analysis than ANOVA, except that it is analysed case by case, and you need distinct groups in order to carry the test out in the first place.

Discriminant analysis may be performed in conjunction with MANOVA, or as a technique in its own right. In the first case, it is usually used – as in the Kashima study – to consolidate the findings of the MANOVA. In other words, it helps clarify what appears to be the case from simply examining the univariate effects and the various multiple comparisons. The overall picture may be unclear when dealing with large numbers of dependent variables, so discriminant analysis offers a tidy way of packaging the important characteristics. It is best used by itself when our hypothesis is too vague for the outcome of a MANOVA to be easily interpreted. In this respect it is something of an *exploratory* technique.

In the Kashima *et al.* study in Chapter 3, DFA was used to separate the five cultural groups after the MANOVA, and it identified two discriminant functions that could be used to differentiate the groups. The first of these was interpreted as 'individualism' and separated the Western and Eastern groups. The second was interpreted as 'relational' and separated the Korean and Japanese groups from each other. In theory this process could have continued until the authors used up all their original groups, although in practice there is not much point in labelling functions that are not significant, and those are usually the first two to be identified.

Some statisticians argue that the two main uses of discriminant analysis – description and prediction – should remain separate from one another, as Descriptive Discriminant Analysis (DDA) and Predictive Discriminant Analysis (PDA). The former is mainly used to confirm the findings of a MANOVA – that specific variables, or groups of variables, have certain effects, while the latter may be used to predict group membership on the basis of a subset of variables. Most textbooks ignore this distinction, but if you are interested in using discriminant analysis a lot, Huberty (1984) is worth reading.

In either case, the dependent variables in DFA are usually referred to as *predictor* variables.

Questions to be answered by discriminant function analysis

How many functions can we identify?

The first function to be identified using DFA is the best discriminator: it is the function that most clearly differentiates the groups, and the best function from which we can predict group membership. In the Kashima *et al.* study, the dimension which seemed to account for the greatest amount of between-group variance was interpreted as *individualism*. In other words, it was the 'individualist' measures which discriminated most clearly between cultures.

The number of subsequent functions that can be identified is determined by the number of groups in the study (k) and the number of predictor variables (p). There is a limit to the number of functions that we can identify, which corresponds to the smaller value of $(k - 1)$ or $(p - 1)$.

The second function to be identified in the Kashima *et al.* study was interpreted as a *relational* dimension. Subsequent functions are assumed to be *orthogonal* to the first: in other words, they are entirely independent dimensions. This function did not account for much of the variance between the Western groups, but sharply differentiated the Eastern ones.

How do you interpret functions?

Discriminant functions can be regarded as 'latent' variables in that they are not measured by the researcher; they are abstract statistical concepts that need to be interpreted in a way that makes sound theoretical sense in the context of the research question and previous theory. (You will encounter many latent variables in multivariate statistics. The most common ones are the principal components that are identified in factor analysis.) It is at times like this that statistics becomes highly interpretative, and not quite as 'objective' as some quantitative psychologists like to think!

Luckily, it is not all guesswork: there are plenty of statistics which can help guide our interpretations. In DFA, the best way of labelling functions is to identify which dependent variables have significantly high loadings on each function. A loading is the correlation coefficient that describes the relationship between the DV and the function. Suppose we subjected the data from the IQ study from Chapter 2 to a discriminant analysis: verbal measures of cognitive ability might load highly on the first function, and visual measures might load highly on the next one. You would interpret the first as a verbal function and the second as a visual one, concluding that the verbal elements of intelligence were better discriminators between your groups than the visual elements.

How well has the analysis classified individual cases?

The next step in DFA is to classify each participant, or case, in the study, by comparing the individual pattern of means with the various patterns of group means for the dependent variables.

Suppose case 13 has the following set of means on four predictor variables:

P1	P2	P3	P4
13	15	17	18

Now suppose that there are two groups in the study, whose overall means are as follows:

group 1				group 2			
P1	P2	P3	P4	P1	P2	P3	P4
18	19	11	10	13	14	15	16

This would be an easy case for the analysis to classify, since case 13 so closely resembles the pattern of means for group 2. However, if there was a third group in the study whose means were exactly the same as case 13's it would be classified as group 3. Normally the match is not so clear and the computer has to guess. At the end of the analysis a hit rate (per cent correct) is calculated, which tells us how clearly the groups were distinguished.

How strong is the association between the DVs and the groups?

Once the functions have been identified, we will be able to say what percentage of the total variance in the data each function 'explains'. All the functions together explain 100 per cent of the variance, but how is this distributed among the individual functions? Suppose, in a three function solution, the first function explains only about 40 per cent, and the variable loadings are small, giving us little information. This would suggest that the groups don't differ in a meaningful way on the basis of the predictor variables. If, however, in a two function solution the first function explains 85 per cent by itself, this would indicate a very strong association between that particular dimension and the nature of the groups.

How important is each dependent variable in the analysis?

Some of the variables may be well represented on the functions; others may barely load at all. With lots of DVs, we might expect quite a high level of *redundancy* – we may not be able to use some of the variables in our analysis because they don't quite fit into the pattern described by the functions. This doesn't necessarily mean they aren't good discriminators – just that other patterns of variables together explain more variance.

A worked example of discriminant function analysis

Imagine you have access to the personnel files of a business organisation and you are interested in seeing what factors are more influential when recruiting new office staff. You have a hunch (it may be more than a hunch if you have found some literature to support it) that the organisation is operating a sexist policy of favouring young, attractive women over older, or less attractive, women irrespective of qualifications and experience. There are all sorts of hypotheses you could generate on the basis of this hunch, but for this analysis you want to reduce your study to one independent variable with two levels – either 'got the job' or 'rejected'.

You might start by gathering together the measures that you are going to enter as your dependent variables. You clearly want a measure of age, some indexical score representing qualifications (perhaps awarding a certain number of points per each qualification at each level), and some measure of experience (number of years at the highest level). You will also need a measure of attractiveness, so you could get an independent panel of judges to rate the candidates' photographs.

As in MANOVA, there are certain restrictions on the ratio of N to p (the number of predictors, or DVs). Stevens (1996) argues that you should have 20 participants for every dependent variable. Therefore, you would need an N of 80 for the four-DV study outlined above. For simplicity we will use a data set of 20 in this example, displayed in Table 4.1, although for a published study this would clearly be inadequate. The usual assumptions of MANOVA (homogeneity of variance, normality, homogeneity of regression) are applicable to discriminant analysis too – and the outlier problem is particularly important here because of the classification of individual cases. Therefore screening of outliers on the pattern of measures, such as Mahalanobis distances, is well worth carrying out.

Testing significance

The preliminary calculations are the same as in MANOVA in that we are dealing with matrices of values that correspond to the sums of squares values in ANOVA. We end up with the **BW** matrix (the between- and within-subject variances), whose eigenvalues (λ) are entered into the following

Table 4.1 Data for discriminant function analysis

Success	Age	Qualifications	Experience	Attractiveness
	24	4	4	9
	21	3	2	9
	20	8	1	7
	22	5	2	7
	25	6	3	5
Got the job	31	5	6	8
	27	3	7	5
	19	5	1	9
	22	4	4	3
	25	7	5	2
	32	8	3	4
	31	7	1	2
	26	2	3	6
	28	1	4	5
	29	1	1	2
Rejected	28	3	6	7
	32	2	2	8
	25	1	1	1
	36	6	1	4
	27	2	2	2

equation to produce Wilk's Λ (r = maximum number of eigenvalues possible).

$$\Lambda = \frac{1}{1 + \lambda_r}$$

Unlike in MANOVA, when the Λ value is converted to an F, in DFA it is converted to a chi-square statistic known as Bartlett's (or Rao's) V, which can be looked up in the tables for significance with *df* determined by $p(k-1)$.

The number of eigenvalues in the **BW** matrix will depend on the number of groups and predictors – this is why we have a limit on the number of functions that can be identified in any given study. For our study there are only two groups, so, regardless of the number of DVs, we can only identify one function. With a three group IV, we would test the two eigenvalues together first and then remove the larger, so that the second function would explain the remaining variance in the solution. This second function is referred to as the *first residual*, because it is examining the error variance left behind after the largest root has been removed. If this is significant, we remove the largest remaining eigenvalue and continue testing the second residual. And so on, until the functions stop being significant (although this is unlikely to be very long unless you have a huge sample). The eigenvalues could be tested separately, although this may well result in functions being overrated (i.e. Type 1 error).

Because there are only two groups in our present example, only one discriminant function can be identified. This has an eigenvalue of 2.87, which is converted to $\chi^2 = 21.65$, which is significant at $p < 0.001$.

Interpreting the functions

The next step is to interpret the function(s). If the χ^2 test was non-significant there would be little point in proceeding further, since there would clearly be no function that explained our group difference adequately. However that is certainly not the case here.

There are two sets of values which we can use to interpret the functions. The first set of values are the *standardised discriminant function coefficients* (sometimes called 'canonical coefficients'). These are *raw* measures of the relationship of each DV to the relevant function, with the effect of the other DVs partialled out. For small sample sizes you need to disregard anything lower than ±0.4. A high, or significant, loading will be one above 0.7 or 0.8, although this depends on sample size too. There is no formal test of significance for these coefficients, so this is another area where the researcher has to rely on his or her interpretative skills. You will notice in Table 4.2 that age has a very high negative coefficient (−1.08) – this indicates that age has an important role in differentiating our two groups. Attractiveness, on the other hand, has a modest coefficient (0.365). Such a figure might be important in a large sample, but not in one with only 20 participants. We can regard attractiveness as a *redundant* variable in our analysis.

The other set of values which we can use are the *correlations* between the variable and the function. These are refined measures of the same relationship that is expressed by the coefficients. They are more useful measures when our DVs are correlated with each other. We use these values to determine which DVs are related to which function (if any), by describing each DV's *loading* on each function. In Table 4.3, age has a loading (correlation) of −0.52 on the function – this would be interpreted as a moderately high negative loading, so it probably tells us something about the nature of the function. Experience, however, has a small loading (0.18), which means that

Table 4.2 Standardised canonical discriminant function coefficients

Variable	Function 1
Age	−1.08
Qualifications	0.81
Experience	0.75
Attractiveness	0.37

Table 4.3 Variable–function correlations

Variable	Function 1
Age	−0.52
Attractiveness	0.29
Qualifications	0.24
Experience	0.18

it isn't very involved with the function. We would have to interpret our function, then, as representing something that is related to age but *not* to experience. The other two loadings are also fairly modest (note how the computer has shuffled the variables into rank order of loading size). What is interesting is that attractiveness, which we have considered redundant, now comes out as second highest on the loadings (albeit at a small figure, 0.29). This suggests that its small coefficient – representing its importance with the other variables partialled out – is due to its high correlation with another variable. A look at the correlation matrix for the DVs suggests that this might be *age*.

Our interpretation of this single function is that it represents age, with a slight nod towards the candidate's attractiveness. We could reject the null hypothesis on these grounds, although our argument would gain more validity if we also ran MANOVA (and, on request, SPSS will supply the relevant statistics as part of the discriminant analysis). In our example we can see that the multivariate test is significant, and this is supported by the univariate tests on age and attractiveness – although the latter is only marginally significant ($p = 0.05$).

Classification analysis

The other important role of discriminant analysis is to provide a *classification analysis*, where it predicts group membership of individual cases from the dependent variables. This is achieved by calculating the group centroid on the basis of the function(s), and then matching each case to the centroids to see which group its pattern of means is closest to. When there are two groups it uses a cut-off point (the midpoint) to sort the cases.

How do we know whether the classification analysis has been a success? We evaluate it on the basis of *hit rate* – how many cases are accurately placed in the two groups (obviously, we can only perform this assessment if we know what the groups are already). In SPSS this information is displayed in a summary table (see Table 4.4) which gives the percentage of correct classifications for each group. In our example you can see that the hit rate is very high: 95 per cent of all cases are correctly classified.

We can find out more by requesting a casewise analysis of classification. This breaks the classification down into individual cases; for each case a group membership code is given, and misclassifications are represented by

Table 4.4 Hit rates for classification analysis

Actual group membership	Predicted group membership	
	Accepted	Rejected
Accepted	10 (100%)	0 (0%)
Rejected	1 (10%)	9 (90%)

an asterisk. (This is known as the *jackknife procedure*). The results are also cross-validated – that is, each case is given a probability of being classified in either group. For example, case 1 has a 92 per cent probability of being assigned to group 1 and a 0.4 per cent probability of being assigned to group 2. Therefore it is a pretty representative member of group 1.

From the output we can see that case 16 is the only one to be mis-classified, though, looking at the raw data, it is hard to see why. One possibility is that the case is an outlier, in which case we can consult the *Mahalanobis distances* listed in the table for each case (recall from Chapter 3 that the Mahalanobis distance (D^2) is a chi-square value relating to the distance of the case from the overall group centroid – the central point of the variable means). Cases 4 and 12 have a D^2 value of 0, which means that their centroid is the same as the centroid of their respective group. Case 19 has a D^2 of 2.7, but this does not quite reach significance. D^2 for case 16 is over 1, but is nowhere near significant. Perhaps some subtle difference in its pattern of scores is responsible for the confusion.

Other features of discriminant function analysis

Stepwise (sequential) discriminant analysis

Like stepdown analysis in MANOVA, it is possible to exercise more control over the entry of dependent variables into discriminant analysis. We could set certain criteria for entry, such as the minimum value of Λ or V. If we ran the previous example as a stepwise analysis, attractiveness (as it is effectively redundant according to its coefficient) would fail to meet the entry criteria and would not be included in the final solution. Stepwise discriminant analysis is also referred to as sequential discriminant analysis, because variable selection can be either forward or backward (we can remove earlier variables from the analysis if they are not contributing anything at subsequent stages).

Stepwise discriminant analysis has been strongly criticised by statisticians, because it can so easily lead to inaccurate conclusions about the relative importance of variables in the analysis, and to variables being needlessly discarded. It has been suggested that the only statistic that can be used to infer relative importance of variables is *F*-to-remove (Huberty 1984). This statistic is provided by SPSS in a table like the one in Table 4.5.

Table 4.5 F-to-remove and lambda for variables in stepwise discriminant analysis of the recruitment bias example

Step	Variables	Tolerance	F-to-remove	Wilk's lambda
1	Age	1.00	13.97	
2	Age	0.88	17.29	0.86
	Qualifications	0.88	5.48	0.56
3	Age	0.67	26.38	0.76
	Qualifications	0.76	8.56	0.44
	Experience	0.73	7.83	0.43

A high *F* statistic tells you how important each variable is to the analysis at each step. For the first step in our recruitment bias example, where age has been entered on the basis of its lambda value, the analysis would be substantially affected if age was then removed and the analysis conducted on the remaining three variables. At stage two, with qualifications in as well, the removal of age would affect the analysis to an even greater degree; even more so with experience in there too. Clearly, for the most important variables, their importance grows relative to that of other, less important variables.

Interpreting more than one discriminant function

This is just a short section on the interpretation of designs which yield a second function or more. Rather than introducing a completely new study, I will run a discriminant analysis on the film × anxiety data from Chapter 3, although as you will see, the analysis is not of much use!

Tables 4.6 and 4.7 contain the important data from the discriminant function analysis. Note that one function accounts for practically all the

Table 4.6 Significance testing statistics for film × anxiety

Function	λ	% variance	Λ	V	df	p
1	1.49	93.6	0.37	12.1	6	0.06
2	0.1	6.4	0.9	1.2	2	0.56

Table 4.7 Structure matrix for film × anxiety

Variable	Function 1	Function 2
Pulse2	0.85	−0.52
Breath2	0.79	0.62
Rating2	0.65	0.63

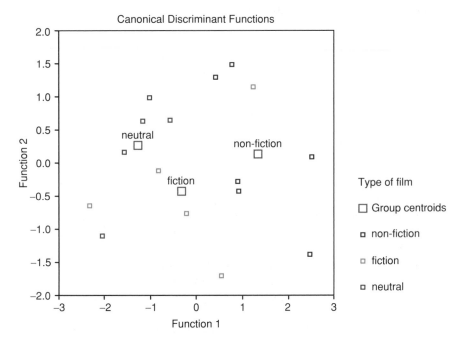

Figure 4.1 Discriminant function plot for film × anxiety

variance – and even that fails to reach significance at 0.05! This suggests that, as we expected from the MANOVA, the multicollinearity is forcing all the variance into one highly correlated function. This is confirmed by the structure matrix, which shows that all three variables load highly on function 1.

These data are easy to interpret: the three variables are all measuring the same thing (anxiety)! That is function 1. Function 2 is so far from significant it is not even worth thinking about, but if we had to label it we would need some sort of concept with an inverse relationship between pulse rate and the other measures. Since it is impossible to think of one (unless the participants were bluffing) then we will move straight to the graphic illustration of this data.

Figure 4.1 contains a discriminant function plot. The individual cases are plotted on both dimensions, with the first function as the *x*-axis and the second as the *y*-axis. It may take a while to interpret if you are not used to this kind of display. We read the first function left to right, so we can see that the non-fiction group centroid – the largest square – is highest on this function (which we have already labelled 'anxiety') and the neutral group centroid is lowest. Then re-orientate to read the second dimension from bottom to top. Here the fiction group centroid is lowest. If the functions were strong predictors of group membership, we would observe a clustering effect, with most of the little squares – the individual cases – nestling around the neutral group centroid, and the other squares around the non-fiction centroid. If our study had a third dimension, you would have to examine two functions at a time, unless you have a software program that produces rotating scatterplots (*DataDesk* is good for creating these).

Example of discriminant function analysis from the psychological literature

McGue et al. *(1999): personality factors in substance abuse*

This paper reports a typical example of a discriminant analysis being used to support a series of MANOVAs. The authors were investigating the role of personality factors in alcoholism and drug abuse, and predicting that the two different kinds of substance abuse would be characterised by different personality traits.

The sample for the study consisted of 1530 controls and 638 individuals with a substance use disorder. The experimental sample was split three ways, into a group with an alcohol disorder only ($n = 212$), a group with a drug disorder only ($n = 153$), and a group with both alcohol and drug disorders ($n = 173$). All participants completed the Multidimensional Personality Questionnaire (MPQ), an instrument which is based around 3 dimensions of personality – positive emotionality (enjoyment of life), negative emotionality (moodiness and negativity), and constraint (caution, inhibition and morality). There are 11 scales in all: the first 4 (well-being, social potency, achievement and social closeness) represent the positive emotionality dimension; the next 3 (stress reaction, alienation and aggression) represent negative emotionality; the next 3 (control, harm avoidance and traditionalism) represent constraint; and the final scale, absorption, is a separate construct.

Results

A 3-way MANOVA, with the 11 scales as DVs, eradicated gender as an important factor, but found significant main effects for drug and alcohol and a significant drug/alcohol interaction. On inspection of the univariate effects, the latter seemed to be based round some of the scales relating to negative emotionality and constraint. On all three negative scales, participants with an alcohol disorder scored more highly than those without; and on all three constraint variables, participants with a drug disorder scored more highly than those without.

Discriminant analysis was used to see if functions could be identified which represented these two groups of variables. The four groups (controls, alcohol yes/drug no, drug yes/alcohol no, and alcohol yes/drug yes) were entered as the independent variable, and the 11 MPQ scales were the dependent variables. The first of three possible functions that was identified had a χ^2 value of 277.5 ($p < 0.01$). For the second, $\chi^2 = 92.1$ ($p < 0.01$), and for the third, $\chi^2 = 9.71$, ($p = 0.32$). Therefore, the third function was not interpreted further.

The scales which loaded most highly on the first function are traditionalism (0.71), control (0.68), harm avoidance (0.51) and aggression (-0.51). Therefore this function appears to be a measure of *constraint*. The highest loadings on the second function were alienation (0.64), stress reaction (0.54), traditionalism (0.42) and aggression (0.41). This then appears to be related to *negative emotionality*.

No classification data are reported in the paper, which is a shame, perhaps reflecting the distinction mentioned earlier between descriptive discriminant analysis (which is used primarily to support MANOVA) and predictive discriminant analysis. It would have been interesting to see how accurately the analysis classified participants with both alcohol and drug disorders.

Summary

This chapter examines the technique of discriminant function analysis, which introduces readers to several more concepts common to many forms of multivariate statistics. Discriminant analysis is used when we have several dependent variables and we wish to use these to sort our cases, or participants, into a small number of discrete groups on the basis of their patterns of response. Often discriminant analysis is carried out to consolidate the findings of a MANOVA, since in some ways it is essentially a MANOVA in reverse. However it is probably best used as an exploratory technique, when we want to examine constructs that underpin the pattern of the data.

Part II

Measures of relationship

Regression techniques

In this part of the book I will introduce a number of statistical techniques which are extensions of the simple linear regression equation. As I suggested at points in Part I, the variants of ANOVA that we have considered so far could also be tackled by using regression techniques. Sometimes they would be *better* tackled using regression, particularly where the independent variables in an experimental design are random rather than fixed. For example, the spelling and visual memory study described in Chapter 2 considers two groups: controls and poor spellers.

An alternative approach is to test the children's spelling and treat spelling as a continuous (dependent) variable, in which case the visual memory and IQ scores could be entered as predictors in a regression equation. I did not use this approach in my study because there is substantial evidence to suggest that spelling ability is not normally distributed within the overall population at any given age, and that there is a small 'hump' at the left end of the bell curve representing a subgroup of children with specific learning difficulties in spelling. Therefore I relied on teachers' suggestions to identify a discrete experimental group of poor spellers.

As the techniques in this section become more and more complex, and we enter the world of structural equation modelling (Chapter 7), these restrictions actually become less important, because the modelling process enables us to play around with all manner of variables, discrete and continuous.

I shall start off by discussing the technique of multiple regression, which is a very widely used approach. In fact some psychologists might not consider multiple regression to be an 'advanced' method at all since it is covered in almost all undergraduate degrees, certainly in the UK. Nevertheless its logic underpins the more sophisticated techniques of logistic regression and structural equation modelling, which makes it a good launching pad for the section.

5 Multiple regression

Multiple regression is a simple extension of bivariate regression. If you have mastered that particular statistical technique, then multiple regression should be straightforward. All the elements are the same: correlation coefficients, prediction and regression lines. The only difference is that there are more of them!

Partial correlation

Before I begin to discuss multiple regression I shall briefly discuss partial correlation, since it is an important concept that underlies most of the principles behind multiple regression and more advanced modelling techniques. Partial correlation performs the same role in multiple regression as 'partialling out' a covariate in ANCOVA (see Chapter 2). Essentially we are reconsidering a relationship between two variables in the light of a third.

Table 5.1 represents an entirely fictitious data set whereby ten different (and rather violent!) capital cities are compared over the period of a month to investigate the relationship between wet weather and homicide (occasionally studies appear which *do* actually support a link, although cause-and-effect are very hard to establish, and this is the sort of problem which can be

Table 5.1 Data for partial correlation example

Rainy days (X)	Number of murders (Y)
4	6
5	3
7	6
8	3
11	8
12	8
14	9
15	8
16	11
18	12

caused when we try to interpret a correlational finding as though it were an ANOVA).

A Pearson's correlation finds that there is a significant positive relationship between X and Y ($r = 0.87$, $p = 0.001$), so by itself, the number of rainy days appears to be a good predictor of the homicide rates of these ten cities.

Now we will add a third variable to the equation. Z is a measure of national homicide rates. Suppose that there is a very high correlation between national and city homicide ($r_{YZ} = 0.94$) and an equally high correlation between national homicide and rainfall ($r_{XZ} = 0.93$). We can enter these figures into the formula for $r_{XY.Z}$ (the city homicide/rainfall relationship *controlling for* national homicide).

$$r_{XY.Z} = \frac{r_{XY} - (r_{XZ} \times r_{YZ})}{\sqrt{1 - r_{XZ}^2}\sqrt{1 - r_{YZ}^2}}$$

$$r_{XY.Z} = \frac{0.87 - (0.93 \times 0.94)}{\sqrt{1 - 0.93^2}\sqrt{1 - 0.94^2}}$$

$$= \frac{0.004}{0.36 \times 0.35}$$

$$= 0.03$$

Therefore, we can say that, when the effects of national homicide rates are controlled for (or partialled out), the relationship between city homicide rate and rainfall is almost negligible.

How could we interpret such a finding? One explanation is that the overall crime figure for the country involved is a much better predictor than rainfall of the murder rate in specific cities (hardly surprising). Perhaps, though, rainfall is the cause of homicide on a global scale, and it is the variation in rainfall that has caused our two sets of murder figures to be so closely related. If that is a likely explanation, then perhaps a partial correlation of this data would not be so useful. Nevertheless, if we wanted to examine this possibility seriously we would need to take into account many more factors, and this is where techniques such as multiple regression come in.

The multiple regression equation

We can begin by considering the multiple regression equation as an extension of the simple linear regression equation. Remember that the equation for predicting a value of Y from a given value of X is:

$$\hat{Y} = bX + a$$

When we are considering the effects of more than one predictor on the value of Y, we need to calculate a value for the slope (b) of each extra variable. Therefore, a multiple regression equation with three predictor variables would look like this:

$$\hat{Y} = bX_1 + bX_2 + bX_3 + a$$

If we return to the imaginary data set in the last section, we might wish to study the combined effect of various meteorological conditions on the homicide rate. Along with our measure of rainfall, we could add the effects of temperature (X_2) and sunshine (X_3) to the equation:

$$\hat{Y} = 0.35X_1 + 0.3X_2 + 0.08X_3 + 0.85$$

In order to predict $\hat{Y}$, we would select any given city in the sample, and insert that city's rainfall, temperature and sunshine values into the appropriate slots in the equation. This would mean that we multiplied each value by the value of the slope – usually referred to as the *regression coefficient* – for that variable. You would find that, given this combination of coefficients, a change in one unit of rainfall is likely to have a more profound effect on the value of Y than a change in one unit of sunshine. This doesn't necessarily mean that sunshine is not any good as a predictor: we need to know what scale it's measured on first. If sunshine is measured by total hours over the month, rather than average hours per day, then 0.08 may not be such a small coefficient after all.

For this reason, regression coefficients are usually standardised – i.e., converted to Z scores. The symbol that is used to represent them is large beta (β), and they are referred to as β *weights*. However, even the standardised weights cannot tell us a great deal by themselves. This is because the overall solution looks at the relationships between the different predictors in order to work out which single variable explains the most variance in Y. The solution as a whole is represented by the *multiple regression coefficient*, which is the square of the correlation between Y and the *best linear combination* of predictors (in other words, $r_{Y\hat{Y}}$). This is expressed as R^2. If, for example, $R^2 = 0.70$, then we can say that the variables in the equation account for 70 per cent of the variance in Y.

The individual coefficients in the multiple regression equation are *partial* regression coefficients. In other words, the partial correlation procedure that we performed on the data to account for the influence of national homicide rates would have been performed on rainfall, temperature and sunshine in order to arrive at the coefficient values in the equation. Therefore, the coefficient for rainfall is arrived at by partialling out the variance which is also explained by temperature and sunshine. On its own, rainfall has a slope value of 0.55. Some of that variance, therefore, must also be

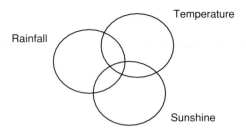

Figure 5.1 Venn diagram illustrating shared variance between three predictors

common to temperature and sunshine. What is left is rainfall's *independent* contribution to the solution.

This situation is typically illustrated by means of a Venn diagram.

In Figure 5.1, the overlapping areas represent the variance shared by rainfall along with both of the other predictors. When rainfall was used by itself to predict the homicide rate, this variability in Y would have been attributed to rainfall, because it had no competitors in the solution. In the three-predictor model, we need to account for the fact that some of the variability in Y is also explained by the variability in temperature and sunshine.

Testing the significance of the regression coefficients

We can determine the importance of our coefficients by testing their significance: the null hypothesis in each case is that the predictor does *not* explain a significant amount of the variance in Y.

The first thing we need to know is the *standard error* of the coefficient, or how much its value is likely to vary over repeated sampling. We then divide the coefficient by the standard error to give us a t statistic which we can then look up in the relevant table using $(N - P - 1)$ degrees of freedom, where P = number of predictors.

So, for the rainfall coefficient, we work out the SE to 0.22, and insert it into the equation:

$$t = \frac{0.55}{0.22} = 2.5$$

If $df = 6$, we find that this is slightly higher than the critical value at $p = 0.05$, and therefore we can say that rainfall contributes significantly to the prediction of homicide rate. The t value will be the same whether we use raw or standardised coefficients (obviously the standard error would be different for the standardised figure). You could, if you prefer, convert the t to an F value by squaring it. You would then use $df (1, 6)$ to look up its significance in the F tables – the 1 indicating that only one predictor is being tested.

Testing the significance of R^2

Once we have devised the overall solution that best predicts Y, we can then put it to the test. We do this by converting R^2 to an F value which can be looked up in the relevant statistical tables. We convert it using the following formula (where, again, P stands for the number of predictors):

$$F = \frac{(N - P - 1)R^2}{P(1 - R^2)}$$

In our earlier example of weather and homicide, suppose we had an R^2 value of 0.70. Therefore we would enter the following values:

$$F = \frac{(10 - 3 - 1) \times 0.7}{3 \times (1 - 0.7)} = \frac{4.2}{0.9} = 4.67$$

Look this figure up in critical values tables using the number of predictors as one of our numerator *df* and $(N - P - 1)$ as the denominator degrees of freedom. The critical value for *df* (3, 6) is 4.76, so we would have to accept the null hypothesis on this occasion. If we had used more cities in our study, an R^2 of 0.70 would almost certainly have been significant.

Sample size: how many cases?

Because sample size is a major consideration when it comes to evaluating the predictive ability of the multiple regression equation, then it's worth looking at the sample sizes recommended by different authors. There are two ways of estimating a minimum N: one is to recommend a minimum number of cases (or participants) per predictor – for example, Stevens (1996) recommends 15 cases for each predictor. Using this rule, we would need to have sampled 45 cities in our homicide example. An alternative way is to recommend a minimum N for any multiple regression study. Harris (1985) suggests that N should always exceed p by at least 50. Ultimately, neither rule is perfect: 15 cases in a bivariate regression model would convince few people; conversely, 70 cases in a 20-predictor multiple regression would seem far too few.

Different types of regression model

How do we decide what represents the best combination of predictors in a data set? The example in this chapter so far has been based on the 'standard' model of multiple regression, where each predictor is treated as though it is the last one to enter the equation. All the researcher has to do in this case is to nominate the set of predictor variables. This isn't as obvious as it might seem, since many multiple regression analyses are performed on huge data sets, where many of the variables would make useless predictors. In any regression analysis, the choice of predictors must be related to the theory underlying the research question.

However, psychologists tend to prefer to use a regression model where the predictors are entered in a sequential fashion. This is referred to as *hierarchical* multiple regression. The idea behind hierarchical regression is that you can control the relative importance of the predictors. For instance, in our earlier example, you might decide that rainfall is the most interesting, or most likely, predictor of homicide, and so this would be the one to enter first. It would have a coefficient of 0.55, because the outcome of this procedure would be identical to bivariate regression. When we come to enter the next variable, then, most of the variance in Y (or a substantial part of it) will have already been explained.

If temperature were to be entered next, its coefficient would be based on its *semipartial* correlation with rainfall – in other words, it would represent the correlation between temperature and the *residual* variance (i.e., the variance in Y that X_1 can't explain). In Figure 5.1, all the common variance shared by the three predictors would be eaten up by rainfall's contribution to the equation. Temperature, as the second entry, would eat up the shared portion between itself and sunshine, so that when sunshine came in at the end it would have very little variance left to account for.

The order of entry of predictors is a matter of some controversy among statisticians. One popular model is *stepwise regression*, in which predictors are selected according to certain statistical criteria. The order in which the predictors enter the equation is based on the correlations between the predictors and the Y variable. As each predictor is entered, a significance value is calculated for the remaining unexplained variance (i.e., the residual), and this determines whether or not the next predictor enters the equation. The process continues until subsequent predictors are not explaining a significant proportion of variance. For example, by the time temperature is entered in the homicide example, there may be so little variance left to explain that there is no point adding sunshine to the equation.

Critics of stepwise regression argue that it is essentially *atheoretical* – in practice, the order of entry, and which predictors we use, should be determined by the research question and not by some spurious set of figures. After all, we may be particularly interested in the effect of sunshine on the homicide rate – it may even be the reason for carrying out the study in the first place! An alternative approach to stepwise regression is *backwards deletion* (elimination). Here, the full set of predictors is entered at once, and then gradually removed to see what effect deletion has on the equation. The order in which predictors are removed is determined by their F or p level.

Finally, if you have the right software, you can perform *all subsets regression*, whereby every possible combination of predictors is tried out, and the best subset is selected using a statistic known as Mallow's C_k (or C_p). This has been criticised on the same grounds as stepwise regression, in that the best set is chosen on an atheoretical statistical basis. However, since the appropriate software is now readily available, there is no reason why researchers need to be stuck with one solution unless it is a solution dictated by the research question. Otherwise, run several combinations of predictors in a different order and decide which one makes the most sense in the theoretical context of your study.

Data screening

As with the multivariate tests covered in Part I of the book, there is a certain amount of data screening that needs to be carried out before we can run a multiple regression analysis. Some of these are the same assumptions as for ANCOVA and MANOVA, although the emphasis may be slightly different, and with regression-based models there are slightly different ways in which you need to deal with violations.

Multicollinearity

As with other multivariate techniques, while we expect our variables to have a linear relationship – that is, we expect the line of best fit to be straight – we do not expect the predictors to be highly correlated with each other. If two predictors have a correlation above, say, 0.9, the chances are that they explain precisely the same variance in *Y* (see Figure 5.2). This is known as multicollinearity. It is represented in multiple regression models by a statistic referred to as *tolerance*. The tolerance of a predictor is calculated by performing a regression analysis in which all the other predictors are regressed on to that one. If the others explain 90 per cent of that predictor's variance, then it would have a tolerance value of 0.10 (i.e., $1 - R^2$). Low tolerance values indicate that a variable is not contributing much to the overall solution.

Another problem with multicollinearity is that highly correlated predictors inflate the standard error of their coefficients. What this means is that the values of those variables are likely to fluctuate greatly across replications of the study. This is known as the *variance inflation factor* (sometimes represented as VIF). This is calculated as

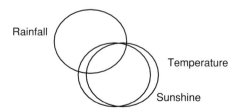

Figure 5.2 Multicollinearity

$$\frac{1}{(1 - R^2)}$$

Therefore, high figures (> 10) are the ones we want to avoid.

There are two usual ways of dealing with highly correlated predictors. The first is to drop one of them from the equation. Obviously this choice should be based on theoretical grounds. The second alternative is to collapse together, or combine, the two variables. A third alternative is to employ a technique known as *ridge regression*, which has been the source of some controversy (see Price 1977, for an argument in favour of this technique, and Rozeboom 1979, for a critique).

Outliers

Because regression is what is known as a statistical *maximisation* process – we are seeking the solution of 'best fit' to the problem – it is particularly sensitive to outliers. These are exceptional data points that may be dragging the solution away from the model of best fit. Outliers may be found on any one of the criterion or predictor variables – for example, an exceptionally tall person, or an implausibly low test score. These are known as *univariate* outliers. Alternatively, we need to look out for *multivariate* outliers; these are cases with an exceptional combinations of values – for example, a six-foot thirteen year old.

Outliers are important for two reasons. First, we may find them more interesting than the rest of the data because they might tell us something about our measures. Second, from a statistical point of view, they may be interfering with our analysis and we may need to do something about them. Apart from anything else, it is always worth screening for outliers, even if you know your data has nothing unusual in it – after all, you might have keyed in the wrong value somewhere (if you were supposed to enter 9, then 99 is very likely to be identified as an outlier!). One way of doing this at the outset of your analysis is to ask your software to draw a stem-and-leaf plot, or a boxplot (where some packages will identify the outliers with a label).

Alternatively, we can ask the computer to produce *diagnostic* statistics for all the data points. These take into account three properties of outliers.

1 *Outliers on Y (predicted)* These are outliers with high *discrepancy*, or distance from the regression line – in other words, they are cases where the predicted value is markedly different from its actual value of *Y*. These can be measured using Weisberg's outlier test, which produces a *t* statistic which can be assessed for significance.

2 *Outliers on the predictors* These are cases which are said to have high *leverage*. This means that they are a considerable distance from the mean of one or more of the predictor variables. They can be identified using a statistic known as *Mahalanobis distance*. This is a statistic based on what are known as 'hat diag' (h_{ii}) values which represent how far each case is from

the *centroid* of the predictors – the combined mean of all the predictor variables. These values fall between 0 and 1. A high value indicates an outlier, and this can be converted to a χ^2 statistic to test significance. (Most computer packages do this automatically.)

3 *Influential data points* High discrepancy and leverage may alert us to the presence of extreme data points. But they do not necessarily mean that these points are affecting the outcome of the regression equation. To find out how much *influence* an outlier is having on the analysis, we need to compute a third measure, known as *Cook's distance*. This combines the discrepancy and leverage information and can tell us how much the regression coefficients would change if a particular case were to be deleted and the regression run again. A value above 1 is an indication of high influence. Cook's distance is a useful statistic to identify influential data points which are high on neither leverage or distance – this is particularly true of multivariate outliers. With large data sets and large numbers of predictors, however, a Cook's value above 1 is very unlikely (because it would take very extreme values to influence the overall solution).

Residual plots

One popular method of screening data in multiple regression is to examine a scatterplot of the *residuals*. The residual, or error, in regression refers to to the difference between Y and $\hat{Y}$ – a measure of the accuracy of our equation's prediction. If we have 50 cases in our data set, there should be 50 points on the scatterplot, and ideally, these should be normally (symmetrically) distributed around the regression line.

However, there are three ways in which this assumption could be violated. The first is through *non-normality*, where the points are much more spread out. This would suggest that the model tends to over- or underestimate $\hat{Y}$ much of the time. The second violation is that of *non-linearity*, where the data fall into a pattern that is meaningful but non-linear – for example, a curvilinear pattern, indicating a quadratic trend (i.e., low and high values of Y are underestimated, but middle values are overestimated). A data set that looks like this would not suit *linear* multiple regression (the sort we are dealing with in this chapter) but could be analysed using logistic regression (see Chapter 6).

The third possible violation goes by the horrendous name of *heteroscedasticity*. It may not help you if I say that this is simply a violation of the assumption of *homoscedasticity*, unless I explain that homoscedasticity exists when the variability of one variable is the same at all levels of another variable. If that's no clearer, then imagine a situation where a gifted schoolteacher takes on a mixed-ability maths class and gets them all through an exam at the end of the year. If we correlated maths ability and time, we would find that the variance in ability was very wide in weeks 1 and 2, but the gap between the children had closed considerably by, say, week 30. The resulting scatterplot would have a strong positive skew and would demon-strate heteroscedasticity. Such a data set may result from having one or two skewed predictors. We could eliminate this by transforming the relevant variables, either by using square roots or by using logarithms.

Missing data

As you begin to deal with larger and larger sets of data, the likelihood of obtaining a complete set of data grows increasingly small. With scales and questionnaires, for example, people are often unable or unwilling to respond to some items. In univariate analyses we can often get round this problem by substituting the mean for the missing value. But with multivariate analyses this is harder to do, because we are interested in the effect of the *combination* of variables – there are any number of means that we could use as a substitute.

Researchers usually resort to one of three options. The first, *casewise (list-wise) deletion*, is the most obvious – just drop that particular case. However, we may be reluctant simply to scrap a whole case, especially if the missing value is just one of a large number of predictors, and we have taken a lot of trouble to assemble our sample. If our sample is on the small side to begin with, we may also be unwilling to sacrifice power by losing another case.

An alternative is *pairwise deletion*, where the correlations involving the missing value are simply skipped, but the rest of that participant's data are kept in the overall equation. We end up with a missing value correlation matrix, which is not ideal, but if the data set is large and the number of missing values is small, then it is a reasonable solution. With small data sets, or variables with lots of missing values (perhaps because a scale or question-naire item did not apply to most respondents), this type of deletion can result in unstable data.

A third option is to create a *dummy variable* which sorts your data into cases with or without missing values, coding them as 0 or 1 respectively. If there is a good reason why some of your data is missing, this variable may by itself turn out to be a good predictor of Y!

Worked example of hierarchical multiple regression

Here I will go through an example of multiple regression using the SPSS program (most software packages will produce similar output). As with the multivariate ANOVA chapters, by-hand calculation of these techniques is very complicated. While sometimes it is helpful to know exactly *how* the calculations are performed, it is by no means essential for interpreting most of the results. If you are really keen you can learn *matrix algebra* – most multivariate statistics textbooks include a chapter on this (e.g., Tabachnick and Fidell 2001).

The data are imaginary, as with all the 'worked' examples in this book, but they are loosely based on an actual survey of health cognitions and behaviours throughout Europe carried out by Steptoe and Wardle (1992). They collected information on various health behaviours from their respondents, and also asked them to complete a questionnaire which looked at their awareness of health risk and their beliefs in the importance of avoiding risky health behaviour. They used the questionnaire data to see which items best predicted actual behaviour.

In this example, I have put together a set of data which includes one criterion variable: number of cigarettes smoked each day; and four predictor variables: *age, gender, risk awareness* and *belief*. Risk awareness is an index of awareness of the various illnesses associated with smoking, and values can vary between 1 and 3. Belief is a rating on a scale from 1 to 10 of how important it is not to smoke. We would naturally expect an inverse relationship (negative correlation) between these two predictors.

In Table 5.2 a portion (the first five cases) of the data set is displayed just by way of illustration. The full data set can be found in Appendix 1.

The first thing to notice about this data set is that one of the predictors – gender – is a *dichotomous* variable; that is, it has only two possible values (0 and 1). Although multiple regression is normally carried out using continuous variables, there is no reason why we cannot enter dichotomous variables into the model, except that it means that the raw coefficients will certainly need to be standardised in order for us to interpret them. Indeed, one advantage of using a dichotomous variable is that we can be certain that it has a linear relationship with the other variables in the data set!

The first thing to do is to inspect the data for multicollinearity. A good starting point is to obtain the correlation matrix (Table 5.3). This will not

Table 5.2 First five cases of the full data set for multiple regression example

Respondent	Cigarettes	Age	Gender	Risk	Belief
1	0	19	0	2.0	10
2	0	20	0	2.2	8
3	0	20	1	2.4	9
4	0	20	0	1.1	10
5	0	18	1	1.6	8

Table 5.3 Correlation matrix

	Age	Gender	Risk	Belief
No. of cigarettes	0.43**	−0.13	0.54**	−0.64**
Age		−0.02	0.30**	−0.06
Gender			0.01	−0.03
Risk				−0.39**

Note: ** coefficient is significant at $p < 0.01$

only alert you to any redundant (too highly correlated) variables in your data but also give you some idea what to expect from the forthcoming analysis.

From this we can see that gender does not significantly correlate with anything else, so is unlikely to play a role in the regression equation. As expected, belief and risk are significantly negatively correlated, while number of cigarettes has significant correlations with age, risk and belief, although the relationship with belief is a negative one (as might be expected). Multicollinearity does not appear to be a problem with this data set.

Performing the analysis using computer software

While statistical software differs slightly in its terminology and design, most programs observe similar conventions. I have used SPSS (version 9.0) throughout most of this book because it is probably the most popular package, although only minor adjustments need to be made for most programs.

Find 'Regression' from the Statistics menu and choose 'Linear'. You are asked to enter one variable as your 'dependent' and as many as you like as 'independent'.[1] You also need to specify which type of model you wish to use. In this case, choose Stepwise, just to see how it works.

The various statistics need to be obtained from the following buttons at the bottom of the screen:

Plots   This offers you a choice of different values for the x- and y-axes of a scatterplot. Select 'DEPENDENT' for the y-axis. If you want a plot of standardised residuals, then ZRESID will need to go on the x-axis. There is a command at the bottom of this screen which will also produce a histogram of the same data if you want.

Save   This command brings up a screen on which a bewildering variety of diagnostic statistics are offered. For simplicity's sake we will just select Mahalanobis and Cook distances, and also 'Dffits' and 'Dfbeta'. These are two sets of values which tell us how great a change will be effected in the results if a particular case is dropped from the analysis. Dffits tells us how much the value of $\hat{Y}$ will change by, and Dfbeta will tell us how much each of the coefficients will change by. Rather than appearing in the Output file, these values are saved to your data file, where they are easier to interpret.

Options   This command is useful for stepwise regression, which is the method we will use to analyse this data. (It also gives you the chance to specify how the program should deal with missing values.) The default settings will serve our purpose adequately, so there is no need to change anything. Simply note that the top two commands relate to the entry criteria for predictors in stepwise regression: the first option (the default) is that variables are only entered into the equation if their F value is significant at 0.05, and removed if their significance creeps below 0.10; the second option enables you to set specified levels of F if you prefer.

Interpreting the output

Regression diagnostics

First of all, return to the data file and examine the diagnostic information. Notice that there are no significances provided for the Mahalanobis distances, so these will need to be looked up in tables. But there is no point doing this unless the Cook distances are above 1, which is not the case with this data. In fact, most of the Cook values are below 0.1.

The next column is 'dffits', the change in $\hat{Y}$ if the case is deleted. Notice there is only one case that will effect much of a change, and that is case number 37, whose deletion would reduce $\hat{Y}$ by −7.8 standard errors. This seems like quite a lot, but Cook is only 0.6. If we look at the data for this case, we can see that it is quite unusual in that both risk and belief, which we know to be negatively correlated, are both very high, and furthermore, it is a 10-a-day smoker. Perhaps this is somebody who is desperate to give up!

'Dfbeta' is stretched across 5 variables, one for each predictor and one for the intercept (constant). These values are not particularly interesting in this data set, because there are no great fluctuations on any one variable.

Scroll down the Output file and look at the residual scatterplot (Figure 5.3). You may be surprised to see that it is somewhat heteroscedastic, with a number of points clustering in the top right hand. It looks as though heavy smokers do not fit the pattern quite as well as moderate smokers. We *could* run the test again, using the WLS command (weighted least squares) – this adjusts the data by using a specified variable as a result. But it's not clear in this case which variable is the culprit. An alternative is to set a limit on number of cigarettes (say, 20). In reality though, we often have to accept that data are never perfect, and that slight irregularities are interesting in their own right. The data here are not *so* irregular that they make linear regression inappropriate.

Stepwise regression

Return to the top of the output file, where details of the stepwise regression analysis are given. The first table, 'Variables entered/removed' tells you the order of entry: belief has entered the model first, then age, then risk. Gender was not used, presumably because it failed to meet the entry criteria.

The next table, 'Model Summary' gives you the R, R^2 and adjusted R^2 at each step in the analysis. When belief was entered by itself, it explained 41 per cent of the variance in cigarettes smoked ($R^2 = 0.41$). In other words,

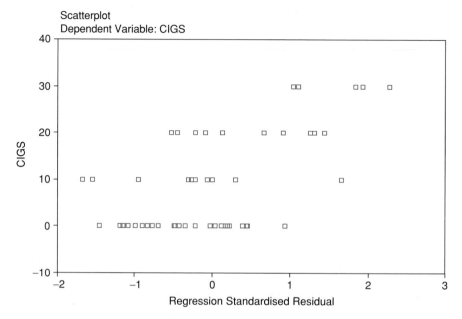

Figure 5.3 Scatterplot of residuals

belief in the importance of *not* smoking is the best predictor of how much our respondents do actually smoke. The addition of age explains a further 16 per cent of the variance ($R^2 = 0.57$). The addition of risk only explains another 4 per cent ($R^2 = 0.61$).

The ANOVA table produces F statistics for each step of the analysis. Not surprisingly, F becomes smaller as more predictors enter the equation, so the third F refers to the predictive power of the model as a whole. With so much variance explained, it is quite high ($F(3, 46) = 23.6$, $p < 0.001$).

The next table, 'Coefficients' provides the B and β coefficients (and *t* statistics for each), which enable us to produce the equation itself:

$$\hat{Y} = (-3.396 \text{ belief}) + (1.806 \text{ age}) + (5.845 \text{ risk}) - 14.45$$

Note how, using the B coefficients, risk has a higher value than belief. This shows why we use standardised weights to interpret the contribution of the different predictors. If we take case #1 and enter the relevant values, this becomes:

$$\hat{Y} = (-3.396 \times 10) + (1.806 \times 19) + (5.845 \times 2) - 14.5$$

$$\hat{Y} = -33.96 + 34.314 + 11.69 - 14.45$$

$$\hat{Y} = -2.406$$

You can check this by requesting predicted values from the 'Save' screen.

The last table indicates the β values for gender were it is included at various steps in the analysis. It also displays the tolerance levels for the predictors (which are mostly very high).

Now, run the analysis again, this time specifying Enter as the model. This is instructing the program to run the analysis with all the predictors in it regardless of entry criteria. You will notice that the overall R^2 is marginally higher (0.625), but slightly less significant ($F = 18.76$). This suggests that the inclusion of gender actually weakens the predictive power of the model. In fact, we might have decided to drop gender after inspecting the correlation matrix. However we may have a good theoretical reason for keeping it in (perhaps as a control variable), in which case the stepwise model would have been unsuitable for the analysis.

Model validation

Once we have decided on the 'best' solution to our regression equation, how do we then decide whether this is any good or not? There are a couple of further analyses we can perform that assess the validity of the model we have chosen, both for internal and external purposes.

Cross-validation

As you will see in Part III of this book, one of the most common ways of evaluating data obtained from a questionnaire or survey is to split the data set into two random halves and see if the overall pattern is the same in each half. This is a realistic alternative to running a second study simply to check whether or not the first one was a fluke. With multiple regression we need to obtain a different solution from each of the two halves, and then see how well each equation predicts the Y values in the other half. We should end up with a cross-validation correlation (R_{cv}^2) which will inevitably be less than R^2, but if our overall model is good, then the difference should not be too great.

Adjusted R^2

A variant on the above procedure is to obtain an adjusted value of R^2 which is an estimate of R^2 if cross-validated with a second sample drawn from the same population. In other words, it takes into account the sample size, and number of predictors, and estimates what value of R^2 we could expect across any number of repeated studies. Wherry's formula is the one used most frequently to calculate this:

$$\hat{\rho}^2 = 1 - \frac{(n-1)}{(n-k-1)} \times (1 - R^2)$$

This figure is produced automatically by most software packages, and is often reported instead of R^2 itself.

An example of multiple regression from the literature

Seibert, Crant and Kraimer (1999): personality and career success

Many studies of multiple regression published in the psychological literature involve vast samples – hundreds of participants assessed on numerous variables. This study is a typical example. The authors wanted to examine the ability of a certain personality type to predict career success. They argued that individuals who display much *proactive* behaviour (always seizing the initiative) would be more successful in their careers than those who were more *reactive* (laid back).

They assessed 496 graduates who had entered a variety of professions. Career success was the criterion variable, and they used three separate measures of this: first, they performed a regression analysis with salary as the Y variable; then with the number of promotions as the Y variable, and then with 'career satisfaction' (an index of a number of ratings) as the Y variable. Therefore they ended up with three separate regression equations. Proactive personality was measured by a 17-item scale.

There were 37 predictor variables in the first two analyses and 39 in the career satisfaction one. The predictors were grouped into five sets of *control* variables: 1) demographic information (age, gender, ethnicity, socio-economic status, married or single, whether spouse employed or not); 2) 'human capital' – this included a lot of dichotomous variables (e.g. whether respondents had a PhD or not, whether they had an engineering qualification or not), plus some continuous ones (years since graduation, etc.); 3) motivational factors (desire for upward mobility measured on a scale, number of hours worked each week); 4) organisational factors (number of employees, whether 'publicly traded' or not); and 5) area of industry (a set of dichotomous variables relating to nature of employment). For career satisfaction, salary and number of promotions were included as control variables.

The control variables are in the model largely because the authors wanted to make it as difficult as possible for proactive personality to have any effect on Y. The controls were entered into the model first, so that most of the variance would already be accounted for by the time personality was entered.

The R^2 values for the three analyses were as follows:

Salary	0.54
Promotions	0.37
Career satisfaction	0.37

Obviously, with a huge sample like this, you would expect much of the variance to be unexplained 'noise', so an R^2 of 0.54 is pretty good going. Having said that, there are some professions where nature of employment alone could predict salary, so for this analysis, perhaps R^2 is not a particularly useful statistic.

Nevertheless, what the authors were interested in was the contribution of proactive personality to the solutions, and they found that, for each of the three analyses, proactive personality had a significant impact on Y. For salary, the standardised coefficient of proactive personality was $\beta = 0.11$, which was found to be significant at $p < 0.05$. The statistic reported in the text is the amount R^2 would change if this predictor was dropped, represented by the symbol ΔR^2 (in this case, $\Delta R^2 = 0.01$). This may not look a great deal, but in a sample of this size, and with this many predictors, it was found to be significant at $p < 0.05$. Proactive personality also emerged as significant on the other two analyses: number of promotions ($\beta = 0.12$, $\Delta R^2 = 0.01$) and career satisfaction ($\beta = 0.3$, $\Delta R^2 = 0.07$). The latter figures are clearly significant, suggesting that personality type is a very good predictor of job satisfaction.

This is a good example of a very complicated study whose complexity is specifically designed to extract the last drop of significance from the predictive model. By throwing in so many control variables, and entering these into the model first, the authors made it as difficult as possible for personality to have a serious impact on R^2. Therefore, although the change it produced in Y was only 0.01, this was deemed to be significant.

Multivariate regression

Although not often seen in the literature, it is possible to carry out a multiple regression analysis with more than one criterion (Y) variable. Such a model would be described as multivariate regression, and has close links with multivariate ANOVA (MANOVA). For example, the authors in the above example could have collapsed their three models together, and obtained a general measure of prediction for career success. This would be expressed as Wilk's Lambda (Λ) – see Chapter 3 for an interpretation of this statistic. The significance of the model for each criterion variable would be given as an F statistic.

Generally speaking, there would need to be sound theoretical reasons for lumping together criterion variables in this way. The arguments for and against such a procedure are essentially the same as those relating to MANOVA. In the Seibert *et al.* study I suspect that separate analyses were preferred because there may be substantial differences at a conceptual level among salary, number of promotions, and career satisfaction (even though the first two were significant predictors of career satisfaction). In taking a broad definition of career success, it is more meaningful to target your analyses accurately.

Summary

The second part of this book deals with techniques which are variations and extensions of the basic regression equation. If you can understand this, it is not too great a conceptual leap to the advanced material, although I have begun this chapter by covering some basic concepts such as partial correlation, which are necessary to understand multiple regression and its variants. One of the most important aspects of multiple regression is data screening, and nobody should ever undertake a regression analysis without first examining the data in case they violate various statistical assumptions. It is also important to design your regression model carefully, ensuring that your choice of predictor variables, and their order of entry, is based on a sound theoretical rationale. This has been a long chapter, but multiple regression underpins so many multivariate techniques that it is necessary to cover as many aspects of it as possible. Even so, there are still some omissions. If you are interested in interaction effects in multiple regression, for example, consult Aiken and West (1996).

Note

1 I have avoided referring to the predictors as 'independent' variables, because I prefer to keep that term for experimental designs where the distinction between IVs and DVs is that the researcher *manipulates* the IVs. With regression models, the terms 'predictor' and 'criterion' variables make much more sense. Within the General Linear Model, however, as far as SPSS is concerned, predictors = IVs.

6   Logistic regression

Logistic regression is a technique which has been popular with health researchers for a long time, and is becoming increasingly popular within psychology (especially in health and medical psychology). It is similar in many ways to discriminant function analysis (see Chapter 4), in that it is concerned with predicting group membership from a set of variables. Its statistical calculation is more like multiple regression, however. It enjoys one major advantage over discriminant analysis, which is that it can deal with any kind of variables – so a lot of the assumptions about data do not apply.

Essential features of logistic regression

The nature of the variables

You may recall from Chapter 5 that multiple regression can handle dichotomous variables on one or more of the predictors. In logistic regression the criterion variable itself (Y) is a dichotomous variable. Rather than predicting the value of Y, then, the object of the exercise is to predict which of two groups each case will belong to. Herein lies the popularity of logistic regression in medical research, where many studies are concerned with predicting whether someone should or should not receive a particular diagnosis, or predicting which factors will predict recovery from a particular illness.

Occasionally a logistic regression may be performed on a Y variable with more than two possible values. In this case it is described as a *polychotomous* variable. However, in this chapter, for simplicity, I will concentrate on models with a dichotomous criterion variable, typically coded 0 and 1.

Like multiple regression, logistic regression has no problem handling categorical variables as its predictors, creating dummy variables for each category. When the data is in this form, logistic regression begins to resemble chi-square, and several of the statistics produced in this kind of regression analysis are distributed on χ^2.

Non-linearity

Because there are only two possible values of our *Y* variable, logistic regression is not bound by the need for linearity which is a feature of most of the multivariate analysis considered so far. In fact the assumption here is that the distribution of data will be best represented by a *sigmoidal* (S) curve, with most cases accurately assigned to one of the two categories.

The logistic regression equation

The equation that is produced for a logistic regression model looks very similar to that for a multiple regression, in that each of the predictors has a coefficient associated with it which can be interpreted in roughly the same way as the β weights. However they represent slightly different information – they refer to the *odds* of a given case belonging to either group 0 or 1. The coefficients are the logarithm of the odds, and are known as *log odds*.

For an example, imagine you were predicting success in a job interview, with experience, qualifications and hair colour as predictors. Out of 50 interviews, 15 people were offered jobs. The probability of success in this sample is 15/50, or $p = 0.30$ – that is, three out of every ten people in the sample were offered a job. The odds, however, as any betting enthusiast will know, refer to the likelihood of success against failure, and so are worked out as 15/35 = 0.43. Turn this on its head, and 35/15 = 2.3. You could say that the chances of rejection are more than twice the chances of getting an offer.

In the logistic regression equation, the odds undergo a *logit transformation* – that is, they are converted into logarithms, which perform the same function within the analysis as the standardised coefficients in multiple regression. Therefore a solution to the above example, where β_0 is the intercept, might look like:

$$\text{log odds} = 0.3\text{experience} + 0.2\text{qualifications} + 0.01\text{hair colour} + \beta_0$$

Each of those weights can be tested for significance using a χ^2 value known as *Wald's statistic*. In each case, we want to know how accurately that variable predicts group membership – therefore, the log odds represent the odds of that variable successfully predicting the group membership of any given case.

Types of regression model

These are pretty much the same as for multiple regression, in that there is a distinction between standard and hierarchical logistic regression, and the stepwise procedure can be used to enter and remove predictors on the basis of specified statistical criteria (significance of Wald's χ^2 in this case).

Worked example of logistic regression

For this example I will return to the study by Seibert *et al.* (1999) described at the end of Chapter 5, and create an imaginary data set from their predictors that could be used to predict personality type in a logistic regression model. As before, I will describe the stages for carrying out the analysis on SPSS, although other software packages are likely to be very similar.

Recall that respondents in Seibert *et al.*'s study were assessed using a 17-item scale of proactive personality. In their study, proactive personality was a continuous variable, measured by a respondent's score on the scale. We will now take this variable and *censor* it – that is, define an arbitrary cut-off point which assigns respondents to one of two groups. Those who scored above this point in the scale are assigned to the *proactive* group (code: 1), while those who scored below the cut-off point are assigned to the *reactive* group (code: −1). Statistically speaking, it doesn't really matter what codes are used, but in this case, there is some logic in having a positive and a negative value.

The predictors in this analysis will be career satisfaction and salary, along with two others: PhD (or not), and geographical location (London, New York and Hawaii). The first five cases of the analysis ($N = 50$) are included in Table 6.1 (the only reason for including geographical location is to illustrate an example of dummy coding). The full set of data can be found in Table A1 in the Appendix.

As with the multiple regression example, we can begin by obtaining the correlation matrix (Table 6.2).

Table 6.1 First five cases of logistic regression data set

Case	Group	Salary	Promos	PhD	London	NY	Hawaii	Location
1	1	20,000	2	0	1	0	0	1
2	0	15,000	0	0	0	1	0	2
3	1	25,000	4	0	0	0	1	3
4	0	27,000	4	1	0	1	0	2
5	1	24,000	1	1	0	0	1	3

Table 6.2 Correlation matrix for logistic regression example

	Salary	Promos	PhD	London	NY	Hawaii
Group	0.3**	0.48**	0.01	−0.29*	−0.29*	0.51**
Salary		0.83**	0.08	0.01	−0.14	0.14
Promos			0.03	−0.15	−0.11	0.24
PhD				−0.17	−0.06	0.28*
London					−0.33*	−0.50**
NY						−0.54**

These data tell us two important things: first, the correlation between salary and number of promotions is high (0.83). A little higher and we would certainly have multicollinearity. We will keep it in, however, because while we would expect these variables to be correlated, we might expect promotions to be a better predictor of proactive personality (after all, a 'reactive' employee may happily settle for a well-paid first post).

The other thing of note is that having a PhD does not seem to have any effect on group. It does have a small correlation with Hawaii, though, so this might be worth entering into the model as an interaction.

Performing the analysis using computer software

Before we run the analysis, we need to decide how we are going to enter our location data (again I am using SPSS version 9.0 as the default). One way would be to enter only the location variable (coded 1–3) and specify that it is a categorical variable once in the program. Alternatively we can enter our three dummy variables as themselves. I would recommend the latter option, because SPSS uses the same strategy for analysing categorical data as it uses for contrasts in ANOVA, and is even harder to interpret in this case.

Choose 'Regression' from the Statistics menu and then 'Logistic'. The main screen is similar to that for multiple regression, except that it calls the predictors 'covariates'. If you want to request an interaction, you need to enter the variables first, and then select your two interaction variables while holding down the Ctrl key. Click on the button marked >a*b> and this enters the interaction into the covariate box. First of all, though, run the analysis with just the six predictors on their own.

Click on 'Save' and ask it to compute predicted membership (don't bother asking for probabilities, because they aren't – they are predicted values, and are redundant with a dichotomous variable). Also ask for Cook's distances. Then ask for a classification plot under 'Options'.

Interpreting the output

Begin by looking at the saved data, which consist of the predicted group membership and Cook's distances. The Cook figures are the only ones to interest us at this stage – and we can spot four influential data points (> 1). One of these, case #47, is not surprisingly influential, because it is a participant with a whopping salary (compared to the rest). The other three simply have salaries or promotions which are slightly different from the rest of their group.

Should we delete or transform these cases? It depends on how important classification is. This is just a harmless exercise, but it may be that classification (e.g. on the basis of some medical predictors) is of tremendous importance, determining, perhaps, whether or not a psychiatric client receives a diagnosis. Then we would need to be much more careful about our model.

The first statistic in the Output file is labelled '-2 Log Likelihood' (referred to as just -2 Log L in most other programs). The value of this is 69.3. What this tells you is how good a fit the overall model is before any of the predictors have been entered. Shortly afterwards, we see how much this figure is reduced with all the predictors in the model (39.2). If the value of -2 Log L decreases (which it should do) when predictors are added to a model, then we can be sure that some of the variance has been explained by the predictors.

Note the comment 'estimation terminated at iteration number 5'. What this means is that the program has to keep adjusting the coefficients until it comes up with the best fitting solution (at which point we say the solution *converges* – any subsequent adjustment will simply repeat the same pattern). This is known as an *iterative* approach to equation solving. In this case, it has taken five attempts (iterations) to find the best fit – although we could have specified a maximum level if we thought too many would overload the program (only necessary with very large data sets).

The -2 Log L is evaluated by a chi-square statistic ($\chi^2 = 30.1$, $p < 0.001$). This is repeated three times in the output (the 'step' and 'block' lines are for stepwise models). Then there is a 2×2 contingency table familiar, I'm sure, from chi-square statistics, which tells you what the accuracy of the prediction is – the hit rate is 80 per cent, which is pretty good. However, if you return to your data file you will see that, where the model has misclassified cases, they are generally outliers.

Then we reach the equation information. The first column (B) represents the log odds (coefficients) for each predictor. Our regression equation could be written:

$$\text{log odds} = (-0.0003 \text{ salary}) + (1.29 \text{ promotions}) - (0.8 \text{ PhD}) \dots$$
$$\text{and so on.}$$

The third column contains Wald's χ^2 statistic for each coefficient. In this example, only the number of promotions is significant ($\chi^2 = 6.25$, $p = 0.012$). The column on the far right contains the odds for each predictor, calculated by taking the exponential (e^x) of the log odds. We can use this information to make statements about our data, such as 'the proactive group on average had 3.6 times as many promotions as the reactive group'.

You have probably noticed by now that the odds on a proactive person living in Hawaii are even higher than those of promotions. Yet Wald's χ^2 for Hawaii is very small (< 1). If you run the analysis again without London and New York you will find that Hawaii becomes the most significant predictor in the equation (you will get the same effect if you enter location as a categorical variable instead of the dummy variables). This is because the three dummy variables are not really independent predictors as such – the value of Hawaii is determined by the value of the others, and so a form of multicollinearity is produced, and all three variables become redundant.

Entering location as a categorical variable is the 'correct' procedure, but unfortunately the program does not present sufficient information to interpret the results.

If you run the analysis again omitting salary, PhD, and all location information but Hawaii, then it improves the hit rate (to 84 per cent) and Hawaii emerges as a powerful predictor of group membership. How could we interpret this result? Perhaps proactive people are more likely to seek promotions, particularly if they are in desirable locations! What this example illustrates is that we may sometimes need to run several analyses on the same data for a coherent tale to unfold.

Two examples of logistic regression from the psychological literature

Rose et al. (1996): predictors of quitting smoking

The first example is an analysis of data that had been collected over several years on attempts to quit smoking by young adults. Over 8,500 people from the midwest area of the US participated in the study at some point over 14 years, although the actual data set in the analysis consisted of a subsample of 700. These were young adults who had been identified as regular smokers in a 1987 survey, just prior to graduating from high school, and who were surveyed again in 1994. All manner of tactics were employed to track them down, from 'motor vehicle bureau information' to ads on local radio.

Two sets of logistic regression analyses were conducted. The criterion variable in the first set was whether or not the respondent had attempted to give up smoking at some point in the previous five years. Of all respondents, 580 had made some attempt. The aim of the analyses, therefore, was to find out which variables best predicted membership of this group.

Five separate models were tested for the first set of analyses. Each model contained the same four control (moderator) variables – level of education, amount smoked, gender, and age of onset. The unique variables for each model were:

1   The likelihood of smoking within the next year
2   Smoking environment – parental smoking, friends who smoke and the perceived prevalence of smoking
3   Various smoking beliefs and general health and lifestyle variables
4   Motives for smoking (various physical and psychological measures)
5   Social roles (age, student, married, employed, living with children).

With the exception of number 2), all of these models were successful predictors of 'quit attempts'. In particular, 3), 4) and 5) had high χ^2 values which were all significant at $p < 0.001$. β weights are given for each individual predictor, and, where significant, the odds ratios are listed. The best individual predictors were education level (significant in two models) and whether or not the respondent was married (odds ratio = 2.08 – therefore married respondents were twice as likely to try to quit).

An interaction was examined for general health beliefs × amount smoked. This emerged as a significant predictor (odds = 1.56). Specifically, heavy smokers were more likely to try to quit if they thought smoking was dangerous to their health, while light smokers were less likely. (Maybe they are more complacent if they think they have their habit under control?)

The second set of analyses used as the criterion variable whether or not respondents had been successful in their quit attempts. Therefore the total sample was slightly smaller for these studies (in fact, listwise deletion was used for missing data, and some analyses had $N < 450$). The 'successful' group numbered 115 in total. All the five models had overall significance, so they were all good predictors of group membership. Level of education was a significant predictor in all the models (the higher the level, the more likely the respondent was to be in the successful group), and amount smoked was also significant in all the models (light smokers were more likely to be successful). A sixth model was tested as well: this was a cluster of variables relating to reasons for giving up. This was the best overall model for predicting 'success' group membership ($\chi^2 = 60.99$, $p < 0.001$). Particularly important were 'sensory' reasons for giving up (odds = 2.51). These were responses to items such as 'I enjoy handling a cigarette'. However, since the direction is positive ($\beta = 0.46$, $p < 0.001$), this is a rather hard finding to interpret!

Scheidt and Windle (1996): alcohol and sexual risk

The second example is a study by Scheidt and Windle (1996) from the same journal. This was a study of users of an alcohol clinic in New York (481 men and 321 women). The main goal of the study was to find out what part alcoholism played in risky sexual behaviour. The data for men and women were analysed separately, and there were two main analyses using roughly the same predictor variables. In the first, the criterion variable was whether the respondent's most recent sexual experience was with a regular or non-regular ('nonprimary') partner. In the second, the criterion variable was whether the respondent had used a condom in that encounter.

Unlike the previous example, the regressions were performed with all the predictors in the model together. Hierarchical regression was used by entering the variables one block at at time. The first block consisted of *individual* variables (age, ethnicity, whether cohabiting or not, presence of antisocial personality disorder, drug abuse, amount of daily alcohol use, how often the respondent drank with strangers, and how much they expected alcohol to enhance sex). The second block consisted of *sexual history* variables (use of condoms, number of partners, sexual disease). The third block related to the most recent sexual *event* (drug or alcohol use during sex, whether or not sexual health was discussed). A fourth block consisted of interactions between the individual/historical variables and the event variables.

For the first ('nonprimary partner') analysis, all the blocks had overall significance except the interaction block (this was true for men and women). Odds ratios are reported for the individual variables, but not β weights – instead the 95 per cent confidence intervals are reported (highest and lowest). Therefore it is hard to comment on the significance of the specific predictor variables. Highest specific predictors for men were alcohol use during the event (odds = 3 or more), and discussion of sexual health. Drinking with strangers (odds = 1.79) was also a good predictor. A similar pattern was true for women, with the addition of anti-social personality disorder. It could be argued that these represent episodes where a casual partner was 'picked up' during a night out.

For the second ('condom nonuse') analysis, the criterion variable of nonprimary partner was added as a predictor. The sexual history block was the most significant predictor for both men and women (χ^2 of 216.34 and 124.71 respectively, both $p < 0.001$). History of condom nonuse was the most significant variable within this block (odds = 6.71 and 5.36 for men and women respectively). The 'Individual' block was not significant for either group, but the 'event' block was significant, though no specific variables had odds > 1. For men, there was a significant interaction between condom nonuse history and nonprimary partner: it appears that men with a habit of casual sex also have a habit of sexual risk taking.

Here is an example of a logistic regression that is entirely suited to the research question: it is important to be able to predict group membership (condom users vs condom nonusers). Then the individual predictors can be identified as targets for 'preventative interventions' such as counselling.

Summary

This rather short chapter has been concerned with logistic regression, a variant of multiple regression which uses similar modelling techniques, but with a different goal. Rather than predicting values of a criterion variable on a continuous scale, logistic regression predicts category membership, so it is a useful technique when you wish to identify single cases which are 'at risk', perhaps. This brings it close to discriminant analysis, and judging by recent trends in the psychological literature, logistic regression appears to be a more popular option. Like multiple regression, logistic regression can also provide information about the relative power of the equation variables as predictors. Most applications of logistic regression in the literature have concerned dichotomous criterion variables, but it is certainly possible to run them on variables with several values, although of course the predictive power of the technique is weakened except with very large data sets.

7   Structural equation modelling

In this chapter I shall attempt to outline the ideas behind, and uses of, a range of statistical techniques which can be lumped together under the general term of structural equation modelling (SEM). This is a set of techniques which have been developed more recently than the other methods discussed so far in this book (originating in the 1960s), and have only just started to become commonplace in psychological research. Indeed, at the time of writing, they are undeniably *trendy* – it has become fashionable for journal reviewers, for example, to advise authors to re-analyse multiple regression data in the style of a path analysis or even a structural equation model. This enthusiasm for sophisticated and impressive-looking analysis may be misguided at times, however, and there are many statisticians and psychologists who are somewhat cautious about the routine application of SEM to psychological data.

To its supporters, SEM might be seen as the culmination of all the methods so far described: essentially, it is a set of techniques for testing a theory by examining correlations, covariance, and even means differences between sets of dependent and independent variables of all shapes and sizes. It can be applied to all manner of data sets, can yield a bucketload of awe-inspiring statistics, and – the most attractive feature of all – can be illustrated using an elaborate and sophisticated form of box-and-arrow model known as a *path diagram*.

You are likely to encounter these with increasing frequency in psychology journals, so it is worth knowing how to interpret them. However, as you might imagine, the actual mathematics involved is frighteningly complicated, so the emphasis in this chapter is more towards *interpreting* uses of SEM rather than actually carrying out the analyses. The added complication is that SEM is not available on general statistical software packages like Minitab and SPSS, and you need to get hold of specialist software to perform it. However I will give a brief overview of the software available at the end of the chapter.

Terminology

One of the most confusing aspects of SEM is that it is not a fixed method like ANOVA, which is basically a simple concept (the *F* ratio) with lots of extra bits attached depending on the types of variable and the complexity of the design. SEM has developed in parallel with other related methods, so that different researchers use different terms to describe what amounts to the same basic technique. Among the other terms you may find are the following.

Causal modelling

This term covers essentially the same territory as SEM, though with slightly more overstated assumptions. As its name implies, causal modelling is about establishing cause and effect through examining the relationship between different variables. There are problems with these assumptions, though, and these will be discussed later in the chapter.

Simultaneous equation modelling, latent variable modelling and analysis of covariance structures

All these terms refer to different aspects of the SEM process. Again, they basically amount to the same thing, but in each case the researchers have highlighted a different part of the process as its most salient feature. (What the terms mean precisely will become apparent – hopefully! – as you work through the chapter.)

Confirmatory factor analysis and path analysis

If the terms defined previously are meant to contain the variety of SEM techniques, then confirmatory and path analysis are more specific terms used to describe certain *types* of SEM. Confirmatory factor analysis is a special application of SEM and will be discussed in more detail in Chapter 9. Path analysis is a simplified version of SEM which is essentially an extension of multiple regression, and will be described in this chapter.

LISREL and EQS

You may find papers which use these terms as though they were statistical techniques in their own right. They are actually specialist software packages for performing SEM. LISREL, in fact, is the brainchild of Karl Jöreskog, one of the original founders of SEM, and it has become almost synonymous with the techniques themselves. However, to say that you analysed a data set using LISREL is (almost) like saying you analysed a data set using SPSS, except that different programs use different equations to perform the calculations.

Basic concepts in structural equation modelling

SEM is used when we want to test an elaborate theory involving several different variables and constructs. It is a complex form of the predictions you made using multiple regression. For example, we might like to expand the study on cigarette smoking that I used as the worked example of multiple regression in Chapter 5 into a general model to predict risky behaviour.

Ultimately we are looking for two things when we carry out an SEM analysis. Firstly, we are testing the 'fit' of our model to the data. This is where the structural equations come in. We start out with a set of equations that we believe to be true, for example:

X_1, X_2 and X_3 predict X;
Y_1, Y_2 and Y_3 predict Y;
X predicts Y.

Then we model these with a data set that we have collected and see how closely the model is predicted by our equations.

If our model is a good fit, then we can interpret the findings more precisely by specifying the parameters of the model – the beta coefficents between the different variables, the relative importance of different 'paths' within the model, the variance explained by different variables, and so on. The best way of presenting this information is in the form of a path diagram.

Path diagrams

I will begin this section by creating two path diagrams which can then be used to illustrate the basic concepts of SEM. The first diagram, Figure 7.1, refers to the cigarette smoking example in Chapter 5. This diagram illustrates the nature of the connections between the variables in the cigarette smoking example. Simply put, the direction of the arrows in a path diagram indicates the implied effect of one variable on another. The arrow leads from risk awareness to cigarettes smoked because we are assuming that the negative correlation between these variables is a reasonable predictor of smoking. The bi-directional arrow linking risk awareness to health beliefs indicates that there is a high correlation between these two variables.

All the boxes in this diagram are rectangular. This is because all the variables in the equation are *measures* of something, and are referred to as measured (or manifest) variables. In more complex analyses we are examining *latent* variables, which are abstract concepts linking together a number of measured variables. They are latent because they are not actually measured; their function in the model is hypothetical. If the fit of the model is good, then we have some statistical evidence that supports the existence of the concept.

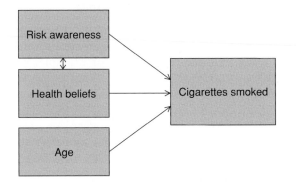

Figure 7.1 Path diagram of multiple regression example on smoking predictors

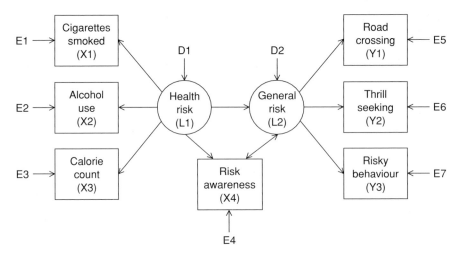

Figure 7.2 Path diagram of hypothetical health risk study

An example of a more complicated path diagram is shown in Figure 7.2. Here, cigarette smoking is one of three measured variables which are linked to the latent variable 'health risk'. Notice how the arrow joining cigarettes smoked to health risk now points towards cigarettes smoked. This indicates that cigarette smoking can be predicted by the more general factor of risky health behaviour. Because it is a latent variable, health risk is represented as a circle or oval. There is another latent variable in this model, which is labelled 'general risk'. This in turn predicts three other measured variables – an observational measure of road crossing behaviour, a scale measure of thrill-seeking and an experimental measure of risky behaviour. Notice that there is a one-way arrow linking health risk to general risk. This suggests that we can predict overall risky behaviour from risky health behaviour.

Although most of the measured variables in the diagram are linked to only one latent variable, there is a measured variable that is predicted by both of them: this is risk awareness. In fact the arrow connecting risk awareness to general risk is bi-directional: this implies that we are not sure in which direction the effect is taking place (does low risk awareness predict general risky behaviour, or vice versa?) Notice also that each measured variable has an arrow pointing to it. These represent the error variance for each variable (i.e., that portion of the variance which is not explained by the latent variable or by other measured variables).

The important thing to remember about SEM is that the path diagrams and goodness-of-fit statistics are dictated by the researcher's own theoretical interests. This may seem an obvious point (indeed it could apply to any method, quantitative or qualitative). However, because these models are sometimes referred to as 'causal models' it is tempting to assume that they are definitive accounts of cause-and-effect processes. Yet almost the first thing we are taught about correlational design is never to infer cause and effect. Therefore, the results of SEM do need to be treated with caution. Of course there are many additional variables which may be involved that the researchers have ignored. In the above example, both health risk and general risk may well be predicted by other factors (e.g., rebelliousness). Ultimately, the latent variables are simply those which the researcher is interested in.

Data assumptions for structural equation modelling

The assumptions of SEM are essentially the same as for the other multivariate techniques – linearity, normality, avoidance of multicollinearity, and homoscedastic residual plots. It is also assumed that the sample size is large, certainly in excess of 100, especially if there are large numbers of measured variables.

Equations

The mathematics for SEM are based on matrix algebra like other multivariate statistics. However there are differences in the equations used by different computer packages. The two most common packages – LISREL and EQS – differ quite markedly from each other in the actual calculations. EQS is based on the Bentler-Weeks method of model specification (Bentler and Weeks 1980). All the variables in the model are referred to either as DVs or IVs, and you devise a set of predictions based on the parameters in the model. In the above example, we would need to specify eight DVs (including general risk) and nine IVs (including error terms for all the measured variables and the error for the latent variable general risk – known as a *disturbance*).

This is effectively an extension of the multiple regression equation, and is expressed as:

$$\eta = B\eta + \gamma\xi$$

In the above equation,

η = vector of the DVs
B = matrix of regression coefficients between the DVs
γ = matrix of regression coefficients between the IVs and DVs
ξ = vector of the IVs

For each variable in the model, this equation allows us to make a prediction about its relationship with other variables. For cigarettes smoked, where * represents an unspecified value, the equation works out as:

$$X1 = (X2)0 + (X3)0 + (X4)0 + (Y1)0 + (Y2)0 + (Y3)0$$
$$+ (L1)* + (L2)0 + E1$$

If you cancel out all the zero coefficients (i.e., where no relationship is hypothesised), you are left with the basic equation:

$$X1 = L1* + E1$$

In other words, the number of cigarettes smoked (X1) can be predicted by the sum of the error term and the predictive value of health risk multiplied by some unknown coefficient (the parameter which is to be estimated). We end up with a matrix with all the coefficients for the IVs, which are then estimated by a series of guesses. These may be based on available data, or suggested by the software. The process then becomes iterative, as in logistic regression, so that various combinations of coefficients are tried out until the solution *converges* and the best fit is found (see Chapter 9 on factor analysis for a more detailed description).

In LISREL the process is similar but more complicated, because, where EQS simply distinguishes DVs from IVs, LISREL draws a distinction between measured and latent variables as well. Therefore a variety of matrices are constructed in order to arrive at the best fit.

There are various estimations of the optimum sample size for use with SEM. These fluctuate according to the exact process in use. Tanaka (1987) discusses this issue in more detail, and concludes that, for a model with one latent variable and four manifest variables, a minimum sample of 50 would be required. Therefore, for most SEM studies we would require considerably more. Generally speaking, sample size is related to the distributional assumptions of the data: if we use a method that allows us to use non-normally distributed data, then we need to compensate by increasing the sample.

Model evaluation

Having carried out our parameter estimates, we then need to evaluate the model of best fit to see if it is indeed a *good* fit. This process involves two stages: calculating an index of fit, and then testing that index for significance.

There are a variety of statistics one can use to express the fit of a model. The most commonly used is the *Comparative Fit Index* (CFI). This is a figure which compares the estimated model to a completely 'independent' model with no relation between the variables, and whose value can range from 0 to 1. The higher the value, the better the fit (> 0.90 is desirable).

An alternative measure is the *Goodness of Fit Index* (GFI) which compares the sample covariance matrix to an estimated population covariance matrix (i.e., the range of parameters we would expect from replications of the study across different samples). The range and interpretation of values is similar to the CFI, and the figure can be adjusted for a more conservative value (AGFI).

Other measures use the residuals as their points of comparison. The *Root Mean Square Residual* (RMR) and its standardised value (SRMR) represent the difference between the sample and population covariances. With this measure, we would be looking for a small value to indicate good fit (preferable SRMR < 0.05).

Once we have decided on our index, we can then obtain a significance level for this value which is expressed as a chi-square statistic. The important thing to remember here is that we are looking for a *non-significant* χ^2, because it is a measure of the difference between the model and the data. If $p < 0.05$, then we would obtain good fit less than 5 per cent of the time, which would not do at all.

Another important consideration here is the degrees of freedom. Because large samples are more likely to yield significant χ^2 values (and large samples are required for SEM), we can look at the ratio of the χ^2 statistic to its *df* in order to interpret it. If the ratio is less than 3, then we usually have good fit.

Two final sets of values are usually calculated. The first is a set of modifications we can make to the model. These are suggested by the *Lagrange Multiplier* test, which suggests additional paths of interest to add to the model, and by the Wald test which suggests which paths could be dropped to improve the fit of the model. These are normally expressed as the *change* in χ^2 observed by adding or removing paths.

Second, we can obtain significance values for the paths that we have specified in our original model. These are obtained by converting the standardised coefficients into Z scores by dividing them by their standard errors. These can then tell us about the relative importance of the paths in the model (for example, which X variable is best predicted by L1?)

Example from the literature of a study using EQS

Rini *et al. (1999): psychological factors in childbirth*

The authors in this study set up a model to investigate a variety of psychological factors in pregnant women that contributed to birth outcomes. Specifically, they hypothesized that 'personal resources' (i.e., coping strategies), stress levels and socio-cultural factors would affect both the weight of the baby and the length of gestation (whether or not the baby was born prematurely).

The main dependent variables in this study were:

*   *Birthweight* (in grams).
*   *Length of gestation*: Gestational age at birth in weeks.

The stress measures were:

*   *State anxiety*: 10-item scale relating to potentially stressful situations encountered in recent days.
*   *Pregnancy anxiety*: 10-item scale relating to stressful aspects of pregnancy (e.g., baby's health, labour, caring for a baby). The authors split this measure into two separate 'parcels' of items because latent variables with less than 3 *indicators* (attached measured variables) are said to be *under-identified*.

The 'resources' measures were:

*   *Mastery*: 7-item scale relating to control over one's personal outcomes.
*   *Optimism*: 8-item scale measuring dispositional optimism.
*   *Self-esteem*: 10-item standard measure.

Finally, sociocultural and other variables:

*   *Ethnicity*: Dichotomous variable – participants were coded either as White (1) or Hispanic (0).
*   *Income*: Measured on a scale from 1 (< $10,000) to 10 (> $90,000).
*   *Education*: Measured in years.
*   *Married*: Dichotomous variable – either yes or no.
*   *Age*
*   *Nulliparity*: Dichotomous variable measuring whether it is the first baby (1) or not (0).

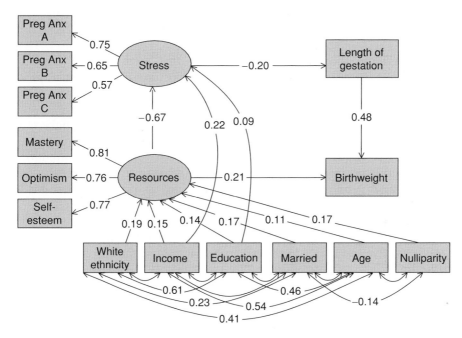

Figure 7.3 Full model, plus parameters, from Rini *et al.* (1999). Copyright © 1999 by the American Psychological Association. Reprinted with permission.

Results

The path diagram for this study is shown in Figure 7.3. Though there are only two latent variables involved, there are 14 measured variables. It is a good example of the role of latent variables in SEM, because although there are only two, the whole model pivots around them. Notice how 'Resources' is predicted by six measured variables and in turn predicts four different measured variables in addition to the latent variable 'stress'. (Also notice the lack of error terms – these would undoubtedly have been entered into the equations, but ignored in the final report.)

The model had a good fit to the data. The χ^2 statistic was significant, the CFI was above 0.90, and in any case, the ratio between the χ^2 value and the degrees of freedom was below 3. These results were reported as follows: (χ^2 (60, $N = 230$) = 140.99, $p < 0.001$; CFI = 0.92, $\chi^2/df = 2.35$).

Use of Lagrange and Wald tests suggested alterations that would create an even better-fitting model. These included setting some of the predictions to zero, for example, the paths from age to resources and education to stress. These are the only coefficients in the diagram which failed to reach significance at $p < 0.05$.

The individual paths in the diagram are indicated by the standardised parameter estimates (coefficients). You should be able to make some sense of these. To start with, look at the two sets of indicators attached to the latent variables. We describe these coefficients as *loadings* on the respective latent variable (a term you will be familiar with if you have studied factor analysis). These values are all high, particularly the resource measures. The fact that they have all loaded highly on the same latent variable suggests that they are closely related. Likewise, the sociocultural and demographic variables are all closely related, as shown by high covariates (coefficients).

The aspect of the model we are most interested in is the predictive power of the measured variables on to the latent variables, which are then linked to the two main dependent variables in the study, birthweight and gestation age. Most of the sociocultural variables make a small, but significant, contribution to the variance in resources, and there is a large negative relationship between the two latent variables, which can be interpreted as suggesting that good resources lead to reduced stress. In turn, stress negatively predicts gestation (e.g. highly stressed mothers are more likely to give birth prematurely), while both resources and gestation make positive contributions to birthweight (good resources and later birth lead to heavier – and therefore healthier – babies).

The role of resources in this study is probably its most interesting aspect. Are there other factors which might contribute to their positive effect? Separate regression analyses found that the effect of resources on birth outcomes was still significant even after the other variables were partialled out. The authors suggest that maybe resourceful women are more likely to practise preventative health behaviours and effect lifestyle changes (e.g. giving up smoking). However, establishing causal relationships – for example, between resourcefulness and stress – is not easy. It is also worth considering what other measures might have been entered into the study (different stress measures, for example).

Example from the literature of a study using path analysis

This next example from the literature involves a study where path analysis was used to predict the response of men with a history of domestic violence to a partner's request that they use a condom (Neighbors *et al.* 1999). Path analysis by itself is rather like SEM without the structural equations. There are no latent variables to examine – all the researcher is interested in is the predictive power of different measured variables on each other. The parameters are still the same (beta coefficients), but they are arrived at using a series of standard multiple regression equations relating to the different paths in the model.

The measures used were as follows:

Outcome variables:

• *Sex with condom*: Indication, on a 6-point scale, of how likely the man was to use a condom following the partner's request that he did so. (A score of 1 actually represents a refusal to have sex at all.)

- *Coercive tactic*: Indication, on a 9-point scale, of how extreme the man's response would be to the request (a score of 1 indicates compliance with the request, while high scores represent violent responses).

Key variable:

- *Positive evaluative reaction*: This was the main DV in the study, measured by a series of items relating to the request to use a condom. High scores, as the label suggests, are positive responses to the request.

Predictor variables:

- *Marital violence*: Men were assigned to three different categories – severely violent, moderately violent, and nonviolent – based on their responses to a questionnaire.
- *Attributions*: These were measured using a 'condom attributions' scale, in which respondents were asked to agree with different interpretations of their partner's request to use a condom. The responses were split into four subscales:
  - *Insensitivity* (towards him)
  - *Health concerns* (e.g., solely for prevention of HIV)
  - *Suspicion of infidelity* (partner may have been infected)
  - *Contraception* (birth control)

Covariate:

- *Social desirability*: This was a measure which was intended to 'screen out' respondents who were simply giving 'socially desirable' answers.

Results

The path diagram for this study is displayed in Figure 7.4. Notice that this display contains both the raw and standard coefficients, and a significance level for each parameter. There are also R^2 statistics given for the outcome and key variables. Notice also that some of the predictor variables are not connected to any other variables. The decision whether or not to include these variables in the diagram is at the discretion of the researcher. In this case (a relatively simple diagram) the researchers were keen to show that social desirability, as a covariate, has no confounding influence on the outcome, and that contraception attribution is not a significant predictor. If you choose to include non-significant variables in the model it does help if you cite the coefficients all the same (but we'll overlook that minor point on this occasion).

What we have left is a trio of multiple regression equations which are then arranged in the most meaningful fashion as a set of parameters. The first parameter regresses all the predictor variables on to Positive Evaluative Reaction. Together the predictors explain 37 per cent of this figure. Three of

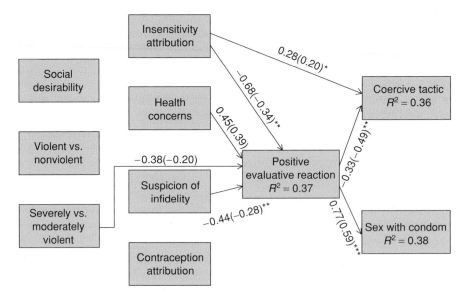

Figure 7.4 Path diagram with raw and standardised coefficients, from Neighbors,
O'Leary and Labouvie (1999).
Note: * $p < 0.05$, ** $p < 0.01$, *** $p < 0.001$
Copyright © 1999 by the American Psychological Association. Reprinted with permission.

the attribution subscales make significant contributions, but contraception
does not. Note how the researchers have treated the 'marital violence' data:
what they have done is to set up (presumably using dummy variables) a
pair of *orthogonal contrasts* – one pits the nonviolent group against the two
violent groups, and the other pits the moderately violent group against the
severely violent group. Only the latter contrast explains a significant portion
of the positive evaluation reaction. This is negative, so we could assume that
severely violent men received a code of 1 and moderately violent men a code
of 0, and so the negative coefficient indicates that severely violent men were
significantly less likely to evaluate the request positively.

The second parameter regresses all the predictors – and positive reaction
– on to 'coercive tactic', i.e., how aggressively the respondent tried to resist
condom use. Altogether, the measures explain 36 per cent of the variance in
coercive tactics, but only positive reaction and insensitivity attribution emerge
as independent predictors. In other words, positive reaction explains the
same variance as do health concerns, moderately vs. severely violent, and
suspicion of infidelity. However, insensitivity makes its own significant contribution to the variance in coercive tactics. We can interpret this by suggesting that insensitivity to the partner's wishes (desires?) seems to cause
more friction than even the suspicion of infidelity.

Finally, all the variables except 'coercive tactics' are regressed on the
respondents' willingness to use a condom. Here the only independent contribution is positive reaction, and this explains 38 per cent of the variance.

While the less complicated path diagram makes path analysis look like a simpler option than full-blown SEM (and, at a mathematical level, it certainly *is* simpler), there is nonetheless a great deal of ingenuity involved in selecting the parameters of interest and entering the variables into the various regression equations.

Problems with structural equation modelling

While SEM may be one of the most fashionable quantitative methods currently in use in psychology, it also has its detractors. Cliff (1983), for example, has identified a number of problems.

Fit assessment

The assessment of models is based on negative confirmation. We consider a model to be a good fit simply because the χ^2 statistic is non-significant: in other words, a good model is defined as such simply for *not* being a *bad* fit. It should be clear that reversing the direction in which we accept significance means that there is a 95 per cent chance of the model fitting. However, we normally avoid this problem by quoting the fit statistics and the degrees of freedom. Nevertheless, we can never be entirely sure that our non-badly fitting model is the best for explaining the relationship between our manifest variables.

Modification of the model

It is possible to use SEM in order to cobble together a theory out of the existing data. If we set up a model and then find that the data do not fit, then we can use the Lagrange multiplier and the Wald test to suggest alternative parameters; we may end up with quite a different set of parameters from those we started out with, and all on the basis of the same data set. Another data set may yield entirely different results. It seems that, come what may, SEM will package our inadequate data into some convenient explanatory pattern (see McCallum *et al.* 1992). Breckler (1990) argues that, unless researchers are required to publish their 'modification history' – a blow-by-blow account of how they have modified their original model – then modified models could easily be passed off as the original. This is a fairly harsh criticism, although at a theoretical level, we could argue that, if our measures are appropriate for the concepts behind our research question, who cares if our model does not prove an exact fit? This should not pose a problem if we see SEM as purely a descriptive statistical tool. However . . .

Implication of causality

This is in my view the fundamental problem facing users of SEM. Clearly a lot of researchers have seized on SEM because it promises to 'uncover' chains of causality between variables of their choice. They have even used the term *causal modelling* to describe it. However, one of the first things students are taught at undergraduate level is that causality cannot be inferred from correlational data. So why make an exception for SEM? The answer lies possibly in the goodness-of-fit assessment – but as we have seen, this method of evaluation is far from perfect.

Ultimately a structural model, like a regression analysis, is restricted to the set of variables entered by the researcher, along with all his or her assumptions and biases concerning the relationships among those variables. Furthermore, the latent variables in SEM are not real measures; they are constructs which are identified and labelled by the researcher (on the basis of biases, assumptions, etc.) This makes it a largely *subjective* measure – a highly ingenious one if applied properly, though hardly sufficient evidence to demonstrate cause and effect among sets of correlated variables.

Alternatives to structural equation modelling

The alternative methods described in this section are not necessarily solutions to the above problems: indeed, in some cases, the alternatives are on even shakier ground.

Partial least squares

Partial least squares (PLS) is a more recent technique than SEM, devised by Herman Wold (1985). Initially the idea was to study relationships between manifest variables without making firm hypotheses about model structure, an approach that became known as 'soft modelling'. More recently, however, Fred Bookstein and his colleagues (see Bookstein, Sampson, Streissguth and Barr 1996) have developed PLS for slightly different purposes.

Bookstein's application of PLS concerns a longitudinal study of fetal alcohol syndrome (the detrimental effects of consuming alcohol during pregnancy). The process entails specifying two sets of manifest variables: in this case a set of measures (Xs) of alcohol consumption – number of drinks per week, binge drinking, etc. – and a set of measures (Ys) of behavioural outcomes, such as IQ and classroom behaviour. Latent variables are then produced from the correlation matrix of Xs and Ys. Unlike the latent variables in a structural model, which are the *factors* which explain the most variance in the manifest variables, these are the *linear combinations* of the manifest variables, vectors which are extracted from the correlation matrix.

Each set of manifest variables has at least one latent variable attached to it. The coefficients between the Xs and the Ys are referred to as *saliences*. If we have assembled our variables in order to predict cause (X) and effect (Y), then we can calculate a score for any X variable which represents the degree to which it explains the variance in all the Ys.

Figure 7.5 displays two X variables from the Bookstein study plotted against two latent variables. The first latent variable (or vector) is plotted

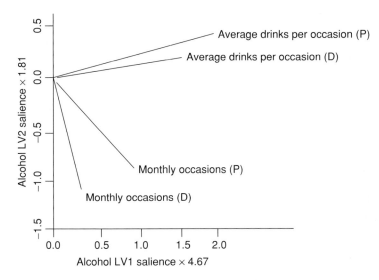

Figure 7.5 Two-dimensional analysis of alcohol consumption prior to the awareness
of pregnancy (P) and during midpregnancy (D) against behavioural outcome, from Bookstein *et al.* (1996). Copyright © 1996 by the American
Psychological Association. Adapted with permission.

along the *x*-axis: it is labelled 'Alcohol LV1 salience × 4.67'. This vector,
which represents the central tendency of the columns in the correlation
matrix, accounts for 75 per cent of the variance in the matrix. We can
compute a value (the salience) for each manifest variable on this vector.
For 'monthly occasions' (i.e. instances of alcohol consumption), the score
during midpregnancy (D) is less than 0.5, but for drinking prior to the
awareness of pregnancy (P), it is higher (closer to 1). For 'average number of drinks' the score during midpregnancy is close to 1.5, but before
awareness it is almost 2.

What this tells us is that alcohol consumption early in pregnancy is a
better predictor of the child's behaviour than alcohol consumption in
midpregnancy (the pattern was similar for most of the other X variables in
the study). It also tells us that the amount of alcohol drunk in a session is a
better predictor of the child's behaviour than the frequency of sessions.
These inferences could be made if the scores were strung out on a single
dimension. The second vector, plotted on the *y*-axis, represents the central
tendency of the *rows* in the correlation matrix. The addition of this vector
increases the amount of explained variance to 86 per cent.

One of the advantages of PLS over SEM is that it can be used with
smaller samples – one rule of thumb is that the minimum sample should be
ten times the number of paths directed at a particular construct. In the condom
example in pp. 90–2, there are potentially *seven* paths aimed at positive
evaluative reaction, so a sample of 70 would suffice for a PLS treatment of
this model. However, some statisticians have argued that PLS can be run on

even smaller samples than this. Another advantage of PLS is that it is a more parsimonious method for use with unwieldy, complicated models.

It has been argued that, because its goal is *prediction* rather than goodness of fit, PLS can be regarded as complementary to SEM, perhaps for exploratory data analysis before the researcher is ready to hypothesise a complex model.

See Miller, Cowan, Cowan and Hetherington (1993) for an example of another study using PLS.

Latent class analysis

This type of analysis is used when the dependent variables of interest are *categorical* and we are interested in predicting group membership. Like SEM, Latent Class Analysis (LCA) is used when a structural (hierarchical) model is hypothesised and can be used to predict the likelihood of the data fitting that model.

An example can be found in Lazar and Torney-Purta (1991), who investigated the development of 6-to-7 year old children's understanding of death. The authors identified four subconcepts of death which needed to be mastered for full understanding: irreversibility (once dead that's it), cessation (of life, person, etc.), causality (death as result of some chain of physical and environmental events) and inevitability (comes to us all). Understanding of these concepts was measured by responses to a structured interview. Children were asked about the death of humans and animals.

The authors were mainly concerned with the order in which these four subconcepts developed during this period of childhood. They specified hierarchies based on the literature and then tested these for goodness of fit. The first hierarchy to be tested had irreversibility as the first concept to be mastered, followed by inevitability, and a two-way possibility for the last concept. This had a χ^2 value of 2.33, indicating good fit (i.e., $p > 0.05$). Then three further possible hierarchies were tested, though these fitted the data slightly less well. They also failed to hold up over time periods and with concepts of death related to animals.

Like PLS, LCA requires the use of specialist software, some of which can be downloaded free of charge, but this is rarely of high quality. In time, these techniques may become available on more general statistical packages such as SPSS. For further reading, see Clogg's chapter in Arminger, Clogg and Sobel (1995).

Summary

I have used this chapter to introduce the reader to structural equation modelling, a multivariate technique very popular in psychology at the start of the twenty-first century. The mathematics involved in SEM is too complicated to describe here, and the software is still somewhat specialised; it has not found its way into the standard statistical packages available to students. Therefore I have focused on the interpretation of studies using SEM, and identifying opportunities when the reader may wish to go beyond conducting a basic path analysis and test models for their overall fit. It is important, however, to be cautious about making grandiose claims for the power of these models as techniques that can be used to establish cause and effect. Because SEM is a complex field, I will leave the detailed description of its application to other authors.

There is a substantial literature on SEM, although most of it assumes extensive statistical knowledge. Two of the more accessible texts are Loehlin (1992) and Hoyle (1995). If you have access to the appropriate software, then the users' manual will be the best reference. However, Jodie Ullman's chapter in Tabachnick and Fidell (2001) contains worked examples using LISREL, EQS, SAS and SYSTAT. A useful introduction to LISREL is Diamantopolous and Siguaw (2000). There are also a number of useful web sites which are worth exploring. Occasionally these will allow you to download demo versions of relevant software or even full-blown packages. However, these are of variable quality, often full of bugs and, more often than not, you require specialist software in order to run them in the first place!

Part III

Questionnaires and scales

Survey design

This part of the book is concerned largely with data that is collected by means of original 'pen-and-paper' measures.[1] I will concentrate on the creation and analysis of single measures, although it needs to be borne in mind that such measures usually form part of a wider battery or selection of measures that together form a *survey*. I have not covered survey design in this book as such, largely because there is so little agreement as to the definition of a survey, and because the design of a survey is entirely dependent on the research context.

Some researchers argue that a questionnaire becomes a survey when it has been distributed to a certain number of people, or to a carefully stratified sample. Or when the questionnaire reaches a particular length. Others would argue that a survey needs to involve more than a single questionnaire, no matter how many respondents, or how representative the sampling. But a single questionnaire can contain so many different sections, and collect so many different types of data, that even the term 'questionnaire' is itself somewhat vague. Many surveys include interviews as well as (or instead of) pen-and-paper measures. As a result, the survey is often regarded as a research strategy rather than a method as such (Robson 1993).

The measures considered in this part of the book are perhaps better described as 'scales', tests which are constrained by the style of their items so that measures of internal reliability can be performed. In a study context, these measures will very rarely be administered without collection of any further data, if only demographic information, so the actual *instrument* that respondents complete is likely to have the appearance of a questionnaire/survey, especially if there are a number of scales completed in the same session. But how many measures you should include in such a study, and what type of measures, are entirely dependent on your research question.

However, it is worth mentioning a couple of features of survey-type designs that are important for all such projects: overall design, and sampling techniques.

Broadly speaking, survey designs fall into two categories: *longitudinal* and *cross-sectional*. This distinction is particularly important in developmental psychology (although, ironically, you rarely see a developmental project referred to as a survey, probably questionnaires are not the most appropriate methodology for studying young children!). Longitudinal designs are useful for studying changes that take place over time, when the same participants are administered a variety of measures (or repeated measures) over a specified time period. This could be anything from a few days to several years, and is often referred to as a *panel* survey. Cross-sectional designs are those in which the sample is tested only once. They are like between-groups experiments in that they can be used to compare responses from different social groups.

Robson (1993) distinguishes between probability and nonprobability samples; use of the former enables you to make inferences from sample to population, and so is more relevant to the types of measures discussed in this section.

Random sampling

Anyone who has studied psychology will be conscious of the fact that 'random' is not the same as 'haphazard', and that random sampling should be based on mathematical principles. This can be done using random number tables or computer programs.

Systematic sampling

A slightly less precise method than true random sampling, although often confused with it. For example, you might select the first name in the telephone directory and then every 50th name subsequently. This is not random sampling because the first name is not chosen at random (indeed, some businesses are deliberately named so that they will appear first in alphabetical lists).

Stratified random sampling

This can be either *proportionate* (where your sample sizes are intended to be relative to the population sizes), or *disproportionate* (if you are especially interested in a particular group). For example, in a study which has gender as the independent variable, you would aim for equal numbers of males and females. Disproportionate samples are more useful when you want to run a small control group for comparison's sake but are not really that interested in their responses.

Cluster sampling

This method applies to situations where true random sampling is difficult; for example, due to geographical reasons. So in a survey which aims to generalise to the population of Britain, you might construct three samples, one in the North, one in the Midlands and one in the South. Random sampling would be near impossible in such a design.

For more detail concerning survey design with specific reference to psychology, see Sapsford (1999).

Note

1 This term is beginning to sound rather old-fashioned, as many questionnaires are now created and distributed via the internet. In fact it is not uncommon for a questionnaire to go all the way from conception to analysis without the involvement of any pens or paper!

8 Scale design and construction

The construction of questionnaires and other scaling instruments has always played a central role in psychological research. Almost every concept in psychology has produced some form of pen-and-paper measure, from the intelligence tests of Binet and Spearman through to modern attempts to measure 'self-construal'. Over the years test constructors have been increasingly concerned with making testing an exact science, and various methodological tools have been developed which enable tests and scales to be validated in order to give them credibility (and, in many cases, enable them to be published at exorbitant prices!).

In this chapter I will discuss the most important steps to take when constructing an original questionnaire or scale. Mostly these relate to issues of reliability and validity, of which you may already have some background knowledge. In the following chapters I will describe a number of statistical analyses which may be performed on tests and scales. Although test and scale data can and have been used with most of the methods presented in the book so far, the techniques in this section are ones which have been developed mainly to examine the internal properties of a scale.

Varieties of tests, scales and questionnaires

In this chapter I will refer to tests, scales and questionnaires interchangeably. Although they are all different types of *psychometric* assessment, and can be bracketed together for analytical purposes, there are considerable differences between the way they are constructed and used. Roughly speaking, we can regard any such measure as consisting of a set of carefully constructed items which is open to analysis of internal and external validity.

Psychometric tests

A psychometric test is typically a list of questions which seek to measure some form of psychological *ability* on behalf of the respondent. The classic psychometric test is the intelligence test, or measure of IQ, developed by

Binet and others at the end of the nineteenth century, which is still in use in modern Western schools. Of course intelligence tests have been considerably developed and refined since the early days, but the idea of a test that can yield an index of ability for a child which is presumed to be fairly consistent over time is still attractive to educationalists. Today children are more likely to be assessed using a *battery* of tests – for example, the British Ability Scales (Elliott 1983), with a variety of subtests measuring reading, spelling, numeracy and various cognitive abilities. Other intelligence tests have been developed which have attempted to circumvent some of the problems of traditional IQ tests, such as Raven's Matrices, a measure of non-verbal intelligence in which the respondent completes a logical sequence of patterns by choosing among a number of alternative patterns.

Intelligence tests, particularly those that are intended for large-scale commercial use, need to go through a range of *standardisation* procedures before they are adopted by educational psychology services. They need to be tested, often across several trials, on large representative samples of different age groups. They need to have excellent reliability and validity, and are often refined several times before they can be published. At a more localised level, a test may be designed for a specific study – for example, a computerised reaction time task. Such tests are rarely subjected to the statistical scrutiny of commercial tests, and even reliability statistics may not be reported in papers where measures are not intended for use in other contexts.

Ultimately, psychometric tests are intended to yield a single score which can be treated as some definitive measure of a psychological ability. This may be a mean value calculated across responses, or a sum total of correct responses, depending on the nature of the test. We would normally expect such tests to have a *single-factor solution* – in other words, most of the variance can be explained by a single construct or factor which underlies most or all of the items in the test. The process for investigating factor structure is explained in Chapter 9.

Questionnaires

Like psychometric tests, questionnaires can either be tightly structured instruments intended for commercial use (such as a personality test), or largely unstructured research tools for obtaining information as part of a survey. The first type of questionnaire requires the same degrees of reliability and validity as an IQ test in order for it to be published. However the second type may be little more than a series of questions designed to elicit a series of responses that has no overall internal consistency. For example, question 1 might ask respondents to write down their age or gender, while question 2 asks respondents to tick a box that represents their salary level. There is no internal connection between these two items, and they would be treated as separate measures for data analytic purposes. Nevertheless, the total collection of items is still treated as a single instrument.

Questionnaires can be designed using a range of different response types. These vary according to the researchers' needs. For a test such as the Eysenck Personality Questionnaire (Eysenck and Eysenck 1975), where the author was interested in comparing individuals on the basis of bipolar personality dimensions, a simple YES/NO response is all that is required. This enables the researcher to compile a score on each dimension for each respondent. Another type of questionnaire might wish to group respondents into a set of categories and so more options would be presented. An unstructured questionnaire might produce a mixture of data types – some questions asking for category information, some for interval data, and so on.

Questionnaires are often divided into *closed-reponse* and *open-response* types of measure; the latter type allows respondents to elaborate, either with lists of answers, or with continuous prose. Clearly these items produce qualitative data which need appropriate forms of analysis. These will be discussed in Part IV of the book.

Scales

While IQ and other psychometric tests are often referred to as scales, I am using the term here to distinguish tests that require a response on a sliding scale (such as a Likert scale) from questionnaires that require 'closed' responses. Typical scale items are *statements* with which respondents are asked to agree or disagree, by indicating the level of their agreement on a set scale.

Scales are different from questionnaires and psychometric tests because they are highly dependent on internal consistency. In theory, a questionnaire or test could consist of a single item. As an example, if you wanted to identify young children who are at risk from developing dyslexia, and a single item discriminates these children from the rest 100 times out of 100, then that single item *could* constitute your test. No other items would be necessary (unless the item only 'works' when embedded in a list of questions). However, the objectives of scaling instruments tend to be broader than those of most tests, attempting to explore a topic in greater depth.

The earliest psychological scales of this sort were concerned with the measurement of *attitudes*. Thurstone and Chave (1929) devised a series of scales where statements were collected expressing a view towards a particular topic (e.g., capital punishment). A panel of judges (probably students) then rated each statement on a scale of 1 to 11 depending on how favourable, or unfavourable, each statement was towards the topic. Each statement received a *scale value* which was the median rating given by the panel. A representative range of statements was then selected as the final set of scale items and then respondents were asked to agree or disagree with these items on a YES/NO basis. A respondent's final score was the median scale value of the items with which s/he agreed.

Subsequent attitude researchers have devised all manner of ingenious scaling techniques, notably Guttman's (1944) scalogram analysis in which the pool of scale items is manipulated by the researcher so that a hierarchy of items can be created which reflects varying degrees of acceptance towards a given attitude. The advantage of this type of scale is that respondents can then be said to occupy a place on a meaningful continuum (e.g., favourable–unfavourable) rather than simply acquiring a score computed from a haphazard assortment of items.

Another popular technique is Osgood's *semantic differential* scale (Osgood, Suci and Tannenbaum 1957). Here the respondent is presented with a set of bipolar adjectives, for example:

happy	:	:	:	:	:	sad
boring	:	:	:	:	:	exciting
careless	:	:	:	:	:	considerate

The respondent is then asked to rate a particular topic or person on each of those dimensions. The scale needs to be designed in such a way that the total, or subtotals, can be used to indicate the respondent's position on the topic or person under investigation – or, in the words of the creators, the subjective *meaning* of the topic.

However, by far the most common scaling technique used today is that pioneered by Likert (1932). Here it is the respondents who choose where to stand on a continuum. A selection of statements is presented and, for each statement, respondents are asked to agree or disagree by indicating their position on a scale. A typical Likert scale contains the following options:

Strongly disagree	Disagree	Neutral	Agree	Strongly agree
1	2	3	4	5

There are a number of variations on this type of response scale. Some scales use 7 options, others 4 or 6. One advantage of using even-numbered sets is that respondents are forced to commit themselves to either a positive or a negative position. However, we might be interested in neutral responses (we might even choose to discard them in our analysis). There is some evidence to suggest that higher numbers of options are less reliable (Chang 1994), but this is hardly surprising – if you give a respondent three 'disagree' options their responses are more likely to vary than if offered just two. Other scales use 0 as the neutral option, with negative and positive values for disagreement and agreement.

Over the century, the study of attitudes has changed considerably. While some researchers have taken the attitude approach to extremes, even producing computational models of attitude development (Eiser 1994), others have criticised attempts to measure attitudes as artificial and simplistic. Nevertheless, the use of Likert-type scales to measure all manner of psychological and behavioural phenomena has remained extremely popular, and so it is this technique which will form the focus of the rest of the chapter.

CONSTRUCTING A SCALE

In this section, I will outline the necessary steps that you will need to take in order to construct an original psychological scale. It must be stressed that, while the construction of *statements*, and the use of a numbered scale as a response set, are unique to Likert-type scales, the steps in creating an item pool, and carrying out reliability and validity checks, are relevant to *all* psychological tests and questionnaires. However, if you are concerned with issues that apply specifically to psychometric tests (measures of intelligence, clinical screening tests and so on), then more detail can be found in Rust and Golombok (1999) and Anastasi and Urbina (1997).

Creating an item pool

The first step in scale development involves the creation of suitable items that will enable you to answer your research question. For research purposes, a scale is usually intended to be the measure of a particular psychological phenomenon (intelligence, personality, attitudes to capital punishment) that you wish to compare with some other measure (age, gender, another scale). For clinical or educational purposes, the scale may be an end in itself – a useful means of assessment – or may form part of a larger battery of tests and scales. It is therefore important to ensure that you create appropriate items, rather than a ragbag of information which may simply produce statistical 'noise' when you come to investigate the structure of the scale.

A good way to start is by drawing up a blueprint of your scale, usually referred to as the *test specification*. This consists of a grid or matrix on which you subdivide your scale into a number of themes ('content areas') and the ways in which these themes might be experienced ('manifestations'). Some of these themes may be more important than others; therefore you might want to devote a larger proportion of items to them. Similarly, the manifestations may be unequally weighted. It is necessary to create more items than you would ideally like in your scale (Rust and Golombok 1999, suggest 50 per cent as many), since you will almost certainly need to drop some items following your pilot study. The initial set of items is referred to as your *item pool*, since it is from this pool that you will select your final set of items.

Example of a test specification

Here I shall describe the construction of an imaginary scale to investigate the phenomenon of academic stardom[1] – that is, the ways in which the role of lecturer is akin to that of a media celebrity (I anticipate colleagues throwing up their hands in horror at the very idea!). The scale is designed to elicit various attributes of lecturers, such as their standing as authority figures and role models: these form the *content areas* of the specification. The key content area in this scale is 'Lecturers as glamour figures', so this receives a slightly higher weighting than the other content areas.

CONTENT AREAS	WEIGHTING
Lecturers as glamour figures	25%
Lecturers as authority figures (commanding respect, and so on)	15%
Lecturers as facilitators (i.e., providing guidance)	15%
Lecturers as experts	15%
Lecturers as friends	15%
Lecturers as role models	15%

The *manifestations* of the scale refer to the quality of interaction students have with their lecturers: intimacy, professional and so on. These are weighted equally:

MANIFESTATIONS	WEIGHTING
Identification (i.e., can relate to the lecturer)	25%
Intimacy (i.e., one-to-one relationship with the lecturer)	25%
Functional (i.e., lecturer just seen as colleague)	25%
Professional (i.e., lecturer evaluated in terms of job)	25%

The number of items in the initial pool will be determined by the weightings for each cell in the grid. You will need at least 12 items in total (Rust and Golombok 1999), and no more than you can reasonably expect respondents to answer. If, for example, you were handing out a questionnaire to shoppers in a busy mall or High Street, you could anticipate a high non-completion rate if you presented them with more than 15 items! By contrast, a postal survey that respondents complete at their leisure could include 50 or more items.[2] Work out the number of items for each content area and then multiply this figure by the weighting for the manifestations in order to calculate the number of items in each cell.

It was decided to create 40 initial items for the academic stardom pool. Using the percentage weightings, this gave a total of 10 items for the 'glamour' content area, and 6 items for the other areas. The manifestations were all weighted equally, so 10 items would need to be created for each one. It is clear in the grid below (Table 8.1) that our calculations for the cell totals do not round off to whole numbers, so I have entered the minimum number of items that would need to be created for each cell. The extra items are free to slot into any cell, so long as the row and column totals end up as printed.

Table 8.1 Test specification for the academic stardom scale

Manifestations	Content area						Total items
	Glamour	Authority	Facilitator	Expert	Friend	Model	
Identification	2	1	1	1	1	1	10
Intimacy	2	1	1	1	1	1	10
Functional	2	1	1	1	1	1	10
Professional	2	1	1	1	1	1	10
Total items	10	6	6	6	6	6	40

Writing items

The next step in scale construction, as directed by the specification, is to write the items themselves. This is not so easy a matter as it might seem. Great care has to be taken with the wording of items, so that they are clear and unambiguous – otherwise the responses you get may not be truly representative of your sample.

Statements for a scale can be generated in a number of ways. Their creation may be driven by theoretical concerns, or from findings in the literature. Sometimes new scales are created by modifying or rewriting items from other scales, particularly in cross-cultural research (often items have to be translated into other languages and then 'back-translated' to see if the translation has worked!). In small group research, items can be generated by 'brainstorming', where different members of the research team can bring all their perspectives to bear.

Perhaps the best way to generate statements is to conduct a focus group interview with participants who are from the same general population as the respondents of the intended questionnaire. This may produce all kinds of interesting data that will inform the scale construction perhaps in ways not foreseen by the researcher. It also ensures that the items can be worded appropriately.

Poor questionnaire/scale items

Complex or compound items

These are items that demand too much from respondents, either because they are unwieldy or because they are effectively two statements rolled into one.

'The royal family are a drain on the national economy and are a relic of a bygone age'

This is a hard item to use because it contains two potential answers. A respondent might agree with the first clause and disagree with the second clause. In this case they are likely to respond with a neutral value (often the central value in a Likert-type scale is headed 'don't know').

Another device to avoid is the double negative:

'People who do not vote cannot expect to have their views represented'

Such questions can confuse respondents and lead to an incorrect answer.

Use of jargon

Questionnaire constructors often forget that respondents are not experts in the field covered by the topic and include technical terms that may be misunderstood or unrecognised. Another potential risk is the use of slang or jargon that might be unfamiliar to the intended population.

Incomplete or ambiguous items

Ideally we want our respondents to be able to answer positively or negatively, but sometimes a statement does not provide enough information for a respondent to make a decision. I recall a student questionnaire in which the following statement produced a lot of neutral responses.

'If I found that my teenage son or daughter had smoked cannabis, I would be horrified'

Many respondents were unwilling to commit themselves to a response because 'teenage' covers a wide age range, and the idea of a 13 year old smoking a joint was more alarming than that of a 17 year old.

Statements of 'fact'

Sometimes respondents are asked to agree or disagree with a statement that appears to be factual, e.g.

'Crime in British cities has increased since the last war'

A respondent may be of the opinion that s/he is simply unable to give an informed answer. There is, however, a fine distinction between a statement that can be confirmed on the basis of the available evidence and one that relies on belief. For example, the statement

'Poverty is the single most important cause of crime'

might elicit a 'don't know' response in *some* respondents, but the 'real' answer is so elusive that any agreement or disagreement will have to be based on belief or opinion. (A philosopher might argue that this is true of *any* statement!).

Sometimes test constructors throw in 'trick' items to make sure that respondents are paying attention, or to deal with the issue of *social desirability*. Often people try to respond to questionnaire items in order to show themselves in a good light, rather than revealing the 'true feelings' that psychological tests aim to elicit.[3]

The most well-known example of this is in the Eysenck Personality Questionnaire (1975) where a subset of 'lie detector' items is included, randomly scattered among items measuring extraversion, psychoticism and so on. Many tests include items which are intended to act as a screening procedure for respondents who are not answering the questions seriously. These are statements that are highly unlikely to be true, e.g., 'I have never made a mistake at work'. It could be argued that such items make particular assumptions about human nature in general (deceit, cruelty, and so on presented as 'normal behaviour'). However, if a respondent has answered positively to *all* such questions, it is likely that they are probably not offering an honest account of themselves, and we may do well to discard their answers.

Organisation and layout of questionnaire

Once we have created our item pool, the next step is to arrange the items in the best possible way to present them to respondents. The order of items may be very important. First, you may need to make sure that respondents are unable to 'guess' the objective of the research. With an attitude scale, this is unlikely to be a problem, but sometimes there are special statements embedded within a scale that are the important measures in the study. In the academic stardom example, the 'glamour' items could be the important ones, and the others mere padding. In fact we could design the scale with only *one* glamour statement, if item analysis proves this to be a good item. However, presenting this as the first statement in the questionnaire would be a very unwise move!

The other important issue in organising questionnaires is to avoid *response bias*. This will occur when a respondent decides to select the same response to most items – strongly agree, for instance. This may happen if a respondent becomes bored with the questionnaire and tries to rush it, or if s/he finds that s/he strongly agrees with most of the items and so tends towards the right hand of the scale for all of them. The way to prevent response bias is to organise your statements so that some of the statements are designed to elicit a positive response and others a negative response, and these are arranged randomly. For example, in a scale measuring attitudes to cannabis, a positive item might read 'Cannabis should be legalised', while a negative item would read 'Cannabis use is likely to lead to the use of hard drugs'. An assortment of positive and negative items forces respondents to read the statements properly, rather than just skimming through.

One major problem with Likert-type response scales is that respondents are often tempted to give neutral or 'don't know' answers down the middle of the scale. You need to be careful here that respondents are aware what a middle value represents: if your scale is supposed to be measuring a *bipolar* concept, like an attitude, where you wish to place respondents at a point somewhere along a dimension (favourable–unfavourable, for example), then the middle value should indicate an indifferent response. However, this is not *necessarily* the same as 'don't know', or 'don't care'. I once used a 7-point Likert-type scale for a questionnaire measuring people's 'parasocial' interaction with TV characters. A number of respondents answered '4' to all the statements, and one or two of these wrote 'don't watch television' at the bottom of the page! I was forced to scrap these replies, since they were clearly irrelevant to the research question. An alternative way of avoiding neutral response bias is, of course, to remove the middle value and simply present respondents with an even-numbered scale (or even a forced choice 2-option response!).

Once you have gathered your statements into an appropriate order, the next step is to design the instrument itself. The layout of a questionnaire is very important because respondents need to be clear about the researcher's requirements. One option is to list your statements on one page and then present the response scale on a separate sheet. Or you may prefer to alternate statements and scales, e.g.

1. Cannabis should be legalised.

Strongly disagree	Disagree	Neutral	Agree	Strongly agree
1	2	3	4	5

2. Cannabis use is likely to lead to the use of hard drugs.

Strongly disagree	Disagree	Neutral	Agree	Strongly agree
1	2	3	4	5

A major drawback of this method is that it is a waste of paper!

Respondents also need to be presented with clear instructions. These should be authoritative but polite, thanking respondents for their time but explaining in a direct fashion what you would like them to do. Below is a typical set of scale instructions. The first part is a brief paragraph informing the respondents about the purpose of the research and assuring them of confidentiality, this is followed by the specific instructions attached to the scale. Figure 8.1 contains the top two scale items as they might be laid out in the booklet.

		Strongly disagree				Strongly agree		
		1	2	3	4	5	6	7
1	My favourite soap opera characters are those who have been in the show for the longest period of time.							
2	I would be upset if my favourite soap opera or drama series was axed.							

Figure 8.1 Scale instructions and suggested layout

This questionnaire is designed as part of a research project investigating people's perceptions of television. For the research it is necessary to collect some basic information about respondents. You may be assured that any information we collect will be treated in confidence and there is no need to disclose your name anywhere on the questionnaire.

The next 35 items are statements regarding people's perception of media and media characters. Please indicate your level of agreement with each statement by placing a tick in the appropriate box on the right-hand scale.

Piloting and item analysis

Once you have designed your questionnaire, you need to carry out a pilot study using respondents who are similar to the eventual target sample. If your eventual sample is expected to consist mainly of students, then use students for the pilot: if you are targeting a specific group (say, mothers with children under six months), then use as close to that group as possible in the time available (mothers with young children of varied ages, for instance). Try to use as large a sample as reasonably possible: if you are aiming at a specific group, the minimum pilot sample is *the number of items in the scale plus one*. If you are just handing out questionnaires to students, try for a somewhat larger sample (unless you have a huge list of items).

After you have collected in all your response sheets and entered your data, the next stage is to carry out a complete analysis of all the items in the scale. This is necessary for you to refine your scale before you carry out your eventual study. There are two useful measures for item analysis – the facility index and the discrimination index.

Facility index

This index is useful in knowledge-based tests where we need to ensure that items are not too easy or too hard. In any sort of test or scale we do not really want items that everyone answers identically, because they are not much use in the final analysis (unless they are special items like lie detectors). The F index is calculated for each item by adding together all the correct responses and dividing this by the number of respondents. The eventual total will be a figure between 0 and 1. A score of 0 would indicate an item that is too difficult to be of use, while a score of 1 indicates an item which is too easy. Ideally we are looking for a value between 0.25 and 0.75.

Discrimination index

Most tests or scales are designed in order that respondents can be ranked on a meaningful continuum (positive–negative attitudes, for example, or

Item	Quartile	Responses (7-point scale)	Total	DP
1	UPPER	$1 \times 1, 1 \times 3, 1 \times 4, 3 \times 5, 3 \times 6, 1 \times 7$	48	1.7
	LOWER	$2 \times 1, 2 \times 2, 3 \times 3, 1 \times 4, 1 \times 5, 1 \times 7$	31	
2	UPPER	$1 \times 4, 2 \times 5, 3 \times 6, 4 \times 7$	60	0.1
	LOWER	$1 \times 4, 2 \times 5, 4 \times 6, 3 \times 7$	59	

Figure 8.2 Example of discriminative power analysis

extraversion–introversion, or good–bad). For statistical purposes, we would expect these qualities to be normally distributed in the population – at least that's how we would go about designing the scale. What we are looking for are items which will discriminate between people at either end of the continuum – on a personality questionnaire we are looking for items to which extraverts will respond differently from introverts, and so on. Items which are answered the same by all respondents are generally of little use.

We can calculate the *discriminative power* of each item by ranking the respondents' total scores and then selecting the upper and lower quartiles (top and bottom 25 per cent). For each item, add together the responses of each group and divide by the number of respondents in the quartile. Then calculate the difference between these figures to give the discriminative power (DP) index.

Figure 8.2 contains two examples of test items analysed for DP. These are data from a study with 40 respondents, so the upper and lower quartiles each consist of 10 responses. Therefore the total value is divided by ten to calculate the DP index. Item number 1 is a good discriminator, since the scores for the upper quartile group are clustered to the right of the scale and the scores for the lower quartile are clustered on the left. We would do well to retain this item. Item number 2 is a poor discriminator – all the responses fall to the right of 3, and there is barely any difference between the upper and lower groups. The DP for this item is practically zero and suggests the item should be dropped. What constitutes a satisfactory DP? It really depends on the scale you are using. For a dichotomous scale (e.g., true/false answers), you could treat the DP almost as a correlational index. For a 7-point scale like the one above, a DP of 7 would be possible for a perfect discriminative item. Of course, any negative DPs are indicative of poor items.

Item–total correlations

More detail on our items can be obtained by examining the correlation between each item and the overall scale total. The logic behind this measure is the same as for discriminative power – that each item should discriminate between high and low scorers on the scale as a whole. Item–total correlations can be obtained by using Pearson's Product-Moment or a point biserial correlation depending on the nature of the response choice. Items with low correlations (≤ 0.2) are probably not telling us much about our respondents.

Measures of reliability and validity

In addition to the above measures, we need to carry out checks for reliability and validity before we can present the questionnaire to our intended sample.

Internal reliability

The internal reliability of a scale is usually measured by a statistic known as *coefficient alpha*. This is a measure of the variance in the test, sometimes referred to as the 'equivalence', or *internal consistency*, of a test. A test is said to be reliable if there is little variance that is specific to certain items (Cortina 1993). Our discrimination and item–total correlation checks should alert us to items with high variance (i.e., where everyone gives different answers regardless of their overall score). An alpha value then gives us a reliability measure for the scale as a whole.

One example of alpha is *split-half reliability* (Spearman-Brown formula). This value is obtained by splitting the test in half (e.g., odd- and even-numbered items), obtaining an alpha statistic for each half and an overall alpha which represents the correlation coefficient of the two halves with each other. The most commonly used statistic is *Cronbach's alpha*, which is effectively the average of all possible combinations of split-half reliability (i.e., splitting the test by every possible combination of items). The formula is shown below, where N^2 refers to the square of the number of items, $M(COV)$ to the mean covariance between items, and $SUM(VAR/COV)$ to the sum of all the elements in the variance–covariance matrix

$$\frac{N^2 \times M(COV)}{SUM(VAR/COV)}$$

What value should we accept as an index of reliability for our scale? Many sources argue that an alpha of 0.8 indicates a reliable test, but lower alphas are often accepted. However, alpha, like so many statistics in psychology, is closely linked to the number of items in the scale. Large scales can produce alphas over 0.7 even where there are low *inter-item correlations* (correlations between items). The factor structure of the scale is also important: alpha is most useful with single-factor tests, where all the items are measures of the same underlying dimension. Where the test incorporates a number of dimensions, we would expect less internal consistency. Nevertheless, if each item is closely related to the other items measuring the same dimension (i.e., is answered in the same way by respondents), there will still be little variance that can be attributed to specific items, and alpha will still be high. Therefore we need to consider what the test is measuring, and how many items it contains, before interpreting the alpha value.

Some computer packages have a very useful output for Cronbach's alpha; on SPSS, for example, it will compute 'Alpha if item deleted' for each item. This tells you what the overall alpha value would be if you deleted that particular item and ran the calculation again. This is a good way of spotting offending items that are dragging alpha down below an acceptable level.

External reliability

Once we have determined that a scale has reliable structure, we then need to investigate its reliability across time. We can do this by means of *test–retest reliability*, where we want to see if respondents will always give the same answer to the questions on every occasion. The external reliability of a test is not related to the items themselves so much as the overall concept under investigation. For example, an attitude scale is based on the assumption that people's attitudes towards a topic are relatively unchanging over time: one's attitude to fox hunting is unlikely to waver from positive to negative in the course of a few days, or even a few months. If attitudes *do* change substantially in this time, we can regard their measurement as unreliable.

To carry out a test–retest reliability check, we need to ensure that we can contact our pilot respondents again some time after their initial completion of the test. This may be a few days later, but ideally you should leave several weeks; otherwise respondents are likely to recall their original responses and simply repeat these. It is not necessary to use the entire group again; perhaps the upper and lower quartiles will suffice. An index of external reliability can then be calculated by correlating the test and retest responses using Pearson's Product-Moment (or, in the case of a forced choice response test, a point-biserial correlation would be more appropriate).

If a test has low external reliability (i.e. a non-significant *r* value) then the whole exercise will need to be reconsidered: maybe the concept under investigation is too unstable to be worth measuring (attitudes to certain topics, such as party politics, might change over a short period following news stories). Normally we would expect fairly high coefficients (0.9 or thereabouts, depending on the size of the scale and the size of the sample).

Refining the scale

Now you have enough information on the scale as a whole and all its items, you can decide how much you want to (or need to) modify it before running the main study. Rust and Golombok (1999) suggest that you would usually retain 70–80 per cent of the original items. Clearly this depends on how many items were initially created, who your respondents are (will they have time to complete a large questionnaire?), and the balance of the items with reference to your original specification. You may find, for instance, that a whole content area suffered badly in the item analysis and you might prefer to drop that cell from the specification. Above all, however, you should never revise your original research question just because of the statistics. If an item is crucial to your study, but reduces the overall scale reliability, then you need to think carefully about how important it is to the scale before dropping it.

Another source of information that may affect your eventual instrument is *respondent feedback*. You may find that the poor performance of individual items is due to one of the problems mentioned earlier in the chapter – the wording is unclear, or the meaning ambiguous. Respondents may indeed mention difficulties they are having with any of the items; you could actively seek this information from your pilot sample by inserting an appropriately worded question at the end of the questionnaire. If your items are failing because of the wording, you may be able to simply rephrase them and keep them in (if they are not important, however, it is probably best to drop them!).

Once you have decided which items to drop for your eventual study, you need to take care that the balance and organisation of the test is not disturbed. For example, a pool of 40 items produces five items with low item–total correlations (≤ 0.1). You decide to drop these items and use a 35-item scale instead. However, when your final set of 300 questionnaires returns from the printer, you realise that the five items were all negatively-worded ones, and there is now a surplus of positively-worded items which could potentially create a response bias! Therefore, it is always a good idea to examine the structure of the test before deciding on the final version.

An example from the literature

Archer and Winchester (1994): pet bereavement

The psychological literature is crammed with hundreds and probably thousands of different tests and scales. Here I have selected an example of scales whose construction was reported in sufficient detail for other researchers to be able to make informed modifications.

The authors created a questionnaire to investigate grief reactions caused by the death of a pet (companion animal). Items were created on the basis of reactions to human bereavement, such as disbelief, avoidance strategies, the 'urge to search for what was lost', and so on. They wrote 40 items and these are reproduced in Table 8.2, grouped by content area. Also included is the number of each item. High inter-item correlations were used to omit a number of items from the final analysis (10, 15, 17, 21, 22, 30, 31, 34, 37 and 40). For example, items 17 and 27 had a correlation of $r = 0.86$, making one of them redundant. The authors used this method because the item–total

Table 8.2 Items from the pet bereavement scale (Archer and Winchester 1994)

Numbness and disbelief (initial reaction)
9   I found it easy to come to terms with the death of my pet*
1   When the death occurred, I couldn't believe it had happened
28   When my pet died I experienced feelings of numbness
15   At first, the loss didn't seem real

Preoccupation with the loss or the lost pet
21   I have found myself reliving the times we shared together
30   I felt the urge to talk about my lost pet
4   I return again and again to thoughts about my lost pet
35   I hardly ever think about my lost pet*
11   I needed to talk about the death and the surrounding circumstances
19   I found I couldn't concentrate for thinking of my pet
33   I found certain habits hard to break, e.g. I have begun to feed my pet or
     called out for them
23   At certain times, the image of my pet seemed so strong that for a split second
     I believed that I had seen or heard him/her in their usual place

Anger, irritability and self-blame
10   I was more irritable after the death of my pet
27   After the death I quarrelled more than usual with my family and friends
12   I felt no anger or bitterness*
17   I flared up more easily after the death of my pet
3   I looked for someone to blame for the death of my pet
25   At times I asked myself if I could have done anything to prevent the death

An urge to search for what was lost
8   I found I was drawn to animals that reminded me of my lost pet
36   I have felt the urge to look for my pet before realizing it was pointless
14   I have never been drawn to their favourite or usual places*
32   At times I have found myself wanting to be near places and objects that were
     closely associated with my lost pet

Mitigating and avoiding grief
26   I have never felt that my lost pet is nearby*
7   I have sometimes gained comfort by pretending that my lost pet is nearby
39   At times I have avoided thinking about my lost pet because it upsets me
18   At times I have deliberately avoided people or situations that act as reminders

A feeling of loss of self
24   When my pet died I felt I'd lost something important in my life
2   When my pet died I felt that part of me had gone

Anxiety and distress
37   Stupid little things upset me after the death occurred
29   After the death of my pet I was always on the go and keeping busy
38   I felt more restless after my pet died
5   After the death of my pet I didn't feel anxious*
40   After the death of my pet I found I was increasingly tense and unable to
     unwind
22   I didn't experience any breathing difficulties*

Table 8.2 (*cont'd*)

Feelings of hopelessness and depression
34 At times I have experienced feelings of hopelessness
16 After the death of my pet I experienced a general loss of interest towards hobbies and pastimes
20 I often had the feeling that things I did were not worthwhile
13 My appetite was affected after the loss of my pet
 6 I found it more difficult to fall asleep after my pet died
31 I did not wake early or during the night more than usual after the death of my pet*

Source: Reproduced with permission from The British Journal of Psychology, © The British Psychological Society.
Note: * indicates negatively worded items: content areas are in italics, items in normal type, item numbers in the left-hand column.

correlations were generally high (mostly > 0.3), and they wanted to carry out a factor analysis on the most reliable items. Cronbach's alpha for the full 40 items was 0.94, which is a high value, although there is a positive relationship between alpha and the number of test items, so we need to be a bit cautious with these values for large scales.

The test scores were then used as the dependent variable in a 2×2 ANOVA where the factors were suddenness of death (yes/no) and whether the respondent lived alone or not. Both main effects were found to be significant (those living alone had higher scores, as did those whose pet died suddenly), but there was no interaction. A 2×2 ANOVA was also conducted for suddenness of death and emotional attachment (high/low); again, both main effects were significant but the factors did not interact.

Summary

The aim of this chapter is to give the reader enough information to construct a reliable psychometric instrument for collecting quantitative survey data. In order to achieve this aim different types of scaling techniques are discussed, of which Likert scaling is by far the most popular today. Then there is a lengthy section containing advice on scale construction, which is necessary for designing a scale which will elicit the data you hope to collect, and not statistical 'noise'. The test specification will help you design a balanced set of items, and the reliability checks are essential if you ever want to publish your data. You might even want make your test available commercially, if it was thought to be useful in a clinical or educational context, in which case you would also need to establish norms on a large representative sample. If you want an existing (published) scale and want to avoid the pitfalls of constructing your own, Maltby *et al.* (2000) is an excellent reference for published psychological tests of all different shapes and sizes, complete with reviews of the tests, their references and use in published research.

Notes

1 Moran (1998) has published on the topic of academic stardom – though in the context of international research fame, rather than localised celebrity among students!
2 See Robson (1993) for a useful series of tips on getting good response rates from postal questionnaires.
3 A precondition for completing a psychometric test is that our respondents are honest. Scientifically speaking, the concepts of honesty, sincerity, and so on are not without their problems. The fact is that we can never *know* whether a person is being honest (and we may not even be aware when *we* are being honest!). Of course, this problem applies to all psychological research, which is why some people prefer to study 'discourse', which deliberately sidesteps the issue of private emotions and opinions. Some would say that it sidesteps the topic of psychology too! But these are issues to be debated in Part IV of the book . . .

9   Factor analysis

Before using an original scale in a major psychological study, there are other measures of validity that a researcher would like to explore. The *factor structure* of a scale or test is an important consideration in assessing whether an instrument is successful in tackling the researcher's original question. For instance, if our hypothesis is rooted in the notion of intelligence as a single, unitary concept, then a test of intelligence should be best described by a *single-factor solution*, with a unique factor underlying all responses, rather than a pattern of several factors which would suggest that intelligence is composed of different subskills.

We can study the factor structure of a scale by examining the correlations and covariance between different items. The purpose of this is to identify which items appear to 'go together' – in other words, if respondents tend to strongly agree with item 1, then they tend to strongly agree with items 3, 4 and 6, but there is no relationship with items 2 and 5. If they disagree with item 2, they tend to agree with item 5. Patterns of response like this can tell us a lot about the structure of the questionnaire. It may be, for instance, that when we developed the grid of content areas and manifestations (see Chapter 8) we had 2 and 5 in a different cell from 1, 3, 4 and 6. We might have organised the questionnaire like this on conceptual grounds (perhaps 2 and 5 are tapping a subcomponent of the overall topic area). These matters are of considerable significance for the development of theory; they are of particular concern in the field of personality research, where the number of personality 'types' is often indicated by the number of factors that can be identified in statistical analysis.

Therefore, most scales will undergo some form of factor analysis (FA) during their early stages. If you have come to this chapter after reading Parts I and II of the book, you will find some of the concepts involved in factor analysis markedly similar to that of other statistical techniques, notably discriminant function analysis (identifying 'functions') and structural equation modelling (identifying 'latent variables'). You will already have encountered concepts such as iterative solutions and eigenvalues. Of course, all these techniques are connected through the mysteries of matrix algebra: to reiterate points for readers who have come straight here, there is no need to understand how the computation is arrived at, so long as you know how to interpret the findings. But to do that requires some understanding of the basic processes involved.

Exploratory factor analysis

First of all, it is necessary to distinguish between *exploratory* factor analysis and *confirmatory* factor analysis. The distinction has echoes of debates touched on previously in the book, such as the essential difference between exploratory data analysis and hypothesis testing. Exploratory factor analysis is a technique for investigating the structure of a data set about which you have few preconceptions – in the case of scale construction, you have designed a questionnaire and collected the data, but you have no idea whether the responses match your original predictions. Confirmatory factor analysis is only used when you have a specific hypothesis that you want to test. You would not perform it on a single scale, but you might want to split a scale into subscales in order to discover what portions of the variance in another measure separate subscales explain.

Exploratory factor analysis can be further broken down into different types of analysis. The differences between these types are fairly minimal, but once you have mastered *principal components analysis* – the most commonly used technique – the idiosyncracies of the other types will make more sense.

Steps in principal components analysis

The most common form of exploratory factor analysis is known as principal components analysis (PCA). The goal of PCA, as with all types of factor analysis, is to reduce a large data set to a small number of general factors that explain most of the variance in the data set. In PCA these factors are referred to as *components*, but I shall try to avoid confusion by referring to both components and factors as factors – this is quite conventional. The real difference between factors and components is marginal, and is to do with some of the values used in the statistical procedure. I will explain the difference in more detail once I have gone through an example of PCA. The procedure in this section is based on Kline (1994), so if the reader requires more detail, this is the next reference to turn to.

The starting point for any type of factor analysis is the correlation matrix between the variables of interest. With a large test, this matrix will be vast and unwieldy, so I shall use a very simple matrix to illustrate the procedure. Table 9.1 contains the correlation matrix for a hypothetical set of exam results on a psychology degree. From the values we can see that some of the subjects correlate more highly than others: Social Psychology and Developmental Psychology have quite a strong positive correlation, while Social Psychology and Statistics have only a very modest positive correlation.

Table 9.1 Correlation matrix for principal components example

	Statistics	*Cognitive*	*Developmental*	*Social*
Statistics	1.0	0.3	0.2	0.1
Cognitive	0.3	1.0	0.3	0.2
Developmental	0.2	0.3	1.0	0.4
Social	0.1	0.2	0.4	1.0
Total	1.6	1.8	1.9	1.7

Two features of a correlation matrix are very important and must be borne in mind throughout: first, half of any correlation matrix contains redundant information; the value in the bottom left-hand cell (0.1) is the mirror image of the top right-hand cell – both cells contain the correlation coefficient of Statistics and Social. Second, the values along the diagonal from top left to bottom right are all 1.0: these cells represent the correlation of each variable with itself. (These features may seem obvious but they are important.)

PCA proceeds by working out how much variance in the matrix can be explained by a general factor. It would seem logical to label this factor 'general psychology ability'.

1   It starts out a little like an ANOVA, by squaring the sum totals of the columns and adding them together ($1.6^2 + 1.8^2 + 1.9^2 + 1.7^2$). This gives you a total of 12.3. Find the square root of this figure (3.5) and then divide the four column totals by it. You should end up with four values: 0.46, 0.51, 0.54 and 0.49. This set of values is referred to as the *first trial vector*.

2   Now you need to multiply the first trial vector by the original correlation matrix. This is done by multiplying each of the above four values by each of the elements in the matrix and then adding together each row, as in Figure 9.1.

3   You should end up with four values: 0.76, 0.91, 0.98 and 0.86. Square these, add them together and take the square root of the total (1.76). Then divide the above values by this figure. You will end up with the set of values: 0.43, 0.51, 0.56 and 0.49. This is the *second trial vector*.

4   The aim of PCA is to find, through repeated analyses, trial vectors that are identical to each other. This is the process known as *iteration*, which I have mentioned occasionally in previous chapters. Keep repeating

$0.46 \times 1.0 + 0.51 \times 0.3 + 0.54 \times 0.2 + 0.49 \times 0.1$
$0.46 \times 0.3 + 0.51 \times 1.0 + 0.54 \times 0.3 + 0.49 \times 0.2$
$0.46 \times 0.2 + 0.51 \times 0.3 + 0.54 \times 1.0 + 0.49 \times 0.4$
$0.46 \times 0.1 + 0.51 \times 0.2 + 0.54 \times 0.4 + 0.49 \times 1.0$

Figure 9.1 Multiplication of first trial vector by the original correlation matrix

the above process with each new trial vector that is produced, until the values match each other. In the above case, trial vectors 1 and 2 are *almost* the same, but not quite: you will need to go through the process again.

5   The third trial vector is a bit different: 0.42, 0.52, 0.57 and 0.48. Keep on plugging away, though, and you will find that the fourth trial vector comes out as 0.42, 0.52, 0.57 and 0.48. Snap! You have identified the *first characteristic vector* of the correlation matrix. At this point, we can say that the iterative procedure has *converged*.

6   Now you need to calculate the *factor loadings* for each variable in the matrix. Factor loadings are very useful, because they tell us how highly each variable is correlated with the factor. To calculate these loadings we need to rewind a little in the process and find the square root of the last sum of squares. In step 3, this value was 1.76, but we have worked out two trial vectors since then. The actual value we need is, however, 1.76, which just happens to be the same. This figure is the first *eigenvalue* of the matrix (sometimes referred to as the first characteristic root). This figure tells us the amount of variance explained by the factor; if we divide it by the number of variables (1.76/4) it tells us what percentage of the total variance in the matrix the factor has explained (in this case, 44 per cent). The factor loadings are calculated by multiplying the values in the first characteristic vector by the square root of the eigenvalue. Therefore:

Variable	*Factor loading*
Statistics	0.56
Cognitive	0.69
Developmental	0.76
Social	0.64

Roughly speaking, the higher the loading, the more the variable characterises the factor. If the factor is indeed one of general psychology ability (and it is up to us to decide whether this makes sense), then we could say that developmental scores are most typical of this ability, while statistics scores are less typical. But generally speaking, loadings of 0.3 or more are considered to be significant. However, we are far from finished yet, and we would certainly never use the unrotated factor loadings to make assertions like this!

7   The next step is to extract the next factor, or component, from the correlation matrix. (In PCA we need to extract as many factors as there are variables, because the goal of PCA is to account for every last drop of variance in the matrix.) However, before we can do this, we need to 'partial out' the variance we have explained through factor 1. We do this by calculating the *residual matrix*. This is done by multiplying all the factor loadings by one another: the resulting values are referred to as the *cross products*. Therefore:

Statistics/Cognitive	0.56×0.69
Cognitive/Developmental	0.69×0.76
Statistics/ Developmental	0.56×0.76
Cognitive/Social	0.69×0.64
Statistics/Social	0.56×0.64
Developmental/Social	0.76×0.64

The diagonal values become the squares of the factor loadings (0.31, 0.48, 0.58 and 0.41). Then we subtract these values, and all the pairs of cross products, from their correlation coefficients in the original matrix, which should leave us with a residual matrix looking like the one in Table 9.2.

Table 9.2 Residual matrix for principal components example

	Statistics	*Cognitive*	*Developmental*	*Social*
Statistics	0.69	−0.09	−0.23	−0.26
Cognitive	−0.09	0.52	−0.22	−0.24
Developmental	−0.23	−0.22	0.42	−0.09
Social	−0.26	−0.24	−0.09	0.59
Total	1.6	1.8	1.9	1.7

8   Now the iterative process begins again in order to extract the second characteristic vector which will be treated as factor 2. This will almost certainly have a lower eigenvalue than factor 1, and therefore will explain less variance in the correlation matrix. The loadings on this factor will be different, and are most likely to have a high degree of polarity, with several negative loadings. The third factor is extracted from the new residual matrix with the variance from factors 1 and 2 partialled out, and this will have a lower eigenvalue still. By the time you reach the final factor the loadings will be tiny and the amount of variance explained will be negligible. However, we are still only halfway there. The next step is to rotate our main factors in geometric space. But before I describe this process I shall say a little about the alternatives to PCA.

Other forms of exploratory factor analysis

The main difference between PCA and other forms of factor analysis concerns the elements on the diagonal row of the correlation matrix, referred to as the *communalities*. In PCA these all have values of 1.0, indicating perfect positive correlations of the variables with themselves. However, in real life we know that this is hardly ever the case: in the previous chapter, I explained how we can sometimes consider a test reliable if it has a Cronbach's alpha lower than 0.8. Many variables have lower alphas than this and are still entered into factor analyses (e.g., rogue test items). This leaves a lot of error variance unaccounted for.

In *common* and *principal factor analysis* an attempt is made to separate error variance from specific variance (i.e., that which is explained by the variable itself). This is done by replacing the 1.0s in the diagonal of the correlation matrix with estimates of communalities: these may be the squared multiple correlation of each variable with the others, or they may be the alpha coefficients (if the variables are tests). As a result, the iterative process is more complicated.

In *minimum residual factor analysis*, the communalities are omitted altogether. However, this creates problems for iteration, in that there is no limit to the number of factors which can be extracted and, unless the matrix has a very clear factor structure, the iterative process could go on *ad infinitum*.

So how does a researcher decide which technique to use? There is no simple answer, and experts in the field of factor and PC analysis simply choose favourites and stick to them. To the casual user, most of the techniques tend towards similar solutions anyway, especially with large data sets. My personal recommendation is that you use PCA for one-off research studies, such as the initial testing of a new scale, but you would be better off using FA for standardising a test or scale. The reason for this is that PCA explains all the variance in the correlation matrix for your study, while FA – through estimating the communalities – is more appropriate for measures which are intended to be generalised to a population.

Factor selection

Once the iterative process is complete, we then need to 'rotate' the factors in an effort to simplify the analysis for the sake of interpretation. Rotation is a complicated business, though, so the simplification needs to begin earlier, with regard to the number of factors we choose to rotate. The two most common ways of selecting factors are Kaiser's criterion and Cattell's scree test.

Kaiser's criterion

The iterative process tells us how much variance is accounted for by each factor, expressed by the *eigenvalue* (λ). The square root of the eigenvalue tells us how much variance in the correlation matrix is explained by that particular factor. Therefore, these values are useful when we need to identify the important factors. Kaiser's criterion (1960) specifies that we only rotate factors with eigenvalues greater than 1.0. It is estimated that a 20-variable matrix will yield 4 to 7 factors with $\lambda > 1.0$ (Tabachnick and Fidell 2001).

In practice, Kaiser's criterion is most useful as a maximum limit: we should never be interested in factors with $\lambda < 1.0$. The number of variables

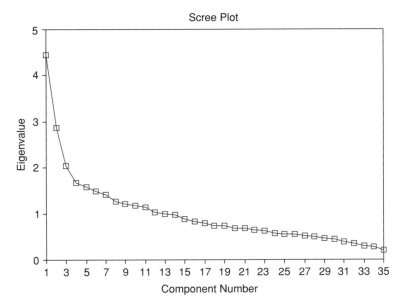

Figure 9.2 Cattell's scree test

is an important consideration. With a small number, this method may be an ideal way of selecting a manageable set of factors; with large numbers (such as 40-item tests), there may be far too many factors with $\lambda > 1.0$, most of them clustering in the $2 > \lambda > 1.0$ region, and we may need to be more discriminating.

Cattell's scree test

The scree test, devised by Cattell (1966), is a graphical way of deciding on a cut-off point for selecting factors. Simply plot the highest eigenvalues on a graph (any computer package will do this) and look for the break in the line that joins them together. This is sometimes referred to as the 'elbow' if you think of the line as a crooked arm. In Figure 9.2 the elbow appears between the third and fourth factors, but not between the fourth and fifth factors, so we would select the first three factors (i.e., the ones on the upper arm) for rotation.

No method is perfect for all occasions. We may have other considerations – for example, our research question or theory may require us to select a certain number of factors because we have predicted a particular structure. For example, we may have deliberately designed a questionnaire to tap five underlying constructs, so a cut-off point of three factors would clearly be inadequate (except that the scree test could be used to demonstrate the different contribution of the factors). Another measure is to work out how

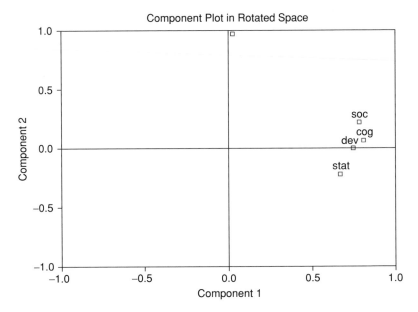

Figure 9.3 Rotation of factors in a two-dimensional plot

much variance we would wish our solution to explain. Take a figure, say, 75 per cent, and select as many factors as explain that cumulative percentage of variance.

Factor rotation

Once we have decided on our number of factors, we then put our factor loadings through the process of rotation. The first part of the analysis was based on matrix algebra, but the next part can be based on either algebra or geometry. The early factor analysts, such as Thurstone (1947), would at this point have set to work through the night using set squares and compasses, but we can do it with a single mouse click.

Essentially a rotation of the solution involves placing the solution in a variety of alternative geometrical positions. With two factors, this is relatively easy – we simply shift the axes round a given angle, as depicted in Figure 9.3, where factors 1 and 2 have been rotated so that variables A and B have new loadings. Add new factors to this graph, though, and the solution becomes far more complicated, with the axes plotted in three dimensions, and a bewildering number of possible solutions. In any new set of positions the factor loadings will change, but still explain the same variance. Therefore the loadings are *relative* values.

The whole point of factor rotation is to see if there is a simpler solution to our analysis than the one arrived at through iteration. The ultimate goal is *simple structure*. In order to reach this simple structure, geometrists would need to plot the rotated factors in an infinite number of alternative positions. Today, however, this result is achieved through a number of criteria which are built into the various computer packages as an algebraic formula; roughly, rotation stops when the simplest solution is found – where the fewest variables load on the selected factors. This means, ideally, that different variables load on different factors, and there is little crossover.

Different types of rotation

Orthogonal rotation

Orthogonal rotation places the factors at right angles to each other. This means that they are uncorrelated and, therefore, this type of rotation should only be selected when you believe this to be the case. In most factor analyses, such as studies of personality tests, it is unlikely that factors would not be correlated. By far the most common software for orthogonal rotation is the *Varimax* program, available with most statistical software.

Oblique rotation

This method is more complicated because it means that the factors can take up any position in three-dimensional space. For reasons mentioned above, though, it is more appropriate in psychological research because we would normally expect some degree of overlap or correlation between factors. As a result, there are a variety of different software packages available. Some are relatively obscure and difficult to use (such as Maxplane and Rotoplot). Probably the most commonly used is *Direct Oblimin*.

Interpreting the computer output

Once we have achieved the goal of simple structure, we still need to interpret the rotated factor matrix. It is important to distinguish between the *factor structure matrix* and the *factor pattern matrix*, both of which are usually produced by the computer. With orthogonal rotation, both matrices display the same information, but after oblique rotation, the structure matrix is the table that you should use for interpretation.

An imaginary structure matrix is laid out as in Table 9.4. At the top the eigenvalues for each variable are shown. The first column, Factor 1, contains the factor loadings for each variable. You can usually specify that it selects only variables with loadings over 0.3 (or your preferred significance level). The next column, Factor 2, contains the loadings for that factor. The same process continues across the table.

The researcher's first task is to supply names for each of the factors. This is done by identifying links between the high-loading variables on each factor.

Table 9.3 Example of a factor structure matrix

Variables	Factor 1 (λ = 3.8)	Factor 2 (λ = 3.1)	Factor 3 (λ = 2.5)
item 17	0.82		
item 15	0.71		
item 3	0.65		
item 14	0.53		−0.33
item 1	−0.44		
item 23	0.32		
item 8		0.78	
item 20		−0.69	
item 2		0.54	
item 13		0.36	
item 9			0.80

What is it, in this case, that items 17, 15 and 3 have in common? Notice how item 1 has a negative loading on factor 1. If the items are statements measured on a Likert-type scale, you might find that people who gave high ratings to statements 17, 15 and 3 tended to give low ratings to statement 1. However there is a less clear pattern between these items and item 8. For item 8 we need to link up with items 20, 2 and 13 to supply a name for factor 2. Factor 3 seems to be largely bound up with a single item (9). This often happens when there are items in a questionnaire with a very clear pattern of response but which are not related to the other items.

Notice how item 14 makes two appearances in the matrix. One of the goals of simple structure is to avoid this type of thing happening. Variables which load highly on more than one factor are known as *complex* variables; we generally try to aim for 'pure' variables, which correlate with only one factor. Where variables load on more than one factor it is customary to talk of *crossloading*.

Example of exploratory factor analysis from the literature

Maltby (1999): religious orientation

Previous research has identified three basic religious orientations: *intrinsic* (internal religiosity, e.g., a personal philosophy), *extrinsic-personal* (religion as a source of comfort) and *extrinsic-social* (religion as a public expression, e.g. going to church). In this example, Maltby (1999) examined a measure of religious orientation, the 'Age-Universal' I-E Scale (Gorsuch and Venable 1983) to see if this scale's factor structure supported the three basic religious orientations.

The scale was completed by 3390 (1408 males, 1984 females) students, non-student adults, and schoolchildren from the United States, England, Northern Ireland and the Republic of Ireland. The full list of items is con-

Table 9.4 Principal components analysis with oblimin rotation of all the items (original item numbers in brackets)

Item	1	2	3	4	5
Intrinsic					
I try hard to live all my life according to my religious beliefs (9)	**0.77**	0.02	0.02	0.03	−0.05
It doesn't much matter what I believe so long as I am good (3)	−0.02	−0.03	0.05	**0.91**	0.04
I have often had a strong sense of God's presence (7)	**0.68**	−0.04	0.04	−0.06	0.15
My whole approach to life is based on my religion (16)	**0.81**	0.05	0.04	0.06	0.01
Prayers I say when I'm alone are as important to those I say in church (19)	0.06	−0.11	−0.12	**0.85**	−0.07
I attend church once a week or more (6)	0.29	0.04	−0.05	0.02	**0.55**
My religion is important because it answers many questions about the meaning of life (11)	**0.79**	−0.12	−0.01	0.01	−0.02
I enjoy reading about my religion (1)	**0.81**	−0.08	0.06	0.03	0.02
It is important to me to spend time in private thought and prayer (5)	**0.84**	−0.06	0.04	0.02	0.01
Extrinsic-personal					
What religion offers me most is comfort in times of trouble and sorrow (10)	0.03	**0.86**	0.11	0.04	−0.01
Prayer is for peace and happiness (13)	−0.04	**0.89**	−0.02	−0.02	0.01
I pray mainly to gain relief and protection (8)	−0.07	**0.88**	0.03	0.03	0.03
Extrinsic-social					
I go to church because it helps me make friends (2)	0.07	−0.02	**0.84**	0.02	0.08
I go to church mainly because I enjoy seeing people I know there (17)	0.04	0.09	**0.90**	0.03	−0.06
I go to church mostly to spend time with my friends (15)	−0.01	0.13	**0.85**	−0.04	0.02

tained in Table 9.4; respondents are asked to say whether each statement is a description of them. Items were scored on a three-point scale (no/not certain/yes). The responses were then subjected to a principal components analysis. The scree test was used to identify the number of components, and on this basis, five components were extracted; these were then subjected to oblimin rotation.

Table 9.4 shows the loadings of all the items on the five components, with items deemed important to the component in bold type. The first column is organised in terms of the religious orientation of the items. At this point, two things are worth noting about the table: first, all items have loadings above 0.5, which is a good sign, indicating that a simple structure has been uncovered which is clear and unambiguous; second, there are no complex items – all loadings above 0.3 are linked to a unique factor.

The first signs are positive: the first component comprises most (six) of the nine intrinsic items, the second component comprises all of the extrinsic-personal items, while the third component comprises all of the extrinsic-social items. This means that the factor structure corresponds roughly to the basic religious orientations.

But what about the other two components that the scree test has identified? What might they represent? We can see from the factor loadings in columns 4 and 5 that three 'intrinsic' items have their highest loadings on these two additional components, which suggests that some other factor explains these items better than 'intrinsic religious orientation'. When this kind of thing happens, the clue usually lies in the wording of the statements.

The item 'Prayers I say when I'm alone are as important to those I say in church' is problematic because it effectively describes two behaviours – prayers alone (a personal activity) and prayers in church (a public activity). Therefore it straddles two of the basic religious orientations. Similarly, the item 'I attend church once a week or more' may reflect a personal commitment to religion (intrinsic) but it may also reflect social expression of religiosity (extrinsic). Therefore these items are probably not good measures of intrinsic religiosity.

All in all, then, the Age-Universal scale seems quite a good measure of the basic religious orientations. Bear in mind too that it was not designed specifically to test these three orientations! When this type of concordance occurs we usually talk about a test having good concurrent validity – it means that, even if we cannot say for certain that it measures what we want it to measure (i.e., has construct validity), at least it concurs with other tests attempting to measure the same thing.

Some issues in factor analysis

First- and second-order factors

It is possible that a set of identifiable components or factors are nested within an overarching single factor (or maybe more than one). In the above example, there might be a general factor separating the careerist items from the rest, which could be gathered together under the general label of 'moral reasons'. Such general factors can be identified in an analysis, in which case they are termed *second-order* factors.

This normally happens when factors are correlated with each other, so if we use an orthogonal rotation we will not have to worry about these. The way to check for second-order factors is by running a factor analysis on the matrix of factor correlations (i.e. the relationship between the first-order factors identified through your analysis so far). However, you need to ensure that your preferred software will allow you to do this.

Second-order factors may or may not be desirable, depending on our theoretical perspective and our initial research question. We might be predicting a single-factor structure and find that items load highly on a number of other factors; here the emergence of a second-order factor might help confirm our initial expectations.

Bloated specifics

Sometimes a factor may look like a general collection of discrete items or variables, but may be no more than a selection of reworded statements that all measure the same thing. In a test I created to measure parasocial interaction (the interaction between viewers and media figures), I included two items that had very similar wording. One was

'If my favourite soap character was ill or in hospital I would send flowers or a card'.

The other was

'If the actor or actress who plays my favourite soap character was ill or in hospital I would send flowers or a card'.

The intention was to tease out the subtle difference between parasocial interaction with a real person (i.e., the actor) and that with a fictional person (i.e., the character). However, respondents tend to fill in questionnaires rather quickly (especially if there are lots of items), and a number of them claimed that the same statement had been included twice in the instrument. Subtlety is wasted on questionnaire respondents! It is a good example of a bad item (or two) with unclear, ambiguous meanings for respondents.

If these two items had loaded on a single factor, then we would have a clear case of a bloated specific. In other words, the factor would be interpreted as nothing other than a single item that was unrelated to other parts of the questionnaire. However, both questions loaded on a factor along with several other items, so this was not a problem for the analysis. Nevertheless, we must always be careful that we do not mistake a bloated specific for a general factor.

Order out of chaos

One of the most common criticisms of factor analysis (research papers are often rejected on this count) is that factor analysis is used as an artificial way of tidying up a sloppy data set. This is particularly true of studies where there is no obvious dependent measure, or where the research is largely exploratory. Such objections to factor analysis tend to come from the school of inferential statistics – academics who would rather see complex phenomena reduced to flawless single-factor solutions than painstakingly dissected in all their messy glory. As descriptive data, factor analysis can be extremely useful; as a rule of thumb, if the factor structure provides an appropriate answer to the research question, then it has served some purpose.

Use of Likert-type data

A frequent criticism of factor analysis (particularly as used by psychologists) is that the data rarely meet parametric assumptions. This is especially true when we are analysing tests and scales. If our variables are whole test scores and other measures, then their derivation is unimportant because the analysis is conducted on the correlation matrix. But when that matrix contains correlations between items with a very restricted range of responses (such as 1 to 5, or even 1 and 2) then the analysis becomes unstable, and little of the variance is likely to be explained by general factors.

The solution may be to use appropriate correlational techniques to produce the initial correlation matrix. For Likert-type scales, a Spearman rank correlation is probably more appropriate than a Pearson correlation, while for dichotomous variables, point biserial correlation would be necessary. In practice, however, the eventual outcome will not be markedly different from using Pearson correlation, so long as a large sample ($N > 150$) is used.

These issues have led to a number of alternative approaches to scale analysis. One such approach is known as Item Response Theory (Baker 1992; Steinberg and Thissen 1996), which is a set of procedures for refining a scale. A related approach is Rasch scaling (Rasch 1960), which attempts to convert Likert-type data to an interval measure, and can be used to examine the bias in a data set created by specific items.

Confirmatory factor analysis

Probably the most frequent criticism of exploratory factor analysis is that it is entirely descriptive. It cannot be used, for example, for hypothesis testing, or parameter estimation. Much of the analytic work relies on the interpretative skill of the researcher, as early in the process as selecting which factors to rotate (essentially, Cattell's scree test is an impressionistic method). Furthermore, the plethora of alternative iterative and rotational procedures leaves non-specialists confused.

Many psychologists would not consider these things problematic – as you will see in Part IV of this book, the same criticisms are laid at the door of qualitative methods. However, an alternative form of factor analysis has recently gained popularity, and this is Confirmatory Factor Analysis (CFA), which *can* be used to test hypotheses (up to a point) and provides rather more in the way of inferential statistics. In fact we have already covered CFA in the book, since it is merely another form of structural equation modelling that can be performed using LISREL or related software, as described in Chapter 7. If you have skipped that section of the book so far, now is the time to go back and read that chapter.

There are two main differences between CFA and structural equation modelling: first, the weighting process (and, therefore, the hypothesis you are testing) is usually informed by the results of at least one exploratory factor analysis. Typically, a CFA is used to compare two or more alternative factor structures using appropriate measures and samples. For example, you could run the Age-Universal religious scale on a different sample (perhaps a non-Christian one, provided the wording is adapted), and include a related measure as well. You would then draw up a set of weights that predicted the three basic religious orientations to see if the same pattern of factor loadings emerged (or, to use CFA terminology, the same 'set of paths'). The idea of CFA is to match a better fitting model, or solution, to the data. It is therefore no different from the goal of SEM.

The only other difference between CFA and SEM is that CFA uses the same terminology as exploratory factor analysis. For 'latent variables' read factors; for 'path coefficients' read factor loadings; for 'manifest variables' read items (or whatever variables you use in exploratory factor analysis). The results are still presented in the form of a path diagram.

Example of confirmatory factor analysis from the literature

Anthony et al. *(1999): symptoms of post-traumatic stress disorder*

In the last two decades there has been a huge interest in the psychological response to traumatic incidents: witness the growth of disaster counselling, which has become *de rigeur* for most large-scale accidents. However, the classification of symptoms for post-traumatic stress disorder (PTSD) has failed to follow any consistent pattern, with a variety of models being proposed. The authors in this study decided to test a selection of these models by using confirmatory factor analysis to identify the best-fitting classification system for PTSD symptoms in a large group of children and adolescents.

The ten models they selected for analysis ranged from a single-factor solution to a four-factor solution. All the models tried to package the same set of symptoms into subgroups, but they did so slightly differently. Model 8, the four-factor solution, identified the following factors:

1   Intrusion (frequent reminders, images, dreams, etc.)
2   Avoidance (thought stopping, etc.)
3   Numbing (isolation, loss of affect, etc.)
4   Arousal (attentional difficulties, insomnia, 'on edge', etc.)

For example, the item *bad dreams* loaded on one general PTSD symptom factor in model 1, on an 'intrusion-avoidance' factor in models 2 and 7, on an 'intrusion-arousal' factor in models 3 and 4, on a single 'intrusion' factor in models 5, 6 and 8, on a combined 'intrusion, avoidance and arousal' factor in model 10, and on a 'sleep/attention' factor in model 9.

The sample for the CFA study comprised over 6000 children from schools in South Carolina, USA, who had been exposed to Hurricane Hugo in September 1989. This hurricane produced 175 mph wind speeds, and a 23 foot tidal wave, resulting in vast damage to property (over $6 billion). Some 35 per cent of the children had suffered 'severe damage' to their homes, many had been unable to return to them, and several of their parents had become unemployed (presumably because of damage to small businesses). Incidence of physical injury is not reported.

The next thing for the researchers to do was to select an appropriate measure – preferably one that has been used in a number of the studies from which the models have been drawn. In this case they chose the Frederick Reaction Index (RI) for children, which presents 20 symptoms and asks the children to rate each symptom on a scale ranging from 1 (none of the time) to 5 (most of the time). These items were then mapped on to the factor sets from the 10 models. In addition, a standard measure of anxiety was completed by the children, along with an open-ended questionnaire which measured degree of 'exposure' to the hurricane (coded according to severity of damage, parental job loss, etc.).

First, using a carefully stratified sample (25 per cent) from the total data set, the models were compared according to their goodness of fit for the RI data. Model 7 (a three-factor solution: intrusion-avoidance, numbing and arousal) produced the highest Robust Comparative Fit Index (between 0.90 and 0.95) and outscored the other models on a selection of similar measures.

Then, using another stratified sample of 25 per cent, the Lagrange Multiplier test was used to identify model improvements to Model 7. This suggested some slight modifications to the paths from the items to the factors, and it also suggested building in a second-order factor to link the three first-order factors together. When added to the model, the first-order factors all had loadings of over 0.8 on this overall PTSD factor.

Finally, the improved model was cross-validated on a further (17 per cent) subsample from the database, and then the full sample was used to relate the RI items to the anxiety and exposure measures. This was done to examine further the validity of the three-factor model, and significant correlations were found between the three factors and the anxiety subscales and degree of exposure. Degree of exposure was found to be most highly correlated with intrusion-avoidance.

In addition to analysing previously proposed models of PTSD, this study also produced useful information for the DSM-IV classification of the disorder, with some of the 'central' symptoms (e.g., attention problems, anhedonia) failing to load substantially on any factor. These findings have important implications for clinical practice, since they are often used to diagnose PTSD.

Summary

Factor analysis is a widely used technique in psychological research, having its roots in psychometric testing, and generally this remains the field in which it is most widely used. Today, of course, psychometric testing has expanded far beyond the measurement of personality traits, incorporating attitude scales and other types of Likert-type scaling methods, but factor analysis is still seen as a useful exploratory method for studying the internal structure of a scale or data set. This chapter has outlined the basic statistical processes involved in the iterative process of identifying factors, although factor analysis is essentially an interpretative method, whereby the researcher needs to apply his or her theoretical knowledge and familiarity with the data in order to label factors or components, and to make sense of the analysis. Confirmatory factor analysis is a different technique altogether, being a variant of structural equation modelling, in which tests of significance are used to investigate the 'fit' of a specified model against a set of data.

10 Other techniques for data reduction

One way of looking at factor analysis is as a means of data reduction – it identifies patterns in a large set of data that make the data easier to interpret. As mentioned in the previous chapter, this can leave us open to the criticism that we are making a silk purse out of a sow's ear, seeing meaning where there is nothing but noise. But such criticisms miss one of the important points of research – namely, if our research question is sufficiently interesting at the outset, and our methodology is not hopelessly flawed, *whatever* data we obtain should be open to analysis. We may not have the evidence to prove or disprove hypotheses, but this certainly does not mean our data are of no interest (often, hypotheses are only advanced when the researcher is highly confident of obtaining a statistically significant result).[1]

Luckily, there are several techniques we can use to 'reduce' data for interpretation. Factor analysis is at its most useful for reducing data obtained from tests and scales, because it looks for patterns that group together several variables (e.g., test items). Often we are more interested in patterns that group together several cases – perhaps individuals who have taken a test, or who have been measured on a number of variables. In this chapter I will describe two types of analysis which identify patterns in the data – cluster analysis and multidimensional scaling – by examining how the data are arranged in geometric space. There is also a section on canonical correlation, a type of analysis which studies relationships between two sets of variables.

CLUSTER ANALYSIS

Imagine a study was carried out to investigate seasonal shopping trends. We might expect the sales of certain consumer goods to fluctuate across months of the year; sales of ice cream would be highest in the summer months, while thermal underwear would tend to be purchased during the winter. Suppose we collected data on the sales figures for these products at three points in the year: January, April and July. We could plot these data on a scatterplot, but instead of representing each value as a cross, it is represented by a code

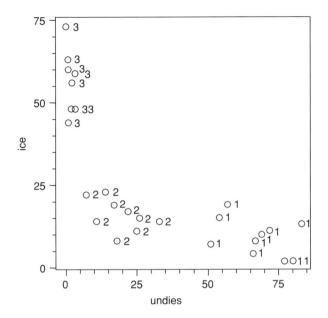

Figure 10.1 Scatterplot of ice cream and thermal underwear sales

referring to the month (1, 2 or 3). The scatterplot might look like the one depicted in Figure 10.1. The clear implication, from looking at this plot, is that the three months form three distinct *clusters* of data points; the threes tend to cluster together, as do the ones and the twos. Now imagine adding several other items to the analysis – say, skiing equipment, tennis racquets, umbrellas, Easter eggs and sunblock. The clustering pattern would probably start to become less clear-cut, and it would be harder to pick out the three months so easily. You would also need a rotating scatterplot representing a number of dimensions to contain data on all those measures.

This is where cluster analysis is a useful technique – for identifying groups of similar cases in data sets which are difficult to portray graphically. The way this is done is to calculate the *Euclidean distance* between each pair of values. This is a measure of the distance between the two points in multi-dimensional space (depending on the number of variables on which the cases are measured). The formula for the Euclidean distance (*d*) between two cases *a* and *b* measured on three variables is given as:

$$d_{ab} = [(a_1 - b_1)^2 + (a_2 - b_2)^2 + (a_3 - b_3)^2]^{1/2}$$

If the variables are measured on different scales it may be necessary to standardise them before performing these calculations. Euclidean distance can be thought of as the distance between points 'as the crow flies' – it is sometimes referred to as *ruler distance*.

There are some other measures of distance that can be used in cluster analysis, most notably *Manhattan* (city block) distance, which could be regarded
as the distance 'by road' between the points. You might use this measure if
you do not wish to standardise the variables. Another measure of distance,
that we have already encountered, is Mahalanobis distance (see Chapter 3),
the distance between the group centroids. However, this value could only be
used to describe the distance between two clusters once the analysis had been
carried out (since we would not know what the clusters *were* at the outset!).

The distances between each pair of cases in the data set are then entered
into a matrix. Let us suppose that sales for the seven sets of consumer items
were standardised, and the distances between each pair of items (across
three monthly points) entered into a matrix (Table 10.1).

Table 10.1 Matrix of Euclidean distances between consumer items

Consumer item	IC	TU	SE	TR	U	EE	SB
Ice cream	0	10.3	11.2	2.3	9.8	5.1	10.5
Thermal undies		0	4.8	9.7	5.5	6.3	0.7
Skiing equipment			0	6.4	7.2	7.9	4.4
Tennis racquets				0	6.5	6.1	2.4
Umbrellas					0	5.5	11.3
Easter eggs						0	9.1
Sun block							0

The distances in the matrix indicate how similar the sales patterns are over
the three months between the items; therefore, there is a strong similarity
between sales patterns of ice cream and sun block, but very little similarity
between umbrellas and sun block. What sorts of question might we be asking of cluster analysis? A store owner might be wondering in which months
to promote certain goods, or how best to organise displays of items – which
items would go best alongside each other?

Hierarchical clustering techniques

Most forms of cluster analysis work through the matrix until all the distances are contained within a single cluster. This approach is known as
hierarchical cluster analysis, because it supposes that the first small cluster
formed is the strongest, and successive clusters are weaker. The simplest
method of doing this is *single linkage* cluster analysis, in which the two cases
that are closest together form the first group, and the next two closest cases
form the second group, and so on until they all merge into a single group.
This is sometimes referred to as *nearest neighbour* analysis.

Complete linkage cluster analysis starts by looking at the matrix and identifying the first group from the matrix, represented by the smallest distance.

In the above example, ice cream and sun block form the first group. The maximum distances between these two items and the others in the matrix are then calculated, and a new matrix is formed (Table 10.2), from which the next group is identified (the smallest distance in the new matrix).

Therefore,

$$d_{(17)2} = \max[d_{12},d_{27}] = d_{12} = 10.3$$
$$d_{(17)3} = \max[d_{13},d_{37}] = d_{13} = 11.2$$
$$d_{(17)4} = \max[d_{14},d_{47}] = d_{47} = 2.4$$
$$d_{(17)5} = \max[d_{15},d_{57}] = d_{57} = 11.3$$
$$d_{(17)6} = \max[d_{16},d_{67}] = d_{67} = 9.1$$

Table 10.2 New distance matrix

Consumer item	IC + SB	TU	SE	TR	U	EE
Ice cream + sun block	0	10.3	11.2	2.4	11.3	9.1
Thermal undies		0	4.8	9.7	5.5	6.3
Skiing equipment			0	6.4	7.2	7.9
Tennis racquets				0	6.5	6.1
Umbrellas					0	5.5
Easter eggs						0

The smallest distance in the new matrix is between the first group and tennis racquets. Therefore, tennis racquets joins the first group, and the maximum distances are calculated again, e.g.

$$d_{(174)2} = \max[d_{172},d_{42}] = d_{172} = 10.3$$
$$d_{(174)3} = \max[d_{173},d_{43}] = d_{173} = 11.2$$
$$d_{(174)5} = \max[d_{175},d_{45}] = d_{45} = 11.3$$
$$d_{(174)6} = \max[d_{176},d_{46}] = d_{176} = 9.1$$

Then, another distance matrix is formed.

Table 10.3 Second new distance matrix

Consumer item	IC/SB/TR	TU	SE	U	EE
Ice cream + sun block + racquets	0	10.3	11.2	11.3	9.1
Thermal undies		0	4.8	5.5	6.3
Skiing equipment			0	7.2	7.9
Umbrellas				0	5.5
Easter eggs					0

Now, the smallest distance in the matrix is 4.8 (thermal undies/skiing equipment). These items form the second cluster. The distance between the two clusters is worked out:

$$d_{(174)(23)} = \max[d_{12}, d_{13}\; d_{42}, d_{43}\; d_{72}, d_{73}] = d_{43} = 11.2$$

And then the process begins again, continuing until we have whittled the matrix down to one element. At this point we need to make some judgement as to which is the pattern of clusters that best describes our data. As with factor analysis, this is where the interpretation of the researcher is paramount: we need to base our decision on the theory underpinning the original research question. To help us, the result of a cluster analysis is often portrayed as a *dendrogram*. If we performed complete linkage cluster analysis on our seasonal consumer items we might find that the pattern in Figure 10.2 emerges.

Rescaled Distance Cluster Combine

```
   C A S E      0         5         10        15        20        25
  Label    Num  +---------+---------+---------+---------+---------+

SUNBLOCK   3    ┐
TENNIS     7    ┤                                       ┐
ICE        1    ┘                                       │
EASTER     6    ────────────────────────────────────┐  │
UNDIES     2    ┐                                    │  │
SKIING     4    ┤───────────┐                        │
BROLLIES   5    ────────────┘
```

Figure 10.2 Dendrogram of cluster example data

From this pattern, it looks as though our three most pertinent clusters are:

- ice cream, sun block, tennis racquets
- thermal underwear, skiing equipment and umbrellas
- Easter eggs

Easter eggs are a cluster by themselves because they are only purchased in April (unless Easter falls in March). However they are eventually incorporated into the winter goods cluster because the summer goods have a very solid identity. How we interpret this outcome depends on the data we have collected – of course, we would need twelve monthly variables to make firm decisions about consumer patterns. And it may be inappropriate to compare impulse purchases like ice cream with investment purchases like sporting equipment!

Average linkage cluster analysis

This technique proceeds in the same fashion as complete linkage until the first group from the initial matrix is compared with the other items in the matrix. Whereas, with complete linkage, we calculate the maximum distance between the first pair of items and the other items in the matrix, in average linkage we calculate the *average* distance.

Therefore, our first set of calculations would be:

$$d_{(17)2} = (d_{12} + d_{27})/2 = \ \ 5.5$$
$$d_{(17)3} = (d_{13} + d_{37})/2 = \ \ 7.8$$
$$d_{(17)4} = (d_{14} + d_{47})/2 = \ \ 2.35$$
$$d_{(17)5} = (d_{15} + d_{57})/2 = 10.55$$
$$d_{(17)6} = (d_{16} + d_{67})/2 = \ \ 7.1$$

And the first matrix would look slightly different. However, the next step would be the same, with tennis racquets joining force with ice cream and sun block. And indeed, the overall outcome is identical if you go on to complete the analysis. Therefore, the difference between complete and average linkage is minimal in practice.

One of the most troublesome aspects of cluster analysis is that there is no hard-and-fast rule for specifying the number of clusters. What is the cut-off point? The answer may depend on the researcher's expectations; in the above example we would be quite happy with three clusters. There are a handful of tests we can carry out to compare cluster solutions. *Beale's F-type* statistic is so named because it is *like* an ANOVA but not quite; the principle is still the same, comparing the sums of squares for the cluster distances between two alternative cluster solutions. If F is significant, this means that the higher cluster solution (i.e., the one with more clusters) is a better one. Alternatively, a *psuedo Hotelling's T^2* statistic can be calculated on two clusters within the same solution to decide whether they should be merged into one cluster or remain separate. Here, a significant value suggests we should keep them separated.

Example from the literature of hierarchical cluster analysis

Mulry et al. *(1997): HIV at-risk subtypes*

Cluster analysis is particularly useful if the goal of the research is the identification of subtypes. The authors of this study attempted to identify subtypes of gay men on the basis of sexual behaviour preferences. It was thought that this information might be useful for HIV prevention.

They recruited 106 sexually active gay men via newspaper advertisements and health clinics, who completed a number of questionnaires:

- *Perceived Sexual Control Inventory* (typical item: 'I forget about safe sex when I am with a new partner')
- *Sexual Sensation-seeking Scale* (typical item: 'I feel like exploring my sexuality')

- *AIDS knowledge test* (24 items)
- *Questions about sexual behaviours*, e.g., have you ever participated in _____?, how pleasurable (1 to 5), and how risky (1 to 5)
- *Relapse reasons* (rank ordering of 4 reasons for not using a condom, e.g., partner pressure)
- *Resist reasons* (rank ordering of 4 reasons for resisting unsafe sex, e.g. fear of AIDS)

From these measures, the following variables were entered into the analysis:

- Overall sexual control score
- Overall sexual sensation-seeking score
- Pleasurability rating of anal sex withdrawing before ejaculation
- Pleasurability rating of rimming (oral-anal sex)
- Pleasurability rating of cuddling

Using *Ward's* method of clustering (which uses squared Euclidean distances in order to identify clusters on the basis of least variance) three similar-sized groups of men could be identified. The first cluster scored low on all except sexual control. This group was labelled 'low sexual'. The second cluster scored moderately but with the highest rating for cuddling. This group was labelled 'sensuous'. The third group scored highly on anal pleasure and sensation seeking but low on sexual control. They were labelled 'high sexual'.

These clusters were analysed using ANOVA to see how significantly they differed in the five variables. All three clusters differed significantly on the anal pleasure variables; cluster 2 had a significantly higher cuddling rating than the others, and cluster 3 had a significantly higher sensation-seeking score. None of the clusters differed significantly on sexual control. The clusters were also compared (using ANOVA) on the remaining measures. Here, men in the high sexual cluster had significantly more partners than the other men, were more likely to use alcohol or poppers (amyl nitrate) prior to sex, and were more likely to relapse into unsafe sex if condoms were unavailable or if pressured by partners.

Although the analysis yielded some interesting data, the researchers are aware of its limitations (relatively small sample, no clear boundaries between clusters, closed-response questions, and so on). Nevertheless, this is an example where cluster analysis can be used in an exploratory fashion at the outset of a research project before moving on to more clearly defined research questions.

MULTIDIMENSIONAL SCALING

Another geometric technique for reducing data sets to make them more interpretable is multidimensional scaling (MDS). The idea behind MDS is to construct a map based on the distances between objects (can be either cases or variables) which plots the objects on two or more dimensions. The most obvious example is that of a map of a country based on road distances between towns plotted on east–west and north–south dimensions.

MDS is useful for analysing certain types of data, particularly sets of *similarity judgements*. A study of the classification of facial expressions can be used here as an example.

Katsikitis (1997): physiological cues to emotional expression

Cross-cultural research suggests that there are six facial expressions of emotion which are recognised the world over: happiness, surprise, fear, disgust, anger and sadness (Ekman 1993). Katsikitis' research attempts to capture these emotions in line drawings in order to work out exactly what pattern of features is involved in each. For example, surprise and sadness are best expressed in the eyebrows, while happiness and disgust are best expressed by the mouth. She and her colleagues produced two sets of stimuli: 23 photographs of actors posing for each emotion, and line drawings of each emotion based on a set of measurements (mouth opening, eyelid/iris intersect, and so on). In addition to the six universal emotions, a set of 'neutral' expressions was also obtained.

Katsikitis then asked a group of 17 volunteers to sort the pictures into the appropriate emotion categories. Table 10.4 contains the data relating to the photographs. These relate to the frequency with which each volunteer placed the photo in a particular pile (for each expression there is a total of 391 observations). From this table we can see that happiness produced a similarity response of 96 per cent – most respondents identified this emotion accurately from the photos. However, fear was only classified accurately on 28 per cent of the occasions (although there were more observations in the 'fear' category than any other). Kappa scores[2] suggested that there were moderate to high agreements for most expressions.

Table 10.4 Frequencies of response to emotion photographs from Katsikitis (1997)

Emotion	Happiness	Surprise	Fear	Disgust	Sadness	Neutral
Happiness	377	46	1	17	0	6
Surprise	3	198	68	9	16	21
Fear	1	41	108	6	16	13
Disgust	3	9	17	128	33	13
Anger	3	11	55	89	58	29
Sadness	0	10	47	48	146	68
Neutral	4	76	95	94	122	241

Calculations in multidimensional scaling

Like ANOVA, MDS is essentially a set of techniques rather than one single formula. However, the sequence of calculations is broadly similar in each case. To begin with, a set of *proximities* is calculated to provide some measure of how alike, or similar, the variables are. These could be correlations between variables, or (as in the expressions study), a *similarity matrix* which contains information about the frequency with which objects are paired with each other.

After this stage, MDS becomes much more complicated than cluster analysis, and we must delegate the number-crunching to the computer. The first thing the computer needs to do is to construct a matrix of distances between the variables, perhaps using the same Euclidean (ruler) distances as in cluster analysis. The central assumption of MDS is that the distances should correspond to the proximities. Programs such as SPSS will provide a scatterplot to demonstrate this relationship. Then some measure of *fit* is computed which best represents the data in multidimensional space, usually referred to as the *configuration*. This is arrived at through an iterative procedure (like factor and cluster analysis) in which the goal is to minimise a value known as *stress*.

Stress is an index of fit: the closer to 0, the better the fit. Typically, MDS proceeds by calculating the stress value for a one-dimensional configuration, then for a two-dimensional configuration, and so on, until the decrease in stress is negligible. In practice, however, we are seeking the most easily interpreted solution, so we would usually settle for a two- or three-dimensional configuration. This is particularly true of a small data set like the one in the expressions study.

Once a solution has been decided on, we can then plot the co-ordinates for our map. In the current example, a two-dimensional configuration was chosen with a stress factor of 0.18. A three-dimensional solution gave a stress factor of 0.13 but was rejected as unreliable. The co-ordinates given by the two-dimension solution enable us to draw up a plot, as in Figure 10.3. For disgust, the co-ordinates are roughly −1 on both dimensions; for happiness, the co-ordinates are between −1 and −2 on dimension 1, but between 1 and 2 for dimension 2.

The whole point of drawing the plot is that it enables us to interpret the dimensions. As with factor analysis, at this point, the interpretation of the solution is entirely up to the researcher. In this example, Katsikitis suggested that the first dimension, which has happiness and fear at its extremities, might be a measure of upper face–lower face dominance, since the eyebrows are most important in the emotions in the top half of the plot, while the mouth is more important for those in the bottom half. The second dimension, which has surprise and happiness at one end and sadness, anger and disgust at the other, can be labelled pleasant–unpleasant.

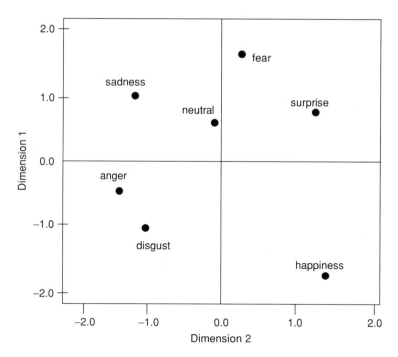

Figure 10.3 Scatterplot of cases on two dimensions from Katsikitis (1997). Copyright
© 1997 by Pion, London. Reprinted with permission.

Evaluating the MDS solution

How do we decide whether our scaling process is any good? In the above
example, Katsikitis was able to examine the two dimensions and fit the
solution into the existing theory simply by looking at the plot. But sometimes this is not so easy: for one thing, when we have three dimensions, the
interpretation becomes harder, so four or more dimensions are very hard to
analyse.

An alternative means of evaluating the configuration is to perform a
multiple regression on the solution. We can do this by choosing a dependent
measure that represents each dimension and then regress the co-ordinates
for the plot on this measure. Of course, this process depends on the data we
have collected, and would be inappropriate for nominal data of the sort in
the Katsikitis study. Therefore, another example from the psychological
literature is needed to describe the use of this approach.

Cole and Bradac (1996) carried out a study into the attributes most valued
in people's *best friends*. They began by asking undergraduates to generate
a list of attributes and ended up with 43 'sources of satisfaction' (e.g.,
independent, committed, ambitious, easy going, not physically violent) which
represented a range of valued qualities of best friends. The next stage was to

ask students to sort these 43 attributes into piles based on similarity. A similarity matrix was then constructed by counting the number of times that different attributes had been included in the same pile. This matrix was then subjected to MDS and the following three dimensional solution was obtained (stress = 0.169):

1   Spontaneous-active (e.g., fun to be around) vs. stable-passive (e.g., admits mistakes)
2   Rational-reserved (e.g., emotionally balanced) vs. emotional-intimate (e.g., share similarities)
3   Ambitious-assertive (e.g., intelligent) vs. easygoing-unassuming (e.g., approachable)

These dimensions may not appear all that intuitive, but they are the labels that the researchers felt best described the items that have clustered around either pole of the respective dimension.

The next step was to evaluate this solution (and the labels) by getting another group of undergraduates to rate all 43 attributes on each of the three dimensions. For example, indicate on a scale of 1–7 how the item 'fun to be around' falls on dimension 1 (with 1 = spontaneous-active, and 7 = stable-passive), and likewise for dimensions 2 and 3.

Therefore, the researchers ended up with three ratings for each item. They then carried out a multiple regression using these ratings as the criterion variable (Y) with the co-ordinates the computer had used to create the three dimensions of the scatterplot as the predictors (X_1, X_2 and X_3). The results of this procedure are displayed in Table 10.5. Each row in the table refers to a different dimension; the columns Dim.1 through Dim. 3 contain the respective *regression weights* for the solution, also referred to as the *directional cosines*. The column headed *R* contains the multiple correlation coefficient for each solution (with the significance on the right).

Kruskal and Wish (1978) specify two criteria for accepting an MDS solution: first, the multiple correlation (*R*) should be as close to 1 as possible (over 0.75 is acceptable); second, each scale should have a high directional cosine on its respective set of co-ordinates (and not on the others). (These

Table 10.5 Regression results from Cole and Bradac (1996)

Dimension	Dim. 1	Dim. 2	Dim. 3	R	p
1 Spontaneous-active vs. stable-passive	**0.806**	−0.551	0.211	0.88	0.001
2 Rational-reserved vs. emotional-intimate	0.426	**0.843**	−0.374	0.82	0.001
3 Ambitious-assertive vs. easygoing-unassuming	0.447	0.135	**−0.864**	0.83	0.001

criteria are obviously closely related – for example, if dimension 1 had a cosine direction of 0.2 on dimension 2, then the overall R would certainly exceed 0.9.)

The researchers concluded from the data in Table 10.5 that their three-dimensional solution provided a good fit with the data. They interpreted the solution as follows:

1   The first dimension (spontaneous-active vs. stable-passive) relates to the *activity* level of the best friend. Attributes such as 'fun to be around', 'activities director', and 'healthy' scored highly on this dimension, while attributes like 'doesn't use me' and 'not verbally abusive' were found at the other pole. (N.B. These dimensions do *not* represent desirable–undesirable attributes – remember, all 43 statements are supposed to be 'sources of satisfaction' with a best friend.)

2   The second dimension (rational-reserved vs. emotional-intimate) is concerned with *closeness*. High scores are associated with intimacy (e.g., 'available', 'share similarities'), while low scores are 'independent', 'emotionally balanced', and 'practical'. This dimension is perhaps less clear than the first.

3   The third dimension (ambitious-assertive vs. easygoing-unassuming) relates to a best friend's *demeanour*. High scoring attributes here include 'serious', 'ambitious', 'independent', while low scoring items are 'flexible', 'approachable' and 'altruistic'.

Canonical correlation

The final technique to be considered in this chapter is less a geometric technique and more a variant on both multiple regression and factor analysis.

Canonical correlation is used when we have two sets of variables and we are interested in how changes in one set might affect the other set. It is rather like a double multiple regression analysis, except that rather than predicting one set of scores from the other, we are looking at correlations between them.

In Chapter 5, an example of multiple regression was given in which a data set where age, gender, risk awareness and belief (predictor variables) were regressed on to the number of cigarettes smoked (criterion variable). We could carry out a canonical correlation study in which we related those 'personal' measures to any number of measures of risky health behaviour. We could add units of alcohol consumed per week, and calorie intake to the smoking data and use these as 'health risk' variables, and then see which changes in the personal variable set were associated with changes in the health risk variable set.

An alternative use of canonical correlation is where you have a set of variables on which you retest participants after a time interval. Suppose you measured a group of people on health risk behaviour twice over five years.

You could then see which of these behaviours had changed over time, and how the pattern of behaviour was related across the two time periods.

Example of canonical correlation from the literature

Finn (1997): personality correlates of media use

The study in this example was designed to examine the relationship between personality and media use. Finn issued the NEO personality inventory (Costa and McCrae 1992) to 219 students and then got the students to keep diaries during eight random days across the academic year. The diary material was then coded as to the type of activity that the student had engaged in. Finn ended up with the following set of activities:

Television viewing	Partying
Radio listening	Spectator sports
Reading for pleasure	Religious activities
Movie attendance	Conversation

These activities comprised the first set of variables in the study. The second set of variables consisted of the five factors in the NEO inventory, notably:

Neuroticism	Extraversion
Openness	Agreeableness
Conscientiousness	

We can begin to analyse the data set by looking at the correlation matrix between the variables. Table 10.6 indicates where significant relationships exist between individual variables. For example, television viewing is negatively related to conversation and openness, while conversation is positively related to openness and agreeableness. Spectator sports are not really related to any of the other variables, so are unlikely to make much contribution to the analysis.

The first procedure in canonical correlation is to find two linear combinations, one from each variable set, which have the highest possible correlation. For example,

$$u_1 = bX_1 + bX_2 + bX_3 + \ldots bX_8 + a$$
$$v_1 = bX_9 + bX_{10} + bX_{11} + \ldots bX_{13} + a$$

so that $r(u_1 v_1)$ = highest possible value. This value is referred to as the *largest canonical correlation* and is represented as R_1. This is also referred to as the first *canonical root* in the overall analysis.

This procedure is then repeated in order to find the next largest canonical correlation, on the assumption that this new pair of linear combinations is

Table 10.6 Correlation matrix for the data in Finn (1997)

Media use	2	3	4	5	6	7	8	N	E	O	A	C
1. TV viewing	0.09	-0.02	0.05	**-0.22**	-0.15	-0.06	-0.03	0.05	-0.15	**-0.20**	-0.13	0.04
2. Radio listening		0.03	0.12	-0.02	-0.10	-0.03	-0.10	-0.06	-0.11	0.02	-0.03	0.03
3. Pleasure reading			0.10	0.06	**-0.19**	-0.10	-0.08	0.08	**-0.23**	0.27	-0.06	-0.12
4. Movie attendance				0.03	-0.08	-0.02	-0.09	-0.08	-0.09	0.12	0.02	-0.02
5. Conversation					0.00	0.04	0.01	0.11	0.07	**0.28**	**0.27**	-0.15
6. Partying						0.10	**-0.20**	-0.01	**0.20**	-0.03	-0.01	0.00
7. Spectator sports							-0.03	-0.05	0.11	0.02	0.09	0.08
8. Religious								-0.11	0.04	**-0.19**	0.08	0.05
Neuroticism									**-0.22**	0.01	**-0.25**	**-0.30**
Extraversion										0.17	**0.23**	**0.27**
Openness											**0.22**	**-0.20**
Agreeableness												-0.02
(Conscientiousness)												

Note: Correlations in bold type are significant at $p < 0.01$.

Table 10.7 Canonical weights for the first two solutions in Finn (1997)

	Root 1	Root 2
Set 1: Communication activities		
Television viewing	−0.16	0.24
Radio listening	0.03	0.23
Pleasure reading	0.60	0.40
Movie attendance	0.16	0.12
Conversation	0.48	−0.69
Partying	−0.21	−0.20
Spectator sports	−0.02	−0.15
Religious activities	−0.39	−0.07
Set 2: NEO personality inventory		
Neuroticism	0.17	−0.35
Extraversion	−0.46	−0.72
Openness	0.92	0.05
Agreeableness	0.11	−0.64
Conscientiousness	0.10	0.22

uncorrelated with the first. (In other words, the two solutions are *orthogonal*.) This second canonical root is represented as R_2. This procedure can continue as many times as there are variables in the smaller set (in the above example, therefore, no more than five solutions can be obtained).

We are then left with a set of *canonical weights* for each solution. These are the coefficients for each set of variables that are entered into the combinations at each stage. In the Finn study, the first two sets of weights are displayed in Table 10.7. These weights are hard to interpret by themselves, even though they represent the contribution of each variable to the relevant solution. At this stage, the most meaningful statistic we can obtain is a measure of the significance of each canonical solution. This is calculated using a statistic called *V*, which is distributed as a chi-square statistic, and can be converted to an *F*. This value indicates whether the two sets of variables are significantly related. If the first canonical root is significant, then we calculate *V* for the next canonical root, and so on until the solutions are no longer significant. For this example, the first two roots were found to be significant at $p < 0.01$, with correlations of 0.50 and 0.38 respectively, but the other three solutions were not.

We can also calculate a measure of *redundancy* which explains how much of the variance in one set is explained by the linear combination of the other set of variables. For instance, in the current example, in the first solution the communication variables accounted for 4 per cent of the variance in the personality set, and the personality variables explained 5 per cent of the variance in the communication set. These values are quite small, but with 13 variables in total, we would not expect them to be high. (A more meaningful

Table 10.8 Structure matrix for the data in Finn (1997)

	Root 1	Root 2
Set 1: Communication activities		
Television viewing	−0.23	0.46
Radio listening	0.11	0.32
Pleasure reading	0.73	0.43
Movie attendance	0.29	0.20
Conversation	0.55	−0.73
Partying	−0.25	−0.35
Spectator sports	−0.06	−0.26
Religious activities	−0.40	−0.10
Set 2: NEO personality inventory		
Neuroticism	0.25	−0.10
Extraversion	−0.32	−0.71
Openness	0.86	−0.26
Agreeableness	0.17	−0.69
Conscientiousness	−0.35	0.13

statistic is 'percentage of trace', which is equivalent to an R^2 in that it explains how much variance in each set is explained by each overall solution. However, the paper's author does not provide this information.)

The best way to interpret the canonical correlations is to carry out a second analysis whereby the canonical weights are multiplied by the original values for each variable. This produces a structure matrix (like the one that you use to interpret a factor analysis) from which the relationship between the variables can be inferred. The structure matrix for this example is displayed in Table 10.8.

In this example, the structure matrix is not all that different to the matrix of weights, although this is not always the case (see Levine 1977 for an example of a structure matrix that is completely different). For the first canonical root, openness is the personality variable with the highest loading, and this is most strongly associated with reading, conversation and (negatively) religious activities. On the second root, both extraversion and agreeableness are related strongly to conversation, and have negative relationships with television and reading. We could use these results to argue that a typical television viewer is less open, introverted and disagreeable! Agreeable extraverts are more likely to spend their time chatting and partying.

Canonical correlation is not a particularly widely used technique in psychological research, but it is worth knowing about it in case you stumble across it in a journal article – and, if you can find the software to run it, it can be useful on occasions. However, Stevens (1996) warns against using it because the solutions are so unreliable, unless vast numbers of subjects are involved.

Summary

Three techniques are described in this chapter, all of which could be described as devices for exploring large and unwieldy data sets. Cluster analysis is particularly useful when we need a technique for classifying data and sorting values into groups of variables or cases based on similarity. Multidimensional scaling allows us to plot such values in geometric space and also provides us with a statistical solution to our data that we can interpret for meaning. Finally, canonical correlation is another variant on the basic regression equation, this time describing the relationship between two large sets of variables. This brings us to the end of the exclusively quantitative part of the book; log-linear analysis and meta-analysis have been held over to go in Part V. Otherwise, I hope I haven't missed anything too important out . . .

Notes

1 Indeed, there is a provocative paper by Dracup (1995), which argues that true significance in statistical analysis should take into account the researcher's track record in obtaining significant results. A good researcher is defined as one who consistently designs studies which allow them to reject the null hypothesis. A bad researcher, conversely, is one whose designs repeatedly fail to hit the jackpot. Dracup's argument has probabilistic appeal – if a researcher cannot design powerful studies then a significant result at the twentieth attempt can be considered a fluke! However, this conjures up a rather peculiar vision of what psychological research, not to mention science in general, is all about. Is the point of research nothing more than being able to say 'I told you so'? Is there really no value in data which reflect the 'real world' instead of conforming to a narrow set of statistically pure criteria? These questions are related to the current obsession some psychologists have with statistical power (see my comments on this in Chapter 1).

2 Cohen's *Kappa* (κ) is a measure of agreement based along similar lines to chi-square: you draw up a contingency table, e.g.

	Happiness	*Surprise*	*Total*
Happiness	377	(46)	423
Surprise	(3)	198	201
Total	380	244	624

and then enter the proportions within the 'agreement' cells (e.g., happiness = 96 per cent) into the following formula:

$$\kappa = (P_o - P_e)/(1 - P_e)$$

This should give you an overall kappa of 0.83. Anything over 0.6 is regarded as 'substantial' agreement.

Part IV

Qualitative methods

11 Qualitative research in psychology

The aim of this part of the book is to give the reader some idea of the important techniques in qualitative research that are regularly used in psychology. The use of qualitative methods in psychology has increased significantly in recent years, and yet to many psychologists, qualitative research is an area of deepest mystery. To others it may even be a source of contempt. Even qualitative researchers themselves argue fiercely about the methods they use, and some prefer not to use the term 'methods' at all (Parker 1992). So complex are the issues around qualitative research that it has become a broad research topic in its own right, with social scientists from various disciplines specialising in the field (Denzin and Lincoln 2000 is a mighty volume gathering together a vast range of writing on the topic).

Given the scope of qualitative research, it might seem surprising that so many psychologists should be ignorant of the area or hostile to its methods, especially since quantitative approaches to psychology have been criticised for a long time.[1] However, there are several reasons why psychology has been reluctant to embrace qualitative methods over the years. To begin with, psychology has spent much of its short history fighting for scientific status. In order to stave off criticism from the established scientific disciplines, it has tended to be rather conservative in its preferred methods, valuing experimentation above other paradigms (especially during the behaviourist era), and insisting on *measurement* as the only way of meeting the criteria for scientific validity.

This has led to what Danziger (1990) has termed 'methodolatry', whereby techniques such as single case studies, commonly used in long-established sciences, have been dismissed as unscientific. It sometimes seems as though what passes for science is what *looks* most like science, so structural equation modelling is worshipped by academic journal editors and reviewers, while other, less ostentatious methods are sneered at. How psychologists 'do science' is far from being a quantitative vs. qualitative debate; as we shall see in Chapter 21, even those most wedded to the statistical approach are locked in a heated debate about significance testing.

Qualitative research has long been held by many psychologists as unscientific because it appears to lack some of the essential features of scientific research. Perhaps the most important of these is thought to be replicability. Michael Morgan, a vociferous opponent of qualitative research in psychology, argues that qualitative research must always rely on subjective opinion because its methods are not sufficiently transparent to enable another researcher to replicate a given study (Morgan 1996, 1998). Qualitative researchers themselves have argued that scientific research is never quite as objective and unbiased as scientists often like to think (Woolgar 1988). In fact, it could even be argued that, for some topics in psychology, qualitative approaches are *more* scientific, since they are sensitive throughout to the influence that the researcher has on the topic under investigation (Smith 1996a). In wishing the researcher away, quantitative approaches (particularly social psychological experiments) often provide misleading data that are too artificial to have any ecological validity, and tell us very little about human behaviour under normal circumstances.

Because psychology has so long been tied to measurement as the principal objective of research, the discipline that has evolved has been irrevocably shaped by the techniques it has employed to this end. For example, it is hard to imagine the study of intelligence without the IQ test, or the study of personality without Eysenck and Cattell's psychometric instruments. In applied areas such as clinical and occupational psychology, quantitative measures have become big business; publishers make a lot of money out of copyrighted test materials. In academia there is much pressure on psychology departments to utilise scientific equipment and resources (laboratories, technicians, etc.) in order to attract maximum financial support. It is not surprising, then, that there has been so much resistance to adopting alternative approaches to research.

Arguments for using qualitative research in psychology

Psychology as a diverse discipline

Probably the most convincing argument for the use of qualitative methods in psychology has come about through a number of challenges mounted on the discipline in recent years. Traditional psychology has been based around two central themes: the establishment of 'laws', or norms, that can be used to predict human behaviour; and the location of psychological processes within the individual human subject (at varying levels of cognition and neurophysiology). An example of the first theme might be the theory of planned behaviour, which is frequently used in health psychology to investigate which variables best predict a particular health behaviour (e.g., smoking or drug use), or, more controversially, the forensic practice of 'offender profiling'. An example of the second theme would be the working memory model, which locates memory processes within the cognitive architecture of the individual, or 'self-esteem', measured using psychometric scaling.

On the face of it, these themes appear uncontestable as the backbone of psychological investigation. Surely there are universal patterns of human behaviour across history and culture? Why locate 'memory' anywhere other than the mind or brain? One of the reasons that such claims are so difficult to challenge is that psychological theory has spawned so much 'common-sense' thinking about behaviour that the terms and concepts used by psychologists have become part of modern Western culture. However, this need not have been the case. The archival research of sociologist Nikolas Rose and others has demonstrated how the course of academic and professional psychology has been shaped profoundly by historical, social and political factors (Rose 1990; Danziger 1990). In recent years, challenges to these traditional themes of psychology have been launched by 'critical' psychologists who have advocated steering psychology along a different course altogether (Fox and Prillitensky 1997; Ibáñez and Iñiguez 1997; Sloan 2000).

Cultural influences on psychology

The theme of normative patterns of behaviour, which can be used to make general, universal, predictions, has come under attack from writers and researchers who regard such generalisations as threatening to minority cultures and lifestyles. For example, some psychologists have criticised the notion of child development as representing a series of normative stages, since any deviations from this path tend to be regarded as 'atypical' and problematic (Burman 1994a). Most contemporary feminist psychologists have adopted a critical approach by examining traditional psychology as representing a predominantly male perspective in which women have been treated as 'other' (Wilkinson and Kitzinger 1996). Others, not necessarily following the critical tradition, have advocated the greater use of idiographic research (the study of the individual) over nomothetic research (the search for universal laws) (Harré 1993; Smith 1995).

At the same time, the second theme of traditional psychology – the study of individual cognitive processes as the dominant mode of investigation – has been challenged by discursive psychologists in the past two decades. While cognitive psychology has treated memory as the property of the private individual, something to be teased out through 'priming', and measured by rigorous laboratory experiments, discursive psychologists have examined the way in which memory acts as a property of *discourse*. Edwards and Potter (1992) argue that, outside the laboratory, we can never know whether an individual is telling 'the truth', and so cognitive psychology becomes fairly redundant in such circumstances as a court of law. But we can investigate how a defendant's plea is put together discursively, and how language is used to construct a particular account of events. Even in everyday situations, such as a group of friends piecing together an account of a drunken night out, the structure of the discourse – perhaps determined by what people *want* to 'remember' – can tell us more about the people involved than an accurate record of events (Giles 1999).

Another area where the focus on the individual mind has been sharply criticised is in the field of attitude research. As discussed in Chapter 8, the psychometric tradition in psychology has been strongly influenced by the use of Likert-type scales to measure attitudes to a variety of subjects. Such methods, with an emphasis on test–retest reliability, presume that an attitude is a fixed, enduring property of an individual (and something that can be quantified). However studies of attitude *talk* in everyday conversation have shown that 'attitudes' are far from stable, and that people tend to shift from one position to another in the course of an argument (Billig 1987; Potter and Wetherell 1987). Again, the challenge to traditional psychology is quite powerful. The study of everyday talk and text, in the shape of discourse analysis, calls for psychologists to get out of the laboratory and study people in everyday settings.

The final challenge to the emphasis on the individual mind has been inspired by anthropological studies of selfhood and personhood in non-Western cultures (e.g., Geertz 1973). Like Rose's historical account of psychology, this work has revealed the culture-specific nature of Western psychology, with its focus on the private individual, by comparing it with notions of personhood in Eastern cultures such as Bali and Java. In these cultures personal identity is determined more by social bonds (to the extended family, for example) than by the cognitive framework of the detached, autonomous individual. By contrast, in Western psychology concepts like self-esteem are located within the individual. However, it is fairly clear that self-esteem, and many other personality traits that have been attributed to genetic inheritance are strongly influenced by group behaviour (we may be inhibited at work and domineering in a relationship, or extraverted in familiar company and introverted with strangers).

More importantly, the location of these characteristics within the individual mind has had a profound influence on Western culture (and vice versa, of course). The explosion of self-help literature in the twentieth century, and the use of pharmacological treatment to deal with mental distress, are just two ways in which psychological theory has shaped the way in which Western society has come to regard the person. An alternative approach that has become popular with some psychologists is *social constructionism* (Gergen 1985; Burr 1995), which is the study of everyday phenomena as objects that are 'constructed' through culture and particularly through language (or discourse). Social constructionists explicitly reject the idea that psychology can be explained through the discovery of scientific 'facts', arguing that issues such as personality and selfhood can only be understood by examining prevailing cultural discourses.

Why should these challenges necessitate a shift from quantitative to qualitative research methods? Some critical psychologists have argued that quantitative methods – including experimental studies – are perfectly appropriate for tackling psychological research from a critical perspective, so long as issues of *reflexivity* are addressed, such as the influence of the researcher (Reicher 1997). Overwhelmingly, though, qualitative methods have been used to explore non-traditional research questions from social constructionist, feminist, and other positions.

There is no reason why the use of qualitative methods should necessarily follow from a critical perspective. Bryman (1988) has argued that the choice of qualitative over quantitative methods in social science is usually the outcome of one of two debates. The *epistemological* debate is essentially the critical perspective; here, the fundamental nature of knowledge is in question, and thus the way of accessing that knowledge (epistemology) is of paramount importance. This debate usually results in a sharp division between quantitative and qualitative research, since the two practices are seen as dealing with incompatible goals. The *technical* debate is one in which qualitative research is seen as a more appropriate approach for investigating certain topics. Following this line of argument, the use of qualitative methods does not need to be predicated on any great challenge to the fundamental assumptions of psychology. However, psychological research – perhaps because of the discipline's history – is rarely quite so straightforward; it is often more important to know when *not* to use qualitative methods to answer particular questions (Reicher 2000).

In the next section I will try to present an overview of the different qualitative approaches that have emerged in psychology over the past two decades or so.

The use of qualitative research in psychology

Qualitative research did not begin to make a major impact on psychology until the 1980s. Before this, it had largely been the concern of social sciences such as sociology and anthropology. The practice of ethnography has had an influence on the development of anthropology as a discipline that is arguably more profound than that of experimentation on psychology. In the UK at least, sociology is now dominated by qualitative research.

For the reasons mentioned earlier, psychology has been much more reluctant to embrace qualitative methods, but the situation changed considerably towards the end of the twentieth century, particularly in the UK, where in 1991, the Scientific Affairs Board of the British Psychological Society commissioned a report (Nicolson 1991, cited in Henwood and Nicolson 1995) which advocated the greater use of qualitative approaches in psychological research. This has been followed by a rapid uptake of qualitative methods in teaching (where a recent 'benchmarking' exercise carried out by the Quality Assurance Agency in higher education stressed the importance of qualitative research in psychology), and by the increasing appearance of qualitative papers in psychological journals. Both the *Journal of Community and Applied Social Psychology* and the *Journal of Health Psychology* published special issues on qualitative research during the 1990s.

By and large, qualitative research has been recruited to service the requirements of psychology, rather than psychology changing to meet the different demands of qualitative research (though the latter has occurred to some extent in 'critical' fields of the discipline). For example, ethnography, despite its long tradition in other social sciences, has played little part in psychology, while discourse analysis, with its natural appeal to psychologists interested in language, has become more popular in psychology than in many other disciplines. Meanwhile, the re-emergence of qualitative research in psychology has revived the popularity of some areas which were originally grounded in that approach – psychoanalysis in particular, but also phenomenology and rhetorical psychology – and helped shape some newer areas, such as 'cyberpsychology' (Gordo-Lopez and Parker 1999) and postmodern psychology (Kvale 1992).

One of the most important issues for psychologists to discuss is whether it makes sense to talk of 'qualitative research' in global terms, as though it were a unified concept. Recent attempts to establish universal criteria for research in psychology (Elliott *et al.* 1999; Yardley 2000) have met with a mixed response (Reicher 2000). Some critical psychologists have resisted attempts to formalise qualitative techniques such as discourse analysis, fearing that they may be turned into 'just another psychological method' (Parker 1992: 20). Other qualitative approaches have been so tightly formalised that they resemble quantitative methods (for example, the hypothesis-testing model devised by Miles and Huberman 1994).

Henwood (1996) has identified three distinct strands of qualitative inquiry that have direct application to psychological research. The first concerns methods which have reliability and validity as a central principle; these are approaches such as the Miles and Huberman (1994) data display model, and qualitative content analysis. The second strand concerns methods whose chief aim is to generate theory from data; these are a variety of approaches which go by the term *grounded theory*. The third strand consists of approaches which are primarily discursive in nature, including several variations of discourse analysis and narrative analysis.

The next three chapters will take a closer look at some of these methods. I shall start by apologising to readers who feel I have left anything out. One of the problems in integrating qualitative methods is that qualitative research is such a broad church there are very few people who would claim to have expertise or knowledge of all of them. As the authors of a book on qualitative health psychology put it, 'whatever claims one may make for or about qualitative research, there are always alternative views and opinions to be found' (Murray and Chamberlain 1999: 8). I have deliberately selected the methods which are most commonly taught at undergraduate level and those which appear most regularly in psychology journals. Nevertheless, many qualitative psychologists will claim that I have overlooked a crucial approach, or neglected their own field of endeavour.

Chapter 12 is exclusively concerned with grounded theory, which figures in a number of publications about qualitative research in psychology, but has taken slightly longer to make its appearance in the research literature itself. However there are signs that this is now changing, perhaps because it is so widely taught (relative to other qualitative methods) at undergraduate level. One of the features that may make grounded theory attractive to psychologists who are relatively new to the qualitative field is that it has a distinct set of analytical procedures which make it easy to teach alongside quantitative research methods, and to squeeze it into standard laboratory reports. However it is an approach that is not without its problems; as Silverman (2000) argues, students often treat grounded theory simply as a means of carving up interview data into 'common-sense' descriptive themes, without performing any meaningful analysis at all. Nevertheless, if it is taught properly, and the procedures followed closely, these criticisms should not invalidate grounded theory as a method.

Chapter 13 discusses the philosophies and practice of discourse analysis, which is by far the most commonly used qualitative approach in psychology. However, the term 'discourse analysis' incorporates so many different philosophies and practices that it would be impossible to cover them all in a single chapter; instead I refer the reader to the many textbooks now published on the topic. Discourse analysis is often characterised with reference to two main approaches – the Loughborough school of discourse analysis and the Foucauldian, or critical realist, approach. I am not sure that this distinction is really all that applicable any longer. The majority of discourse analytic studies published in recent years tend to draw on both traditions, or specialise yet further; a recent guide to discourse analysis identifies five separate models (Wetherell *et al.* 2001a, 2001b).

In Chapter 14 I take a briefer look at a variety of other methods that have appeared in the psychological literature in recent years. These include qualitative content analysis, conversation analysis and ethnography.

Then, finally, Chapter 15 considers how to write qualitative research reports and how to evaluate qualitative research. Report writing is one of the most difficult aspects of qualitative research to convey to students who have hitherto been trained solely in the use of quantitative methods. The standard experimental laboratory report format is often followed so rigidly that they have difficulty adapting the method and results sections to more complicated quantitative techniques such as surveys and scales, let alone discourse analysis and grounded theory. In addition, there are extra criteria, such as a consideration of reflexivity, which may be required for a qualitative report. These, and some other issues around reliability and validity, are discussed here.

Summary

This part of the book introduces the reader to qualitative research in psychology, and this chapter begins by outlining the rationale for using such methods to carry out scientific research. It is increasingly being recognised, by bodies such as the British Psychological Society, that qualitative research can make an important contribution to psychology as a discipline. However this progress will only continue if rigorous standards are maintained for conducting and publishing qualitative psychological research, and it is important to be familiar with the theories and philosophies underpinning the field. I have tried here to give as simple an introduction to these ideas as possible, since many psychologists have never studied qualitative research and may have some difficulties mastering the jargon in specialist textbooks.

Note

1 Within social psychology at least, criticism of quantitative methods has been voiced regularly since the 1960s, largely as a result of the 'crisis' that had built up surrounding the ethical and theoretical doubts about experimentation in this field (Harré and Secord 1972). This period heralded a 'turn to language' for some social psychologists, and by implication, a paradigm shift towards the use of qualitative methods. This shift is often characterised as 'new paradigm' research.

12 Grounded theory

Grounded theory is both a means of generating theory and a set of techniques for conducting qualitative research. As such, it is a difficult topic to pin down; a novice researcher is confronted with reams of jargon, varying descriptions of methodology, and little clear guidance about how to conduct grounded theory research, how to evaluate it, and – perhaps most vexing of all, how to actually report the results. However it is becoming increasingly popular as a qualitative method in psychology, having already established itself in certain areas of social science, notably nursing and health research.

The popularity of grounded theory for theory generation is probably down to its intuitive nature. It rejects the received (scientific) wisdom that the study of a given phenomenon needs to be rooted initially in the theoretical literature, and that existing theory should indicate which methods and research questions are most appropriate. Instead, by contrast with the use of data to test a given hypothesis, theory is said to be 'grounded' in the data itself. This makes it a useful method when there is a lack of literature on a topic, but also when a researcher wishes to move away from a particular model or theory that has become established (and perhaps outdated) in the research literature.

It is often described as a 'naturalistic' approach to research in that it requires the researcher to enter the field and observe what is 'really happening in everyday life', far away from the laboratory or university library, and use this data to generate theory rather than relying on a set of preconceived notions. With regard to psychology, this approach is attractive because it moves away from the reductionist approach of experimental methodology (where the researcher attempts to isolate human behaviour from its social context in order to control specified 'variables') towards a more *contextual* approach to behaviour. Not all grounded theorists working in psychology are in agreement with this description, however, and, as I shall discuss later, there are an increasing number of departures from the original philosophy behind grounded theory among qualitative researchers.

The popularity of grounded theory as a series of techniques for carrying out qualitative research is due partly to the explicit attempts to systematise and clarify the processes involved, and also to their applicability to many kinds of qualitative research. It is not surprising that psychologists have started to pick up on grounded theory, since it is more attractive to researchers trained in the natural science model of research (e.g., experimentation, psychometrics), with clear guidelines for data collection and analysis, than approaches such as ethnography, which can sometimes appear to have no obvious 'methods' at all. However, there appears to be something of a gap at present between describing the procedure of a grounded theory study (or teaching students how to do it) and actually publishing grounded theory research in psychology journals.

It is perhaps no coincidence that the first paper to be published in a British psychology journal on the topic was a theoretical article (Henwood and Pidgeon 1992). Reports of research conducted using grounded theory methods are currently rare in psychology journals, but are beginning to appear gradually (e.g., Clegg *et al.* 1996; Burgoyne 1997; Costain Schou and Hewison 1998; Tweed and Salter 2000). One reason for this may be that grounded theory is most commonly used to conduct large-scale research, and does not lend itself to short research reports in the same way as, say, experimental research, or even a qualitative approach like discourse analysis. Strauss and Corbin (1990) recommend publishing short papers which focus on specific aspects of the analysis, and this appears to be potentially the most fruitful avenue for publication in psychology (see Clegg *et al.* 1996 – discussed later in this chapter – for a good example of this type of article).

In the rest of this chapter I will attempt to clarify the grounded theory approach as usefully as possible for anyone who would like to consider using it for research or teaching purposes. For further details I will refer the reader to specialist sources whenever appropriate.

Background to grounded theory

The history of grounded theory begins with a research project conducted in the United States in the 1960s by Barney Glaser, a sociologist trained in the quantitative tradition, and Anselm Strauss, a researcher with a background in symbolic interactionism, on the awareness of dying in terminally ill patients (Glaser and Strauss 1965). The methods used in this study then formed the basis of a book entitled *The Discovery of Grounded Theory* (Glaser and Strauss 1967), which has since become extremely influential in qualitative research in the social sciences.

The basic idea of grounded theory is that, rather than using data to test hypotheses derived from the previous literature on a topic – as in most quantitative research – it generates theory from the data themselves, usually verbal accounts of people's experiences. Typically, data in grounded theory consist of transcribed interviews, but fieldnotes, official documents and other archival material may be used as well as, or instead of, interviews. These data are then subjected to a continuous process of coding and categorising known as *constant comparative analysis*, starting with a large set of descriptive codes which are gradually reduced to a series of analytic categories, and then, in most versions of the technique, refined to a central, or core, category. The ultimate goal of this analysis is to generate a set of theoretical concepts (or, in some versions, a central process) that best explains the data.

The most difficult aspect of grounded theory to grasp for psychologists with a quantitative science training is the *non-linearity* of the process (Charmaz 1995). As with much qualitative research, the chronological distinction between data collection and data analysis is blurred, with analysis beginning much earlier in the research process than would normally be the case in a quantitative study, and no obvious end point (Rennie 2000). However, the general principle is that data are studied initially at a descriptive level, and as the analysis continues and the data organised into smaller and smaller units, the organising concepts become increasingly abstract and explanatory, until they can be interpreted by one overarching framework or process. As Henwood and Pidgeon put it, the analysis moves 'towards a conceptually rich understanding' (1992: 103). By this point the research has finally moved from data analysis to theory-building.

In addition to following the basic grounded theory procedure, there are a number of techniques which researchers need to perform in order to address issues of reliability and validity. These include full documentation of the entire research process (in the form of 'memos'), techniques for organising the data into meaningful categories (e.g., 'saturation'), and various means of assessing the robustness of the analysis (such as 'theoretical sampling' and 'negative case analysis'). This is where many qualitative researchers find themselves in disagreement with the basic assumptions of grounded theory, which some see as over-reliant on positivistic concerns with objectivity. It is also a point of departure for some grounded theorists, and some recent modifications to the methodology are discussed later in the chapter.

Figure 12.1 illustrates the process of grounded theory research – how the data collection and analysis phases interact, how specific techniques contribute to the analysis, and how analysis proceeds from initial coding to theory-building.

Perhaps it is important to add at this point that the developers of grounded theory never intended the techniques to be prescriptive; they regarded the procedure as a model for good practice in qualitative research in general (Rennie 1998a). Perhaps the best way of looking at grounded theory is as an *evolving* method, which can be modified and adapted to serve different purposes according to the perspective of the researcher and the topic under investigation (Chamberlain 1999).

HOW TO PERFORM A GROUNDED THEORY ANALYSIS

In this section I will outline the procedures at each stage of a grounded theory study, drawing on published work to illustrate the stages and techniques,

DATA COLLECTION   **DATA ANALYSIS**

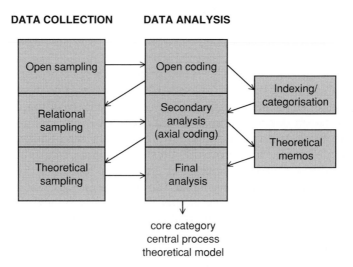

Figure 12.1 Stages in the grounded theory process

particularly from a study by Orona (1997) on the loss of identity in Alzheimer's disease, which is very explicit about the grounded theory process and contains some excellent examples.

Data collection

As mentioned above, the data in a grounded theory study are usually collected in the form of interview transcripts, although other texts can certainly be used – ethnographers may use extensive fieldnotes that they have taken during observational work, and media texts can also be used (for an example of a grounded theory study using newspaper articles, see Burgoyne 1997).

One of the most difficult questions at the outset of a grounded theory study is to know where to find the first data. Given that grounded theory specifically avoids the use of previous literature to guide the data collection process, the initial stages of a study are usually exploratory in nature. Chamberlain (1999) specifies three types of sampling used in data collection at each stage of the grounded theory process. In the initial stages, *open sampling* is used to gather enough data to begin coding. After the initial coding phase, *relational sampling* uses the initial codes as a basis for gathering further material; in the final phase, *theoretical sampling* is used to gather material to help construct your core category or overarching theory.

Therefore, initial data collection is not quite as important as in a tightly-structured quantitative study; the entire focus of the study may change halfway through. As Charmaz (1995) argues, analysis should begin as soon as possible in the study, to avoid wasteful data collection. The sooner you can identify a focus for your study, the more useful your data collection will become.

Orona (1997) describes how she came to begin data collection in her study of identity loss in Alzheimer's disease. The study derived from her work as a sociologist in a team working at an adult day health centre, where she observed many instances of the illness and became interested in the caring experiences of relatives. Eventually she organised five interviews with carers in their own homes, each interview lasting between 1.5 and 4 hours, gathering as much material as possible about their experiences. These data then formed the basis for the initial coding process.

When grounded theory is carried out as part of a larger project, an ethnographic study, for example, participant observation is often used as a means of locating the initial sample. Torsch and Xueqin-Ma (2000) did this in their cross-cultural study of health perceptions in Chinese and Pacific Islander older adults. Where a researcher is starting from scratch, they may aim for as much variety as possible in their initial data collection, either in an attempt to collect a representative sample, or simply to gather as wide a variety of cases as possible. A study of bullying experiences among schoolchildren is unlikely to begin simply by looking solely at fee-paying schools; you would normally set out to sample from as many different types of school as possible.

Having collected the initial sample of data, the next step is to prepare it for analysis. In interview-based studies, this of course means transcribing several hours of audiotape. The important thing at this stage is to ensure that you get as much material on paper as possible – you never know what will turn out to be significant, or useful. You also need to ensure there is enough room in your transcript for extensive notes, so leave wide margins and, preferably, $1^{1}/_{2}$ line spaces between the lines.

Initial analysis

Open coding

The best way to start the initial coding process is to read through your transcripts a few times and make some notes in the margin whenever you see something of interest. This will give you some idea of the kinds of descriptive *themes* that are likely to shape your analysis.

Then you will need to carry out more intensive coding of the data. This usually involves the inspection of chunks of data and the generation of a number of descriptive codes which best sum up the content of the text. Charmaz (1995) refers to this as 'line-by-line coding', although there will be many lines in your transcript which fail to suggest any codes at all; indeed, Rennie (2000) prefers the term 'meaning units' to codes. Nevertheless, this intensive approach to coding allows the researcher, in Charmaz's terms, to get closer to the data and to avoid bringing their own preconceptions and biases to bear on the analysis. Above all, it forces the researcher to avoid taken-for-granted or common-sense meaning, taking 'the familiar, routine and mundane and [making] it unfamiliar and new' (Charmaz 1995: 38).

The important distinction between grounded theory and a purely descriptive form of coding such as that found in content analysis (see Chapters 14 and 16) is that the codes are not pre-determined. Content analysis usually proceeds through the use of a fixed schedule based on previous theory or research. Grounded theory is much more creative, although the analysis will only 'work' if the researcher remains as close to the data as possible, and is able to move from the descriptive towards the conceptual.

In Orona's (1997) study, one of her initial codes referred to the comment 'She used to like coffee' (spoken by the daughter/carer of an Alzheimer's sufferer). An initial skim through the data might ignore such a seemingly bland, run-of-the-mill comment, and extracting it from the text makes it seem even more pedestrian. However, as the researcher worked through the coding process, she would have found other, similar comments, which contrasted the carer's descriptions of her mother *now* with the life-long perceptions that had shaped her mother's identity. Therefore, the expression 'used to' suggests that *time* is an important factor in identity loss.

Focused coding

Once the initial set of codes has been generated, the second step is to attempt to integrate these codes into broader, conceptual, *categories*. An example from Orona (1997) shows how this process may take place. Initially, she identified a number of codes from her interviews with Alzheimer's carers such as 'memory', 'clock' and 'rituals', which she then gathered together into the category labelled *temporality*. Below is a list of data fragments in which the italicised words or phrases had been coded in relation to time; all these were then collected together as examples of the 'temporality' category.

> It was *the time of year* when nobody goes in the yard anyway.
> *More and more*, he was leaning on me.
> *Before*, she would never be like that.
> She *used to* love coffee.
> Even on *free days*, you're always up *against the clock*.
>
> (Orona 1997: 179–80)

As you begin to categorise your initial codes, it is essential that you develop some form of *indexing system*. Pidgeon and Henwood (1997) suggest the use of 'category cards' on which you collect all the examples you have found in the text. Alternatively, you may use computer software to sort your data. There are various programs which can do this, such as QSR NUD•IST (see Gahan and Hannibal 1998, for a usable handbook), WINMAX, or CODE-A-TEXT (see Seale 2000, for a useful overview of using computers for qualitative analysis). A word of caution, however; while computer packages can sort text into categories on the basis of descriptive information (e.g., searching for text segments which contain specified words or phrases), they cannot do your conceptual work for you!

The types of category produced through initial coding are the foundations of the grounded theory. If codes are essentially descriptive in nature, categories are basic attempts to structure the data at a more abstract level. Categories like Orona's 'temporality' are *interpretative* categories; they link the initial codes together in terms of key ideas. However, this type of category can be contrasted with *in vivo* categories, which are suggested by the language in the text – perhaps phrases or metaphors that participants have used frequently (Charmaz 1995).

How many codes constitute a category? Clearly, qualitative analysis resists any temptation to quantify this kind of process. Instead, grounded theorists talk of *saturation*. Think of a concept card that has been labelled – perhaps Orona's 'temporality' category – and is gradually filling up with all the fragments of text that relate to that category. At some point you will find that each fragment is simply a duplicate of a fragment already on the card. This would seem to indicate that saturation has occurred – there are no new variations on the theme. If your list of fragments seems rather thin on the ground this might suggest that the category is too narrow, or too similar to another, related category. These are minor concerns at this stage.

By this point, your analysis is finally beginning to take shape. However, it may be that the categories which best explain your data are nothing like those you had in mind at the outset of the study. Interesting themes or concepts have appeared which could have been explored more fully in your initial data set. It may be time to collect more data, in which case you would need to conduct more interviews, or gather together more texts, which enable you to fully explore some of the ideas you are pulling together. Then try applying the categories from your initial set of data to the new data. You may find that the new data simply repeat the pattern; however, with a new set of interview questions, you may find some categories expanding, or new ones emerging.

Again, a question that psychologists with a quantitative background are liable to ask is: how do you know when you have enough categories? Rennie (2000) argues that this really depends on the types of category you have – if your codes are mostly of the 'in vivo' type (i.e., closely rooted in participants' language) you may have a very large number (up to 100), but if they are more abstract (e.g., 'temporality') you could aim for around twenty.

Secondary analysis

The next stage of analysis occurs when you have sorted most of your data into basic categories. This has been described by Strauss and Corbin (1990) as 'axial' coding, where you are working at a higher level of abstraction, and your codes are *concepts* rather than mere descriptions. The goal at this stage is to reduce your initial set of categories to an explanatory framework of higher-order categories by linking them together in some way, or even breaking them down into more manageable units. Of course, not all categories will necessarily be linked, but you will find that some of them share certain properties and can be collapsed; other categories may appear to be simply descriptive, or not adding very much to the overall analysis.

This stage of analysis is usually carried out through the use of *theoretical memos*, which are pieces of writing by the researcher to explain *how* higher-order categories have been generated. This is often a hard concept for students to grasp because, even more than coding, memo-writing is a creative process, and different approaches will work for different researchers. Rennie (1998a) describes memos as a kind of 'research diary', part of the documentation of the whole grounded theory process. Karen Henwood (Pidgeon and Henwood 1996) presents an example from her own research into mother–daughter relationships in which she used ideas from discourse analysis to split an unwieldy initial category ('relational closeness') into two categories ('closeness' and 'overcloseness').

Orona (1997) describes three different uses of memos in her Alzheimer's study. First, she used memos to 'free associate', jotting down any thoughts that occurred to her as she read through the transcripts. A second use was for 'unblocking', setting up a dialogue with an imaginary person (e.g., a professor) that enabled her to work through problematic issues. Finally, she used them to track ideas from germination in the coding process through to higher-order category development. These uses may not work for everyone, of course; some researchers prefer more formal record-keeping.

Students often fail to grasp the point of memos, although it is good research practice in any methodology to keep some kind of log of ideas; certainly it is essential for quantitative studies involving model-building or exploratory analyses, such as multiple regression, structural equation modelling, or factor analysis. The main difference between those studies and grounded theory is that, in quantitative research, memos are treated as overly subjective, scraps of paper to be discarded after the report is written, and superfluous to the data analysis. Probably nobody ever thought to formalise them as part of the analytical process; grounded theorists use them as part of an analytical audit trail, providing evidence of the theory-building process.

Ultimately, memos may have an important part to play in the creation of higher-order categories; indeed, Rennie (2000) suggests that the sorting of memos is the best way of achieving this aim. However the most common practical function of memo-writing is to assist the researcher in the eventual report of the study. Charmaz (1995) suggests that, while initial memos may be informal jottings that are solely of use to the individual researcher, as time goes by they can be gradually polished until they can be used in the eventual report.

Another useful device for generating higher-order categories is the use of *diagrams* to illustrate the links between initial categories. Diagrams can take a number of forms, such as flowcharts, matrices, and networks. They can be used simply as a way of structuring the associations between categories solely for the researcher's benefit, or they may play a central role in the theory-building process. In her study, Orona (1997: 181) used diagrams 'to see the interaction between the players and to graphically document the process as it moved temporally and existentially', in other words to structure the typical course of identity loss described by the carers across time.

Final analysis

At some point, the grounded theorist needs to know when to draw the analysis to a close. Having generated a small number of higher-order categories, the researcher needs, in Rennie's (1998a: 103) words, to identify 'the key concept that organises the theory'. This concept is usually an even higher-order category described as the *core category* (Glaser 1978), in which case the researcher's task in this final stage is simply to identify the conceptual thread that ties all the higher-order categories together.

The core category may be a way of explaining the data by way of a central (psychological) *process*. Here, the researcher, usually with the aid of a flowchart, demonstrates how the higher-order categories link together to produce the phenomenon under investigation.[1] Or it might be some form of structure like a model or typology (see the Clegg *et al.* 1996 study later in the chapter), or even a 'storyline' (Strauss and Corbin 1990) common to most cases in the study. Alternatively, the researcher might select a core theoretical category *and* demonstrate a central process, as in the Tweed and Salter (2000) study reported later in the chapter.

Ultimately, the choice of core category or process is down to whatever makes the most sense for the researcher. Like labelling factors in factor analysis, the decision is entirely interpretative. However, Strauss and Corbin (1990) suggest some criteria for evaluating grounded theory: first, it is *representative* of the phenomenon in reality (the data being drawn from as wide a variety of sources as possible); second, it should be *comprehensible* to people in the area, both participants and researchers; third, it should provide *generality* (i.e., it should be sufficiently abstract to be applicable in a variety of other contexts), and fourth, it should provide a basis for *action* in the area (at least, it is capable of acting as a model for future research). However, not all grounded theorists are in agreement on these criteria (particularly the representation and generality issues).

There are also a number of final 'checks' which can be carried out to cement the final analysis. First, you may wish to collect yet more data to help confirm the core category or process – for example, there may be a critical question that you could ask participants that has been missing from the earlier transcripts. This is known as *theoretical sampling* – you are selecting your participants, or texts, solely on the basis of your emerging theory. Second, one way of 'testing' your emerging theory is to conduct *negative case analysis*, where you search through your data to discover an instance which does not fit into the central process, or suggests that another category may ultimately be more important than the core category you have identified. Here, you need to decide whether these are 'exceptions that prove the rule', or critical cases which require you to reformulate your theory.

Writing the grounded theory report

Having finally selected a core category or process for your theory, you will then wish to present your findings to the world. At this point, psychologists from a quantitative background may panic: I have no literature review; no hypothesis; the method and results don't fit into two separate sections; and so on. I will discuss qualitative report writing in more general terms in Chapter 15, but one or two issues are especially relevant to grounded theory.

The use of literature is perhaps the most difficult aspect for novice grounded theorists to grasp, as the whole approach is concerned with avoiding the theoretical literature as a basis for method. Nevertheless, no psychological journal will accept a paper, whatever its methodological orientation, if it does not have any conceptual link with academic literature. Traditionally, psychology research papers, in common with the discipline's dominant natural science approach, have been very instrumental with regard to existing literature, using previous findings to formulate precise hypotheses. In grounded theory (and other qualitative research) the literature review acts more as a background to the area that you are researching rather than a collection of 'findings' that you are using as justification for your hypothesis.

Therefore, where traditionally psychologists are expected to carry out a literature review before collecting any data, grounded theorists – while having (one hopes) a broad grasp of the topic area to begin with – rarely begin to consult the literature in any great depth until they have entered into the business of theory-building. For example, if 'temporality' has emerged as your core category, you might start looking for other instances of temporality in relation to the phenomenon under investigation. Inevitably this means that your literature review, when it appears, may be somewhat 'post hoc' – this is perfectly acceptable as long as you remember what it is you have done, and avoid making false (and, in the case of grounded theory, inappropriate) claims, such as 'I decided to investigate the issue of temporality in X'!

Another important issue is the use of *data* in the final report. Whereas quantitative researchers can demonstrate their findings by providing numeric tables and citing test statistics and significance values, qualitative researchers are obliged to present raw data as evidence to help the reader evaluate their analyses. In discourse analysis, where language is of paramount concern, authors are expected to provide large chunks of transcript; however, grounded theorists differ in the amount of raw data they include in the report, prioritising *concepts* over examples (Charmaz 1995). Ultimately, the amount of data you present depends on the nature of your study – in psychology, where you may have interesting case studies to use as illustrative material, grounded theorists are likely to present more data than in other fields.

Finally, there is the issue of methodological clarity. One of the most striking features of many grounded theory studies in areas outside psychology is the apparent lack of methodological detail. Indeed, Strauss and Corbin (1997: 63) argue that 'grounded theory methodology and methods are so much a part of some researchers' thinking that they don't bother especially to address them when writing up their research'! However, if you are writing for a psychological audience, particularly in a mainstream psychology journal, the reviewers will expect you to provide quite a lot of explicit detail in your report (remember, many mainstream journal editors still don't accept qualitative research as at all rigorous, or even worthwhile). It might be an idea to consult one of the papers described in the next section as an example of how to write up a grounded theory report.

Examples of grounded theory from the psychological literature

Clegg et al. (1996): carer–client relationships in a learning disabilities unit

This study, from the *British Journal of Clinical Psychology*, is part of a larger project which also uses quantitative methods to study the quality of interaction between direct care staff and their adult clients in the learning disabilities units of four different clinical services (one residential, three day centres). For this study, a number of interviews were conducted with care staff at the various units (twenty in total).

Unusually for a grounded theory study, this is very much a team effort: the interviews, for example, were conducted by a trained psychology assistant who, after transcription, took no further part in the analysis. The first author then coded the transcripts, and checked the initial analysis with other professionals in the area, along with some of the participants and other care staff (this is sometimes referred to as a 'member check' – a validity procedure in qualitative research). Then the first two authors took the analysis through the theory-building stages.

Initial coding provided 27 categories, including 'comprehending aloneness' (how aware, or affected, are clients), 'boundaries of relationships', and 'staff as instruments of other professionals'. Axial coding then integrated these; for example, 'staff emotional response' was integrated with related aspects of other initial categories, such as 'risk of rejection' and 'risk of over-involvement', producing the higher-order category of 'ambivalence towards the keyworking relationship'.

The final analysis in this study produced a typology of relationships as its integrating theme. Four types of carer–client relationship were suggested:

- *Provider*: an instrumental relationship, typically with younger clients, with few positive features
- *Meaning-maker*: where the carer makes a continual effort to understand the client, most common with severe disability
- *Mutual*: the most positive relationship, usually with healthy clients, where the carer perceives the relationship as a friendship
- *Companion*: typically with older clients, a more 'existential' relationship, based on trust and shared time

In addition to these basic types, four basic propositions were made about carer–client relationships: first, that some of these types are better than others; second, that achieving *control* in the relationship is important for staff; third, contact with clients' families may improve relationships; and fourth, professional commitments often drained the emotional resources of carers, interfering with their relationships with clients.

The practical applications of this study are important in terms of placing clients with particular carers, and the need for carers to have more detailed information about the clients' histories. As a piece of grounded theory, the most telling justification for the methodology comes from a comment by the authors that the typology offered initially by learning disability experts and staff comprised 'friend, mother, teacher, advocate'. Attempts to force the data into these pre-set categories (as in, say, content analysis) may well have resulted in an artificial analysis, lots of unplaced but important data, and few practical uses for the research.

Tweed and Salter (2000): non-attendance by the clients of clinical psychologists

This next paper is not unlike the first in terms of setting and topic, but produces a somewhat different type of analysis. Without going into much detail, the study consisted of interviews with six clinical psychologists in the British health service about situations where their clients had failed to meet an appointment. The core category identified by the authors was 'responsibility', the concept which seemed to underpin all six accounts, whether in relation to the client, the health service, or themselves as good professionals.

With their remaining higher-order categories, the authors produced a process model that could be applied to the subject of client non-attendance, illustrated in Figure 12.2. Starting with *non-attendance*, the key issue here concerns whether it could be predicted or not. This determines the *affective reaction* of the psychologist; if unexpected, the psychologist is likely to experience a state of 'flux'; in either case, the psychologist's affective reaction

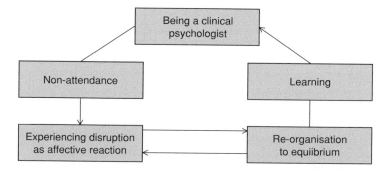

Figure 12.2 Process model pertaining to non-attendence, from Tweed and Salter 2000. Reproduced with permission from The British Journal of Medical Psychology, © The British Psychological Society.

is important (e.g., were they relieved at not having to deal with that client at that point in time?).

This leads on to (but is affected by) the *re-organisation to equilibrium*, which involves a number of factors: what to do next (write to the client?); attributing responsibility (is it me? them?); and plain therapeutic curiosity (why?). These things contribute to the professional learning process, and are all part of being a clinical psychologist. Clearly other factors influence this category, such as professional guidelines, and/or the policy of the health service, or the specific psychology department.

Debates and developments in grounded theory

Since the publication of Glaser and Strauss's 1967 book, the principles behind grounded theory, and the precise methods advocated, have been hotly debated – not least by the original authors themselves. Something of a rift in the grounded theory literature was opened up by the publication of Strauss and Corbin's (1990) *Basics of Qualitative Research*, in which Strauss (along with Juliet Corbin) suggested a number of modifications of the methods outlined in the Glaser and Strauss (1967) text. Among the most radical were the use of data fragments to test hypotheses of theories emerging from the data; the use of *introspective* data for theory-building (i.e., reflections on the data drawing on the researcher's personal experience); and the use of a 'conditional matrix' for generalising the application of the overarching theory or process (Rennie 1998a).

In a later text, Glaser (1992) attacked these modifications on a number of grounds, chiefly epistemological. Hypothesis-testing went against the whole ethos of grounded theory, he argued, since it is essentially a *positivistic* method (i.e., used by quantitative researchers to establish facts about an objective 'reality'). Similarly, the principle of generalisability itself owes much to positivism (e.g., the use of probability to infer statistical findings from sample to population). By contrast, the use of introspective material as data is essentially a *relativistic* method (where 'objective reality' might be regarded as the construction of the individual researcher within a specific culture). David Rennie (1998b: 131), in a consideration of the Glaser/Strauss debate, comes down firmly on Glaser's side, employing a technique derived from the philosophy of science ('methodical hermeneutics') to argue that Strauss and Corbin's (1990) modifications are logically inconsistent, and 'promote a drift into subjectivity that undermines groundedness'.

While on the face of it, this debate might appear to be somewhat esoteric, it has important implications for the use of grounded theory, and taps into wider debates about the use of qualitative research in psychology which will become more apparent in Chapter 13. Just to give a flavour of these debates, here are two key issues relating to grounded theory.

The status of verbal data

Suppose you are coding transcript of an interview with a psychiatric patient and you come across the statement 'I am being oppressed'. How do you treat that statement? As a clinical psychologist, you might consider it as a symptom of a paranoid disorder (since you infer from the speaker's identity that s/he has received a clinical diagnosis). As a social realist, you might consider it a statement of fact, and attempt to deduce from the transcript who – or what system – is responsible for the oppression. Both these positions are essentially realist positions – the belief in an external reality which can be studied empirically, either through measures of psychological dysfunction, or through observation of social (or political) systems.

A third position, though, is the relativist position, where you refuse to take 'I am being oppressed' as a statement of fact and treat it as a manner of speaking, a rhetorical device, or a 'discourse'. I will go into greater detail on this issue in the next chapter; here, consider it an important issue for the sort of claims we make about verbal data, and the sorts of theory we can build from texts and transcripts. Do they tell us about an external reality, or are they tied firmly to the context of the individual speakers?

Reflexivity vs. emergence

If the above issue can be described as the 'realism vs. relativism' debate, then its counterpart is the 'objectivity vs. subjectivity' debate in grounded theory. This is less to do with the status of the data than with the status of the theory. A common question in the literature is: 'What grounds grounded theory?' (Henwood and Pidgeon 1992). Many grounded theorists talk of categories 'emerging' from the data, as though they are lying buried beneath the surface, waiting for a researcher to discover them. This is clearly an 'objective' position, but to an extent it is one of the core assumptions of grounded theory methodology, and the degree of rigour involved. On the other hand, a 'subjective' position, which regards the analysis as solely the product of the individual researcher's perspective, calls into question many of the techniques in grounded theory (such as negative case analysis).

As a result of these debates, a number of researchers have attempted to modify grounded theory to suit their own needs. While clearly such departures need to be justified, this practice is entirely in keeping with the original tenets of grounded theory, which has always been seen as an *evolving* method (Chamberlain 1999).

Departures from traditional grounded theory

One such departure addresses the realism vs. relativism debate as presented above; this is the *radical constructionist* approach of Madill *et al.* (2000). Here, the authors seek to develop a version of grounded theory which assumes neither a) an internal consistency of participants' accounts, nor b) an essentialised model of subjectivity (2000: 16). In other words, they want to treat participants' accounts as 'discourse' rather than statements of fact, but at the same time avoid the 'drift into subjectivity' as described by Rennie (1998b). Rather than this being a straightforward case of realism or relativism, however, Madill *et al.* make an important distinction between the positivist school of realism (i.e., the natural science approach) and the 'radical constructionist', or 'poststructural' position, whereby many of the assumptions of positivism (e.g., about language as a representation of reality) are distrusted.

Madill *et al.*'s solution is to develop a more explicit approach to coding, where rather than just treating text as a collection of meaning units that can be broken into fragments, texts are read closely, either for 'macro discourses' that shape the underlying assumptions of participants' accounts, or for rhetorical devices that are rooted in participants' language use. This approach to grounded theory is strongly influenced by discourse analysis, and a number of qualitative researchers have attempted to reconcile the two methodologies (see, for example, Willott and Griffin (1997) in the next chapter). However, there remain queries about the use of grounded theory as a vehicle for this type of analysis – particularly since, in the 'radical' version of grounded theory, concepts such as objectivity and reliability are treated as 'rhetorical devices', effectively paying lip-service to traditional science.

A second departure from traditional grounded theory has been suggested by Schatzman (1991), who introduced the idea of *dimensional analysis*. In some respects, this is the reverse of the radical approach, in that it seeks to tighten up some of the 'mysterious' analytical procedures in grounded theory (Kools *et al.* 1996). Dimensional analysis is concerned with identifying a *perspective* from which to view the data, expressed through the use of an 'explanatory matrix'. The analysis builds up to this point by identifying dimensions, rather than categories, which eventually form a 'critical mass', at which point one is selected to provide the overarching perspective from which the data can be most usefully understood. As yet, there are relatively few examples (particularly outside health research) of grounded theory conducted in this way; it remains to be seen whether dimensional analysis becomes popular or whether, as Chamberlain (1999) suggests, it is regarded as simply replacing one set of prescriptive practices (or jargon) with another.

Finally, there is some indication that specific techniques from grounded theory may be starting to find their way into other forms of qualitative research. Constant comparative analysis is one such technique which occasionally informs other approaches (Chamberlain 1999). Again this is entirely in keeping with the original aims of grounded theory. It seems almost certain that, with qualitative research gaining increasing popularity in psychology, researchers will find many different ways to adapt the approach to their own needs.

Summary

Grounded theory is starting to make a small impact on the psychological literature after having established itself as a major method in areas such as health studies and nursing. It seems likely that it will continue to be influential in many areas of psychology beyond the health and clinical literature. Here I have tried to outline the steps behind conducting grounded theory research in as straightforward a manner as possible. One of the most important features of grounded theory, and qualitative research in general, is that the data collection and analysis are conducted throughout the research process, rather than in two separate stages as in most quantitative research. Newcomers to the technique often struggle with identifying categories, and constructing theories; I hope I have supplied enough examples to help with these problems.

Note

1 Charts and diagrams are widely used in qualitative research, partly as an aid to the reader, which is sensible if you have a great many categories that are conceptually linked, and partly as an aid to the researcher. Very often your analysis only begins to make sense once you can see it diagrammatically (depending on your preferences for displaying information, of course). Some qualitative researchers have gone so far as to build a whole research paradigm around the use of data display models; Miles and Huberman (1994), for example, argue for the use of matrices, flowcharts and other diagrams as the end-product of the research process, and even as hypothesis-testing devices (though I know few qualitative researchers who would endorse this use of qualitative data). On a more cynical note, the popularity of flowcharts and diagrams in qualitative research may also have something to do with the fact that, like path diagrams in structural equation modelling, they make a research paper *look* scientific!

13 Discourse analysis

It is probably fair to say that discourse analysis has been the most commonly used qualitative approach in psychology over the last decade. Since the publication of Potter and Wetherell's 1987 book *Discourse and Social Psychology: Beyond Attitudes and Behaviour*, discourse research has evolved rapidly, along several different methodological and epistemological lines, and a recent pair of textbooks on the subject identify no fewer than six different versions (Wetherell *et al.* 2001a, b). Admittedly, these texts cover discourse research in a variety of social science disciplines; however, for various reasons, the discipline boundaries are sometimes blurred in the field of discourse analysis.

As a result of this rapid expansion, and so many differing perspectives, the novice researcher is – as with grounded theory – suddenly presented with a minefield of jargon to pick his or her way through. However, discourse analysis is more than about simply acquiring a new set of analytical methods. In psychology, it requires a radical re-evaluation of the subject under investigation. Being aware of what discourse analysis *cannot* do is almost as important as appreciating its potential. Research questions are invariably determined by the methods available, so traditionally, psychologists have couched their hypotheses in terms of cause and effect (the experimental approach), or influential factors (multivariate analysis), or between-group differences. However, discourse analysis (and, indeed, most qualitative research) will not help you answer these questions. It is necessary to understand some of the theoretical ideas behind discourse analysis before attempting to put the techniques into practice.

The first section of this chapter, then, looks at some of the philosophical and theoretical ideas that have informed the practice of discourse analysis, as well as charting the history of its development. I will then present a short guide to carrying out an analysis before addressing some of the more specific debates.

Ideas behind discourse analysis in psychology

Discourse analysis in psychology is an approach which has become established largely in Europe (particularly the UK), but is gaining in popularity elsewhere. It has been influenced by two broad traditions: first, the (largely North American) field of conversation analysis; and second, European philosophy, particularly the work of the historical philosopher Michel Foucault.

Development of the discourse analytic tradition

Philosophers have always been interested in language, and so the true origins of discourse analysis lie behind several centuries of scholarship. However its story, for our present purposes, begins in earnest somewhere around the 1960s, with the emergence of 'ethnomethodology' and the technique of conversation analysis. I will discuss this technique in more detail in Chapter 14, although some discursive psychologists would argue that its influence is so pervasive in discourse analysis that, as Jonathan Potter (1996: 132) has argued, 'a basic practical understanding of conversational analysis is a prerequisite for producing high-class discourse analysis'. However, many other discourse analysts would disagree – this is a very diverse field – and so I will try to keep my coverage of it here to a mimimum. Indeed, while some forms of discourse analysis are barely distinguishable from conversation analysis, other forms barely acknowledge it.

Conversation analysis was established as a field following a series of lectures given by Harvey Sacks during the 1960s and 1970s (collected in Sacks 1992). These lectures developed the idea that systematic analytical procedures could be applied to mundane, everyday talk, and that these analyses would reveal the ways people negotiate their understanding of the world through social interaction. In the following decades conversation analysis has been applied to all manner of phenomena, such as turn-taking, hesitation, humour, questions and answers, and to all manner of conversational settings, from the classroom to the workplace (see Drew and Heritage 1992).

Potter and Wetherell's (1987) book suggested ways in which some of the principles of conversation analysis might be applied to traditional psychological phenomena, such as the formation of attitudes. Their approach was also strongly influenced by Steve Woolgar (1988) and Gilbert and Mulkay's (1984) work in the sociology of scientific knowledge, which developed the idea of the 'interpretative repertoires' on which scientists draw to justify the creation of 'facts' and to undermine rival theories. Another important influence in this emerging field was the study of rhetoric (Billig 1987, 1991) – how argument is constructed – and these parallel but complementary bodies of work led to the establishment of the Discourse and Rhetoric Group at Loughborough University in the English midlands, which has had a substantial influence within European social psychology.

However, it is probably Michel Foucault – the French philosopher and historian – who is most responsible for bringing the term 'discourse' to the forefront of social scientific research (although linguists might have something to say on the matter). He offered a definition of discourse that extends beyond language to the operation of society as a whole. In a much-quoted passage, he argued that 'discourses are practices that systematically form the objects of which they speak' (Foucault 1972: 49). Such practices need not be linguistic in nature but may involve the manipulation of symbols (think, for example, of political symbols from the Union Jack to the swastika).

This approach to social scientific research has been picked up widely within the social sciences, but has been popularised in psychology by the work of Ian Parker and others working within the field of critical psychology (see Parker 1992; Burman and Parker 1993). Their approach to discourse analysis has been somewhat different from that of the Loughborough school in that, rather than studying the use of language within different contexts, they study 'discourses' as broader social and cultural practices which manifest themselves in 'texts'. In a now-infamous chapter of a textbook, Parker (1994) demonstrated how it was possible to perform a discourse analysis on as apparently innocuous and mundane a text as the instructions on a packet of children's toothpaste. He showed how this short piece of text (which, in addition to the words also incorporates other elements of packaging, such as images and logos) 'contains' a number of broad discourses – pertaining to the family, medicine, education and development – which are historically and culturally situated.

While Foucault-inspired discourse analysis has produced a number of important studies (typically referred to as 'archaeological' analysis), it has influenced the practice of discourse analysis in psychology in general, so that researchers have applied its principles to a variety of different texts, and drawn on broader concepts of discourse than just the use of language within a specific context.

Implications for psychological theory

Discourse analysis is an approach very much in tune with the school of thought known as *social constructionism* (Gergen 1985; Burr 1995), which is an understanding of the world (i.e., 'reality') as the product of historical, cultural and social interaction, rather than fixed, universal 'essences'. The impact of social constructionist thought on psychology brings into question a lot of the phenomena which the discipline has traditionally taken for granted: the notion of fixed, biologically inherited, 'personality'; its focus on the individual, private self across the lifespan (and therefore, the relevance of concepts such as self-esteem); the search for universal, unchanging 'cognitive architecture'; the idea of 'attitudes' as fixed, tangible essences controlling behaviour; the ability to 'measure' all of these things (and the meaning, and use, of these measures); and, therefore, the (often uncritical) application of these measures to areas such as clinical, occupational and forensic psychology.

Instead of speculating about mental processes and properties of 'mind', social constructionism turns the spotlight on to cultural and discursive practices as the focus of psychological study. Very often this involves a challenge to the categories that we use to make sense of the world; think, for example, of the number of times students construct hypotheses for research projects which compare males and females! A good example of how categorisation influences social practice is in the evolution of the social category 'homosexual'; as Foucault and others have pointed out, the notion of a *person* as being homosexual is a historically situated phenomenon – before recent centuries, homosexuality was spoken about as a practice rather than an identity. We might engage in a homosexual *act*, but not be thought of as 'a homosexual'. The attribution of consistent, even biologically fixed, 'sexuality' that determines the course of our social life is a fundamentally modern phenomenon, one that would have made little sense in earlier times (Burr 1995).

Such arguments fail to make much impact on traditional psychologists wedded to the positivist ideas of truth and linear progress. So what if such phenomena are historically located, they might argue; previous generations did not possess our technological capabilities, our rigorous methods, or our research literature. However, time is not the only dimension along which our ideas of the world vary; anthropological research has also revealed profound differences in psychological understanding between different societies and cultures (Geertz 1973). As much as anything, discourse analysis reveals *how*, rather than *if*, the world (or 'reality') is constructed through discourse – how social interaction actually *works*. This is what is so badly missed in experiments and questionnaires. Since, as social constructionists argue, language (or discourse) is the primary communication medium, then its analysis can tell us how social life is performed and how identities are negotiated.

Social constructionism is less explicit in terms of methodology than some approaches in psychology, and effectively embraces both traditions in discourse analysis as outlined in the previous section. It is also compatible with many other qualitative methods, including grounded theory and conversational analysis, not to mention quantitative methods, although these are rarely used by psychologists with a constructionist bent, probably because they are too closely associated with the positivist tradition which social constructionism seeks to challenge (however, see Reicher 2000).

Often, psychologists in this area use the term *deconstruction* to describe the analytical work they are doing (e.g., Parker *et al.* 1995; Burman 1994a). This is a separate tradition deriving from literary theory, which argues that the 'meaning' of a text is not fixed by its author but through the act of reading (Derrida 1976). Applied to social scientific research, this practice typically involves dismantling a phenomenon – literally, studying *how* it is constructed. This can certainly be done through discourse analysis, whether in the Foucauldian tradition of genealogical research, or in the way that phenomena are constructed through language at the level of talk and text.

STEPS IN CONDUCTING DISCOURSE ANALYSIS

In this section I will take the reader through the process of carrying out a discourse analysis. This is certainly not intended to be a prescriptive guide, since there are so many different approaches to the practice. However, it is difficult for a novice to embark on the process without some idea of the steps involved which are common to most forms of discourse analysis. Often beginners are taken through the conversation analysis-inspired Loughborough approach and the Foucauldian approach separately. However, in practice, these approaches are so often integrated by researchers that separating them at the methodological level may impose unnecessary restraints on the research process. Therefore, I will follow the example of Coyle (2000) in presenting an integrated model which can be adapted for different texts and topics.

Identifying and collecting data

Discourse analysis is similar to other forms of qualitative research (e.g., grounded theory) in that the collection of data is less easily abstracted from the research process than in most quantitative research, where data collection forms a discrete stage in between formulating a hypothesis and performing data analysis. Nevertheless, the type of data used in discourse analysis is dependent upon the broad approach the researcher is adopting, the research topic, and on the kinds of questions s/he is looking for the analysis to answer – which are, of course, all closely related.

Unlike grounded theory, discourse analysis does not rule out the use of previous theory or literature in guiding the research. Many popular psychological topics already have a research history in discursive and critical psychology: racism (Wetherell and Potter 1992); memory (Middleton and Edwards 1990); stress (Brown 1999); identity (Antaki and Widdicombe 1998). Furthermore, several journals cater exclusively for discourse analytic research, such as *Discourse and Society* and *Discourse Studies*, or regularly publish work conducted in that tradition (*British Journal of Social Psychology*, *Feminism and Psychology*, *Journal of Community and Applied Social Psychology*). In addition, discursive papers are beginning to appear in other journals, in areas like health and clinical psychology.

The previous literature on a topic may well determine the type of data you use. For example, discursive studies in the conversation analytic tradition (the 'Loughborough school') often use the same kinds of data as conversation analysts prefer to work with – those described as 'naturally occurring talk and text' (Potter 1996). Such data often come in the form of tape recordings of everyday activities that have been made available to researchers; for example, a group therapy session with teenagers (Sacks 1992), police interviews (Auburn *et al.* 1995) or telephone conversations (see Edwards 1997).

Other material used as 'naturally occurring' text can be drawn from media sources, either in the form of political speeches or televised interviews (e.g., Abell and Stokoe's (1999) use of the BBC interview with Princess Diana), or the content of newspapers and magazines. While the former data can certainly be used to investigate the structure of talk, there is some doubt as to what extent such material can be extricated from its (mediated) context. But this concern is part of a wider issue about the status of text (Giles 2002). Often the goal of discourse research is to investigate discursive phenomena within a given context, such as Steven Brown's (1999) study of the discourses around stress found in the self-help literature, or Sunderland's (2000) study of fatherhood as constructed by parenthood texts.

A large number of discourse analyses are performed on original data collected by the researcher, usually in the form of interviews. These present a number of additional issues for researchers to consider. First, a research interview is not exactly 'naturally occurring' data, unless you are studying the structure of the formal interview itself, so the possible influence of the interviewer on the discourse becomes a feature of the analysis. If you are interested in the dynamics of conversation within groups of speakers, the use of focus group interviews is recommended, particularly where the participants form a natural group (friends, colleagues, etc.).

Second, interview data then present the researcher with the arduous task of *transcription*. Finely detailed transcription is more important here than in grounded theory, especially if you are interested in the finer details of talk, and there are quite explicit guidelines for preparing text for analysis, that have been developed by conversation analysts, notably Gail Jefferson, within discourse analysis (the transcription conventions are usually referred to as 'the Jefferson system'). These guidelines, which I will outline in the next section, often make transcribed material difficult to read, but may be essential for analysis. They are also very time-consuming for researchers to prepare; nevertheless, as Potter (1996) argues, even if it takes 20 hours to transcribe every hour of tape, this should not be seen as 'dead time' – indeed, transcription work often provides analysts with their initial insights.

One might question whether it is really necessary to record every minor detail of recorded speech; indeed, the paralinguistic features of talk (pauses, emphasis, etc.) frequently go ignored in more Foucauldian discourse research. Nevertheless, as Potter (1996) argues, the transcription should be as close as possible to the tape, since quotations from the transcript constitute the 'evidence' a reader will use to evaluate the analysis, and they require as faithful a record of the original talk as possible.

Transcription conventions

The following extract comes from an interview carried out with myself and some female students. We were talking about early experiences with alcohol. The names are pseudonyms (apart from my initials), which is a standard convention in discourse analysis (and other qualitative studies which use interview data) to protect participants from being identified from the report.

1	DG (to Donna):	So was this the first time you got drunk too?
2	Donna:	I think (.5) really <u>really</u> drunk yeah. I was just
3		(.) just (.) kept ↑crying. I locked <u>these</u> lot
4		out of the room. Cos I didn't really have any
		<u>control</u> over myself.
5	DG:	What were you drinking?
6	Donna:	Just [vodka].
7	Emma:	[vodka]
8	DG:	Was this the first time you'd tried it?
9	Donna:	[Yeah] (.) °yeah°.
10	Emma:	[Yeah]

Numbering

The first thing to comment on is the numbers along the left hand margin. It is customary to number each line of your transcript – largely as a reference for yourself when performing the analysis. However, if you are writing a report for publication, where you would not include your full transcript in the appendix, you need to use a numbering system that corresponds to the extracts in the text itself. In my actual transcript, this exchange occurred on about page 3, but I have renumbered the lines to fit in with your reading of the chapter.

Pauses

In line 2, Donna pauses three times. The last two pauses are short enough to make timing pointless, so they are recorded as (.). The first pause is, however, long enough for its length to be recorded (.5 of a second). The fact that she has paused for half a second may not seem remotely relevant to your research, but you might be interested that the significant pause follows the expression 'I think'.

Emphasis

There are three different types of emphasis recorded in this extract. A distinction is made between volume and pitch. The first comes in line 2, where 'Donna' stresses the second 'really', indicated in the transcript by an underline. This tells the reader that the second really was uttered at a greater *volume* than the preceding speech. Some discourse analysts might argue that there is a difference between stress and volume (louder speech may be indicated using UPPER CASE letters). In line 9, Donna's second 'yeah' is flanked by two degree signs, indicating a marked quietness. In line 3, an upward arrow (↑) indicates that the following word ('crying') was uttered at a higher *pitch* than the preceding speech. Had the pitch of her voice lowered at this point, it would be represented by a downward arrow (↓). Our interpretation of these changes in emphasis might or might not be relevant; for example, the fact that Donna stresses the second 'really' may indicate that she feels it necessary to distinguish between different levels of drunkenness.

Overlapping speech

On two occasions in this extract, two of the interviewees talk at the same time. This is indicated in the text by square brackets. Overlapping speech is a frequent hazard in focus group transcriptions, where you may have several people excitedly talking together and interrupting each other. Such situations prove a nightmare to transcribers. Much of the time we are trying to guess what is being said; but it helps if a) there are not too many participants in the group; and b) the speakers have distinctive voices. One useful tip is to get each member of the focus group to identify themselves individually at the start of the recording. This way you have a record of each participant's voice.

'Stage directions'

In line 1 I have remarked on the fact that my question is addressed to 'Donna'. This is important – the wrong person might have been answering the question! Asides such as these are particularly important if there are non-verbal or group reactions – for example, laughter, or a bodily gesture. In the latter case, we may have to take a note of this behaviour (since it will not necessarily produce a sound).

In addition to the symbols in the earlier extract, there are a number of other conventions which are worth knowing about, which I have listed in Appendix 2. For further detail on transcription issues and conventions, you could refer to ten Have (1999) or Atkinson and Heritage (1984).

Analytical techniques

At some point, the data collection process needs to move forward to analysis. As in grounded theory, data may be gathered at any stage of the analysis to explore the ideas that your initial analysis has produced, but this is less often done in discourse analysis because so often the researcher is examining the structure of specific texts rather than exploring a phenomenon which can be generalised to other contexts. Thus, as one author puts it, gather 'sufficient text to discern the variety of discursive forms that are commonly used when speaking or writing about the research topic' (Coyle 2000: 256). You could go on collecting data until the discourses begin to repeat themselves, or, as grounded theorists would say, achieve 'saturation', although representativeness is usually less of a concern in this type of research.

Actually performing the analysis is a difficult business for beginners, and it is often made harder by some of the mystery that surrounds the process. Potter (1996: 140) refers to discourse analysis as 'a craft skill, like riding a bike or sexing a chicken', which can only be acquired through practice. Others talk of acquiring a sensitivity to the data, or an 'analytic mentality' (see Coyle 2000), though how this is done is not disclosed. Indeed, method is often rather opaque within the discourse analysis literature (as with much grounded theory), maybe because 'scholarship' is sometimes preferred to systematic procedures of analysis. It is important to have some background knowledge of the topic under investigation; indeed, it is essential for genealogical research in the Foucauldian tradition. Nevertheless, some authors have managed to outline a stage process of sorts in discourse analysis.

Step 1: Coding

Both Gill (1996) and Coyle (2000) identify *coding* as the first step in a discourse analysis. This parallels the initial coding stage in grounded theory, which is largely a matter of identifying descriptive categories in the data. It is therefore important to read the transcripts or texts several times initially, to 'immerse' yourself in the data. Gill (1996) draws on her study with radio broadcasters in which she was interested in how the scarcity of female broadcasters was justified by (mostly) male disc jockeys and producers. She began by highlighting all the references in the transcripts to female broadcasters. Her next step was to pursue themes at a higher conceptual level – in this case, references to the qualities expected of broadcasters which betrayed assumptions about gender.

Step 2: Identify patterns and functions in the data

Once you have worked out which parts of the data are likely to be of interest, the next thing is to investigate how these data function as discourse. Gill (1996) points out that, typically, reading text is concerned with extracting the *gist* from the actual language used. However discourse analysis is about going beyond the taken-for-granted aspects of language use, often by taking apart some of the most mundane and apparently uninteresting constructions.

One of the most important features of language is the use of *rhetorical devices*, figures of speech which perform actions within the talk or text. For example, discourse analysts have identified the following devices:

- *Extreme case formulations*: Exaggerations, hyperbole, to make a point (e.g., 'But Mum, everyone at school's got one')

- *Stake inoculation*: Devices which deflect attributions of interest, or 'stake' away from the speaker, which may take the form of systematic vagueness, e.g., 'I dunno' (Potter 1997)
- *Use of authentic detail*: To strengthen argument – use of precise details such as names, dates, statistics (e.g., in political speeches).

Carrying out this stage of a discourse analysis involves the simultaneous search for *consistent* patterns of language use (which may be labelled 'discourses') and context-specific, *functional* aspects of language use, which comprise interpretative repertoires and rhetorical devices which may be employed at different points in an argument by the same speaker. One way of doing this is to consider what particular problems the discourse may pose for the speaker. In Gill's (1996) research, male broadcasters were discussing the absence of female broadcasters but were concerned not to appear sexist. How they managed this 'ideological dilemma' became a central part of her analysis. Nevertheless, it is important at this point in the analysis not to impute motives to individual speakers, or speculate about the internal disposition of a speaker. You can only work with what you have on the page.

Step 3: Contexts, positions and the unsaid

Most discourse analyses are likely to proceed through the first two steps outlined here. However, different researchers will be interested in different aspects of the discourse, and it is hard to provide a comprehensive outline for the latter stages of the analysis. Nevertheless, many analysts may, at this point, like to step outside the arena of language and try to locate the text in front of them within the wider world of social activity.

First of all, we might wish to examine the historical, cultural or social context in which the discourses are embedded. A good exercise for performing this type of analysis (depending on the time of year) is the study of Christmas cards, in which a variety of discourses can be identified – in addition to the obvious Christian themes of the nativity, there are other historically located discourses, such as Victorian paraphernalia (from customs like Christmas trees and crackers to Dickensian imagery, such as olde shoppes and plum duffs), and more general seasonal imagery (holly, robins). But where does snow fit in, given its rarity in modern Britain?

A second consideration is positioning. *Subject positions* are ways in which an individual is constructed through discourse (Davies and Harré 1990). There are two contexts in which this can occur: in talk, where speakers create subject positions for each other; and in text, where the reader may be 'positioned' by the author. In a study of friendship groups discussing drunken nights out (where 'memory' is something pieced together through conversation), I examined the way in which one particular group positioned one of its members as a 'wild drinker', according him a consistent identity which he adopted when drunk – usually out of control, and willing to do anything for a laugh (Giles 1999).

When an individual is positioned within a discourse, s/he has two options; either to accept the position, or to reject or contest it. 'Sven', the drinker in this group, took up both of these options within the same conversation. At certain points he challenged his 'wild drinker' identity by accusing his friends of exaggeration, but at other times he was willing to accept the position, perhaps because of the macho status it afforded him within the group, or because he did not wish to make an issue out of seemingly harmless banter. Of course, readers of texts have more room to reject the subject positions created for them; I often wonder, for example, what a burglar might make of an informative advertisement for the latest security device, where the text clearly positions the reader as a home-owner seeking to protect their property. Of course, identities are flexible; an individual may be both burglar and home-owner.

Third, we may be interested in what is *unsaid* in a piece of talk or text. This may involve studying euphemistic language use (for example, ways of avoiding using pejorative terms like 'fat', or overtly racist or homophobic language). Or it may be a matter of identifying alternative discourses that are available to speakers, and why this particular discourse was chosen on this occasion.

Step 4: The report

Finally, you will need to turn your ideas about discourse into a formal text in its own right – as a research report. Many of the remarks in the previous chapter about grounded theory can be applied to discourse analytic papers. The usual lab report format will provide you with an appropriate overall structure, but you may choose to merge together the results and discussion sections because so much of your analysis will need extensive commentary.

The main difference between the traditional (experimental) lab report and a discourse analysis is that quantitative researchers rarely present raw data in their results section, whereas discourse analysts are required to present as much of the text as they can, to provide readers with a flavour of the material that is used to construct the analysis. Discourse papers may contain several large chunks of interview data which are then examined in great detail. It is important that you provide these chunks with meaningful line numbers so that you can refer to points in the extracts in your commentary. It is also important that your commentary is incisive and analytical, and does not simply repeat or reword the material in the extracts.

Discourse analysts tend to be a lot less explicit about their methods than quantitative researchers, or even grounded theorists (although these vary tremendously). It is rare to find a report which takes you step by step through all the stages involved in putting the analysis together, largely because it is assumed that readers will be far more interested in studying the examples of text, and what you have to say about them. This sometimes leads to the criticism that discourse analyses are 'impressionistic', but it is usually more important that they resonate with the intended readership of the journal than satisfy the sceptic.

Two examples of discourse analysis from the psychological literature

Lawes (1999): the social construction of marriage

This paper is an example of a discourse analysis which is based on a critique of recent mainstream psychological research – in this case research that tries to account for the apparent decline in popularity of marriage based on social statistics (however, as the author points out, there is some disagreement on this matter).

The Method section outlines a research design that follows explicitly Potter and Wetherell's (1987) steps for conducting discourse analysis – focusing on 'resources that participants draw on to construct their talk'. A total of twenty interviews were conducted altogether, a sample size which the author describes as 'generous' given that language is the focus of the study. All the participants were born between 1961 and 1971 (a generation which has been used by the media to epitomise the declining popularity of marriage): 12 were male, 8 female; 6 were married, 4 not involved in a romantic relationship at all, and the others either dating or co-habiting; all were heterosexual. The interviews, transcribed, came to a total of half a million words.

The analysis itself is described and discussed over the remainder of the paper. Twenty extracts from the interviews are cited in this section (the extracts range from four words up to twenty lines), although only ten of the interviews are cited. The analysis begins with some 'introductory observations' (for example, the difference between marriage in theory and marriage in practice as characterised in a number of accounts), and introduces the notion of 'interpretative repertoires', of which two are singled out for further investigation: the *romantic* repertoire and the *realist* repertoire.

There follows a section on each repertoire. An example of the romantic repertoire, in which the idealistic account of marriage is worked up, is the comment by 'Theo' that divorce can occur when partners 'grow apart and lose interest . . . but if that happens you probably haven't got married to the right person in the first place' (Lawes 1999: 7). The idea that people can be 'right' for each other, and that marriages are successful if you work at them, places responsibility with the individuals involved and promotes the idea of marriage as an ideal state of being.

The realist repertoire, on the other hand, constructs marriage as vulnerable to the hand of fate. In this repertoire, as 'Catherine' argues, divorce can be justified 'if you don't love the person any more' (11). If it's just that your partner snores, she argues, 'that's ridiculous', but you shouldn't stay in a relationship 'because you feel sorry for them or you know that kind of comfort love'. This repertoire is distinct from the romantic one because here aspects of marriage are discussed as being beyond the responsibility of the partners. Snoring can be worked on, but simply 'not loving' your partner is ineffable and uncontrollable. In this repertoire, there is no obvious distinction drawn between marriage and co-habitation; marriage is just a piece of paper. Indeed, 'Theo' claims that the best thing about marriage is that, if he died tomorrow his wife, rather than his mother, would be next of kin!

Lawes makes the important point that these repertoires are 'not a matter of personality or individual differences' – as the quotes from 'Theo' above demonstrate, an individual is free to select any repertoire as a resource 'depending on the rhetorical effect that was to be achieved at a particular moment in the conversation' (10). In the 'final considerations' section she looks at more specific rhetorical devices that are used by participants, such as 'particularisation' – typically, claiming that yours is an exception (one participant agrees that the chances of divorce are high, but that her relationship is a special one).

Finally, the author makes some more general claims about the concept of marriage in the light of her findings. The 'institution' of marriage, Lawes argues, 'does not demonstrably exist outside of the discourse in which it is referred to' because the wedding ceremony and the divorce courts are themselves 'discursive practices'. As a result, talk of 'the future of the institution of marriage' is rather pointless. Ultimately, the research here challenges the argument that marriage is a common-sense category with a fixed and universal meaning; the author has advanced the research by identifying a *vocabulary* of marriage in the way it is talked about.

Gillies (1999): discursive positions of female smokers

Whereas the Lawes paper above is typical of the Loughborough 'school' of conversation analysis-inspired discourse analysis, this study of female smokers' discourse by Val Gillies is conducted from a critical realist perspective (Parker 1992), with the deliberate aim of seeking to empower its participants – in this case, working-class women who smoke. Specifically, the research has an applied objective; to inform the content of health promotional literature on smoking.

The data in this study were taken from four one-to-one interviews with working-class mothers in North London. Gillies began by isolating all the references to cigarettes and smoking and then identifying themes which were either consistent or contradictory. She then used as her analytic tool Parker's (1992: 5) Foucauldian description of a discourse as 'a system of statements which constructs an object' to identify links and networks of 'discursive meanings that construct the activity of cigarette smoking' (Gillies 1999: 70). This enabled her to identify specific discourses and make 'hypotheses . . . concerning [their] functions and effects'.

The discourses that were identified included the following:

- *Addiction* (smoking as a 'bad habit', biologically induced helplessness, physical craving)
- *Control and self-regulation* (coping, can say 'no')
- *Agency* ('it's a choice as to whether you smoke or not')
- *Responsibility* (e.g., respecting non-smokers' wishes, smoking less harmful cigarettes)

In addition, Gillies identified a number of constructions smokers used to counter the argument that smoking is unhealthy: denial (the hazards are exaggerated), case studies (older adults who have smoked for years and are still alive), extreme case formulations (everything is harmful to some extent). Furthermore, some discourses constructed smoking as beneficial – as 'therapeutic', or a way to combat stress.

Gillies argues that, as an application of her work, health literature that concentrates on topics like physical addiction may actually achieve the reverse effect from what is intended; her data demonstrate that the addiction discourse can be used to justify smoking as much as giving up. Instead, she suggests that anti-smoking literature focuses on smoking as a *pleasurable* activity, perhaps by presenting some healthier alternatives.

Some debates in discourse analysis

The model I have presented above is, of course, an over-simplified one, but should contain enough ideas for a beginner to start thinking about what topics to explore. In addition to the techniques of discourse analysis, there are also some extra considerations that must be taken into account when performing this sort of research, and these issues may shape the nature of the analysis itself. Here I will outline some specific debates that discourse analysts of different shades find themselves embroiled in from time to time.

Cognitivism/agency

At many points in your analysis, particularly if you are analysing interview data, you will be tempted to speculate about the *intentions* of a speaker. If you are examining the function of language use – and particularly as a psychologist – it is very hard to avoid. I have some great interview data in my cupboard from an undergraduate project about phobias (Hood 2000), but I have never been able to turn it into discourse analysis because every time I end up speculating about how speaker A's spider phobia is clearly related to the presence or absence of her boyfriend, or how speaker C's fear of baked beans (I said it was great data) seems to be linked with his initial experiences of living away from home. In narrative analysis or life history, such speculation is permissible. In discourse analysis it risks slipping into psychoanalysis, or cognitivism, and speculation about the unconscious, or internal states and private motives (Coyle 2000).

As a result, many discourse analysts prefer to talk about the *effects* of discourse rather than the intention behind specific utterances. Specifically, the emphasis is on the effects that can be observed within the text (rather than assumptions about the emotional or cognitive 'effects' the discourse has on readers or speakers). Nevertheless, it is often impossible to ignore completely the issue of cognition or agency (i.e., speakers as 'free agents', individuals with private motives). Edwards (1997) discusses this in relation to the practice of speakers 'fishing' for information, where language seems to be a tool for personal gain. His advice is to suspend judgement on private motives, not because it is wrong but because it is impossible given the nature of the data and the research. Nevertheless, many discourse analysts are uncomfortable with such a position. As Madill and Doherty (1994) argue, if analysts ignore such matters, readers may simply fill the gap with their own speculations about mental states.

Criticality and application

One of the most important debates within discourse analysis concerns the ideological position of the analyst. Many versions of this debate are similar to the realism vs. relativism debate covered in Chapter 12; simply, Loughborough-style discourse analysts argue from a relativist perspective – where language is the primary medium – while Foucauldian-inspired discourse analysts such as Ian Parker (1992) argue from a 'critical realist' perspective from which discourses are seen as constructing 'real' objects. Parker uses as an example the British National Health Service; alternatively, think of UFOs as 'objects' that you and I can describe in detail without (necessarily) ever having seen one.

In addition, there is a form of discourse analysis that has been called 'critical discourse analysis'. This is research conducted from an explicit ideological perspective – as van Dijk (1993: 249) puts it, 'the point of critical discourse analysis is to take a position'. Specifically, this form of research investigates the exercise of social power by elites and institutions, and the way in which language is used to achieve ideological effects. Not surprisingly, much of this research has focused on media texts (e.g., Fairclough 1995).

Critical discourse analysis differs from the Foucauldian variety largely because its focus is very much on language use (its roots are in 'critical linguistics'), and from authors such as Edwards and Potter (1992) because of its realist perspective. While many psychologists who use discourse analysis (particularly of the 'critical' variety) envisage explicitly political applications of their work, they have tended to follow the Foucauldian strand (see Willig 1999).

Ethical issues

One of the greatest dilemmas facing discourse analysts using interview data concerns their responsibilities towards participants. Typically, ethical concerns in psychological research relate to the data collection itself – experimental deception, informed consent and so on (see Chapter 20). While some of these concerns are also relevant in qualitative research, the use of raw data in reports, and the interpretative gloss put upon those data, are contentious issues.

In some forms of qualitative research, such as ethnography and grounded theory, it is thought to be good practice to carry out a 'member check', where the researcher allows participants to inspect the data – for purposes of reliability – and even the analysis (particularly where 'empowerment' might be a research aim). However, some topics investigated through discourse analysis make such member checks difficult to carry out without threatening to jeopardise the whole venture. One example is Wetherell and Potter's (1992) research on the racist discourse of white New Zealanders, where the authors identified various rhetorical devices that their participants used to present their 'racist' arguments as 'nonracist' or commonsensical. For example, variations on the phrase 'I'm not racist, but . . .' were often used as the preface to views which the authors regarded as explicitly racist – therefore the opening disclaimer is interpreted as an attempt to save face.

Condor (1997) raises a number of problems with this type of research. First, she argues, the researchers act in such a way as to create a particular subject position for their participants (i.e., as racists desperately attempting to save face), which is implicitly contrasted with their own subject position (i.e., as sensitive nonracist academics exposing oppressive practices). The participants (who may be trying hard to avoid expressing objectionable views within their own idiom) are thus overruled. The authors 'inform the reader explicitly how they should interpret quotations from [these] interviews . . . furthermore, in order to access these snippets of stories, readers must first open a book with the word "RACISM" emblazoned in large letters on the cover' (Condor 1997: 125).

Such conflicts of interest certainly raise the importance of subjectivity in discourse research. Authors are often advised (see Chapter 15) to state their theoretical perspective at the outset of a report as a means of countering accusations of bias (another disclaimer of sorts). Nevertheless, such disclaimers may fail to appease participants whose words are interpreted as offensive. Does this mean that such research is unethical, or are there certain research findings which are so important that we should waive normal ethical conventions in the interest of public awareness? It is hard to say – although we await the first instance of a writ being served against a discourse analyst whose interpretation is deemed slanderous!

Relation between discourse analysis and grounded theory

I conclude this chapter by linking it with the previous one, since one of the most frequent complaints by students in qualitative research is that they cannot tell the difference between discourse analysis and grounded theory, and one of the most common errors by students when producing qualitative work is that they blend the two approaches inappropriately.

Several authors agree that there should not necessarily be a sharp divide between the two approaches. Pidgeon (1996), for example, sees the constructionist version of grounded theory as quite similar in its aims to discourse analysis, and sees no reason why the two approaches should not evolve alongside each other. Others have explicitly drawn on the two approaches simultaneously in their research. Perhaps the best example is Willott and Griffin's (1997) study of unemployment and masculinities.

The authors initially coded their data (focus group interviews with unemployed men) using 31 'in vivo' themes taken from the participants' language, such as references to 'going out'. They then identified different ways in which these themes were talked about; 'going out' was talked about in 17 different ways, from 'pub means going out properly to a man' to 'men go out and women stay at home' (1997: 112). They then mapped out the relationships between these themes in order to produce a hierarchical structure of categories, by taking each theme in turn and seeing if the ways in which it was talked about could be applied to the next theme, and so on. Rather than ending up with a core category, the authors ended up with two dominant categories which they labelled 'discourses': 'domestic provision and public consumption' and 'unemployment and disempowerment'.

Summary

Discourse analysis has been one of the most exciting fields in psychology in the decade before this book was written. I hope I have given readers enough encouragement in this chapter to give the technique a try. The different 'versions' of discourse analysis that are found in the literature at present often confuse beginners, so here I have attempted to synthesise the major approaches without compromising the underlying philosophy of either. I have perhaps said less about collecting data than some readers would like; the answer is that there are so many different approaches that it would be hard to narrow them down into a paragraph, so you are advised to consult one of the specialist texts cited in this chapter if you need more information.

14 Other qualitative approaches

I have concentrated on grounded theory and discourse analysis because they are the most widely taught, and most widely known, qualitative approaches within mainstream psychology at present. In this chapter I will discuss briefly a few other approaches which make occasional appearances in the psychological literature, and which may yet become more popular.

QUALITATIVE CONTENT ANALYSIS

Typically, content analysis in psychological research is carried out to prepare data for statistical analysis, and I will discuss this usage of the method in Chapter 16. It has been less popular in qualitative research, possibly because it is seen as a less rigorous method intellectually than more sophisticated techniques like discourse analysis and grounded theory – indeed, a common criticism of poor grounded theory is that the researcher has 'simply' done a content analysis. What this usually means is that the initial descriptive codes have formed the basis for the analysis, rather than the researcher going on to integrate the categories at a more abstract level.

There are occasions, however, when a 'simple' descriptive analysis is the required outcome of the research. Whereas previous theory or research on a topic is not consulted until near the end of a grounded theory study, it often forms the basis for a content analysis, by providing the categories that the researcher will use. An example could be Livingstone and Green's (1986) study of gender portrayals in UK television advertising, where an important consideration was how to group together different types of ads (is it enough to create a category such as 'advertisements for alcohol', or do you need to break this down into beers, wine, spirits, and so on).

Content analysis has a fairly long history in social science research, particularly in media and communications. Berelson (1952) was the first author to devise a systematic method for this area, which involved exhaustive coding of verbal and visual data for statistical treatment, with the emphasis firmly on objectivity. Later writing on the topic has relaxed some of Berelson's demands, although still recommending quantitative analysis of the data.

Even where content analyses include much qualitative detail, frequency counts may be published. Recently, however, a number of qualitative researchers have re-evaluated the approach as a qualitative method (Thomas 1994; Berg 1995), and the availability of computer software for use with qualitative data (see Chapter 12) may well make content analysis an increasingly popular option.

Because there are so many different possible uses of qualitative content analysis, depending on the theoretical rationale and the nature of the data, the best way to describe it may be to examine two examples from the psychological literature, one from feminist psychology and the other from health psychology.

Chatham-Carpenter and DeFrancisco (1998): women and self-esteem

This study is a nice example of a content analysis that has been conducted from a critical perspective – by taking a concept from traditional psychological theories of self and personhood and examining its social construction. Self-esteem has, of course, a long history within psychology, with numerous psychometric scales and other measures. The authors argue that self-esteem is a problematic concept because it is assumed to be a fixed property of the individual (hence the need for test–retest measures of reliability), and yet this approach ignores the importance of social context. The research in this area has found that men obtain significantly higher scores than women on most self-esteem measures – in the absence of any underlying biological substrate to explain this, it would seem that the social environment (sexism in particular) may explain the difference.

Chatham-Carpenter and DeFrancisco decided to examine what self-esteem actually *means* for women, in order to suggest alternative approaches to studying it. With a diverse range of women of different age and ethnic backgrounds 59 one-to-one interviews were conducted by four interviewers. Then the authors coded half of the data set in terms of the answers to two broad questions: a) how did the interviewee *define* self-esteem; and b) what characteristics did she associate with *high* self-esteem? The codes were then applied to the remaining data. Thirty categories were initially drawn up; these were refined to twelve, and later refined further, to three 'overarching themes'. Finally, comments were compared between interviewees according to ethnicity, age, and life experience to identify any further connections within the data.

The three overarching themes all related to the women's conception of high self-esteem: first, not being afraid to voice an opinion; second, an association with a strong 'inner self'; and third, concern and respect for others (i.e., no need to exploit others). A clear theme that emerged from the data in terms of age difference was that younger participants found it easier to supply definitions of self-esteem. Older participants regarded it as a modern, or 'trendy' concept, and one in particular summed up the social constructionist perspective on self-esteem in a nutshell by stating, 'that word wasn't in the dictionary and so it wasn't one of your worries' (ibid. 1998: 472).

This research is useful because it identifies the need for self-esteem to be rooted in a cultural and/or social context; we could regard it as a first step in 'deconstructing' the concept.

Yardley and Beech (1998): deconstructing dizziness

On the face of it, Chatham-Carpenter and DeFrancisco's version of content analysis sounds remarkably like grounded theory, the only difference being that the 'theory' was driven by ideological (feminist) concerns, and by established psychological theory (on self-esteem). Yardley and Beech offer a somewhat different treatment, albeit one which derives from a similar epistemological background.

Their study examined experiences of dizziness in a sample of 25 women and 10 men who had consulted a doctor on account of vertigo. Again the authors began their analysis by sorting statements on the basis of two responses: a) how the person coped with dizziness; and b) what they perceived as the cause of their dizziness. In their study, however, they treated these as two broad categories, which they proceeded to break down into subcategories, based on frequency counts – effectively grounded theory in reverse. The next stage was to 'deconstruct' the accounts of dizziness in terms of the function and effect of the discourses on which the participants drew. Ultimately, the broad finding of the study was that the language of Western medicine creates something of a dilemma for sufferers: powerlessness in the face of physical 'facts' that only a qualified doctor can treat; yet capable of exerting 'mind over matter'. This leads other people to pose the question: are they 'real' victims, or 'poor copers'?

This use of content analysis sets it up as quite a different method from the quantitative variety. In one respect, it is simply a technique that has been borrowed here, to be used in conjunction with other borrowed techniques (discourse analysis, deconstructionism). One might ask: why not just use discourse analysis from the outset? Perhaps a clue lies in the author's use of inter-rater reliability, 'as a useful way to collaboratively refine classifications and to make explicit coding decisions' (ibid. 1998: 316). Given the authors' critical realist approach, this attention to representativeness and objectivity seems appropriate, in conjunction with their use of codes drawn from traditional psychological theories of health and illness.

Conversation analysis

Conversation analysis (CA) has already been tackled, in the previous chapter, as a major influence on discourse analysis. Since the latter has become such a broad church, and has incorporated perspectives that are not compatible with some of the principles of CA and ethnomethodology, there seems to be something of a revival of interest in psychology in 'pure' CA (see the debate between Schegloff and Billig in the 1999 volume of the journal *Discourse & Society*).

CA initially grew out of a number of different traditions in 1960s sociology in California. Goffman's work on social interaction, Garfinkel's practice of *ethnomethodology* (common-sense reasoning in everyday activity), and Sacks' interest in the sequential organisation of talk, merged to form a 'new paradigm' of sociological research. This later split into two distinct strands – the analysis of talk in institutional settings such as law courts, and 'pure' CA, looking at turn-taking and other micro-level features of talk. In addition to the study of talk, conversational analytic method has been applied to other data, such as video footage (e.g., Heath 1997).

In psychology, CA has been highly influential in the development of discourse analysis in the 'Loughborough tradition', where researchers from diverse backgrounds have applied its principles to a number of psychological topics. However, something of a schism has opened up within discourse research in psychology between researchers with a relativist orientation such as Edwards and Potter (1992), and those from a critical realist tradition (e.g., Parker 1992). Other researchers within the Loughborough school have also queried the relativist nature of CA and its ability to tackle topics of ideological concern, such as feminist issues (Billig 1999). In many respects, the adoption of 'pure' CA principles raises questions about whether or not they are compatible with psychology as a discipline, since they explicitly reject all speculation about mental or cognitive processes, or the study of the individual across different social and discursive contexts.

Nevertheless, the use of CA methods has produced many important insights about taken-for-granted aspects of traditional psychological theory. A good example of this is in the work of Charles Antaki and colleagues on the discursive construction of identity, discussed in more detail below. Whether or not this type of analysis is really 'doing psychology' may be irrelevant: its importance is that it flags up problem areas within the discipline and suggests alternative ways of developing psychological theory.

Much of the data used in CA research comes from databases of tape-recorded interviews and conversations, usually referred to as 'naturally occurring' data because they are not obtained as part of an explicit research interview. This lends the research greater ecological validity, and moves away from the subjectivity of much qualitative research, although (as will be discussed in the next chapter) this is a matter of much controversy within the field. For similar reasons, a thorough transcription of the data is required for CA, employing all the symbols used in the Jefferson system (see Chapter 13 and Appendix 2).

For a detailed account of the stages in conducting CA research, ten Have (1999) is an excellent source. He suggests that an analysis would begin by selecting a single fragment of data (typically about 50–100 lines of transcript) and examining it for four types of interactional organisation:

- *Turn-taking*: How is this managed by speakers? Do speakers 'select' one another, or do they 'self-select'?
- *Sequential organisation*: study of 'adjacency pairs' such as question-and-answer routines and violations.
- *Repair*: Where one speaker attempts to guess, or fill in, another's contribution, or requests clarity.
- *Turn design*: The 'packaging' of turns in order to 'shape' the interaction (e.g., to produce a preferred response).

In the next stage of the analysis, the researcher then applies these findings to multiple data fragments in order to build up an overall picture, or story, of the interaction that is taking place. The analysis then proceeds to a more abstract level which draws on methods such as deviant (negative) case analysis and theoretical sampling, which we encountered in grounded theory (Chapter 12). The eventual aim of CA very much depends on whether you are interested in the data as a representative sample of everyday talk-in-interaction, or whether you want to develop theory within a specific context (e.g., forensic psychology or clinical interviews). An example from the psychological literature of the former type of analysis is described below.

Antaki et al. (1996): shifting identities in talk

Like the two examples of content analysis discussed earlier in this chapter, this study takes a well-established psychological topic – social identity – and raises problems with its assumed status as a concrete, universal phenomenon. Social identity, like self-esteem, has typically been seen as a fixed quality of an individual, part of a coherent self-concept that is partly dependent on group membership, and ultimately measurable using psychometric scales.

Antaki *et al.* discuss the notion of identity within a short conversation taken from a large corpus of 'natural English conversation' recorded and transcribed by Norwegian linguists in the 1970s. The speakers in this interaction are three young professional people who are discussing their occupational and philosophical interests. Most of the conversation in the analysis is focused on 'Charly', a male doctor, who is discussing various aspects of his medical training. As a young practitioner, he is still learning his trade and is not fully qualified, thereby raising something of an identity dilemma (given the implications of identifying oneself as either a 'doctor' or a 'student').

The authors' analysis of this extract of talk demonstrates how Charly's identity fluctuates through the course of the conversation. For much of the time he has set up an identity for himself as a 'successful-if-cynical-medical-student', an identity that works well given the setting (i.e., with two non-medics). However, as the talk turns more to specific topics in medicine that are personally salient for Charly, his identity 'footing' becomes less certain. For a start, in trying to distinguish between a 'sign' and a 'symptom', he says:[1]

> Yes we don't use {s} the same I mean in medicine a symptom is something the [kerm] patient complains of . . . the sign is something the

Charly starts off by referring to medical experts as 'we', but swiftly changes to a passive form of voice in order to make his point (either because he does not want to sound pompous or immodest, or because the objective, factual tone is more convincing, but these motivational considerations are usually suppressed in CA which prefers to locate the 'action' within the talk itself and not in the speakers' heads).

Shortly afterwards, Charly unapologetically uses the 'we' to refer to doctors:

> (...) I mean we write down symptoms . signs you know I mean they're they're they're so different .

But probably the most emphatic declaration of his identity as a doctor comes when he is forced to draw a distinction between personal and professional judgement:

> JOEL   your distinction between sign and symptom . {wi} which
>   I find fascinating
> CHARLY it's not *my* distinction [it's it's
> JOEL   [no . all right – – erm (...)

In making this distinction, Charly clearly aligns himself with the medical profession, thus drawing a line between himself and the other speakers (a teacher and an academic).

Throughout this paper, the authors demonstrate how Charly's identity positions progress from 'just qualified' through to 'doctor' not in a series of tactical moves, but simply as the result of accomplishing the business of the conversation. This is the value of CA in psychology, setting up problems for traditional notions of fixed aspects of selfhood open to measurement, thus making a strong point for the greater use of tightly analysed interview data in research.

ETHNOGRAPHY

I discussed those last two approaches in some detail because they have become increasingly popular in the psychological literature. Alas the same cannot be said for ethnographic research, and there are numerous reasons why this is the case. For a start, ethnography requires an entirely different approach to research from the methods usually employed in psychology – both in terms of timescale and data collection – and as such is difficult to teach to students in the context of research methods at undergraduate level. However it is probably the oldest and most widely used approach within qualitative research, and merits some attention. Furthermore, as qualitative methods become more popular with psychologists, the ethnographic approach will undoubtedly gain more followers within the discipline.

Ethnography's origins lie in the disciplines of anthropology and sociology, where a typical field study for an anthropologist might involve the researcher travelling well away from his or her institution and living in the field setting for many months or even years. Some of the first ethnographic studies in the early twentieth century (notably the work of Malinowski), were carried out by Western academics in the highlands of New Guinea and some of the islands (such as the Trobriands) between New Guinea and northern Australia. The emphasis in those early studies was, however, quite different from many of today's studies; much of the data collection, for example, was closer to that of geology or natural history, gathering samples of clothing or sacred objects for later scrutiny and speculation in the laboratory. Today, ethnographic research is just as likely to be carried out in a setting within the researcher's own geographical environment, so long as s/he enters that environment with the consent of the participants and with clear research aims.

Anthropologists use ethnography in order to provide what Clifford Geertz (1973) referred to as 'thick description' of the ways in which societies operate. In the course they often discover things about psychology too. Geertz's research found that concepts such as privacy, and the individual self, differed enormously between the US and Far Eastern cultures such as Bali and Java. There is no reason why an anthropologist should have made these findings rather than a cross-cultural psychologist, except that the practice of visiting different societies and conducting qualitative fieldwork has not traditionally been part of psychology's methodology.[2]

Closer to home, there is clearly a role for ethnography in understanding behaviour in specific contexts. This is most apparent in areas such as health and clinical psychology, and occupational psychology, where the object of the study is an institution and the aim is to see how people adapt to changing conditions within that institution (such as a switch in a company from single offices to open plan offices). Depending on the research question, it is also legitimate to carry out fieldwork in other areas, such as nightclubs, pubs, and even private homes, although the smaller the social unit the greater the likelihood of *reactivity* to the researcher (i.e., the researcher's presence has a substantial effect on behaviour). A famous example of local ethnographic research is the study of football hooligans by Marsh *et al.* (1978).

Locating the field

Most ethnographers are fiercely opposed to the idea of reducing their methods to a set of simple steps. They argue that the richness of the data produced by ethnography would be impossible to obtain if researchers were following a rigid procedure. This makes it very frustrating for students who are new to the subject. However, there are plenty of guides to carrying out an ethnographic study; Hammersley and Atkinson (1983) is the most well-known, and is readable and straightforward; see also Fetterman (1989) for a step-by-step guide, and Hobbs and May (1993) for some examples of ethnographic studies.

Two essential considerations in ethnography are *setting* and *access*. The first things to think about are: where you are going to carry out your research, who you are going to research, and how you will go about gaining access to the setting and participants. The setting that you choose may almost certainly be dictated by the research question. If you wish to observe interaction in a casino, then you will not answer your question by placing yourself in a betting shop. The next step is to gain access to your setting. The important consideration here is the role of *gatekeepers*. If you have chosen to study an elite casino, where access is restricted to members, you will need to negotiate access via the management. However, this may cause problems: perhaps the manager of the casino does not like the idea of a psychologist working on the premises, possibly disturbing customers; perhaps this means that access is only granted if you agree not to speak to gamblers (which would severely restrict data collection). If the gambling environment is illegal, there will be concerns about the use of the data – will the establishment be guaranteed anonymity? This is not always such a simple matter as it seems: often places can be easily identified from certain details in the report.

An alternative way of gaining access is to carry out *covert* investigation. Here the problem is one of ethical concerns regarding the uses of deception. Is it fair to your participants to pretend to be a fellow mental health service user, a fellow gambler, or a fellow political activist? There is no easy solution to this problem. Bulmer (1982) contains a number of examples where researchers justified the risk of 'going undercover' on ideological grounds: for example, it was necessary to infiltrate the ranks of the fascist UK organisation The National Front because of the political implications of their activities. Approaching gatekeepers as a sociologist may not have met with much success on that occasion!

One need not practise deception in order to bypass gatekeepers in gaining access to participants. Much research on gang culture and football hooliganism in the 1960s and 1970s was initiated by researchers striking up acquaintances with gang members and other individuals by 'hanging out' in the research setting on enough occasions for the participants to feel comfortable with their company and to trust them. Very often all it takes is a single breakthrough with one individual for a 'snowball' effect to be set in motion, where the researcher is gradually introduced to a variety of important contacts. For a very readable non-academic account of this type of research, the sociologist Laurie Taylor's book about his criminological research with former convict-turned-academic John McVicar (Taylor 1984) is an excellent source.

Once you have gained access to setting and participants, it is still important to maintain good relations with your contacts (otherwise known as *field relations*). This is particularly true when you have gained access through mingling with participants rather than through official gatekeepers (although these need to be kept 'sweet' too). It is no good striking up a working relationship with a petty criminal only to drop them once you have struck up relationships with the big shots you are really interested in. If your research involves illicit activity, staying on the right side of the participants could be a matter of life and death!

Data collection

Probably the hardest aspect of ethnography for psychologists to grasp is the nature of data collection. Most research methods are largely designed to produce an identifiable data set, be it a table of numerical values or an interview transcript. Both these types of data may be obtained during the course of an ethnographic study, but only as supplementary to the notes you have been taking during the investigation. These are referred to as *fieldnotes*.

A typical ethnographer will record his or her fieldnotes using either notebooks or, more recently, a dictaphone. They consist of observations made while the researcher is 'in the field', either watching, or talking with, participants, which contain sufficient detail for the researcher to use as data in analysing the results of the study. Fieldnotes may be taken as events are occurring: these are sometimes referred to as 'scratch notes', in that they are scribbled down in a notebook while still fresh in the researcher's memory, usually while 'in the field'. Sometimes this needs to be done surreptitiously, in a toilet or other place on the periphery of the research environment.

A second set of fieldnotes may be taken in the form of a day-to-day diary. This is normally done when one is in the research setting for a long period – for example, when studying a culture at a distance from the researcher's normal environment. Like memos, the diary serves as a useful 'aide memoire' when it comes to writing the report, but it also provides rich information about the researcher's feelings and experiences as they happen, which enables the writer to produce a full account of the research.

Along with fieldnotes and interview material, ethnographers often make use of archive data: these may consist of any printed material that is relevant to the research (local newsletters or handbills, for example). How much of this you collect, or include in your analysis, will be determined exclusively by the nature of the study.

An example of ethnographic research with relevance to psychology

May (1999): taverns and television

This can be regarded as a classic example of a local ethnographic study. Reuben May is a sociologist who at the time of the research was working in Chicago. He was interested in the way regular drinkers in a 'tavern' (bar) in Chicago used television as a tool for social interaction.

May's first task was to identify his research setting. He chose the tavern because it is regarded as a 'third place' (between work and home) where much social interaction takes place. This ties it in with other published literature examining public drinking and social interaction. He selected a tavern in a middle-class African American neighbourhood. His report contains considerable detail about the tavern (identified by the pseudonym Trena's), from the music available on the jukebox to the position of the televisions. The social mix at Trena's is of great importance, so this is discussed in some depth. May was most interested in the 'regulars', a group of around 35 mostly male customers who drink in Trena's during the day (for various reasons, the evening crowd are less interested in television).

The next part of the report describes May's access to the setting, which he negotiates by 'becoming a regular' at Trena's, drinking there three or four times a week until he is recognised by the other regulars. In order to gain the confidence of his participants, he begins by identifying a gatekeeper – in this case, the barmaid, with whom he strikes up a rapport. Gradually he begins to be regarded as a regular, although the others are aware that he is carrying out research. The study itself covered 18 months (which must have cost a fair sum in beer money!). May recorded his data using scratch notes, some of which were taken in the 'rest room' under the pretence of the call of nature.

Little attention is paid to methodology in the report, although Glaser and Strauss (1967) are cited. May's approach seems to follow the grounded theory procedure ('theoretical sampling, coding and analyzing data to generate theory' – May 1999: 78), although the remainder of the paper consists of examples of three core concepts.

* *Personalisation of television thematic content* This concept concerned the use by patrons of television themes as cues for discussion topics. For example, when watching a talk show on casual sex, two of the patrons would strike up a conversation about their experiences of one-night stands, and other patrons used this as a cue to join in.
* *Parasocial relationships* Here, viewers used their imaginary relationships with figures on television (which could be celebrities, or soap characters) as a resource for social interaction. Soap characters' morality might be discussed in such a way that enabled the speaker to demonstrate a particular moral stance.

- *Challenge, evaluation and media information*   In the same way, the life-styles of celebrities were criticised by viewers in order to elevate their own moral status. For example, the talk show host Phil Donahue is criticised because he dominates his guests on the programme. This in turn reinforces the expectations of behaviour in the tavern (i.e., not allowing an individual to dominate the conversation).

Overriding these core concepts were a number of related aspects of tavern culture that determined the way patrons watch and use television. For example, certain social norms and conventions were constantly reinforced. Being a strongly male environment there was a concern with maintaining traditional ideas of masculinity. Effeminate or ineffectual male soap characters were the butt of jokes or slights; if there is any deviation from this position, 'patrons are quickly guided back to the "appropriate" cultural position' (1999: 94).

An important feature of interaction in Trena's is the disclosure of personal information. This enables the regulars to ascribe certain identities to one another. May describes how, during an early visit, the conversation moved on to the topic of teenage girls on television. May commented on his own daughter, which established his identity as a parent; subsequently, jokes concerning patrons 'with kids' would be pushed in his direction.

This study discloses some useful findings for anyone interested in media psychology or social interaction. But it is a very good model for anyone who wishes to carry out an ethnographic study of this kind, particularly with regard to the research setting and conducting the study. One example of good practice is outlined in the report: May takes his first draft of the data back to some of the regulars to test the accuracy of their conversations (all recorded using scratch notes). This technique is known as *member validation*. The patrons are satisfied that his notes offer an accurate account (1999: 77): one even goes so far as to joke 'You put everything I said in here . . . I'm a have to get my 38 [pistol] and shoot you'!

IDIOGRAPHIC APPROACHES

In some respects, the idiographic (case study) approach is the opposite of ethnography, which is mostly concerned with societies. Indeed most qualitative research, deriving from the social sciences, has been used by psychologists in order to deflect attention away from traditional psychology's emphasis on internal cognitive processes towards social interaction. However, perhaps the oldest use of qualitative methods in psychology can be found in *phenomenology*. This is the study of personal experience, and subjective perceptions of phenomena (rather than objective 'truths' about those phenomena). For a full range of approaches to research in phenomenology, see Moustakas (1994), but here I will describe a contemporary variant that is starting to become quite widely used in psychology.

Interpretative phenomenological analysis

This technique is largely the work of Jonathan Smith and colleagues, who needed a qualitative research method that could be used to explore people's perceptions of health, illness, and other phenomena, but which did not rule out consideration of the individual, or of cognition (Smith 1996b). Interpretative phenomenological analysis (IPA) offers an approach to analysing interview data which keeps the focus on the experiences of the participant, whereas discourse analysis restricts its focus to the talk itself, preferring not to speculate about private matters. This is an important distinction, particularly in health research, since there is no other way of establishing the nature of physical illness except through objective (observational) methods, thus ruling out psychological factors altogether, except for the 'reality' produced in consultation and other practitioner–patient interaction.

IPA as a technique sounds very much like grounded theory in its application: the researcher begins by coding the interview data into descriptive themes and then abstracts these into higher-order categories, or a 'master list' of themes, potentially (though not necessarily) towards a single superordinate theme (Smith *et al.* 1999). In addition, the use of theoretical memos and diagrams is advocated for use in theory-building.

The point of departure between the two methods is that IPA may be used to examine a single case rather than attempting to build a theory that covers multiple cases (or that can be generalised beyond the data). One application of the method, as suggested by Smith *et al.* (1999) is to perform data analysis on an individual case, and then build the analysis by comparing that case with the rest of the group. Inevitably, additional themes will emerge, and then these can be referred back to the original case – the analysis effectively operating as a cyclical process.

Clearly, IPA is not compatible with the Loughborough strand of discourse analysis, since the status of cognition is so different in each method. A recent study of psychotic delusions used a combination of IPA and grounded theory (Rhodes and Jakes 2000), and IPA may well become popular outside health psychology where qualitative researchers want to retain a focus on the individual without taking the more radical route of discourse analysis and all the challenges to traditional psychological thought that it throws up.

Narrative psychology

A second method that can be used to examine case studies brings together a number of diverse approaches: narrative inquiry, 'narratology' (Murray 1995), and biographical or life story research (Wilkinson 2000). Again these approaches derive largely from phenomenology, with a strong emphasis on the subjective experience of the individual. The main focus in this case is the way that experience is ordered by the individual into a chain of causal events that is strung together as a *life narrative*, in which we make sense of our personal experiences.

Approaches to narrative psychology vary tremendously between different research traditions. The journal *Narrative Inquiry* deals with largely quantitative analyses of narrative data (in the style of quantitative content analysis), and similar approaches have become popular within relationship psychology (e.g., Vangelisti *et al.* 1999). Elsewhere, cultural psychologists have employed qualitative analysis of narratives within a more ethnographic framework, in the study of cultural identity as expressed through life history (Gone *et al.* 1999).

Crossley (2000) argues that narrative psychology is essentially a social constructionist approach in that it is rooted in the use of cultural materials – notably, story-telling traditions from fairy stories to soap operas – as a means of constructing self and identity. Like IPA, the narrative approach solves many of the problems psychologists have with discourse analysis because of the status afforded to individual subjective experience and meaning-making. Most importantly for psychology, it is the telling of our autobiographies that creates our sense of self and identity: 'our present activity only makes sense . . . in terms of a vast array of interrelated memories from times past and anticipations of and for the future' (2000: 535).

While there is already a well-established field of autobiographical memory research, it may well be that narrative inquiry is one of the fastest growing areas in a number of different fields in psychology over the next few decades. The next step may be to graft one of the systematic qualitative methods, perhaps IPA, on to the study of life history – a potentially fruitful exercise for a budding qualitative researcher.

BROAD APPROACHES

I will close this chapter by considering two approaches to research which have nothing to do with qualitative methodology in the technical sense, although for various epistemological and ideological reasons, have preferred to use qualitative approaches.

Action research

Like ethnography, action research has yet to take off in psychology on a large scale, probably because the two approaches share a research philosophy which is anathema to the way most psychological research is conducted. Both approaches tend to deal with much longer-term data collection than is traditionally the case in psychology, and, to the quantitative researcher, both may appear overly subjective. In some respects, action research goes even further against the grain than ethnography: here, not only is the researcher actively participating in the phenomenon under observation, s/he is attempting, as a primary objective of the research, to *change* that phenomenon.

The term 'action research' was first coined by Kurt Lewin in the 1940s as a means of empowering participants so that they benefited from research findings rather than simply treating them as passive 'subjects' in controlled experiments. Social scientists have since developed action research in a variety of settings from schools to the police to voluntary organisations. In psychology, the most likely areas where action research could be useful are counselling, education, occupational psychology and health psychology (Curtis *et al.* 1999). In each case one of the aims of psychological research is to effect change in participants' behaviour, and to some extent this is true of most applied research – except that action research makes the change an explicit objective rather than a happy by-product of the study.

Taylor (1994) identifies five types of action research:

- *Direct change* The purest form of action research, which makes an intervention to bring about change; for example, developing a support group for victims of sexual harassment.
- *Participatory research* This is where the aims of the study are driven by the interests of the participants; an example is Moore, Beazley and Maelzer's (1998) work with families and disability.
- *Needs assessment/prevalence* Again, participants' interests provide the focus of the research, but this is determined by the researcher on the basis of who will benefit from the intervention.
- *Evaluation research* An exploratory approach where a number of options are tried out (e.g., most effective strategies for women for dealing with unwanted sexual attention).
- *Demystification* The least direct type of action research, where simply conducting the research, and disseminating the findings (through the right channels), is enough to effect change.

Ultimately, action research derives from a realist (empiricist?) perspective, since it is oriented towards establishing cause and effect – arguably, it is a benign form of social experimentation. As a result, it is not intrinsically qualitative in nature, and may involve collecting quantitative data (through surveys, etc.) (Uzzell 2000). This raises the question of how the researcher can determine whether or not the intervention has produced the desired change. One such hypothesis-testing approach is the 'action research spiral', where different interventions are tried out until the original objectives have been met; the success of the venture is determined by participants' responses (either quantitative, such as scale data, or qualitative).

One major drawback with this type of research is that, given its fundamentally experimental nature, it is sometimes necessary to exert some degree of control over confounding variables. Real-world research has long been mindful of the 'Hawthorne effect' (the well-known phenomenon by which awareness of the experimental intervention itself brings about the change, even though it is attributed to the nature of the intervention). There is every likelihood that participants will modify their behaviour in the knowledge that they are participating in a research programme. This is where a reflexive awareness of the role of the researcher is essential, and becomes part of the research design itself.

Feminist research

Probably the area of psychology where action research has most potential for development, and is already an established approach, is in feminist psychology. This is an area of the discipline which has expanded rapidly in the last two decades, and its rise roughly parallels that of qualitative research in psychology. Like action research, feminist research has no specific commitment to qualitative methods, although for various reasons they have been preferred to quantitative approaches by the vast majority of feminist psychologists.

Burman (1994b) has argued that there are no such things as 'feminist methods', and that feminist research is characterised by a commitment to the purposes and goals of feminism, which vary according to time and context. In some situations, quantitative methods are useful; perhaps, in demonstrating inequality between men and women, or in challenging myths about issues like menstruation and its effect on performance (Sommer 1992). However, there is a tendency to reject quantitative methods in feminist psychology, seeing them as intrinsic to the male-oriented traditions of the discipline. For example, Nicolson (1995) discusses the male bias in traditional experimental psychology, where more often than not, the researcher is a man and the 'subject' a woman – a fundamental inequality which has led to the pathologisation of women.

Ussher (1999) identifies four main strands of feminist research: *empiricist* research (dedicated to revealing inequalities, often using statistical methods); *critical realist* approaches (e.g. Ussher's own work on pre-menstrual tension, which studies both material symptoms and the discursive context); *postmodernist* research (e.g., social constructionism); and *standpoint theory* (Harding 1987), an approach to research that attempts to view the world through the eyes of women, and seeks to bring about change. This is effectively the same thing as action research, except with explicitly feminist objectives – 'research for rather than on women' (Ussher 1999: 110).

Qualitative feminist psychological research appears regularly in the journal *Feminism & Psychology*, among other more mainstream journals; for an overview of research in this area, see Wilkinson (1996). What methods are best suited to feminist objectives? The answer clearly depends which version of feminism you prefer; recently, Wilkinson (2000) carried out a study of women's accounts of breast cancer that explicitly compared three qualitative approaches on the same body of data, concluding that discourse analysis was more useful in addressing women's perspectives than either content analysis or narrative/biographical analysis. Nevertheless, different techniques serve different purposes, and a multimethod approach may sometimes be the most rewarding.

Summary

I have used this chapter to give a fairly brief introduction to a number of qualitative approaches which may, or may not, become popular in psychological research over the next decade or so. Content analysis in its qualitative guise may be useful for researchers who want to make sense of a dataset without performing grounded theory or discourse analysis. Conversation analysis has become almost synonymous with some forms of discourse analysis, but has a long tradition in its own right which is worth exploring if you are interested in working closely with naturally occurring talk. Ethnography has yet to take off in psychology, but cross-cultural research is at least one field which would benefit from its contribution. Of all the methods in this chapter it is IPA and narrative analysis which show signs of the fastest adoption in psychology; IPA has been developed within psychology itself, while narrative analysis seems to offer psychologists more potential options than approaches like discourse analysis, which have caveats relating to individual psychology. Finally, action research and feminist research are covered in this chapter, largely because both approaches make considerable use of qualitative techniques, although neither can be reduced to a 'method' as such. Interested readers should consult texts that specialise in these approaches; for action research methods, see Whyte (1991) and Stringer (1996), and for a general overview of feminist research methods, see Reinharz (1992).

Notes

1 Note slightly different transcription symbols here from those outlined in Chapter 12, particularly the use of curly brackets {} around incomplete words. The authors state that they simplified the conventions in the interests of readability, so they may have been transcribed differently by the linguists.
2 Indeed, to date the field of cross-cultural psychology has been heavily dominated by psychometric approaches, and statistical designs in which 'culture' exists primarily as an independent variable. The Kashima *et al.* (1995) study described in Chapter 3 is a typical example. Such studies make valuable contributions to research, but the field as a whole would benefit from drawing on a wider range of perspectives, of which ethnography would seem to be a logical choice.

15 Reporting and evaluating qualitative research

This final chapter in Part IV contains a relatively short discussion concerning the outcomes of qualitative research, and the criteria that might allow us to evaluate a piece of qualitative work. These two issues are both very important in psychology. First, the way in which qualitative research is reported is slightly different from the standard psychological 'lab report', whose structure is based on the information produced in an experimental study with a statistical analysis. The standard lab report is typically laid out with a Method section containing subsections headed Design, Participants (or Subjects), Materials (or Apparatus) and Procedure. This is followed by a Results section and a separate Discussion.

None of this should be new to the reader of this book; indeed, this type of structure is demanded in basic psychology teaching to an extent that is often overly prescriptive. When students are confronted by the differing requirements of, say, a questionnaire or interview study, they frequently insist on using the same (in such contexts) inappropriate subsections. Therefore, the demands of reporting qualitative studies are likely to cause even more consternation for those who are dependent on the regular structure of lab reports, even more so because writing in qualitative research occupies a more central role than in objective science where the observation and the report are much more easily separated (Burman 1994b).

Second, it is vital for qualitative psychologists to defend the quality and merit of their work against criticism that qualitative research lacks rigour, fails to address issues such as reliability and validity, and is unscientific as a result (Morgan 1996, 1998). In the academic world, psychology departments are usually funded on the basis that they are 'doing science', which is an easy position to defend if your teaching and research requires expensive technical equipment for physiological and neuropsychological measurement, but qualitative psychologists' bids for scientific status need to be based on the rigour of their methods. I will try to furnish the reader with some of the arguments that have been put forward recently by qualitative researchers for evaluating research in this field, although the situation is complicated by differing objectives among qualitative researchers themselves (as you will undoubtedly have noticed in the previous chapters).

Writing the qualitative report

Chapter 22 contains many general principles for writing psychological papers. Most of these principles are relevant to qualitative as well as quantitative research, so I recommend that you read that chapter before attempting to publish your research. However there are a number of features of report writing that are of particular importance in qualitative research, which I will discuss here.

The most important difference between a qualitative report and a quantitative one is that the role of the researcher – and therefore the writer – is much more explicit in qualitative research. This is perhaps most obvious in the 'voice' of the qualitative report, where authors are encouraged to use the first person ('I' or 'we') rather than the third person ('s/he' or 'they'), and the active voice rather than the passive ('I decided to . . .' rather than 'it was decided to . . .').

Quantitative psychology generally works from the assumption that the author is a neutral voice, relaying facts obtained though systematic observation of the natural world. From this perspective, writing in the first person and the active voice is considered to weaken the degree of scientific 'authority' carried by the report. However, this tendency to overlook the human context of the research may obscure important details of the study itself, even in quantitative research. As I have suggested elsewhere, qualitative research is sometimes *more* 'scientific' than quantitative research through its acknowledgement of subjectivity, and its elaboration of the measures taken to account for it.

Use of the first person is a case in point: authors frequently refer to their own research in the third person; if I were to write 'as Giles (2000) has argued' anywhere in this book, it might initially appear authoritative, but on reflection it would seem just plain silly. As Cook (1992: 97) puts it, 'ironically, in view of their pretensions to objectivity, these habits imply a belief more in keeping with magic than with science: that a particular form of words somehow alters what happened, deleting the real agent as well as the grammatical one'.

There is an increasing awareness in mainstream psychology that the first person is more appropriate for various kinds of research report (APA publications manual 2001). At the same time, it is important not to get carried away with first person voice, to the extent where the report becomes overly casual and confessional, like a personal diary. Getting the balance right between reflexive awareness and scientific authority is a difficult skill to perfect.

Introduction

The introduction of a qualitative report is not so different from a quantitative report in that the essential information is the same: why you have chosen to research a specific topic, what other researchers have said about that topic, and how your research will contribute to the literature. The main differences concern the reasons for choosing a particular methodology, and the status of the hypothesis, or research prediction.

Qualitative researchers in psychology have needed to be much more explicit about their choice of methods than quantitative researchers, usually because they are publishing in journals whose editors may be sceptical or ignorant about qualitative methods. Therefore it is important in the introduction for you to spell out the precise nature of the research question, and why a qualitative approach (or whatever approach you are taking) is the most appropriate method of answering that question.

In much qualitative psychology, particularly research with a more 'critical' bent, the methodology is often suggested by the literature review. A glance back through some of the studies described in the previous chapters will show how many critical studies take the traditional (quantitative) literature as their starting point (e.g., Yardley and Beech in Chapter 14). Here, the justification for using qualitative methods is part of the rationale for conducting the research, and the literature review will be broadly critical of the methods used previously. It is important not to be *too* negative about the shortcomings of more traditional methodologies, unless you are writing for a critical audience (e.g., a journal like the *Annual Review of Critical Psychology*). Often such criticism is interpreted as professional disrespect and may reduce your chances of getting the report published (Fischer 1999). Respect and *agreement* are not necessarily the same thing.

One of the questions often asked by novice qualitative researchers is: what about the hypothesis? Hypotheses have a troubled history in psychology, partly due to misconceptions about the status of the null hypothesis (see Chapter 21). These have resulted in the belief that the hypothesis is a statement about relationships between quantifiable variables on which you are going to perform an inferential test. Using this definition would render hypotheses meaningless for qualitative research. But of course in most instances a hypothesis is simply a prediction about the research question that you are trying to answer, and seen in this light, would suit many types of qualitative report (obviously not grounded theory, but might be appropriate in some forms of discourse analysis). Qualitative researchers have mixed views about the term; some advocate 'hypothesis testing' as part of conducting research, others reject the term outright for its connotations with quantitative science.

Whatever your views on hypotheses, it is nonetheless important to begin your report with a clear statement about the problem that you are trying to solve. Whether this is couched in the form of a hypothesis, or as a more general research question, is up to you. The main thing is that you allow the reader to determine whether a) it is a question that your data will enable you to answer; and b) you have eventually succeeded in answering it.

Method

The method section in a qualitative report will be dictated largely by the requirements of the outlet. If you are hoping to publish in a journal that specialises in qualitative methods, you may not need to include much technical detail about the steps you have taken in conducting the study (as I point out in Chapters 12 and 13, many studies using grounded theory and discourse analysis say very little about method at all). However, mainstream psychology journals that usually publish quantitative research will require much more detail, and at times qualitative researchers feel they have to crowbar their work into an artificial structure (for an example of a discourse analysis in a mostly quantitative journal whose format seems forced and inappropriate, see Francis 1999).

If the journal guidelines state that you should present your research in the standard lab report format, then your participants section is likely to be considerably more detailed than for a quantitative study (although here again, psychologists in general are being increasingly encouraged to provide more detail). Your materials section, on the other hand, will look somewhat thin (and students often have nothing to report other than the make of the dictaphone!) unless you are analysing textual materials, in which case you will need to provide a context and sampling information. Your procedure will normally contain details about the setting, although again this will vary; an ethnographic study would require much more information than an analysis of newspaper reports. However, you might use this section to outline your coding procedures, although many researchers prefer to do this in the next section of the report.

Results/analysis

This is the section of a report that students new to qualitative research experience most difficulty in writing. In quantitative research there are usually strict conventions for reporting statistical results, and, provided you have presented descriptive statistics, reported test results and performed some basic interpretation, you cannot go too far wrong. In qualitative research, you are starting from a blank slate.

The first thing to do is to give the reader some idea of how you have gone about conducting your analysis. Again the amount of detail will vary according to the demands of the publication (or course). There are so many different ways of reporting this information that it is probably best to consult a few of the references relevant to the method you are using and the field in which you are hoping to publish before deciding on the most appropriate mode of presentation. Generally speaking, you would be expected to describe the higher-order categories, or 'discourses', that you have identified, and possibly illustrate your analysis with some form of diagram, or series of case studies.

The most striking feature of a qualitative report is the use of raw data, often in large, detailed chunks. This is essential for your analysis to be evaluated by the reader, especially where you are performing a very close reading of verbal data, such as in conversation or discourse analysis. By presenting your data in as readable a format as possible (this may require modifying the transcription conventions in the manner of Antaki *et al.*'s study in Chapter 14) you provide your reader with as much information as they need to decide whether your interpretation makes sense and addresses the research problem in a convincing manner. Even if you are not performing as detailed an analysis, you will need to provide enough detailed information to keep your reader interested; here, concrete examples and case studies are essential ways of illustrating your analysis and grounding your data in real life experiences.

Another characteristic of qualitative reports is that the results section is typically much longer than that of a quantitative report. This is due partly to the inclusion of raw data, and the fact that the data are accompanied by a detailed commentary which often needs to go beyond the study context itself (for example, if you have identified a discursive phenomenon which relates to previous research). For these reasons, many qualitative researchers prefer to bundle their results section together with their discussion in one long section headed 'Results and Discussion'. Even if retaining the overall 'lab report' structure, others prefer to avoid the term results, with its connotations of a 'mechanically processed product' (Fischer 1999: 115) in favour of 'analysis' or 'findings'.

Discussion

Whatever structure you have used to report your analysis, you will need a discussion section that relates your findings to your research question and to the previous literature on the topic. Sometimes novice qualitative researchers use the 'Results and Discussion' format as an excuse not to discuss their results, creating the feeling that nothing has been found!

The main purpose of the discussion in a qualitative report is to explain to the reader *how* your analysis has helped address your research question. This will be relatively easy if your methodology is rigorous and your explanations are meaningful. However you may also need to be honest about your research, and careful to discuss any limitations of the study, if only to ward off criticism – for example, you may wish to point out that it was not the intention of the research to produce generalisable findings. Again, these details are included for accuracy's sake as much as anything, as they would be in a quantitative study that had not included a potentially relevant variable. You might also wish to make it clear who will benefit from the findings of your research, and how.

Criteria for evaluating qualitative research

Parallel with the writing-up of qualitative research are the criteria that are required to enable the reader to evaluate the study. This is especially important for reports in mainstream psychology journals, and it is notable that in recent years a number of journals have begun to develop guidelines for the publication of qualitative research – the *British Journal of Clinical Psychology* (Elliott *et al.* 1999) and *Psychology and Health* (Yardley 2000) to name but two.

Both sets of guidelines, along with most other writings on the subject, are clear about two things. First, there is a clear need for rigorous standards of analysis and reporting that are convincing to those who are sceptical about the merits of qualitative research. One vocal critic of qualitative psychology has stated that 'I have yet to be convinced that the techniques go beyond those of good investigative journalism' (Morgan 1998: 483). While many qualitative researchers simply reject such criticisms out of hand as the result of misunderstanding, ignorance, or incompatible epistemology or worldview, they are nevertheless prevalent in mainstream psychology. Furthermore, even if qualitative psychologists simply find (or set up) other journals to publish in, as Silverman (2000) points out, we still need to convince both funding bodies and beneficiaries of our research (professional bodies, etc.) of its merits.

Second, the authors of guidelines for evaluating qualitative research are clear about the fact that 'radically different' criteria need to be employed (Henwood and Pidgeon 1992). These have led to some differences of opinion among qualitative and/or critical psychologists; indeed Reicher (2000) goes so far as to suggest that there are different 'qualitative psychologies' that themselves require radically different evaluative criteria. Most of the disagreement surrounds the archetypal scientific considerations of reliability and validity, so I will discuss these in some detail before looking at the controversies.

Reliability in qualitative research

At this point I will return to Michael Morgan, critic of qualitative psychology, and his claim that qualitative research is unscientific because of its disregard for 'replicability', the bedrock of quantitative methodology. The function of replicability is usually that the method section of a report carries sufficient detail to enable another researcher to conduct the same study using a different sample. The study should be designed so rigorously that the second researcher obtains near-identical results to the first. If this is not the case, the conclusion is drawn that, either the design of the original study was flawed in some way, or the second researcher failed to carry out the research as described, or the explanation given for the first set of results overlooked some confounding variable. Hence the need for sufficient detail in a report so that, in Morgan's (1996: 32) words, 'if [researchers] make false claims they will, sooner or later, be found out'.

The need to avoid 'falsity' of claims made in qualitative research, and the question of how other researchers would 'find them out', invokes long-running debates about the nature of truth and knowledge. Qualitative research is not in the business of establishing 'facts' about the world, however, so the worst that can be said about a claim is that lots of people disagree with it. As a result, some qualitative researchers argue that it is enough that the findings of a study 'resonate with readers' (Elliott *et al.* 1999), and are sufficiently coherent and intelligible as to make a clear impact on the literature, and suggest practical application.

Again, it is important that the report is tailored to the particular audience. Clearly the above criteria will suffice for journals which have a strong critical flavour, but may not convince editors and readers of more mainstream publications. For these outlets, it is important to ensure that there is full documentation of the research process. Such procedures are an integral part of grounded theory methodology. Other conventions to this end include the thoroughness of the transcription procedure in discourse and conversation analysis, and the inclusion of substantial chunks of raw data in results sections of reports. In addition, Henwood and Pidgeon (1992) advocate the use of a reflexive journal, or research diary, that documents each step of the project.

One objection to such detailed documentation might be that it is largely cosmetic; sure, the researcher might claim in a report that s/he kept a research diary, but how do we know? Furthermore, how representative of an interview transcript are the extracts in the report? Might the researcher not simply have waded through one transcript after another until they discovered a single instance of the phenomenon they are interested in? These criticisms are hard to refute, except that the researcher should always be willing to release such documentation on request (indeed, the same goes for quantitative data). Reicher (2000) has suggested that such information might be placed on the World Wide Web, which seems a sensible requirement for research of all kinds, although great care would be needed with regard to confidentiality and ownership of data.

Validity in qualitative research

While the reliability issue in qualitative research is relatively easy to deal with, the question of validity is more problematic. Any amount of documented data may fail to convince a sceptic who simply fails to agree with the researcher's interpretation of them; how far we go to convince the sceptics about our findings may depend on whose interests the research is intended to serve – the psychological community in general, a funding organisation, a small readership of critical psychologists, or a lay community with preconceptions about academic research and the nature of knowledge?

Perhaps the best way of tackling the validity issue is to imagine that you are preparing a research proposal to present to a funding body (see Chapter 23 for more general issues about getting research funded). The funders may well send your proposal to at least one sceptical quantitative researcher, who will need to be convinced that your findings will produce some degree of 'truth' about the phenomenon under investigation: what might you include to satisfy their demands?

One common way in which qualitative researchers press validity claims for their research is through *triangulation*, effectively the use of a variety of different perspectives on the research question. Tindall (1994) outlines four different types of triangulation that might be employed in a research project:

- *Data triangulation* This is achieved through interviewing different participants, or through carrying out interviews in different settings – or even collecting different types of archival data for a textual analysis. The Chatham-Carpenter and DeFrancisco research described in Chapter 14 is a good example of a study which takes the former approach. In their case, the objective was to see how women *in general* talk about self-esteem, so it made sense to sample as widely as possible. Another approach is 'respondent validation', or 'member checks', where the researcher returns to the participants to check if the data are accurate (especially if interviews were recorded as fieldnotes), or even if the analysis is meaningful to them (the Clegg *et al.* study in Chapter 12 used this method).
- *Investigator triangulation* Validity claims are less easily disputed if the research is carried out collaboratively. Collaborative research has plenty of advantages; it enables more data to be collected in a shorter time, it allows more ideas to be generated in analysis, and a wider range of insights to be brought to bear on the research. Even if the research is necessarily independent, such as a student project, other researchers can be involved at certain stages – initial coding for example.
- *Method triangulation* A 'multimethod' approach is often advocated in qualitative research, although this can be extremely time-consuming if one is following through complex procedures like grounded theory. Wilkinson's (2000) work on breast cancer is a good, although rare, example of a study employing three different methods on the same data.
- *Theoretical triangulation* For a thorough overview of a topic, approach it from a number of different perspectives. This might be more useful at the outset of a research project, where a multidisciplinary perspective is often a very good way of enhancing the quality of the study. Much research (quantitative in particular) suffers from being too restricted in terms of its theoretical and disciplinary focus.

Not all qualitative researchers agree that triangulation is a good means of achieving validity. Rennie (2000) argues that data triangulation often results in less coherence, since it is simply piling up yet more 'accounts', themselves open to yet more interpretations. Investigator triangulation may work against the accumulation of valuable insights where teams of researchers censor individual contributions in favour of group consensus (although 'risky shift' theory might suggest otherwise!). Silverman (2000) suggests that the best way of ensuring validity in qualitative research is to adopt a 'refutability principle' based on Popperian logic (i.e., that scientific progress is made through aiming for falsification). One way of doing this is the constant comparative analysis of grounded theory – continually checking theory against the data to ensure perfect 'fit'. Another approach, also from grounded theory, is the use of deviant case analysis (find examples that don't fit, and ask why). Negative case analysis, used by discourse analysts, serves the same purpose.

Reflexivity

If 'reliability' and 'validity' are simply too redolent of quantitative science to be acceptable as criteria for evaluating qualitative research, then it may be that the most important thing a researcher can do is to exercise reflexive awareness at each appropriate point in a study. Wilkinson (1988) suggests three ways in which this might be done:

- *Personal reflexivity*   concerns the 'voice' of the individual researcher and the awareness of the influence that they have on the research itself. This may be expressed in 'owning one's perspective' (Elliott *et al.* 1999) – an important criterion for evaluating qualitative research. Here, the researcher is expected to describe how they came to be interested in the topic of the research, and what particular biases or expert knowledge they can bring to bear on the study. For example, a feminist researcher would be expected to make her theoretical position clear at the outset of a report; this information would either indicate her sensitivity to the context (important for a feminist reader) or alert a sceptical reader to the presence of potential bias in her interpretation. Either way, it gives the reader more information they can use to evaluate the research.
- *Functional reflexivity*   concerns the role of the individual researcher in shaping the course of the study. For example, if you are carrying out an ethnographic study of house burglars you would need to describe in some detail how you negotiated access to your participants. This may require all kinds of information regarding interviews with 'gatekeepers', how you as a researcher arranged to meet the participants, what sort of things you talked about while 'in the field' and so on. Negotiating access, and maintaining good 'field relations' is such an important part of ethnographic research that it an essential part of the procedure of the study.
- *Disciplinary reflexivity*   concerns the contribution made by the individual researcher *as a psychologist* (or sociologist, or whatever). This may seem less important than the other two types, although given the status of qualitative research in psychology, it is often necessary to point out why, and how, you are challenging existing theory. The Yardley and

Beech paper (Chapter 14) is a good example of a study where the researchers' reconceptualisation of the topic (coping with dizziness) serves to empower their participants. By contrast, the authors argue, traditional psychology and medicine's treatment of the topic perhaps causes as many problems as it solves. Nevertheless, the fact that the authors are psychologists may or may not lend weight to their claims (if they were sociologists or cultural scholars, we might simply regard their arguments as typical interdisciplinary squabbling).

The reflexivity issue is one aspect of qualitative research about which there is considerably diverse opinion; to some, conversation analysts for example, it barely merits a mention; to others, for example ethnographers and action researchers, it is a key principle in reporting research. Ultimately, the value placed on reflexivity is a measure of how objective the researcher is attempting to be.

Summary

This part of the book finishes with some considerations about reporting qualitative research. A qualitative report varies somewhat in style and structure from the archetypal lab report that most (all, I suspect) psychologists have been introduced to in the early stages of their degrees, and so putting findings into print is often an anxious time for novice qualitative researchers in psychology. Ultimately the only way of learning how to write qualitative reports is to read other reports of a similar nature – otherwise it is like learning a language before visiting the country, or learning to drive before encountering other traffic. Any of the journal articles I have cited in Chapters 11–15 will be good models. You will be surprised at the variety of styles and structures, and while at first this may seem a bit bewildering, it simply demonstrates the *flexibility* of the qualitative report. The other key consideration is to pitch the report at the right level for the audience. But then this is a factor in any research writing, as I explain later on in Chapter 22.

Part V

Other approaches

I have given this section of the book the rather dull title 'other approaches' either because the methods and techniques covered do not fall easily into the categories quantitative or qualitative, or because they have a slightly problematic status. Content analysis deals with qualitative data, usually in the form of interview transcripts or other verbal texts, but the final analysis is not usually qualitative; the majority of content analyses involve sorting data into pre-existing categories, followed by some inferential testing. This does not usually consist of anything more advanced than basic chi-square, but in recent years log-linear modelling has become popular for more sophisticated analysis of categorical data. This technique could have been covered in Part II of the book along with logistic regression, since the mathematics are similar, but since its most likely use is with data derived from some form of content analysis, I decided to slip it in here. Apologies to any visiting statisticians.

In Chapter 17 I introduce an approach to research which straddles the quantitative and qualitative divide, Q methodology. An integrationist might cite the Q-sort as evidence of a quant/qual marriage, showing how the two need not be diametrically opposed. However, in practice Q-sorts are used to vastly different ends by researchers with different orientations, and so it should really be classed as a 'hybrid' method. Meta-analysis (Chapter 18) could be regarded solely as a statistical procedure for combining effect sizes from a number of completed studies, but it has evolved as a glorified literature review (traditionally, a qualitative approach to theory-building). Ultimately, this book is about methods in their application, and for this reason meta-analysis is hard to place in the other sections.

Chapter 19 looks like a bit of a ragbag, but perhaps the thing holding diary studies, photo essays and repertory grids together is the active role of the participant, who is effectively generating data for the researcher to work with. For this reason, the qualitative/quantitative distinction is less important (and, like Q-sorts, repertory grids have an established tradition of both types of analysis). Perhaps the overall message carried by this part of the book is that the quant/qual distinction is essentially a matter of the researcher's own interests, and the research tradition that s/he has chosen to work with.

16 Content analysis and log-linear models

Content analysis

Content analysis is a suitably vague term that is usually taken to mean a quantitative analysis of data which started life in qualitative form. An example could be a set of interview transcripts, or open-ended questionnaires, which were designed to collect richer information on a topic than could be yielded from closed questionnaires or scales. In either case, the researcher's orientation is quantitative; s/he will be seeking to produce a table of frequencies which may well be analysed using a statistical test appropriate for categorical data.

There are two main approaches to (quantitative) content analysis. The hypothesis-driven approach requires that you set out your codes in advance, because you are very clear about the nature of the data you are collecting. Some clinical interview schedules are designed to elicit data in this way. The alternative approach is to conduct interviews on a topic of interest and then to code the transcripts in a way similar to the 'in vivo' style of grounded theory (see Chapter 13). However the codes in this case will be numerical categories – for example, each time a particular word, topic or phrase is used, it is coded as a single occurrence of that word or phrase. You might interview two groups of people and compare the number of times they refer to a particular concept. An example of data analysed this way might be the study of 'internal state language' (Bretherton and Beeghly 1982) where mother–child talk was analysed for the number of words referring to feelings, emotions, and cognitions. The actual categories for these words would have been derived *ad hoc*, although some categories could have been predicted in advance (e.g. words like 'happy' and 'sad' would clearly be labelled 'emotion words').

One area in which content analysis is frequently used is in media psychology, where television programmes, advertisements, magazines and newspapers provide many verbal and visual data that lend themselves to numerical coding. Kaufman (1999) is an excellent example of a content analysis of men and women appearing in advertisements, where instances were counted of men and women appearing alone with or without children, or men and women appearing together with children, across a number of different types of ad and at different times of day. She ends up concluding that the so-called 'new man' of popular culture is not at all represented in adverts, since men are rarely portrayed as taking part in child care – in most cases their involvement with children is entertainment (play, dining, and so on), while the hard work is still left to the woman.

An example of content analysis from the psychological literature

Weisman et al. (1998): expressed emotion and schizophrenia

This example is a mixture of both types of content analysis in that it uses preconceived codes based on diagnostic symptoms but does not state a directional hypothesis. Expressed emotion (EE) refers to the attitude of the family towards its member with schizophrenia. High-EE homes are those where the environment is critical, hostile or 'overinvolved'. Generally, it has been found that patients who return to high-EE family environments are much more likely to relapse (i.e., require hospitalisation again) than those who return to low-EE environments.

The researchers were interested in what factors determine whether families are high- or low-EE. One possibility was that the patient's symptoms might be influential; those in high-EE environments were more likely to have negative symptoms (e.g., catatonia, flattened affect) than positive symptoms (hallucinations, thought disorder). The reason for this, they suggested, was that family members are more likely to attribute positive symptoms to (external) factors beyond the patient's control, while blaming negative symptoms on (internal) dispositional factors.

The data in this study had been collected some years earlier by means of a standard semistructured interview, the Camberwell Family Interview (Vaughn and Leff 1976). This is an interview in which relatives of the person with schizophrenia are asked questions about attitudes and experiences of that person's illness. In this study, forty people were interviewed, each one being a relative of a different patient. Using a coding scheme devised by one of the authors in an earlier paper, the interviewees were classified as either high-EE or low-EE, depending on the number of critical or hostile comments s/he had made in the interview.

Then a 'trained coder' extracted all the instances from the interviews of critical comments. A second trained coder then sorted each comment into one of the seven categories listed in Table 16.1. The categories in the analysis were not *ad hoc* ones created by the researchers during coding: they were taken from sources such as the DSM-IV (Diagnostic and Statistical Manual of Mental Disorders), and published scales for assessing positive and negative symptoms of schizophrenia. (This is an important contrast with qualitative interview analysis, where categories are determined from the data set itself.) For inter-rater reliability, 10 of the interview transcripts were coded

Table 16.1 Descriptive statistics of criticisms by symptom-behavioural category

Symptom-behavioural category	Mean	SD
Enduring personality traits (e.g., stubbornness)	2.05	2.42
Negative symptoms (e.g., blunted affect)	1.70	1.85
Other nonsymptomatic behaviours (e.g., patient's vocational choice)	0.97	1.17
Other symptoms (e.g., obsessive-compulsive behaviour)	0.81	1.13
Anti-social behaviour (e.g., stealing)	0.32	0.71
Positive symptoms (e.g., delusions)	0.30	0.74
Substance abuse (e.g., alcohol, drugs)	0.16	0.44

by four trained undergraduate coders along with one of the authors. Kappa coefficients (see Chapter 10) were generally in the range of 0.79 to 0.88.

As predicted, most critical comments concerned negative rather than positive symptoms. An unrelated t-test was conducted on the means which found this difference to be significant ($t(36) = 4.15$, $p < 0.001$). It was also found that high-EE relatives criticised negative symptoms more frequently than low-EE relatives ($t(35) = 2.67$, $p < 0.05$), and this was particularly true of personality characteristics. These findings, and a further analysis of the interview data, suggested that a crucial factor was the degree of control the patient was perceived to have over his or her symptoms. Positive symptoms (such as hallucinations) were seen as beyond the patient's control, while negative ones, and enduring personality characteristics, were seen as things that the patient could control if s/he so desired.

LOG-LINEAR ANALYSIS

Underlying principles

Usually, content analysis produces categorical data which lend themselves to nonparametric tests such as the chi-square test of independence. In fact, the Weisman *et al.* data reported above could well have been tackled using a two-way contingency table (high-/low-EE relatives, and positive/negative symptoms). For this reason, I shall now elaborate on a technique that has become increasingly popular for analysing more advanced sets of categorical data – *log-linear analysis*.

Many of the features of log-linear analysis will be familiar to experienced statisticians. First, the terminology, and overall concept, are similar to that of factorial ANOVA (factors, main effects, interactions). Second, the modelling procedure resembles that of SEM covered in Chapter 7, notably the search for the best-fitting model. Third, the use of logarithms, and odds ratios, relates back to logistic regression (Chapter 6), another technique concerned with categorical variables.

Let us imagine the Weisman *et al.* data set could be transformed into frequency counts, to give us the following 2 × 2 table (Table 16.2).

Table 16.2 Two-way contingency table for symptom vs. relative data

Relatives	Symptoms		Totals
	Positive	Negative	
High-EE	20	40	60
Low-EE	10	15	25
Totals	30	55	85

A chi-square test on this data would be carried out in order to discover whether or not the two factors (symptom and relative) were independent of each other. If this was not the case, the χ^2 value would be high, and the *p* value would be low, indicating that the factors are related in some way. This is very similar to the process of studying interaction effects in factorial ANOVA designs. We would calculate it by estimating the expected frequencies for each cell, then using the standard formula

$$\chi^2 = \Sigma \frac{(O - E)^2}{E}$$

to work out how far the observed values deviate from these. The higher the deviation, the higher χ^2, and the worse the fit of the expected values to the data. We would find, in fact, that the χ^2 value is far from significant, and therefore the factors are independent – more negative symptoms than positive symptoms are criticised regardless of the EE status of the relatives.

The chi-square test gives us enough information about our data when there are only two factors involved. Suppose, however, we were to add a third factor, the socio-economic status of the relatives, so that we have a three-way contingency table (Table 16.3).

Table 16.3 Three-way contingency table for symptom vs. relative vs. status data

Relatives	SES	Symptoms		Totals
		Positive	Negative	
High-EE	Low	10	30	40
	High	10	10	20
Low-EE	Low	5	7	12
	High	5	8	13
Totals		30	55	85

This new information lends a different appearance to our data. It looks as though there is a relationship between socio-economic status and the tendency for high-EE relatives to criticise negative symptoms. In short, the effect of symptom disappears for the high status, high-EE families. A chi-square test would not allow us to interpret the result in this way, however, so we need a more sophisticated test, which is where log-linear analysis comes in.

The most fundamental difference between chi-square and log-linear analysis, certainly from the perspective of calculation, is in the use of natural logarithms instead of observed frequencies. We begin our example above by transforming our data into logs in order to begin the analysis. We would end up with the values shown in Table 16.4.

Table 16.4 Three-way contingency table with natural logarithms of the observed frequencies

SES	Relatives	Symptoms		Totals
		Positive	*Negative*	
Low	High-EE	2.3	3.4	2.8
High		2.3	2.3	2.3
Low	Low-EE	1.6	1.9	1.8
High		1.6	2.1	1.8
Totals		1.9	2.4	2.2

Note: Values in the 'totals' cells are the mean logs.

The transformation to logs has the effect of turning our nominal data into a set of linear values resembling interval data in that the values are relative to each other (i.e., measured on the same scale). This enables us to perform the same sort of analysis on our data that would be carried out when parametric assumptions are met.

The next step in the process requires the formulation of a series of *models* that can be tested against the data in the table. These models are a series of expressions similar to the equations used in multiple regression. They predict certain patterns of association in the expected frequencies and we are interested in models that deviate from the estimated expected frequencies. However, because of the number of factors (and therefore the number of possible main effects and interactions) involved, we need to be very precise in our model *specification.*

Models are usually expressed in a formal way; typically, there is a hierarchy of models which can be set out like the rows of the ANOVA table. For the above example, let symptom = S, relative = R, and socio-economic status = O. The symbol $\bigcirc$ stands for the overall mean (of all the logs in the table), and $\bullet$ refers to the parameter for the respective factor or interaction.

Model 1: $\bigcirc$
Model 2: $\bigcirc + \bullet^S$
Model 3: $\bigcirc + \bullet^S + \bullet^R$
Model 4: $\bigcirc + \bullet^S + \bullet^R + \bullet^O$
Model 5: $\bigcirc + \bullet^S + \bullet^R + \bullet^O + \bullet^{SR}$
Model 6: $\bigcirc + \bullet^S + \bullet^R + \bullet^O + \bullet^{SR} + \bullet^{SO}$
Model 7: $\bigcirc + \bullet^S + \bullet^R + \bullet^O + \bullet^{SR} + \bullet^{SO} + \bullet^{RO}$
Model 8: $\bigcirc + \bullet^S + \bullet^R + \bullet^O + \bullet^{SR} + \bullet^{SO} + \bullet^{RO} + \bullet^{SRO}$

The parameter values ($\bullet$) are obtained by an iterative process which you can comfortably leave to the computer. However, it is important to understand what each model is actually specifying, to enable you to interpret the results.

Model 1 consists solely of the grand mean, which is clearly never likely to be the case, since it would require all cells to have equal values. Model 2 estimates the expected frequencies when there is only a main effect of symptom (e.g., a disproportionate number of negative symptoms are criticised), but no effect of relative or status. Model 3 estimates the expected frequencies where symptom and relative both display effects, but independently (rather like the two-way table discussed earlier). Model 5 estimates main effects for all three factors plus an interaction between symptom and relative. Model 7 estimates main effects for all factors and all possible two-way interactions, while Model 8 estimates all main effects and interactions in the data. This last model is referred to as the *saturated model*, and always fits the data perfectly.

The task now is to decide which model provides the best description of the observed values. In order to find out, we need to carry out a test of fit. This is not the chi-square test of independence, but the *likelihood ratio* (usually expressed as χ^2, but sometimes as G^2).[1] This yields a value for each model which is then tested for significance. Table 16.5 contains the likelihood ratios and significance levels for our eight models.

Table 16.5 Likelihood ratios for the three-way symptom vs. relative vs. status table

Model	Likelihood ratio (χ^2)	p
1	–	1.00
2	1.98	0.92
3	0.63	0.99
4	0.51	0.97
5	0.48	0.92
6	0.37	0.83
7	0.19	0.66
8	0.00	0.00

Remember, as from previous modelling techniques, that you are looking for non-significant values as indicators of good fit. It is through this process that we can begin to select the best-fitting model to explain our data. Some authors argue that you should choose the most parsimonious (i.e., simplest) model that fits the data, in which case Model 3 (which just predicts main effects for two of the factors) looks to be the best bet. However, since we are interested in interactions, we clearly do not need to be so conservative.

Following from this, we can draw a distinction between *symmetrical* and *asymmetrical* designs. Symmetrical designs are ones in which we are not making any prediction about the direction of the effects, rather like a 2-tailed hypothesis. Where this is the case, we need to treat all the factors as dependent variables. An asymmetrical design is much more common, however, because we usually have some expectations about relationships between the factors. Here you would expect one or more factors to explain differences in other factors. In our example, symptom might be seen as a *response* variable (roughly equivalent to a dependent variable) while the other factors are *explanatory* variables (roughly equivalent to independent variables). The nature of the design may dictate which effects we test; if, for example, we had an experimental design with two between-subjects explanatory variables, we would not be interested in the interaction of these variables.

With very large tables (four-way, five-way and so on), it is much simpler to specify in advance the effects we are looking for. One way of doing this is through a stepwise procedure similar to that in multiple regression, where we add or delete effects according to the significance level. SPSS does this in a backward fashion, testing the maximum interaction first, then deleting any effects which only explain small changes, until all the effects left are significant.

Other issues in log-linear analysis

Sample size

The issue of sample size is important in log-linear analysis just as it is for most statistical techniques. The main difference is that our 'sample' does not always consist of people so much as observations (instances of a certain word, for example, or, in the above example, criticised symptoms). Therefore, unlike in an experimental design, we may find ourselves left with empty cells, where we failed to observe a particular combination of factor levels. In these cases, it is sometimes better to collapse across categories, which has the effect of increasing the power of the test. Likelihood estimation is based on the assumption that we have a large sample; some authors recommend that we should aim for a sample size of at least 4 or 5 times the number of cells in the table.

Further analysis

Where there are more than two levels of a factor, a simple main effect or interaction does not give us any information as to which factor levels are implicated. Therefore, as with ANOVA, we need further analysis to determine differences between factor levels. These can either be planned comparisons or *post hoc* tests, where a *z* test is carried out on the logs of the observed frequencies to see if they are significantly different.

Green (1988) discusses at some length the use of log-linear models for testing *ordinal* variables. (The term 'ordinal' here is used to refer to factors whose levels are artificial cut-off points on a continuous scale, for example the factor age with three categories, 8–9, 10–11 and 12–13.) The argument is that, in converting observed frequencies to logs, we have data that can be used to study linear trends and other associations (such as cubic and quadratic trends). This is especially important in developmental psychology where we are studying changes over time.

For a two-way contingency table, a *linear row effects* model might be added to the standard hierarchy of models. This is a supplemented model which tests the likelihood of the observations increasing in a linear fashion along the row. If this model is found to produce a significant change to χ^2 for that model, then we can state that there is a significant linear association between the two factors. For a three-way (or higher) table, we would need to select two factors and specify a *linear by linear association* model, which computes the change to χ^2 for those two factors.

Two examples using log-linear analysis from the psychological literature

Both these examples come from the same issue of the *Journal of Child Psychology and Psychiatry*, which gives an indication of the popularity of log-linear analysis at the time of writing, and of its prevalence in developmental psychology.

Jenkins and Buccioni (2000): understanding of mental states in marital conflict

This study was an experiment concerning the effect of age on children's interpretation of marital conflict and the marital relationship. Children aged 5, 7 and 9 (equal numbers of boys and girls) were read a number of vignettes involving parents, and then were asked questions which tested their understanding of the characters' interaction. The first vignette concerned a boy whose mother was preventing him from playing hockey, but whose father overrules the mother and grants him permission to do so. Children were asked questions about the parents' relationship following this scenario; it was predicted that the younger children would regard the conflict as resolved because the child had been granted his wish, while older children would be able to anticipate the continued parental conflict that results from one parent siding with the child. These predictions were made on the basis of previous research into the development of the understanding of others' mental states.

The second vignette presented an argument between a mother and father over the decision whether or not to move to a new house. The participants were then asked how the conflict could be resolved. It was predicted that the older children would be more likely to suggest a resolution in which one parent was persuaded to change his or her mind. Younger children would offer 'behavioural' resolutions in which the parents simply stopped disagreeing, or one parent moved and the other stayed behind.

Following coding of the interview data, the following categorical response variables were defined:

- *Conceptions of marital conflict* What's going on here? Answers were coded either 0 (where one parent was said to be right), or 1 (where the issue was explained in terms of conflicting goals).
- *Parental resolution* How can the parents resolve their dispute? Answers were coded 0 (behavioural change) or 1 (change of mind).
- *Children's role in facilitating resolution* How could the children help their parents resolve their dispute? Answers coded as above.

This coding produced three separate contingency tables with age and gender as explanatory variables.

An initial log-linear analysis was conducted with gender as a factor. Gender failed to make a significant effect on any of the models, and was subsequently dropped from the analysis. Age, however, was found to have a significant effect on all three tables.

- *Conceptions of marital conflict* In this table, the effect of age was so strong that it was impossible to perform log-linear analysis because of empty cells in the age 9 condition (i.e., all those children gave 'conflicting goals' responses). Instead, two chi-square tests were performed, which demonstrated significant differences between the answers at all three age levels.
- *Parental resolution* Here, the best fitting model specified main effects of age, parental resolution and the interaction between them. z tests showed that, as predicted, the older children were more likely to say that a change of mind was necessary to solve the dispute. The difference was significant across all three age levels.
- *Children's roles in facilitating resolution* Here again, the best fitting model specified main effects and interaction for age and children's roles, with the older children indicating the need for a change of mind. However, the difference was only significant for the 5 and 7 year age groups,

suggesting that the realisation that children can effect a change of parental mind occurs just before the realisation that parents can change their minds by themselves!

Antrop et al. *(2000): environmental factors in ADHD*

This study was concerned with a particular theory regarding ADHD (Attention-Deficit Hyperactivity Disorder), the formidably entitled 'optimal stimulation-delay aversion hypothesis'. This theory argues that ADHD is strongly influenced by environmental factors, notably the amount of stimulation that is available. In 'stimulus-poor' environments, children with ADHD will display an increase in activity. This is particularly related to unfilled time intervals, where it is suggested the perception of passing time is different in ADHD (i.e., the interval is overestimated).

To test these ideas, an experimental situation was set up in which a child was taken into a room in order to watch a video but was then made to wait while the researcher pretended to have forgotten the tape and left the room in order to find it. A 2 × 2 independent groups factorial design was employed, where the factors were:

- *Group*   (30 children aged 6–12 with ADHD and 30 age- and gender-matched controls).
- *Condition*   (Either high-stimulation, where the child watched a different video while waiting for the researcher to return, or low-stimulation, where the time interval was unfilled).

While the researcher was out of the room, the child was observed through a one-way mirror, and a video recording was made of his or her behaviour. A pair of trained coders then watched the video and noted the occurrence of a long list of behaviours, falling into the following categories: gross motor activity (e.g., walking, running); minor motor activity (each limb movement); self-occupation (touching self or other objects, or stretching); sounds, and situation-specific behaviour (opening door or leaving room).

An ANOVA was conducted on most of these categories; however, the researchers found that not all the categories met parametric assumptions. Instead, log-linear analysis was applied to these categories. The three factors of group, condition, and behaviour category were tested using a backwards-elimination technique.

Several two-way interactions were found: for example, there was found to be an interaction between behaviour and condition for repetitive movements with objects (LR $\chi^2 = 1.542$, $p = 0.821$). A higher rate of behaviour was found in the low-stimulation condition. The same pattern was also found for 'gymnastics', non-verbal sounds, and vocalisations. A two-way interaction between behaviour and group was found for running and opening the door. For the category of non-intentional movement, two two-way interactions were found: behaviour × condition and behaviour × group. More activity was observed in the low-stimulation condition and among the ADHD children.

Notice how the three-way interaction model was not tested here. This is because, as the design was asymmetrical, group and condition were specified as explanatory variables. However, a separate analysis was performed on the low-stimulation condition data alone; this found higher activity scores for ADHD children on opening the door, running, and talk (all LR $\chi^2 = 0.000$, $p = 1.00$). Here, the saturated model provided the best fit and the most appropriate explanation.

Summary

This chapter began by discussing content analysis as primarily a quantitative method, in contrast to the qualitative version described in Chapter 14. Typically, an interview is conducted, or texts sampled, and the researcher sorts the verbal data into a set of categories that may be previously defined. The result is usually a table of frequencies, which may be analysed using chi-square tests, although most content analyses yield a lot of categories that may be beyond the reach of chi-square. This is where log-linear analysis comes in, and I have described its logic and application here. Like structural equation modelling, log-linear analysis involves the testing of several models to examine which model best 'fits' the data; this allows the researcher to conduct much more sophisticated analyses than would be possible with simple chi-square tests. Nevertheless, it must be recognised that, as with SEM, complex analyses are not necessarily superior to simple ones. Many content analyses aim for nothing more than descriptive data, and such studies can still make a valuable contribution to the research literature.

Note

1 In practice, there is rarely much difference between the chi-square statistic and the likelihood ratio. The distinction may only prove important in cases of borderline significance (where some discretion should normally be applied anyway).

17 Q methodology

Q methodology emerged from the same school of psychometrics as factor analysis, but its founder, William Stephenson, viewed it capable of answering radically different questions about the nature of psychology. After its conception in the 1930s, however, it declined in appeal for a while (not being remotely suited to behaviourism!) and has since re-emerged in two separate guises. The technique is the same in both: in the Q-sort, a method which I shall shortly describe; however, there is a distinct difference in the uses it is put to by the British school of Q methodology, who claim it as part of the 'critical' approach to psychology, and the North American school, who use Q-sorts as a standard statistical tool and correlate the data with other scales and measures.

Q methodology: the basic idea

Stephenson (1935) developed Q methodology while working alongside the likes of Spearman and Burt in Britain in the 1930s, at a time when the development of psychometric testing was starting to gain popularity along with the associated technique of factor analysis. The Spearman/Burt approach is often referred to as R methodology, after the correlation statistic that underpins most of the analyses. R methodology was, and is, mainly concerned with identifying differences between individuals from performance on a variety of scales and tests. Factor analysis is performed on the data in order to discover which tests, or items, are related to each other.

The basic idea behind Q methodology involves turning R methodology on its head, so that, rather than studying differences *between* individuals, you study patterns of response *within* individuals. This is achieved by analysing the way a person organises a selection of items, which can be statements about a topic (as in a Likert-type scale), or other stimuli, such as pictures, or a list of names. This activity is known as a Q-sort. Once a number of Q-sorts have been carried out using the same stimuli, the ratings obtained by the different sorts can be entered into the computer and factor analysis can be performed on the data. However, whereas factor analysis in R methodology groups together different measures, in Q methodology it groups together different sorts, i.e. the cases – the people who have performed the Q-sorts.

As you can imagine, this approach to data collection and analysis requires that we ask quite different questions about psychology than those tradition- ally studied by R methodologists. R methodology works on the assumption that individuals are characterised by varying quantities of different 'traits' which can be objectively measured – for example, extraversion, or intelligence. Q methodology – like personal construct theory (see Chapter 19) – deals with individuals as active organisers of reality rather than the passive recipi- ents of biology and/or environment. Therefore it is interested in the way the person perceives the world, rather than measuring the existence of hypo- thesised properties. The factor analysis, sometimes referred to as Q pattern analysis (Stainton Rogers 1995), groups together people who view the world in the same way.

The Q-sort: a worked example

A positive feature of using Q-sorts as a methodological tool is that they are generally much more fun for participants! This may be because, rather than hav- ing to select a value from a limited range of responses as in a Likert-type scale, there is an element of creativity in the sorting process (although in effect, it is just a roundabout way of assigning a rating to each item in the study).

What are the most appropriate items for a Q-sort? A typical Q-sort starts life rather like a scale in that a large pool of items needs to be selected, which will eventually be whittled down to a given number for the study itself. If those items are statements concerning a particular topic, then they should be drawn from relevant sources (focus group interviews, perhaps, or press coverage, or even existing scales and questionnaires). It is equally appropriate to use pictorial material (e.g., photographs), or lists of names (e.g., celebrities, or names of countries). Of course, the choice of stimuli depends on the research question.

The next step is to ask participants to sort the items into some form of hierarchy. This is usually done by printing each item on a separate piece of card and asking each participant to organise the cards according to a scale. If the items are statements on a particular topic on which we would expect our participants to have an opinion, such as capital punishment, then we might ask them to sort the statements into piles along a scale from −6 (most disagree) to +6 (most agree). However, some restraints are usually imposed in order to ensure that our data fall into a distribution that approaches normality. Many Q-sorts are performed using a grid that forces participants to organise all the items into a normal distribution; others are more flexible. In some studies participants are required to sort the items into a non- normal distribution; for example, Westen *et al.* (1997: 431) designed a grid resembling 'a flattened right tail of a normal distribution' based on findings from clinical ratings of the same items.

In this worked example, our participants are asked to sort nine chocolate bars (referred to as A, B, C, etc.) in order of preference, to fill the grid in Figure 17.1:

Figure 17.1 Empty grid for Q-sort example

Each participant would need to select one most preferred bar and one least preferred bar, three bars in the neutral pile and then two bars in the moderately preferred and least preferred piles. Most Q-sorts are, of course, more complex than this, using anything up to 100 items, but this example has been chosen for its convenience.

We can then get any number of participants to perform the sort. Generally speaking, it is a good idea to have more participants than items, although one of the features of Q as opposed to R methodology is that the practice of generalising from sample to population is not observed, and so the idea of 'representation' is more flexible. However, we need to tailor our sample to the research question, so let that be your guide: if your participants need expert knowledge to perform the Q-sort, then of course it is impossible to make generalisations to a lay population. If the sort simply consists of tasting chocolate bars and indicating a preference, then you might prefer to select them on number alone. For convenience in this example we will settle for a sample of nine students.

Table 17.1 lays out the sort data as you would input them to the SPSS program. You will notice immediately that the layout does not suit SPSS, where the rows are numbered automatically – this is because it is used to

Table 17.1 Data for the Q-sort worked example

Bar	Sort								
	1	2	3	4	5	6	7	8	9
A	2	2	1	2	1	0	1	−1	−2
B	1	0	1	1	2	1	−2	0	1
C	1	1	2	0	1	2	−1	0	−1
D	0	0	0	0	0	−2	2	−1	2
E	0	1	0	1	−1	−1	0	2	1
F	0	−1	−1	−1	0	0	−1	−2	0
G	−1	0	0	−2	−2	0	1	0	0
H	−1	−2	−2	0	−1	1	0	1	1
I	−2	−1	−1	−1	0	−1	0	1	−1

treating each row as a separate participant, or case, in the study. However, because in Q methodology the data matrix is 'inverted', the rows now become the items in the study (in this case, the nine different chocolate bars), while the columns represent the participants, or, more precisely, the sorts (it is perfectly legitimate for participants in this type of study to perform more than one Q-sort each[1]).

The next step is to perform a factor analysis, or pattern analysis, on the above data matrix. In relation to computer software, this is no different from performing a factor analysis on standard test data – mathematically the principle is the same, so long as you keep in mind the fact that the matrix is inverted and that the 'factors' equate to the sorts and not the items. This reversal in thinking can be quite tricky if you are an experienced factor analyst.

For this example, a principal components analysis was performed with Varimax rotation (in Q analysis the factors are always assumed to be orthogonal, or independent of each other – after all, they usually correspond to participants in the study). Four factors were extracted with eigenvalues > 1, which together explain 87 per cent of the total variance. The rotated component matrix is displayed in Table 17.2. This shows the loadings for the nine participants on each of the extracted factors (for simplicity, only loadings above 0.5 are included). The first five sorts all load highly on factor 1, although sort 5 is crossloaded on to factor 2 as well. However the loadings for sorts 6 and 7 are far higher on this factor, and sorts 8 and 9 load singly on to the remaining two factors.

How do we begin to interpret this analysis? First of all, it helps to know something about the bars themselves. The bars were selected for this imaginary study according to their flavour and then arranged in order of sweetness, with bar A having the highest sugar content and bar I the lowest. If you look at Table 17.1 you can see that the first four participants all tended to give positive ratings to the sweet bars and negative ratings to the less sweet bars – therefore factor 1 appears to have identified this 'sweet tooth' group among

Table 17.2 Rotated component matrix for Q-sort worked example data

Sorts	Components			
	1 ($\lambda = 3.3$)	*2 ($\lambda = 2.0$)*	*3 ($\lambda = 1.3$)*	*4 ($\lambda = 1.3$)*
1	0.88			
2	0.82			
3	0.76			
4	0.89			
5	0.65	0.51		
6		0.84		
7		−0.94		
8				0.99
9			−0.88	

our sample. The other factors are less easy to interpret without knowing the precise content of the bars, although it could be that other ingredient preferences determined our participants' sorts (nuts or raisins, or whatever).

This pattern analysis lends itself to two possible implications: the first, in line with Stephenson's philosophy, is that no two people are alike in the way they perceive or construct the world. Rather than imposing a pattern upon people in the way that a typical psychometric test might, we are better off asking our participants to organise our materials for us. Any correlations that emerge can then be attributed to shared worldviews or understandings. Therefore, the same chocolate bar can have strikingly different meanings for two different individuals, but there are trends within our sample which show some individuals to be alike in the meanings the bars hold for them.

The second implication, and the one which many postwar Q studies have tended towards, is that our sort has identified a pattern of response that can enable us to identify subgroups in the population as a whole. Of course, a Q-sort itself does not enable us to make such claims, but there are many other measures that we can introduce into our study in order to provide supporting evidence. For example, there is a theory that preference for sweet food is related to the stimulation of the nervous system (Cloninger 1994), and that it can be related to the personality trait of extraversion (also believed to originate from stimulation levels). Therefore, we might also like to have our participants complete the extraversion scale from the Eysenck Personality Questionnaire (Eysenck and Eysenck 1975) to see if our factor 1 participants score the highest on extraversion. This would in turn bolster support for this theory.

These two very different uses of Q-sorts are clearly opposed at an epistemological level, and for that reason we must be aware of the different 'dialects' of Q methodology that have emerged over the years (see Stainton Rogers 1995 for a discussion). Here I have characterised the dialects as respectively North American and European: this may be unfair in some cases, but I will try to emphasise the exceptions to this generalisation.

The European 'dialect' of Q methodology

The European (mostly British) dialect has emerged from the 'critical psychology' movement and emphasises the radical stance taken by Stephenson in developing Q methodology. This fits in with the general approach taken by critical psychologists towards mainstream psychology, particularly the rejection of 'essentialist' psychology, the idea that humans are reducible to a mixture of traits which are, to varying extents, determined by biology. (For a general discussion of 'critical' themes, see Chapter 11.)

In the worked example above, I showed how we could interpret the data either as evidence of the complexity of human experience, or as evidence for subgroups, in this case based on a preference for sweet foods. Many psychologists would be unsatisfied with the former interpretation (statistical complexity is often referred to, sneeringly, as 'noise'). However, critical psychologists using Q methodology see this as its advantage over other statistical techniques, mainly because its complexity is attributed to the freedom of response which participants are given. Like qualitative research in general, they prefer to see the Q-sort as a celebration of 'mess' rather than a tidy-up technique. Probably the best way to explain this is to present an example from the literature.

Stenner and Stainton Rogers (1998): jealousy as a complex phenomenon

This paper is a good example of a contemporary study using a Q-sort in the European tradition. This study is concerned with people's understandings of the concept of *jealousy*. In the introduction the authors argue that mainstream psychology characterises jealousy as a negative emotion that is a *problem* and that psychology's role is to deal with it and somehow contain it. Whether or not this is a good thing for society (and why not, let's at least see if we can prevent jealousy from getting out of hand) is irrelevant if we fail to pin down exactly what constitutes jealousy. The authors argue that mainstream psychology's attempts to reduce jealousy to simple, uncomplicated individual or social processes (or even genetics) fail to capture the complexity of the emotion. Before we can attempt to 'do' anything about jealousy, we need to understand it fully.

The purpose of their study is, therefore, to demonstrate the variety of shared understandings people hold of jealousy – the authors refer to this as a 'manifold' of understandings. Participants were recruited for the study first through an advertisement placed in a local newspaper, and then by using a 'snowball' sample, where respondents to the advert were asked to distribute materials to family and friends. Eventually 47 completed Q-sorts were returned. The participants were drawn from a wide variety of occupations and ages (to give as great a variability of response as possible in such a small sample).

Participants were asked to generate a short scenario depicting an act of jealousy performed by a specific individual, henceforth referred to as 'person X' (the scenario could be either real or fictitious). The Q-sort itself consisted of 54 statements relating to jealousy, which the participants were asked to relate to the person X in their scenario – for example 'X is just being selfish' – which were sorted into a normal distribution provided by an appropriate grid. Participants were asked to sort the statements on the scale most disagree (−5) to agree (+5). The statements were initially selected from a pool of several hundred statements drawn from a 'concourse' of interview data, media coverage, and even role-play scenarios concerning jealousy.

The factor analysis of the sort data was performed in the same way as in our worked example. The loadings of the sorts on the factors enabled the authors to cluster the participants into different groups based on the content of their scenarios: from this point on, the actual sorts are largely neglected (although they can be used to check the validity of the factor interpretations). These factors were not selected on the basis of eigenvalues or scree tests, but on their distinctiveness. This was assessed by asking an independent panel of 51 judges to read three scenarios per factor where two belonged to the same factor and one to another factor. If the judges were able to identify the odd one out (at an above-chance level of agreement), then that factor was retained for interpretation. In total, the authors regarded 10 factors as sufficiently distinctive for interpretation. Here are the characteristics of the first four:

- *Factor 1* appeared to group together participants whose scenarios involved men acting in aggressive or violent ways. In each case, the 'person X' is regarded as overly possessive towards a female, and this is indicative of chauvinistic attitudes towards women.
- *Factor 2* grouped together participants whose scenarios involved female actors who were justly piqued at being betrayed, for example, finding out about a husband's infidelity. The authors go on to link factors 1 and 2 as 'anti-naturalist' approaches to jealousy: in each case, the participants treat jealousy as something which is attributable to political or moral situations (power, for instance) rather than individual or essential qualities of human beings.
- *Factor 3* grouped together participants whose scenarios were more ambiguous, and seemed to be indicative of the state of an unequal relationship rather than individual responses, or responses to a particular situation. For example, person X is jealous because s/he perceives her or his partner as more desirable and responds by acting defensively and insecurely. The authors regard this factor (in conjunction with a lesser factor) as an example of 'naturalistic' jealousy – in other words, it is a natural and understandable response to a situation.
- *Factor 4* is concerned with overreaction: here the scenarios describe individuals who, because of personality factors, blow trivial situations out of all proportion. This is grouped together with a lesser factor by the authors as examples of 'essentialist' jealousy – that which is attributable to the make-up of the individual rather than social or natural factors.

The authors regard this 'manifold' of jealousy as evidence for the complex nature of the phenomenon. They found that the Q-sort patterns provided by participants were indicative of the nature of their scenarios and that the interpretation of the factors was therefore robust. They argue that the different themes in the scenarios and sorts demonstrate a variety of different accounts, or discourses, of jealousy that can be found in modern culture. Therefore, treating jealousy simply as an individual, consistent and predictable response to a consistent and predictable set of stimuli is a misguided approach to dealing with the emotion.

The North American 'dialect' of Q methodology

I shall begin this section by apologising to North American researchers such as Steven Brown, a former student of Stephenson, who is as devoted to the original aims and philosophy of Q methodology as any of the British 'critical' psychologists using Q-sorts. He is not alone; after all, Stephenson emigrated to the United States after the war, partly because of his isolation at the hands of the R methodologists, and still has a large following in that country.

However, the popularity of Q-sorts in modern psychology largely derives from other, later uses of the technique, most of which largely dispensed with the underlying philosophy and used Q-sorts simply as an extension of R methodology. Most of the research published in psychological journals in North America today tends to hark back to the development of the California Q-set (Block 1978), a sorting instrument which was devised largely for the purpose of identifying clinical subtypes. In fact it is not the persons themselves who sort the materials in this procedure, but the clinicians (or the 'informants'), who sort 100 descriptions (e.g., 'is verbally fluent: can express ideas well') on an agree/disagree scale as they are applied to the client in question. As you can imagine, the methodology underlying this technique is vastly different to the 'empowering' one envisaged by Stephenson and promoted by critical psychologists in Europe.

Creed and Funder (1998): concordance of perspectives on behaviour

This example from the literature involves a study to examine the reliability of clinicians' sorts on the Californian Q-set by correlating informants' sorts with those carried out by the participants themselves using the same materials. In this study the participants were 149 undergraduates, and the informants were family members or friends who the participants chose to take part in the study. These two sets of data were also correlated with an original set of items which were sorted by the researchers on the basis of observing participants' behaviour in social interactions (the behavioural Q-set). The participants also completed Fenigstein *et al.*'s (1975) self-consciousness scale.

First, the authors found that there was a high correlation between many of the self-reported items on both the scale and the Q-set. The authors were particularly concerned with the issue of social anxiety; they found that items such as 'is uncomfortable with uncertainty and complexities' were rated highly on both instruments, while 'is a talkative individual' received high negative ratings.

The next analysis was to compare the correlations between scale scores and Q-sets for men and women. This was done by computing a *vector correlation*, where the male data and the female data are correlated in their entirety (i.e., the correlations are correlated). There was found to be a high degree of similarity in male and female Q-sorts, at least on the social anxiety items. The next step was to compute a vector correlation of the informants' Q-sorts along with the participants' Q-sorts. Here again there was high agreement between informants and participants.

Finally, the authors examined the behavioural Q-sort to see if the observers' sorts of the statements were successful in distinguishing socially anxious individuals. Here, almost half the statements were successful in discriminating between socially anxious and socially comfortable individuals. In the interactions observed, the participants' partners were also rated, and it was found that the behaviour of the participants was strongly contrasted; for example, socially anxious individuals tended to allow the other person to dominate the interaction, and were generally rated as less likeable and less enjoyable to interact with.

Once again, we have an example of a use of Q-sorts which is vastly different from that of the British work, in which the Q data simply serve as another measure to be correlated with other measures instead of acting as an end in themselves. Of course there is nothing intrinsically 'wrong' with such use of the technique, except that it does not employ the factor analytic approach which was so useful in identifying types in the Stenner and Stainton Rogers (1998) study. Perhaps more widespread use of, and knowledge of, Q methodology would enhance the status of the Q-sort as a technique in its own right, and not just another measure in a correlational study.

Summary

Q methodology is an approach to collecting and analysing data that was developed in the 1930s by William Stephenson as an alternative to factor analysis (or 'R methodology'). It has since been appropriated by two diverse groups of researchers, crudely characterised as the North American and European dialects of Q methodology. In the North American dialect, the Q-sort, the principal method, is used as a correlational technique for items which are sorted in a particular pattern along a scale by participants. In Europe (and by some psychologists elsewhere, including the US), the use of Q-sorts sticks closer to Stephenson's original aims of a factor analysis which identifies groups of people rather than groups of objects (e.g., scale items). It has to be said that my example using chocolate bars doesn't really translate into either dialect, but I hope it gets the statistical principles across.

Note

1 For an example of this type of study, see Stenner and Stainton Rogers (in press). This paper reports a Q study in which each participant sorted the same set of items four times. Each sort was done in relation to a different emotion (love, jealousy, joy and embarrassment), the object being to show how emotion words or concepts take on different meanings when applied to different emotions.

18 Meta-analysis

For statisticians, the term 'meta-analysis' refers solely to the statistical technique of combining effect sizes in order to test a specific research hypothesis. In this sense, a researcher could carry out a number of studies using the same variables and combine the results within a single research paper. This practice is extremely rare, and I have yet to see such a paper published in a psychology journal. By far the most common use of meta-analysis in the psychological literature is to combine data from a large number of published studies by different authors. This is a very different approach from the usual application of statistics in psychology. However the use of published literature for theory-building is very common practice. Indeed, two of the most prestigious journals in psychology (*Psychological Bulletin* and *Psychological Review*) are devoted mainly to scholarly reviews of the literature on a specific topic, where the author has written a timely round-up of related studies in that field, or has advanced theory by identifying a neglected link between different research literatures, or has devised a new theory or model based on published work.

Such reviews are unquestionably *qualitative* in nature, where the subjectivity of the author is a key factor in the conclusions that s/he draws, and acknowledged as such by editors and readers alike. Of course, such reviews are open to criticism, and are often followed by a number of critical commentaries from peer researchers. Meta-analysis is a move away from that type of dialogic approach towards a finite, objective statement about the collected data on a specific topic – effectively, quantifying material that has traditionally been dealt with in a subjective, interpretative way. As a result, its statistical sophistication has lent it great credibility with journal editors and reviewers, and meta-analyses are now appearing with increasing frequency in the literature.

If one selects the appropriate studies, applies the correct checks and carries out relevant statistical tests, one is in a much firmer position from which to draw conclusions about the nature of a phenomenon. Meta-analyses are rarely followed by commentaries because, if the researcher has done his or her statistics right, there is no room for further debate; if the statistics are wrong it would not have been published at all. To many, this development is yet another example of positivism devouring all in its path; however, meta-analysis is an undoubtedly powerful tool, and, used alongside qualitative reviews, it can only enrich the literature. However we need to be careful – as with structural equation modelling (Chapter 7) – that we acknowledge its limitations and steer clear of making unsubstantiated statements about causality.

What does meta-analysis allow us to do?

Forms of meta-analysis have existed as long as there have been applications of statistical significance and effect size. Early twentieth century statisticians such as Fisher, Pearson and Cochran all devised ways of comparing data collected in different studies with different samples and dependent measures. The term meta-analysis was first coined by Glass in the 1970s and has been developed since, most notably by Hedges and Olkin (1985), Hunter and Schmidt (1990), and Rosenthal and Rubin (1994).

Essentially, a meta-analysis is a set of statistical procedures that are carried out on a collection of published studies in which appropriate data are reported. It enables a researcher to test a hypothesis about a particular psychological phenomenon where there may be diverse or even contradictory findings in the literature, or simply to explore the effect of different factors on a wide range of studies involving different populations and methodologies. Of course, in either case it is important that the data collection and statistical analysis are tailored precisely to the research question.

Many of the statistical tests performed in meta-analysis should already be familiar to readers. For hypothesis testing, measures of pooled significance and effect size have been devised, which are relatively straightforward to calculate, while more exploratory or predictive analyses tend to employ standard regression approaches (these are also used in hypothesis testing too, but not without a degree of caution).

In addition to these statistics there are other measures that can be applied. First there are various corrections that are required to account for variations in sample size or reliability. There are also techniques for dealing with missing information (such as test statistics or reliabilities). Then there are other interpretative statistics that can help add to the picture, such as the coefficient of robustness which is based on the homogeneity of the studies in the analysis (i.e., if the studies are very different in terms of variance and sample size, the analysis will be less 'robust').

Ultimately, the success of a meta-analysis depends on the relevance of the research question, the thoroughness of data collection and coding, and the appropriateness of the statistical procedures.

Worked example of a meta-analysis

The use of a worked example is probably less useful in this chapter than the others. This is because the data tend to be messier in reality than in this absurdly simple case, and part of the skill of meta-analysis lies in the ingenuity of coding moderator variables and compensating for varying degrees of statistical information reported in the studies. However it should give you some idea of the steps (and issues) involved in carrying out a meta-analysis.

Our example concerns a hypothetical phenomenon in the cognitive literature known as the Mr Blobby effect. A theory states that, if the participants in a memory experiment are interrupted by the appearance of the absurd pink and yellow spotted character from BBC children's television, performance on the memory task will be enhanced (unlikely, perhaps, but I'll try to avoid complicating the issue . . .) Our goal in conducting a meta-analysis is to see how powerful the Mr Blobby effect is across a range of research settings. For example, is the stimulus important (the effect might work with memory for words but not with pictures)? Does it work with children as well as adults? Does the length of Mr Blobby's interruption have an effect? You can see that the research questions are largely exploratory in nature. However, the usefulness of a meta-analysis is that it enables the researcher to draw inferences about a phenomenon that would require a hugely complicated one-off study (in our case, one with several factors). This is especially true when looking at cross-cultural phenomena.

Data collection

The mode of data collection is vitally important for evaluating a meta-analysis. Clearly it helps if the research question is relevant to a wide range of studies, though in effect there are no real guidelines about the appropriate number of studies (most published reports tend to include at least twenty or thirty). More important is the significance of the research question – generally speaking, a research question that drew on only a small selection of studies might be regarded as inappropriate at this point in history.

You also need to have some idea of the discipline boundaries you are working with. Many phenomena in psychological research are not restricted to the psychological literature alone; they may have been researched by academics in other disciplines (e.g., biology, sociology, education), in which case you will need to access other databases as well. Alternatively, they may have generated research in many specialist multidisciplinary journals which are not covered by databases such as PsycInfo.

Selection criteria

Once you have assembled a database of all the studies that have been carried out on the topic of interest, you then need to decide whether to use all the studies in the meta-analysis, or whether you need to be selective. There may be important reasons why you need to exclude certain studies. Unless you are studying a well-defined experimental procedure or phenomenon, there is likely to be some degree of uncertainty over whether the studies you have assembled are relevant. Even relevant studies may not lend themselves to meta-analysis because of missing information, or unusual features that are likely to interfere with the comparison process.

A major problem may be that the topic under investigation has generated an enormous body of research and that you have to narrow this down. For example, if you were studying gender differences in risk-taking, you might exclude certain experimental designs, or only consider studies with adult participants. Alternatively, you might find surprisingly few relevant studies and have to broaden your criteria to include studies which have used different designs, or are carried out in a related field.

As an example, Jenkins *et al.* (1998) carried out a meta-analysis exploring the question: are financial incentives related to performance? Clearly, this question is sufficiently broad to include vast numbers of studies which need to be reduced by considering issues like how to define a financial incentive, or what exactly constitutes 'performance'. Eventually they used seven decision rules (which one of the authors had drawn up for a conventional literature review on the topic some years previously). These were:

- Studies carried out after 1960 (earlier ones lacking 'scientific rigour')
- Empirical studies only (not case studies or anecdotal accounts)
- Studies using 'hard' measures of performance (i.e., where a numerical value is assigned)
- Studies where financial incentive is offered to individuals, rather than groups
- Studies with a control group or condition
- Studies using real monetary incentives rather than symbolic or hypothetical incentives (e.g., imagine if . . . ?)
- Studies using adult populations

In our hypothetical example, we have found five studies to date which have investigated the Mr Blobby effect. This is too small a number for a full meta-analysis, but I have used it simply for convenience here. (There is no specified minimum number of studies to use, but most published meta-analyses usually include at least twenty or thirty studies.)

Once you have retrieved as many relevant studies as you can find, the next step in conducting a meta-analysis is to gather together the detail in which you are interested. Broadly speaking, there are two stages of recording information: collecting statistical data, and coding 'moderator' variables. I will deal with these two stages separately, because they form quite distinct aspects of the procedure – although you need to use the two in harness to carry out your eventual analysis.

Statistical data

Probably the biggest headache in conducting a meta-analysis is the attempt to achieve some degree of uniformity over a vast range of studies using different methodologies and therefore conducting different analyses. It is this aspect of meta-analysis which baffles most people on their first encounter with the technique: on the face of it, it seems an impossible task. However, some ingenious remedies have been suggested across the years.

Obviously, there will be some studies in your collection which are unfit for inclusion. A qualitative study on the phenomenon in question would of course be entirely inappropriate in an analysis of this kind (this is one case where meta-analysis needs to be supplemented with a traditional literature review). However, many quantitative studies do not report sufficient data to carry out meta-analysis. This tends to happen when there are non-significant results in a study, and the authors simply report that 'none of the other comparisons reached significance', or words to that effect.

We would usually require the following data: sample size (and relevant group sizes, etc.), descriptive statistics (mean and standard deviation at least), inferential test statistics (e.g. F, t, r), and results of any additional analyses, such as linear contrasts in ANOVA. As your research methods lecturers will undoubtedly have insisted, these details are minimal requirements for a quantitative report – but you'd be surprised how often they are missing in the literature!

Meta-analyses work by calculating a single statistic for each study that represents its findings. This is usually an effect size statistic. Many studies use Cohen's d statistic (as suggested by Hunter and Schmidt 1990). If you have t, F, or r as a statistic, you can convert these to d using the following formulae:

$$t \qquad d = \frac{2t}{\sqrt{df}}$$

$$F \qquad d = \frac{2\sqrt{F}}{\sqrt{df\,(error)}}$$

$$r \qquad d = \frac{2r}{\sqrt{1 - r^2}}$$

If these statistics aren't available, there is a basic formula for d which you can use so long as you have the standard deviations and the participant numbers in each group or sample. First of all, you need to calculate a single value representing the total variance in the study: for this you will usually calculate the *pooled* standard deviation (the square root of the pooled within-subjects variance). This figure is obtained using the following formula, where e = experimental group, and c = controls:

$$s_p^2 = \frac{(N_e - 1)s_e^2 + (N_c - 1)s_c^2}{(N_e + N_c - 2)}$$

And then you can enter the square root of s_p^2 into the following formula:

$$d = \frac{X_e - X_c}{s_p}$$

This way, you now have an effect size for each of the studies you have included which can be used to compare them in the overall analysis. In addition to effect size, some studies also carry out a power analysis or calculate confidence intervals for each study included.

Moderator variables

The other important part of the meta-analysis procedure is the coding of specified 'moderator' variables which are normally tied to the effects you are interested in studying. For example, the phenomenon under investigation may have been explored using different experimental paradigms, or different populations, or different experimental stimuli. This information needs to be coded so that we can compare effect sizes across different types of study.

In our hypothetical example, the Mr Blobby studies are coded on each of the following variables:

- Stimuli (used in the memory experiment)
- Length of interruption
- Design (between- or within-subjects)
- Age of participants

As you may recall, these variables are all of interest in the meta-analysis, since the rationale is rooted in accounting for differences between studies which may be attributed to any of these factors.

The variables in this example are easy to code, largely because it is only a matter of recording detail provided by the authors. This is not always the case: often, coding of moderator variables is a contentious issue, and it may be necessary to employ a number of researchers to code data in order to evaluate the reliability of the coding scheme. Codes are entered into the data file as category variables; interval data, such as the interruption time, are entered as normal.

Our Mr Blobby data may end up looking like the arrangement of data in Tables 18.1 and 18.2. Clearly some of these variables will not contribute all that highly to the variance in effect size: most of the designs are between subjects, and most of the interruptions are similar. Nevertheless, the participant age and stimuli variables might be worth exploring.

Table 18.1 Summary of imaginary studies for meta-analysis

Study	Stimuli	Interruption	Design	Participants	N	d
Edmonds (1990)	words	30 secs	BS	adults	50	0.25
Edmonds (1992)	pictures	30 secs	BS	adults	60	0.17
Blackburn and Chegwin (1994)	words	30 secs	BS	children	40	0.45
Chegwin et al. (1996)	pictures	30 secs	BS	children	65	0.55
Edmonds et al. (1998)	shapes	45 secs	WS	adults	50	0.12

Table 18.2 Data file for computer analysis of the above information

Case	Stimuli	Length	Design	Age	N	d
1	1	30	1	1	50	0.25
2	2	30	1	1	60	0.17
3	1	30	1	2	40	0.45
4	2	30	1	2	65	0.55
5	3	45	2	1	50	0.12

Carrying out the full analysis

Once the information is entered into a data file, we can now look at the overall analysis of our selected studies. However, it is not worth conducting an analysis on such a small data set as the one in the example above, so from now on I will refer only to real studies from the psychological literature.

Diagnostic tests

Because meta-analysis involves throwing together so many data that we know relatively little about, we need to be even more careful than usual that our analysis is not spoiled by extraneous factors. There are a vast number of screening tests available for countering all forms of error and missing data. Rosenthal (1995), in his guide to reporting meta-analytic studies, lists most of them, but I shall discuss a few key ones here.

We might begin by carrying out some corrections on our raw data to account for the error variance that is undoubtedly present in such a diverse data set. The most common sources of error variance are: *sampling error* (due to a wide range of sample sizes), *measurement error* (particularly where different instruments are used), and *range departure* (where scores on a measure do not fall perfectly within a normal distribution). There are various formulae we can use if we wish to correct for these sources of error; if you are keen to carry out these modifications, you are best off consulting a specialist text (e.g., Hedges and Olkin 1985; Hunter and Schmidt 1990).

There are alternative approaches to dealing with these types of error. First, sampling error may not be a major problem unless there is a disproportionately large sample in the analysis (say, a study with 3,000 participants where the mean sample size is around 200). One recommendation here is to run the analysis with and without this study and see what effect it has on the results (Rothstein and McDaniel 1989). Measurement error may be a problem where different authors have used variations on the same basic questionnaire or scale; however, papers that report the use of scale data usually include reliability statistics which can be entered into the analysis. There are corrections that we can apply for this too (see Hunter and Schmidt 1990).

One statistic that is often reported is a measure of heterogeneity of effect sizes, represented by the test statistic Q. This has a chi-square distribution, so that a significant result indicates that our effect sizes are not homogeneous, and that it is worth exploring differences between them (although as Rosenthal 1995 points out, there is no reason why a non-significant Q should deter us from probing further).

Inferential statistics

By far the most common statistical treatment of meta-analytic data is some form of regression analysis. Typically, the moderator variables are entered into an equation as predictors, with the effect size as the criterion variable. In the Mr Blobby study, we might choose to enter stimuli, length of interruption, design and age as predictors. Oddly enough, Rosenthal (1995) in his guide to writing meta-analytic reports, fails to mention regression analysis, although at least one analysis of this type is conducted in almost every meta-analysis I have seen in psychological journals.

Examples of meta-analysis from the psychological literature

I have selected two examples to describe here, partly because they deal with different areas of the discipline, but mainly because the type of regression analysis is different in each case. There are many other contrasts between these two studies, which if anything suggests how complex the practice of meta-analysis has become, and how broad the range of techniques that are accepted as part of the procedure. In each case, however, the authors have chosen to explore a classic phenomenon across several decades of research.

Bond and Smith (1996): a cross-cultural analysis of Asch's line judgement task

All psychologists will be familiar with Solomon Asch's famous series of studies in which, on a simple line judgement task, a group of mock participants is able to persuade a naïve participant to give false answers in order to conform with a majority decision. Since Asch's original studies in the 1950s, the basic procedure has been repeated in a variety of cultures using many different populations, with varying degrees of success – although the elements of conformity are usually displayed by a substantial number of participants.

Rob Bond and Peter Smith, cross-cultural psychologists from the University of Sussex, were interested in the effect of social norms on the Asch experiment in different types of cultures. They argued that, in some cultures, conformity is regarded more positively than others, particularly in societies with a 'collectivist' nature, where the individual self is strongly related to other members of the society (e.g., in East Asian cultures). In 'individualist' societies such as the United States and Great Britain, conformity is seen as a more negative attribute: we tend to laugh at the duped participant for being fooled into cowing submission to the majority. In other cultures the sacrifice of the individual self in a situation such as the Asch experiment might be seen as entirely understandable.

In order to test this hypothesis (which, in a nutshell, predicts that we would find higher effect sizes in collectivist cultures on the Asch task) Bond and Smith assembled 68 studies which contained a total of 133 separate experiments with a total of 4,627 participants. Of these experiments 97 were conducted in the United States using different experimental paradigms and a range of populations. However in the other studies, as many as 17 different countries were represented.

Because so many different variants on the original task have been used in subsequent studies, it was important to restrict the number of moderating variables. Therefore, strict criteria needed to be drawn up to avoid cluttering the data. Studies were only included if:

- The task involved judging which of three lines was the same length as a target line
- The 'group pressure' paradigm was used in which the majority makes a false judgement
- The naïve participant was alone against a majority
- The majority consisted of at least two people
- The participants were all adults
- The participants were not suffering from a clinical condition
- The answers were given verbally by the participant
- No rewards were given or offered
- The stimuli were not removed before the response was given
- No other interfering tasks were used

This narrowed the search down somewhat; even so, there were still a large number of moderator variables to enter into the equation. These, along with other coded information, constituted the following list of variables:

- Country in which the study was conducted
- Year in which the study was conducted (as opposed to the year of publication; this was calculated as being roughly two years prior to this)

- Type of experimental paradigm (either the original Asch paradigm, or the Crutchfield paradigm in which the participants are seated in individual booths so that they cannot see each other)
- Majority size
- Relation of majority to participant (acquaintances, strangers, in- or outgroup members)
- Whether the participant's response was available to the majority
- Stimulus materials (in some variations, the distance between the lines is greater, and the majority make different responses)
- Total number of trials
- Ratio of critical trials (i.e., those on which the majority makes an error) to the total number
- The average error in inches (this is a measure of stimulus ambiguity)
- The percentage of female participants
- The participant population (e.g., students)

The authors provide a stem-and-leaf plot of effect sizes, which shows a slight positive skew, with four very high effect sizes; the overall mean effect size was 1.06 (unweighted), or 0.92 (weighted).

A series of regression analyses were conducted on the data. First, the studies conducted in the US were analysed separately. There was a significant interaction between experimental paradigm and stimulus materials: with the original Asch stimuli, the Asch paradigm produced higher effect sizes, however, with modified stimuli, the Crutchfield paradigm produced higher effect sizes. There was also found to be a significant effect of majority size (the larger the majority, the greater the effect), of stimulus ambiguity (the more ambiguous, the greater the effect), of the relationship between the individual and the majority (less conformity when the majority are outgroup members), and of gender (the more women, the more conformity). There was also an effect of time: the later the study, the less conformity, perhaps suggesting that the US is becoming increasingly individualistic as a society.

A second set of analyses were conducted using the data from different cultures. An index of individualism–collectivism was used, based on large-scale survey data (Hofstede 1980), by which each culture could be assigned a value. As hypothesised, this measure was a significant predictor of effect size, with collectivist cultures showing the highest effect sizes. Other indices of individualism–collectivism were also entered, based on various cultural values, and these were found to be significant as well.

Bond and Smith argue that the findings support their contention that conformity in this situation is related to cultural values; indeed, they go so far as to say that we should not regard the performance of non-Western participants as a measure of conformity – it might be more accurate to call it 'social sensitivity' or 'tactfulness'. This is a classic example where Western psychology needs to be aware of the limitations of the appropriateness of its terms and concepts.

Marcovitch and Zelazo (1999): a logistic meta-analysis of the A-not-B error

One of the most famous of all Piagetian tasks involves an infant searching for a hidden object. Typically, the child is shown a toy which the adult then 'hides' in a specific location (A), say, under a blanket. After a short delay the child is allowed to search for it. After a number of trials at location A, the toy is then hidden in a different location (B). If the child goes back to location A in order to find the toy, this is referred to as the *A-not-B error*. Piaget argued that this error is evidence that the child has failed to develop the concept of 'object permanence', although many subsequent theorists have suggested alternative cognitive and motoric explanations.

Marcovitch and Zelazo's study was a follow-up of a meta-analysis carried out in 1986 by Wellman, Cross and Bartsch, who collected data from 30 studies and carried out two linear multiple regressions: one with the proportion of children who committed the A-not-B error as the criterion variable, and another with the proportion of children who searched correctly on the first B trial as the criterion variable. The significant predictors in each case were: age (in line with Piaget's stage theory); delay before the child is allowed to search (suggesting the contribution of short-term memory); the number of hiding locations (added confusion?); and the distinctiveness of hiding locations. However, the number of A trials was not a significant predictor.

Marcovitch and Zelazo wanted to follow up Wellman *et al.*'s study by including data collected in the following decade. But they also wanted to make a slight modification to the analysis. They argued that linear multiple regression was not an entirely appropriate test for proportional data, because the values of the criterion variable are 'bounded' – in other words, they can only fall between the values of 0 and 1. In a sense, this is not a major problem, since most data are bounded in some way, and these issues are usually resolved by standardising the values. The authors' argument was that a logistic regression would be more sensitive in identifying significant predictors. (Logistic regression, as you may recall from Chapter 6, is a regression analysis in which the criterion is a dichotomous variable (all values 0 or 1), and the other variables are used to predict membership of the two groups.)

The authors removed some of the original studies from their analysis because they introduced too much variation into the standard A-not-B task. They added another 14 studies to the analysis, including a couple that the previous authors had either missed or excluded. Altogether this yielded a total of 33 studies, although many of these had several conditions across which the key variables were manipulated, so in total there were 107 cases. The six predictor variables were:

- Age
- Number of hiding locations
- Distance between locations

- Delay between hiding and search
- Number of A trials
- Distinctiveness of covers or backgrounds (either distinctive or not)

Two analyses were run, as in the original study, with the criterion variable as either: correct (i.e., the child either searched at A or B, and if B, the response was judged as correct), or incorrect ('perseveration' – i.e., they continued to search at A). In addition, the authors ran linear multiple regression using the same predictors, and with the proportional data as criterion variables as in the previous study.

(At this point I should warn most readers from following up the source of this study, because it is very complicated mathematically. The authors chose to use a connectionist network to perform their logistic regression analysis rather than a statistical software package, so they could make it more complex and therefore more sensitive.)

A number of findings were reported in the Marcovitch and Zelazo study that were different from the earlier meta-analysis. First, the number of A trials emerged as a significant predictor on both linear and logistic analyses. The more A trials, the higher the likelihood of error. Second, the number of hiding locations was a significant predictor of membership of the error (perseverance) group. Again, this had a negative coefficient, so that the more locations, the greater the likelihood of error.

There were also slight differences between the linear and logistic analyses. The logistic analysis also identified distance between locations as a significant predictor. Examining the coefficients also highlighted differences between the analyses. For example, with correct search as the criterion, age has a coefficient of 0.01 for linear regression, but 0.21 for logistic regression. This is explained by the authors as a reflection of the logistic model's sensitivity to extreme data points: there is one study which used children of around four years old. These outlying points weaken the contribution of age in the linear model but not in the logistic model. (An alternative, when using linear regression, would be simply to remove those cases from the analysis.)

Ultimately, Marcovitch and Zelazo do nothing *spectacular* to the analysis by choosing logistic over linear regression. It would also be interesting to see what results they obtained by using a statistical package rather than their connectionist network. However they make the point that, if meta-analysis is worth doing at all, it is worth doing as thoroughly as possible.

Problems with meta-analysis

Like most relatively new approaches to carrying out research, there are almost as many critics as advocates of meta-analysis. Most of the arguments against it are variations on the initial scepticism of most people, that it seems almost impossible to lump together a load of other people's data and carry out a meaningful statistical analysis. Here are some of the more specific points though.

Sampling bias

By far the most common criticism of meta-analysis is that the samples used are intrinsically biased towards finding significant results. There are two reasons for this. First, when taking the decision to publish an article, most psychology journals have a bias towards significant results. Negative findings are not generally viewed as significant theoretical advances (despite the claim by Karl Popper and others that science progresses through disconfirming hypotheses). As a result, our meta-analytic data file tends to contain data that have been selected for their significance, rather than being in any way representative of the population under investigation.

Marcovitch and Zelazo, in the study reported above, claim to have got around this problem by including unpublished data (for example, from conference papers that did not find their way into journals, and by contacting researchers in the field for any additional data that they had not written up). However it remains a major problem for meta-analysis, and suggests that we need to take significant results with a pinch of salt (or maybe at least an increased alpha level).

Inclusion criteria

How do you decide which studies to include in your analysis? This is a particularly taxing question for meta-analysts, and one to which there is no easy answer. Of course, your selection will be based entirely on your interests and your initial research question, although here again there is an opportunity for bias to sneak in. This is one of the reasons meta-analysis must still be regarded as a hybrid technique rather than a pure quantitative method – ultimately, the subjective interests of the researcher leave their stamp all over the analysis. As long as you justify your inclusion criteria, however, they will be taken seriously by people interested in your study.

There is still the problem of missing data. This is compounded by the tendency for authors not to report non-significant test statistics, leading to the studies being omitted from the final analysis. Therefore, in addition to the publication bias discussed above, we are always liable to be left with a disproportionate number of studies with significant results even among the ones we have selected from the published literature. This suggests that we should try as hard as possible to extract every piece of relevant information from the data that we have.

Reliability and validity

One of the attractions of meta-analysis at the moment is the diversity of approaches with which people have carried it out. The Marcovitch and Zelazo study is a world away from the Bond and Smith one: both share similarities but the data they collect and the way they are treated are completely different. Also, the former study looks nothing like the type of report advocated in Rosenthal's (1995) guidelines!

However it is always worth considering issues of reliability and validity in regard to meta-analysis. Zakzanis (1998) is a useful study of reliability across a number of undergraduate dissertations using the same data. This study found generally very high intraclass coefficients between the analyses (mean coefficient 0.94). However, all the students had been taught meta-analysis by the same lecturer, and other findings may have been obtained across different institutions using different methods.

There are also problems of validity when conducting more than one meta-analysis using the same data. It may be that you have assembled a vast number of studies that can be split into two or more groups (for example, half of them use children as participants and half adults). Here you would be justified in carrying out separate meta-analyses on each group of studies. However there might be a temptation to split your data on some other measure in order that you get some significant findings! Of course you should only do this if you can fully justify it in the light of your research question.

A good way of testing the validity of a meta-analysis is to perform cross-validation on your sample. Marcovitch and Zelazo do this by withholding a (randomly chosen) subset of the data and running the meta-analysis with, and without, this subset. If the inclusion of the subset has a major effect on the overall analysis it may be that there are inconsistencies within the data.

Establishing causality

A final point to be made about meta-analysis is simply a variation on an old theme – that, where the data are correlational (which is essentially the case in most meta-analyses), causation cannot be inferred simply from the significance level of a predictor variable.

This point is made forcefully in a meta-analysis by Knight *et al.* (1996). They were concerned that a number of meta-analyses concerning gender differences in cognitive and social task performance seem to have identified date of study as a significant predictor: in other words, the more recent the study, the lower the effect size. These reviews have been seized upon by theorists who argue that gender differences are the result of the environment rather than evolutionary genetics, and, since the environment is becoming more egalitarian, the differences between men and women are growing increasingly small.

Knight *et al.* argue that we should treat these results with caution. First, this is because the authors' own study of gender differences in aggression show the reverse trend (i.e., the effect size gets greater over time). Second, however, they argue that the date of study effect in many of the analyses is a secondary finding that is not part of the initial research question: in other words, there is insubstantial theory to support it. They argue that this is a case of researchers discovering significant findings by chance.

Knight *et al.* have a point. The most convincing meta-analysis would be one in which date of study was the sole focus of the study, and in which a vast array of data were included. The selection criteria would need to be extremely strict, and precisely defined by theoretical literature. It is hard to see how it could be narrowed down to manageable proportions, but might be worth a try. My own feeling on this matter is, however, that the choice of predictor variables is not entirely haphazard, and that it is unlikely that all the studies cited by the authors happened to stumble across the 'date of study' effect by accident. Further, the authors seem overly concerned that such an explanation draws researchers away from considering genetic explanations of behaviour. I fail to see why this should be a problem for anyone engaged in scientific discovery, least of all psychologists.

Summary

The technique of meta-analysis has transformed the literature review from an exercise in theory-building from published research (not unlike grounded theory in some respects) to a systematic statistical exercise in pooling reported findings and testing hypotheses. In this chapter I have tried to give readers enough information to carry out a meta-analysis of their own, while presenting several examples of the technique in practice from the published literature. I have touched only lightly on the potential criticisms of meta-analysis as a tool for psychological research, and I suspect that many of these will be forthcoming over the next few years. When used on appropriate data, it is an extremely valuable tool, but meta-analysis is often guilty of smoothing over some gaping cracks in methodology which can persist throughout an entire literature. The examples I have cited from the literature in this chapter are precisely the sort that meta-analysis is equipped to deal with, where the same methodology has been used with different populations or materials. However, where methodologies vary wildly, yet all studies claim to be measuring the same phenomenon, we must handle the results with extreme caution.

19 Self-generated data

I have called this chapter 'Self-generated data' because I wanted to find some way of lumping together research methods in which the participants are responsible for generating data that require more input than simply ticking boxes or circling numbers on a Likert scale. Of course, it could be argued that interviewees provide most of the data in an interview study, but spoken information only becomes data once it is recorded and transcribed by the researcher – hence it becomes, to cite a glib phrase, 'creata'. In the techniques described in this chapter, participants actually go off and create data themselves, and the researcher (apart from initiating the data collection itself) only becomes involved at the analytical stage.

By far the most common form of self-generated data is the diary study, which has been used throughout psychology's history as a means of collecting data in both longitudinal and cross-sectional research designs. Like interview transcripts, these data can be treated in a multitude of ways, and we shall look at a few instances from the literature here. I have also described in some detail the construction of a repertory grid, used to study personal constructs. This technique is still very popular in the clinical field, although its use in academic research is comparatively rare. Then I look at a different example of self-generated research – the photo essay, which has become increasingly popular.

THE DIARY METHOD IN PSYCHOLOGICAL RESEARCH

The diary method is similar to the interview method in the sense that it is a very flexible tool. In fact you could classify diaries in the same way as interviews, ranging from unstructured (just ask the participants to write down what happened each day) to structured (where an identical questionnaire is completed at a set time each day). The uses of, and justifications for, either approach will be the same as with interviews – you collect unstructured data if you are interested in carrying out an interpretative analysis in which language, or discourse, is the focus of interest, and you structure participants' responses when you want to control variables and carry out statistical analysis.

Since there are no specific guidelines which one can follow when designing a diary study other than those which apply to other forms of interview and questionnaire research, it may be more useful to look at a selection of studies which have used diaries to investigate psychological phenomena.

Coxon (1988): the sexual diary

Strictly speaking, this is not a 'psychology' study as such (it is a 'research note' published in a sociological journal), but the research question, and the nature of the data collected, could certainly form part of a psychological study looking at sexual behaviour and/or HIV risk. Coxon describes here the development of a method for collecting 'systematic' data relating to sexual activity. Essentially this consists of a (fairly) elaborate coding system which allows diarists to record the specific details of their activity without having to catalogue mundane and repetitive information in prose form.

If, as a diarist, your sex life consisted of nothing more than the occasional quickie with the spouse beneath the sheets on a Saturday night, any kind of coding system would be pointless, and your sexual diary would hardly be a riveting read. However, Coxon's research was specifically focused on gay and bisexual men engaging in highly promiscuous sexual activity in which many aspects of the behaviour might constitute risk. For example, some of the 'toys' used to enhance arousal, such as whips, nipple clamps and dildoes, might be shared, with the possibility of exchanging blood and lubricant. Therefore, quite a lot of detail needs to be recorded at each encounter for the researcher to estimate the degree of risk.

As an example of the coding system, the following entry (vicars are advised to turn the page immediately) might read:

> I fucked him; I came to orgasm wearing a condom, he didn't come. Then I was sucked (no condom, i.e. removed), and then I wanked off using a lubricant.
>
> (1988: 360)

However, the coded version would simply run:

AFOX/c + PS + SWO/l

Coxon lists a number of advantages of diaries for collecting this type of information. For one thing, retrospective accounts of behaviour (of any type) are heavily reliant on accurate memory. This is a potential problem with any research into autobiographical memory, of course. However, if the researcher requires (more or less) accurate details of behaviour, then – short of carrying out a different type of study, such as an observation – a daily diary would be a sensible alternative to retrospective interviews or questionnaires. (Obviously, for Coxon's research, a naturalistic observation might prove rather difficult to set up!) Another advantage of the diary is that it allows greater detail to be collected (particularly by use of this type of coding scheme). For example, the term 'sexual partner' in a questionnaire is open to such a range of interpretation that it may elicit meaningless information.

At the same time, it is not always possible to verify the information provided by participants in this type of study (as indeed is the case with any self-report data). Coxon does suggest that ideally, data should be collected from both partners in this type of study – although this may not always be possible especially when there are many different partners involved.

Tidwell et al. *(1996): attachment and social interaction*

This study concerns another topic which is frequently researched using questionnaires where the reliability of respondents' accounts is hard to establish. Tidwell *et al.* were interested to see how people's attachment styles influenced the quality of their social interactions. Collecting this type of data using a retrospective questionnaire would be problematic in that, again, you would be relying on participants having sufficiently accurate memories to allow them to recall events from several weeks previously. However, a diary detailing each day's interactions would minimise the effort required.

In this study, 135 undergraduates on an American university campus completed interaction diaries over a week, where they were asked to record the details of every social interaction that lasted for more than ten minutes. Interaction was defined as 'any social encounter in which participants were responding to one another' regardless of context, whether face-to-face or by telephone, or whether conversation took place (although it is hard to imagine a completely silent 10-minute interaction).

An example of a sheet completed for each interaction is contained in Figure 19.1. Instantly you can see that it looks more like a questionnaire than a diary, and, in many respects, the term 'diary' is perhaps a bit misleading to describe this type of study. After the data had been collected for a week, participants were asked to complete two measures of attachment style, and also had their photographs taken so that a measure of attractiveness could be derived (another group of undergraduates rated the photographs).

To prepare the data for analysis, participants' attachment styles were classified as *avoidant*, *anxious-ambivalent*, or *secure* (a fairly standard classification). The interactions were classified as:

* *all interactions*
* *same-sex* (diarist plus 1–3 others of the same sex)
* *opposite-sex* (diarist plus 1–3 others of the opposite sex)
* *mixed-sex* (diarist plus 2–3 others, including one of each sex)
* *groups* (diarist plus more than 3 others)

Date:_____   Time:_____ a.m. or p.m.?   Length: ___hrs. ___mins.

Who initiated the interaction?
_____ I did.   _____ Other did.   _____It was mutual.

Was this a phone call?_____Yes _____No

Initials of other(s):   ____ ____ ____

If more than three others, number of:
Sex of other(s):   ____ ____ ____ males ____ females ____

Intimacy..................................	superficial	1 2 3 4 5 6 7	meaningful
I disclosed..............................	very little	1 2 3 4 5 6 7	a great deal
Other disclosed........................	very little	1 2 3 4 5 6 7	a great deal
Quality (how pleasant was it?)......	unpleasant	1 2 3 4 5 6 7	very pleasant
I helped/supported other.............	very little	1 2 3 4 5 6 7	a great deal
Other helped/supported me.........	very little	1 2 3 4 5 6 7	a great deal
Degree of disagreement/conflict	very little	1 2 3 4 5 6 7	a great deal
Degree of closeness/camaraderie	very little	1 2 3 4 5 6 7	a great deal
Who mainly influenced or controlled the interaction?........	I did	1 2 3 4 5 6 7	other did
My level of satisfaction...............	dissatisfied	1 2 3 4 5 6 7	very satisfied
I got from the interaction.............	less than expected/ hoped for	1 2 3 4 5 6 7	more than expected/ hoped for

Nature of interaction: Job___ Task____Conversation____Leisure activity___
Other:_____

Approximate content of the interaction (what you were doing and talking about):_____
_____
_____

During the interaction (or immediately after), how much did you feel...

happy/encouraged....................	not at all	1 2 3 4 5 6 7	a great deal
sad/disappointed......................	not at all	1 2 3 4 5 6 7	a great deal
frustrated/irritated....................	not at all	1 2 3 4 5 6 7	a great deal
rejected/left out........................	not at all	1 2 3 4 5 6 7	a great deal
comfortable/relaxed..................	not at all	1 2 3 4 5 6 7	a great deal
needed/appreciated..................	not at all	1 2 3 4 5 6 7	a great deal
bored/distant...........................	not at all	1 2 3 4 5 6 7	a great deal
caring/warm.............................	not at all	1 2 3 4 5 6 7	a great deal
hurt/treated badly.....................	not at all	1 2 3 4 5 6 7	a great deal
worried/anxious........................	not at all	1 2 3 4 5 6 7	a great deal
stimulated/invigorated...............	not at all	1 2 3 4 5 6 7	a great deal
tense/ill at ease.......................	not at all	1 2 3 4 5 6 7	a great deal
successful/productive...............	not at all	1 2 3 4 5 6 7	a great deal
sexually interested/aroused.........	not at all	1 2 3 4 5 6 7	a great deal
envious/jealous........................	not at all	1 2 3 4 5 6 7	a great deal
accepted/like you belonged.........	not at all	1 2 3 4 5 6 7	a great deal
embarrassed/self-conscious.......	not at all	1 2 3 4 5 6 7	a great deal
disgusted/disappointed..............	not at all	1 2 3 4 5 6 7	a great deal
ashamed/guilty.........................	not at all	1 2 3 4 5 6 7	a great deal
imposed upon/intruded upon.......	not at all	1 2 3 4 5 6 7	a great deal
tired/low in energy....................	not at all	1 2 3 4 5 6 7	a great deal

Figure 19.1 The modified Rochester Interaction Record, Reis and Wheeler (1991) as used by Tidwell *et al.* (1996). Reprinted with permission from M.P. Zanna (ed.) *Advances in Experimental Social Psychology* (Vol. 24, pp. 269–318). Copyright Academic Press.

- *same-sex best friends*
- *same-sex others*
- *opposite-sex romantic partners*
- *opposite-sex others*

Then, to reduce the interaction quality ratings to analysable components, principle components analyses were conducted separately on the 11 rating scales and the 21 emotion scales. The quality scales were reduced to three factors: intimacy, promotive interaction (relating to support and disclosure) and enjoyment. The emotion scales were reduced to two broad categories of positive and negative emotions.

Overall, it was found that the quality of social interaction was different for avoidant participants compared with the other two attachment groups. Avoidants reported more negative emotions, particularly in opposite-sex interactions; with romantic partners they reported lower levels of intimacy. Where no romantic partner was indicated, avoidants did not seek to attain intimacy with other kinds of partner. This finding suggests that the avoidant attachment style is related to intimate contact rather than social interaction *per se*.

Clearly a problem with this type of study is – as with the Coxon data – a lack of partner data which could validate the accounts provided by individuals. The same criticism is often levelled at attachment research in general; rather than offering a description of objective attachment behaviour, attachment data may simply present us with an account of participants' own perceptions of their behaviour. Given this limitation, there is an argument for the use of qualitative diary data in this type of study, with the participants' accounts featuring as the focus of the research. However, using an *event-sampling* technique such as the interaction diaries described here, at least the confounding factor of selective memory is controlled, so the data are more accurate than those obtained from retrospective interviews or questionnaires.

Conner et al. (1999): stress and snacking

While Tidwell *et al.*'s diary looks more like a series of questionnaires than a prose diary, the next study moves even further away from the traditional qualitative diary to a kind of quantitative log book where simple details are recorded at the end of each day. In this particular study the focus was on the relationship between daily 'hassles' (i.e., minor stressful events) and between-meal snacking (e.g., bags of crisps, sweets, and so on). Sixty students were asked to record at the end of each day, for a week, what hassles they had experienced, and – on a 3-point scale – how severe a problem each had been, and also to record what snacks had been consumed that day.

Whereas the previous study used an event-sampling method, this study uses a *time-sampling* method. The difference is simply that, while Tidwell *et al.*'s participants were asked to fill in a sheet each time an interaction occurred, Conner *et al.*'s participants were only required to fill in one sheet each day. The advantage of the former method is that memory is ruled out as a factor, whereas the time-sampling method does not control for this, so that a participant with a poor recall of the day may fail to record some of the details.

Analysis of the data showed that there was a moderate positive correlation between the number of hassles and the number of snacks consumed each day. Participants also completed a questionnaire regarding eating behaviour, and this showed that this relationship was strongest among those people with a high *external* style of eating (i.e., eating in response to external cues and not to internal cues like hunger).

One potential problem the authors identify in this study is that of social desirability, that participants may guess the purpose of their study and modify their behaviour accordingly. They suggest that this is unlikely in this study because the moderator variables in the analysis would not be obvious to participants. However it does highlight a major hazard with all diary studies – that of potential *reactivity*. Reactivity refers to the tendency for research participants to modify their behaviour, perhaps unconsciously, simply as a result of participating in a research study.

In a qualitative diary study this would be a major research design issue, since participants may find themselves contemplating their behaviour throughout the period of the study, and this self-reflection may actually produce changes in their behaviour. If the study is part of an action research programme in which the purpose of the study is actually to bring about changes in behaviour, then reactivity would be a reliable indicator that the study is working. In other studies the reactivity itself may be of interest to the researcher, in the case of dream diaries for example.

Another way in which social desirability may contaminate any self-report data is where participants simply fail to record accurate details for reasons of personal pride. The classic example of this concerns questionnaire items relating to alcohol consumption. How many times have you lied when asked the question: how many units of alcohol do you consume each week? The reason *why* we lie – even on quite innocuous questionnaires – to this item is more often that we are made to feel ashamed of our alcohol consumption, partly because the 'acceptable limit' cited by health literature is so much lower than many people's level of consumption. I am of course aware that this is a highly culture-specific example! Nevertheless it is typical of the kind of self-denial that can operate when completing questionnaires or participating in other self-report studies.

This kind of behaviour raises interesting questions about the whole nature of diaries and why people keep them. In a sense they are a problematic research instrument precisely because they are such an egocentric activity. If you have ever kept a personal diary, it is worth considering a few questions: why did you keep that diary, and who did you expect to read it? If the answers are that you kept the diary purely for your own consumption, then it is also worth considering what factors influenced your choice of words and your selection of events and emotions. A typical feature of personal diaries is that we are always aware of the possibility that they will be discovered and read by other people, and that many such 'private' diaries are subsequently published for universal consumption! Ultimately we have to wonder why something so personal should be committed to paper at all; I have a sneaking feeling that no diarist ever imagines that he or she is the only person who will ever read those words.

REPERTORY GRID TECHNIQUE

Repertory grids share some characteristics with open-ended diary studies in that participants have a high degree of control over the material included. However, unlike all but the most structured diaries, the repertory grid is a fixed format with its own unique procedure and method of analysis.

The origin of the repertory grid lies in George Kelly's well-known 1955 publication, *The Psychology of Personal Constructs*, where he outlined his unintentionally(?) sexist concept of 'man the scientist'. Kelly's basic idea was that human beings are continually engaged in the process of devising theories, testing hypotheses based on these theories and acting on the findings. Because we are not all trained scientists as such, we do not use scientific discourse to articulate our theories. Nevertheless, it should be possible to guide non-scientists by providing them with a framework on which they can then structure their own personal science. Kelly described this science as personal construct theory – essentially, we all have our own set of constructs on which we base our knowledge of the world. The framework for articulating these constructs he called the *repertory grid*, a technique which allows its users to build a system of personal constructs which reveal the way they organise their social world.

Today, repertory grids are still used in clinical psychology, where they help psychologists to understand their clients through a more formal system than the standard interview. They are also useful because the grid is an indirect assessment which may allow access to aspects of the client's private world which s/he is not able or willing to articulate in an interview setting. Ultimately, repertory grids are an interpretative technique in that they still require subjective analyses from the researcher. However they are often used in academic research to provide data for quantitative analysis: a couple of examples are reported later in the chapter.

Constructing a repertory grid

The repertory grid is a table, or matrix, which may contain either qualitative or quantitative data. Its columns consist of elements, which define the area of study, and its rows consist of constructs, which are themes linking the elements together. The grid may be constructed by a participant working alone under the instructions of the researcher, or by the researcher and participant working together, or by pairs or even teams of participants, depending on the research question.

Choosing elements

The first activity required of the participant involves drawing up a list of *elements*, which define the topic under exploration. Elements can be anything that the participant has an opinion about. For example, a grid could be designed in order to discover the way a person with an eating disorder construes food, in which the elements might consist of things like cream cakes, celery, bread and chocolate. However, in most uses of repertory grids, the researcher is interested in the participant's *social* world, and so the elements are likely to be people that he or she interacts with, or – in a clinical setting, perhaps – important figures through the lifespan. Kelly's original proposal was to create elements based on specific role titles, for example, 'a teacher you liked', 'your mother', or 'the most successful person whom you know personally'. He suggested 24 role titles originally, which are listed in Table 19.1. The total number of elements you end up with is not important, so long as you keep your research question in mind when choosing them (it is important not to have irrelevant elements in there). Once the elements have been listed, these comprise the columns of the grid. The next stage is to design the rows.

Construct elicitation

The rows of the grid consist of the *constructs* that make up that person's view of the world. These are *elicited* through using the elements, and there are a number of ways of doing this. The most common is the *triadic* method. Three elements are selected from the list and the participant is asked to specify some important way in which two of them are alike and different from the third. The triad can be chosen by the researcher or the participant; in some variations the participant is asked to select 'myself' as a member of each triad. Alternatively s/he can specify a context (e.g., a family meal) and identify the most important three elements involved.

The similarity between these two elements is referred to as the *emergent pole* of the construct; the difference between these two and the third element is the *implicit pole* of the construct. This ensures that all the constructs elicited are bipolar in nature (like the traits in trait theories of personality). As an example, suppose that your participant has chosen brother, mother and father as elements. S/he might decide that brother and mother are both argumentative, while this description would certainly not apply to father. Therefore, 'argumentative' becomes the emergent pole; perhaps 'passive'

Table 19.1 Specific role titles suggested as elements (after Kelly 1955)

Role no.	Role title
1	A teacher you liked (or the teacher of a subject you liked).
2	A teacher you disliked (or the teacher of a subject you disliked).
3	Your wife/husband or present girlfriend/boyfriend.
4	An employer, supervisor or officer* under whom you worked or served and whom you found hard to get along with (or someone under whom you worked in a situation you did not like).
5	An employer, supervisor or officer under whom you worked or served and whom you liked (or someone under whom you worked in a situation you liked).
6	Your mother (or the person who has played the part of a mother in your life).
7	Your father (or the person who has played the part of a father in your life).
8	Your brother nearest your age (or the person who has been most like a brother).
9	Your sister nearest your age (or the person who has been most like a sister).
10	A person with whom you have worked who was easy to get along with.
11	A person with whom you have worked who was hard to understand.
12	A neighbour with whom you get along well.
13	A neighbour whom you find hard to understand.
14	A boy you got along well with when you were in high school (or when you were 16).
15	A girl you got along well with when you were in high school (or when you were 16).
16	A boy you did not like when you were in high school (or when you were 16).
17	A girl you did not like when you were in high school (or when you were 16).
18	A person of your own sex whom you would enjoy having as a companion on a trip.
19	A person of your own sex whom you would dislike having as a companion on a trip.
20	A person with whom you have been closely associated recently who appears to dislike you.
21	The person whom you would most like to be of help to (or whom you feel most sorry for).
22	The most intelligent person whom you know personally.
23	The most successful person whom you know personally.
24	The most interesting person whom you know personally.

Note: *In the early 1950s, young American men were required to undertake a year's service in the armed forces.

Emergent pole	1	2	3	4	5	6	brother	mother	father	10	Implicit pole
argumentative							⊗	⊗	○		passive

Figure 19.2 Example of item in repertory grid

could be the implicit pole. These poles form the ends of the first construct in the grid, and would be represented as in Figure 19.2. S/he would then place a tick under each element that agrees with the emergent pole of the construct.

Continue building the grid in this way until you have generated as many constructs as possible (within reason). You would expect to have at least ten or so in order to perform a meaningful analysis.

The constructs elicited in this way are referred to as *subordinate* constructs. This is because they are relatively superficial in that they are derived to some extent from free association of the data. We may decide, however, that these are sufficient data to move forward to the analysis stage. This is particularly true if we are hoping to combine data from a sample of different grids to search for more general patterns of response (in this context, the grid operates more like an attitude scale than a personal construct technique).

However, we may wish to delve deeper into the private worlds of our participants, and in this case we may attempt to identify *superordinate* constructs, which can be elicited using Hinkle's (1965) *laddering* technique. This is effectively an interviewing technique where the participant is probed on each subordinate construct. Using the above example, you might wish to probe your participant on the construct of argumentativeness–passivity. First of all, which of the poles is preferable? Why? Your participant may reply that argumentativeness is preferable because it displays spirit, or 'mettle', while passivity is a sign of bland acceptance of the way things are. From this point, then, we could move to a superordinate construct with 'challenging' as the emergent pole and 'accepting' as the implicit pole. Then, ask the participant why challenge is important. S/he might say that we live in an unfair world full of cheats and charlatans: this may elicit the superordinate construct of 'just–unjust'.

The point about superordinate constructs is that they may link together a number of subordinate constructs. You might find that the superordinate construct 'just–unjust' also covers two or three other subordinate constructs besides 'argumentative–passive'. This gives you a broader picture of the way your participant constructs his or her social world.

Analysing the grid

If you prefer to use repertory grid technique as a qualitative method, you may find that the creation of subordinate and superordinate constructs is sufficient for your analysis. However, personal construct theory, despite its surface similarities to approaches like social constructionism,[1] was actually developed during a 1950s academic climate that was heavily concerned with quantification, and Kelly himself proposed several statistical techniques that could be used to analyse grids. He saw the grid itself as 'premathematical', on which all manner of analyses could be carried out.

A simple approach is to ask your participant to *rate* each element on each construct, say, on a scale of 1 to 5. You could then perhaps carry out correlation analyses between different elements and different constructs in order to develop a clearer picture of the participant's personal constructs. An alternative approach is to *rank* elements and constructs. This is done by selecting the first construct and asking the participant to place the elements in rank order (1st = most characteristic of the emergent pole, down to, say, 15th = most characteristic of the implicit pole). Repeat this process for all the constructs in the grid. Again, this data lends itself to (Spearman) correlational analysis.

It is perfectly legitimate to carry out factor analysis of the grid, although statistical purists would probably object! Kelly suggested a nonparametric form of factor analysis in his original work, although sadly this idea seems not to have been taken up by subsequent theorists. As it stands, factor analysis of grids seems no more or less valid than factor analysis of Likert-type scales, since both types of data set are constrained (ranked grids more so). One suggestion is that the data set can be made more stable if the number of elements is substantially greater than the number of constructs. This depends, however, which way up we wish to study the matrix. We *could* invert the matrix, as in Q methodology, and search for principal components underlying the constructs. This approach would underline the essential similarities between Stephenson's and Kelly's methods.

An alternative statistical approach is to provide a graphical representation of the participant's personal world. This can be done using multidimensional scaling, which is probably more appropriate than factor analysis when analysing ranked grids, or cluster analysis. See Chapter 10 for further elaboration on these methods.

One other use of statistical analysis is to combine the data collected in a variety of grids. This is more likely to form the basis of an academic research study than a clinical interview technique (more typical for the use of individual grids). An example of each type of approach is listed below.

The individual grid: an example from the clinical literature

Pollock and Kear-Colwell (1994): violence against partners

There is no reason why the use of individual grids should be confined to the clinical literature, except that this is the most common field in which they are presently used. This study used grids to investigate the 'personalities and perceptions' of two women who had committed serious violent offences against their partners.

In both cases, the researchers used role construct repertory grids similar to that devised by Kelly, and elicited constructs using the triadic method. Each element was rated on a scale of 1 to 7 and the matrices were individually analysed using principal components analysis. The resulting factors were then used to identify superordinate constructs, with the factor loadings indicating how strongly each element was related to that construct.

For example, in case 1, the first component to be identified incorporated the subordinate constructs whose emergent poles were 'emotionally close', 'kind', 'taking responsibility' and 'liking self'. The highest-loading elements on this component were 'father', 'successful person', 'ideal self' and 'person never in trouble'. From the therapist's point of view, this was a very significant finding, because the client's father had a history of sexual abuse against her.

In case 2, the first component incorporated the subordinate constructs whose emergent poles were 'law-abiding', 'guilt free', and 'respected'. The element 'myself as a victim' had a high negative loading on this component, as did 'a person who feels guilty' and 'myself seen by others'. The authors take this finding to suggest that the client feels guilty about her sexual victimisation by others (she also had a history of abuse, this time by a stepfather, who emerges a lot more negatively from the grid than case 1's father).

In both cases, there was a tendency for the client to feel guilt as an offender and to deny any causal link between their offences and their previous sexual victimisation by others. The authors embarked on a programme of cognitive-analytic therapy which was intended to break down the structure by which these women viewed each relationship by casting themselves in the role of either 'abuser' or 'victim'.

A year later, the clients were presented with their original grids and asked to complete them in the same way. This time, the elements 'myself as I am' and 'myself as an offender' were much further apart than on the original grids, and 'myself as a victim' had become much further away from 'person who feels guilty'.

This study offers a good example of the positive role that repertory grids can play in the clinical setting, and also of the appropriateness of using factor analysis as an alternative to laddering to identify superordinate constructs. Those with a more qualitative leaning, however, may feel that it is preferable to arrive at these through interview rather than statistical analysis.

Comparisons using grids

Smith (1994): psychological construction of home life

This example ties together repertory grids with the diary techniques discussed earlier in the chapter. These techniques were used to explore the psychological construction of home life. The data collection and analysis for this study took place in a number of stages. First of all, 19 married or cohabiting heterosexual couples (all undergraduates) completed diaries over a 24-hour period where concurrently, but separately, they described the physical location, activity, social context, duration, and their mood for each meaningful piece of activity. A content analysis was then performed on these diaries, and 25 items were derived for use as elements in the repertory grids. Some examples of the elements include:

- *Ironing, folding clothes*
- *Laundry; washing; hanging out clothes*
- *Listening to radio or music*
- *Drinking tea/coffee/juice/beer/wine*
- *Gardening, watering garden, mowing lawn*
- *Being intimate with partner*[2]

A member of each couple was then asked to select the elements (printed on individual cards) that applied to their home life. They then elicited a set of constructs, by the triadic method, using these elements. To aid this procedure, they were encouraged to separate the elements into two separate piles representing similar or different items. This process continued until the participant was unable to supply any more meaningful constructs, or all the different items had been accounted for by constructs. The average number of constructs generated by each participant was 9.2, the range being from 5 to 16.

The constructs in this study were treated rather differently than in traditional repertory grid design. Rather than treating them as essentially bipolar, the emergent poles of each construct were regarded as the 'more important' end of the construct, and the elements were scored as either 1 (associated with the important, or emergent, pole), or 0 (associated with the other end).

This procedure prepared the data for multidimensional scaling. The grids of 0s and 1s are described as *binary similarity matrices*, which were analysed using a program called SSA (Similarity Structure Analysis, Borg and Lingoes 1987). This produces a plot of points on a selected number of axes, and then computes a statistic (K) to describe the goodness of fit for that description of the data (the implication is that, if a grid is featureless and tells us little about the participant's perceptions of home, it will not produce a neat pattern of points on a scale).

The individual grids were then compared using a 'centroid configuration' technique, PINDIS (Procrustean Individual Difference Scaling) (Lingoes and Borg 1976). This transforms the configurations of all the individual grids (necessary because each participant generated their own unique set of constructs), to identify a common pattern among the different elements. This analysis allowed four distinct clusters to be identified. These were defined as:

- Recreation (reading, listening to music, watching TV, sleeping)
- Social interaction (being intimate with partner, talking to partner, entertaining, caring for children)
- Chores (eating alone, tidying, dressing, gardening)
- Housework (laundry, ironing, cleaning, cooking)

These clusters were differentiated according to psychological factors such as the degree of control which people can exert. This may distinguish activities in an obvious way (say, between reading and washing up), but also identifies more interesting contrasts (for example, 'eating a meal alone' is clustered with chores, whereas 'eating a meal with partner' is clustered with other social interaction activities).

Further analyses were carried out using information based on sex, gender role, and presence or absence of children. These found slightly different patterns for women and men, with the personal control factor being more salient for women. However, men with children were more like women in this regard than men in childless couples.

This study offers an interesting use of repertory grid technique, although it has taken the application and analysis of grids in a slightly different direction from Kelly's original purpose.

OTHER METHODS USING SELF-GENERATED DATA

There are potentially as many methods of getting participants to generate their own data as there are different research studies. Technically, it could be argued that a technique becomes a method only after it has been replicated by another researcher (which rules out a lot of qualitative research, and on both sides of the divide there are those who would argue that this is fair enough). Every now and then a method becomes popular in a specific field, and I shall end this chapter with a brief description of the *photo essay*, which has been used by a number of researchers studying gender and self-concept.

Photo essays were first described by Ziller (1990), and subsequently used by Dollinger and Clancy (1993) to identify differences between the ways men and women define the self. The technique involves asking participants to create a description of 'how you see yourself' by taking twelve new photographs and arranging them in a booklet along with a caption for each picture and a brief essay discussing how (and if) the photos achieve this goal. Photos used depicted the participant in various settings – at home, at work, with friends – and provide interesting information such as physical characteristics, dress, social relationships, hobbies and interests. Clancy and Dollinger found that men used significantly more photos of themselves alone than women did, thus supporting the hypothesis that men have a more independent sense of self (or 'self-construal') than women.

Lippa (1997) used this technique to study the concepts of masculinity and femininity. They got 189 psychology students to create photo essays and then asked an independent panel of undergraduates to rate the essays on 38 characteristics using a 7-point scale. The characteristics were a mixture of personality terms and words which are intended to be characteristic of either masculinity or femininity, such as 'anxious', 'athletic', 'creative' and 'family-oriented'.

The ratings were found to have high reliability, although this was more true for male essays than female ones, and higher for surface traits such as attractiveness than for inferred traits such as 'calm/relaxed' and 'unconventional'. The ratings were then correlated with the participants' own self-reported personality measures such as the Bem Sex Role Inventory (Bem 1981). High correlations were reported for femininity and masculinity in men, but not in women. This suggests, interestingly, that the masculine–feminine dimension might be a descriptive term for men alone rather than a point of difference between the sexes. When applied to women, it seems to offer primarily a description of physical attractiveness rather than behaviour. The study as a whole suggests that photo essays are a reliable way of providing information about the self that is relatively consistent with performance on standard personality measures.

Of course there is no reason to suppose that self-generated data like the photo essay might not be analysed at a qualitative level. There is plenty of scope for research using these types of open-ended methods.

Summary

The methods covered in this chapter present the researcher with some different challenges from the more traditional type of design. Diaries encompass a wide range of approaches and in some studies may be little more than questionnaires that participants complete more than once. In others (dream diaries, for instance) they are as 'open-ended' as any method, giving the participant full control over data generation. I have said little about analysis in this section, unusually in the scope of this book, because there are as many potential techniques as there are data that can be applied in this area. Repertory grids differ from diaries in that they conform to a regular and rigid structure, but this structure is ingeniously designed to elicit as rich a data set as possible within the confines of a formal scaling method. Again, analytical procedures are flexible, and, like Q-sorts can be qualitative or quantitative. There are plenty of other self-generated methods I have not discussed here – story completion tasks, for instance, occasionally appear in the literature, and of course there are many projective techniques from clinical and psychoanalytic fields. But it is time to bring the methodological content of this book to a close, and start to consider some of the things we might do (or not do) with the data we have collected and analysed.

Notes

1 It is important to distinguish between social constructionism (the philosophy behind most forms of discourse analysis) and *constructivism*, the philosophy deriving from Kelly's personal construct theory. The two terms are frequently used interchangeably, especially by people who are not familiar with one or the other (or either!) There are subtle but important differences between the two, as I hope this book makes clear.
2 It is assumed, though not explicitly stated, that this refers to physical intimacy, since there is a separate element 'talking with partner'.

Part VI

Uses and abuses of research

Most of the chapters in this book so far have been concerned with conducting research and analysing data, but I want to end by considering a number of important issues that confront psychologists during and after the research process itself. The first of these is ethics. Increasingly, researchers are asked to consider the ethical implications of their work, and university psychology departments in the UK now have internal ethics committees which screen proposed research for potentially problematic issues that might arise. Chapter 21 is concerned with the debate about the use of null hypothesis significance testing, and some alternative (or supplementary) approaches that have been proposed. The book finishes with two chapters concerning issues which are essential for survival in the modern academic world – writing research papers for publication, and writing proposals for research funding. Increasingly academics are being assessed on these two skills alone, so it is important that they are acquired as early in the research career as possible.

20 Ethical issues in psychological research

Introduction

Every undergraduate will be familiar with the need to observe a code of ethics when carrying out research in psychology. However, they may not always pay much attention to this code. It is tempting to see ethical concerns as peripheral to the real business of intellectual endeavour and empirical investigation, and ethics panels as party poopers and spoilsports. But ethics panels would not exist in a world where all researchers were as concerned for the welfare of their participants as for their research ratings. It is also easy for researchers to forget some of their basic responsibilities – notably, the reputation of their research institution, and, even more importantly, the reputation of their discipline.

In this chapter I will discuss some of the central ethical concerns in contemporary psychology research, and suggest ways of tackling these without compromising the basic research questions, or the scientific status of the research. I have narrowed the concerns down to five broad areas that are relevant across most branches of contemporary psychology, though they manifest themselves in different ways according to the nature of the research. Many of the ideas in this chapter are discussed in greater depth by Kimmel (1996).

Deception

I shall start with the most controversial of the issues, the use of deception in psychological research. Deception is largely used in experimental settings, although there are issues relating to survey research as well. It is a problematic area because many researchers would argue that it is an essential characteristic of a successful psychology experiment. Without deception, they might say, we would need to close down the laboratories and carry out all research observing naturally occurring behaviour in the field. Therefore, when addressing the issue of deception, we need to consider how necessary it is for experimental participants to be kept naïve, and on which occasions some mild deception might be acceptable.

In many forms of experimental psychology, deception is liable to be harm-less, consisting of little more than naïveté to the experimental condition, unexpected delays between stimuli and response, or 'distractor' tasks. Most of the time, the issue is one of *incomplete* disclosure rather than outright deception; if participants were given constant feedback about the purpose of the experiment and the manipulations involved, the experiment would have no ecological validity at all, and participants would find the experience thoroughly tedious. However, throughout the last century the use of decep-tion in social psychology has been a major bone of contention, and has at times threatened the fabric of the (sub)discipline itself.

Probably the most famous case of deception in social psychological re-search is the series of studies carried out in the 1960s by Stanley Milgram, where naïve participants were led to believe that they were administering lethal electric shocks to a fellow participant as 'punishment' for making errors on a learning task (Milgram 1974). In fact, the 'fellow participant' was an actor, employed by Milgram to bellow as though in pain each time the real participant pressed an appropriate switch. While participants were debriefed at the end of the experiment, during the trials many became seriously dis-turbed by the whole experience. This did not always prevent them from continuing with the punishment until the voltage read 'XXX: certain death', and the actor's bellowing had diminished into ominous silence.

Milgram's studies were instrumental in awakening the discipline of psy-chology to its responsibilities towards the welfare of research participants. In 1973, the American Psychological Association (APA) published a set of ethical principles for human participants in research which drew special attention to the use of deception. They stressed the responsibility of the investigator to justify the use of deception in terms of the value of the study, to consider alternative procedures, and to debrief participants as soon as possible (APA 1973).

Milgram defended his use of deception on each of these counts. First, he argued that the findings of his experiments were of great value to society because they revealed some of the processes that lead ordinary human beings to carry out unreasonable or even extreme acts when ordered to do so by an authority figure. He drew a parallel between the compliance of his naïve participants and the carrying out of atrocities in wartime. Critics argue that the artificial setting of the laboratory at Yale made it impossible for Milgram to apply his findings to natural environments, and that the bond of trust established between participant and experimenter is short-lived compared to the more complex relationships between military personnel in wartime. There are also suggestions that participants were likely to have suspended disbelief during the trials, even in modifications of the original experiment where the naïve participant was required to force the actor's hand down on to a 'shock plate'.

It is extremely unlikely that any ethics panel would grant Milgram permission to carry out his research today without making fundamental alterations to his procedure. How might we address the issue of obedience *without* deceiving participants? One way would be for an experimenter to issue a series of increasingly unreasonable demands, and to find out at what point a participant refused to comply. In essence this would be no different to the Milgram study, except that one of its characteristics was the experimenter's cue 'You have no choice; the experiment requires that you continue'. Most ethical guidelines now emphasise that participants have the right to withdraw from a study at any point they choose, so the act of withdrawal itself could be treated as the dependent measure in such a study.

An alternative approach might be to *simulate* a situation under which participants were required to carry out orders. Today, many simulation studies involve the creation of 'vignettes', or stories, where participants are asked to respond as though they were the person in the situation described. However, such studies are far from naturalistic and are extremely vulnerable to social desirability effects. The same criticism could also be directed at role-playing studies, although these are hardly free from ethical problems. A classic example of a role-playing study that caused great psychological distress to the participants is the famous Stanford prison experiment (Haney *et al.* 1973).

Gross and Fleming (1982) reviewed over 1000 research papers in leading social psychology journals over a twenty year period, and found that over 60 per cent involved some kind of deception. By far the most common, and a characteristic of more than 80 per cent, was a 'cover story', or false purpose. False information was present in 42 per cent, and the use of 'confederates' of the experimenter as false participants was present in 29 per cent.

It is often assumed that the problems of deception are a quirk of psychology's history, and that contemporary studies are all carried out with respect to the participants' welfare. However, Adair *et al.* (1985) found that, many years after the publication of the APA's ethical guidelines, plenty of cases of unjustified deception could be observed in leading journal articles.

Experimental settings are not the only places in which research participants may be deceived. In Chapter 8, I discussed the lengths to which test constructors may go in order to conceal the true nature of their measures, such as embedding the real question within other, less interesting, items. Many questionnaires are designed in such a way as to elicit information that, with full awareness, respondents might be less keen to impart. A good example, provided by Kimmel (1996), is the use of 'date of birth' rather than 'age'. Also, the use of leading questions may be problematic. Survey designers usually cover themselves in these situations by promising confidentiality and anonymity to participants; however it may be possible to use certain types of demographic information to identify individuals. If you have distributed a questionnaire to a lecture room consisting of 99 school leavers and one mature student, you have unwittingly breached your promise of anonymity if your instrument includes any sort of question concerning the respondent's age! Again most test creators now include a statement to the effect that the respondent may omit certain items if s/he prefers.

The studies discussed earlier in this chapter are, admittedly, extreme examples of deception. The effects of such research are hard to identify, because they rely on interpretations of such terms as 'loss of dignity' and 'psychological harm'. These issues will be discussed in more detail later in the chapter. Probably the greatest harm caused by deception, however, is that relating to psychology as a discipline. One of the biggest problems facing undergraduates at project time is the daunting task of participant recruitment. If there is a danger that they will suffer humiliation as a result of being deceived in a psychology experiment, the very idea might dissuade them from participating in *any* psychology research.

On the contrary, it could be argued that psychology participants *expect* to be deceived as part of the experimental procedure, and that much of the enjoyment in participating comes from trying to work out the purpose of the experiment. I remember participating in a study of group processes as an undergraduate in a laboratory with a one-way mirror (a symbol of deception if ever there was one!). Halfway through the (false purpose) task, we suddenly cottoned on to the purpose of the study and spent the rest of the trial trying to find out who was behind the mirror. As first year psychology undergrads we were hardly naïve participants, but this raises questions about the validity of findings from studies where deception plays such an important part.

The downside of these expectations, though, is that participants become suspicious even of genuine emergency situations. Kimmel (1996) reports a study in which, during a jury simulation study, a participant suffered a seizure. Luckily, a fellow participant had received medical training and was able to administer first aid. However, other members of the mock jury later admitted that they doubted the validity of the seizure and thought it might be part of the experimental deception. Unfortunately for experimental social psychologists, the word has got out: never trust those experimenters.

Protection of participants

The most important issue surrounding the Milgram studies concerns the lasting 'effect' of the experience of participating. There are numerous studies, most of them from the 1970s, which argue that there are very few long-lasting effects of deception in psychology experiments (see Kimmel 1996 for details). In surveys of undergraduates (a typical participant population), respondents generally agreed with the arguments behind the need for deception, and when experimenters who employed deception followed up their original participants, only a small percentage (under 10 per cent) regretted taking part.

It may, of course, be necessary to protect that small percentage from any adverse effects of participating in your study. One of the most important procedures when undertaking research is to identify potentially vulnerable participants, especially if the study involves anything that might cause offence or distress. This is particularly important for the institution that is responsible for the research, such as the university whose staff are conducting the study. Many psychology departments rely on good relationships with local schools and hospitals which are essential for recruiting research participants. Any complaints regarding experimental procedures or questionnaire items might result in the loss of that important link. In some cases (with special client groups, for example), this could threaten the future of a whole research centre.

There is a problem, however, in accurately assessing the degree to which psychology studies are likely to affect participants. Most of the guidelines regarding ethics are suitably vague on the unwelcome outcome of ethical violations. Ethical codes are littered with ambiguous terms such as 'dignity', 'stress', and 'psychological harm', and are largely open to interpretation. Also, while participants may be reminded of their rights regarding voluntary withdrawal, there may be individuals who are placed in a dilemma because they feel they are letting the researchers down by depriving them of a case, and persevere despite feeling uncomfortable. A solitary researcher might, in his or her eagerness to collect data, overlook such feelings. However, when research is carried out by a team, it creates more opportunities for identifying participant discomfort and to act accordingly.

The issue of participant protection is at its most important when the participants are unable to withdraw from the research setting for various reasons. Children are especially vulnerable, although most developmental psychologists are careful to make the research experience as enjoyable as possible for participants, and often parents are on hand in case of potential distress. The situation becomes more complicated when dealing with special adult populations, such as clinical samples. However, participants in these settings are usually protected by separate codes of ethics drawn up by clinics or hospitals.

Informed consent

The deception and protection problems are compounded by the need for studies to contain unexpected elements, without which it may be impossible to examine certain phenomena (implicit memory, for example). Nevertheless, participants should be given some idea of the nature of the study in advance, and some indication of any potentially unwelcome activities.

In the previous section, the topic of voluntary withdrawal was discussed in the light of participants experiencing discomfort in the research environment. This situation might be avoided if participants are given sufficient information at the point of recruitment. Levine (1975, cited in Kimmel 1996) lists eleven types of information that can be communicated at this point.

- Overall purpose of research
- Role of participant in the study
- Reason for choosing the participant
- Procedure, setting, length of participation and others involved
- Risks and discomforts
- Benefit of participating
- Alternative procedures (if relevant, unlikely in psychology research)
- Answers to any questions
- Suggestion that participant may like to discuss potential risks with other researchers
- Rights of withdrawal at any time
- Assurance of full debriefing following participation

It is unlikely that all these points would need to be addressed in a single study. Some points represent little more than good manners, such as explaining to a participant why s/he has been selected. If a researcher is handing out questionnaires indiscriminately in a public place, it may be polite simply to explain the nature of the recruitment to potential respondents, if only in the instructions at the top of the page.

Sometimes, however, there may be more mercenary reasons for recruitment. Many university psychology departments operate 'participant pools' where students are required to participate in research in exchange for course credit. Typically, credit is awarded per hour of participation, and students have to collect researchers' signatures in order to qualify. The alternative is often a mundane piece of written work, and the pool is 'sold' to the students as valuable research experience, so the vast majority are content to comply with it.

There are a number of sensible reservations about student participant pools, such that the APA felt it necessary to issue guidelines for running them in their 1982 revised code of ethics. Chief among the concerns is the lack of information given to participants, particularly at the outset of the study. Often students are not debriefed to the same extent as participants from outside the department. The APA guidelines highlight most of the points regarding informed consent listed earlier in the chapter, but also include items about treating student participants with 'respect and courtesy', and giving students the opportunity to feed back their views on the participation, particularly if there are any problems.

In addition to ethical concerns, criticisms of student recruitment pools are aimed at the use of students in psychological research in general. Very often students are used because they are cheap and available, particularly when researchers require data from the overall population. Clearly there are many reasons why psychology undergraduates are not representative of the population as a whole (entry criteria for university being simply part of the problem). Some journals now insist that authors present a strong case for the use of students as participants when submitting research papers.

Finally, there is even a query concerning volunteer participants in terms of their representativeness. Rosenthal and Rosnow (1991) list a number of characteristics of volunteer research participants. In the main they tend to be well educated, with high socio-economic status, intelligent and sociable. Perhaps most problematic of all, they also tend to be 'approval-motivated', therefore vulnerable to social desirability effects. Again it must be questioned whether research findings obtained with volunteers can be generalised to the overall population with as much confidence as researchers would like.

Right to privacy

Most of the issues discussed so far in this chapter are most relevant in the case of laboratory-based or survey research. When psychologists venture 'into the field' they encounter a whole new set of ethical dilemmas that need to be considered. These mostly concern the investigation of naturally occurring behaviour in observational studies, although increasingly, similar issues crop up in qualitative research, where single cases often form a large part of the reported data.

The classic ethical problem in field studies concerns privacy. If naturally occurring behaviour is the object of investigation, and researchers wish to remain unobtrusive, then it is important that the privacy rights of the people under observation are fully respected. It may seem surprising that privacy should be an issue when conducting an observation on a busy city street (for instance), but people can feel uncomfortable if they become aware that they are the object of a psychological study.

In this respect, privacy is closely related to *anonymity*, which is usually one of the assurances given to participants in questionnaire and interview research. Often trouble is taken to ensure that individuals are not easily identified from the data. This may be easy in the case of a test or a scale, where respondents are not required to write their names and may be asked to provide little in the way of demographic information. However, the more individual data are reported from the study, the more it becomes possible for participants to identify themselves (or, more worryingly, be identified by others).

Interview participants are routinely given pseudonyms in research papers, although the subject matter of the reported speech may make their real identities obvious to readers. Imagine a situation in which a participant is asked to give details of an extramarital affair. Their partner may happen to read the paper at some later date, and be horrified to find details of their relationship recounted in sufficient depth to identify them as well as the participant! From the researcher's viewpoint, one way of protecting yourself against any ethics-related charge is to allow participants to read the transcript before publication and grant consent for it (or specified parts of it) to be used. An experimental situation in which anonymity might be compromised is where a film is made of the study in which individual participants can be clearly identified by viewers. Famous footage remains of many classic experimental studies, but again it is necessary to obtain consent from participants at the end of the study before committing it to videotape.

However, it is less easy to guarantee privacy to participants in natural observational settings. The ethical issues are foggier here than in other types of research, which may be one reason why this type of study has become less popular over recent decades. Informed consent is impossible if we want to avoid *reactivity* (where the knowledge that people are under observation may cause them to behave differently from usual). Debriefing is problematic because – as with deception in laboratory settings – we do not wish to arouse suspicion in the general public. I teach once a year at a university summer school whose neighbourhoods are repeatedly under scrutiny by psychology students (often quite visibly) carrying out observational studies. We are never certain how much awareness local residents have about this annual activity!

Honesty

The last topic relates less to the conducting of research than to its dissemination. A researcher may well have carried out a study with impeccable attention to the welfare of his or her participants, only to invent an entire additional set of data in order to get the results published in a journal. Authors are rarely asked to provide evidence of collected data, and it is certainly possible for an entire study to be a complete work of fiction.

Many of the concerns about this type of 'unscientific conduct' date from the famous 'Cyril Burt affair', where a leading British educational psychologist was accused posthumously of fabricating data in order to create support for his theory of inherited intelligence (Kamin 1977). Not only were some of Burt's correlational data implausibly consistent, it now appears that he also 'invented' co-researchers to lend weight to his findings, since two of the cited authors on his research papers have never been traced.[1]

A number of safeguards have been put in place to try to prevent fraudulent data from being published. First, the scientific method insists on full procedural details of studies to be provided in the Method section of research reports. Any study whose results are doubted can be replicated by researchers in order to challenge its findings. In reality this very rarely happens, although this may be due mainly to the bias exerted by journals in favour of significant results, so many 'reversals' of published effects may go unpublished.

A second safeguard, against corruption in general, is the *peer review* process that authors undergo in order for a journal to publish a research paper. I will say more about this process in Chapter 22, but in short, a paper in a leading journal usually needs to be read by at least two experts in the field under investigation before the editor will agree to publication. Editors try to send papers to a broad range of referees rather than associates of the author, to avoid biased findings from slipping through, although this may not always be possible with studies on highly specialised subjects on which there are a small number of leading authorities who are all close friends!

Other safeguards concern the exploitation of data. One stipulation made by journals is that the data reported in a paper have not been published previously in another journal. Another precaution is that authors are asked to ensure that the same paper is not submitted to more than one journal at any time (see Chapter 22 for an explanation). Many researchers get round this stipulation by repackaging data, or by saving different analyses for separate publications. Most academic journals have such small readerships that such duplications tend to go unnoticed, unless the authors are well known, or the research is particularly noteworthy.

On the other side of the coin, there are instances where funding organisations have been known to block the publication of data that they consider to be against their best interests. This is more likely to occur with commercially funded research, where the funding body, or its products, are shown in an unflattering light by the findings of the study. In these cases, researchers need to decide how much their future careers depend on the investment of such organisations. It may be a case of balancing the importance of the findings against the wrath of the hand that feeds you – an ethical dilemma not unlike the others discussed throughout this chapter.

Summary

My intention in this chapter was to discuss ethics in such a way as to raise their importance throughout the research process, from recruiting the sample to publishing the data. Deception is a major problem for experimental psychologists, particularly those studying social phenomena, and poor attention to ethics here threatens the validity of the research. Participation in a psychological research project should be in some way beneficial; researchers are obliged to explain to their participants what they can get out of the experience, and consent should be based on reliable information at the outset. While most participants are flattered to think that their contributions will eventually appear in print, the findings may not necessarily be complimentary, and so privacy and confidentiality are essential. Finally, any research report should be as truthful as possible. Oscar Wilde once made the point that bad writing and immoral writing were pretty much the same thing, and this applies to research too; an unethical design is a bad design, as culpable as unforeseen and confounding variables in an experiment, or an inappropriately applied statistical test. Unethical studies are normally defended on the basis that they are 'good science'; Nazi experiments on prisoners of war were often conducted with rigorous application of scientific criteria, but whether we can regard these as 'good' science is another matter. As much as anything, ethics are about the *purpose* of research.

Note

1 The case of mystery research assistants raises another important ethical issue, to do with the *ownership* of the research in a published article. Most postgraduate researchers who have collected publishable data will hope to report their findings in a publication of some sort. They will usually write papers based on their findings, and a good supervisor will contribute to this process, offering guidance all along the way. In most cases, the first named author on a paper is the person who has written the paper. If the paper reports data collected as part of a research degree, the supervisor is entitled to be named as one of the authors, usually second (or third, in a case where the data were collected jointly perhaps between the student and a research assistant). Unfortunately, there are many cases where such papers end up being sent to a journal with the supervisor's name as first author even if the supervisor had done no more than stick his or her head round the door to answer a question. Few (if any) guidelines exist regarding protocol in these situations. Worse still are cases where undergraduate data (e.g., from a final year project) are reported without the student even receiving an acknowledgement, let alone an authorship.

21 Issues in design and statistics

Introduction

Ask a British psychologist what s/he considers to be the hottest topic in psychological research methods at present, and s/he is most likely to answer something along the lines of 'the qualitative/quantitative debate'. Judging by the content of *The Psychologist* (the journal of the British Psychological Society) during the 1990s, this would appear to be the case. The pros and cons of qualitative methods gained more coverage than any other methodological issue during that decade. Meanwhile, the American Psychological Association's journal – the *American Psychologist* – ran many articles on a quite different methodological debate; whether or not null hypothesis significance testing should remain the dominant statistical approach in psychology.

In some respects, this comparison is a reflection of the relative status of qualitative methods in psychology in Britain and the US. In both cases, however, the debates are central to the sort of psychological questions we wish to answer. The quantitative/qualitative 'debate' is a non-starter in many respects because we should not regard qualitative methods as an alternative set of techniques for exploring questions which are couched in the language of quantitative research (e.g., 'what is the effect of X on Y?'). Similarly, the abandonment of null hypotheses would eventually lead to psychologists asking different questions, since for so long we have been concerned with 'significance'. Perhaps we would start to design studies with a more exploratory flavour. Perhaps it would further increase the popularity of the qualitative approach.

In either case, the debate centres on the development of psychology as a discipline that behaves as if it were a physical science, in which there are knowable 'truths' and exact ways of measuring human behaviour. It is becoming increasingly clear that, whether we use quantitative or qualitative methods, we need to become a bit more honest about what it really is that we are researching. This is why I have emphasised the need for *appropriate* forms of investigation throughout the book.

Because most of the qualitative issues are covered in Part IV of the book, I will use this chapter to focus on the significance issue. For quantitative psychologists, this will be one of the most important methodological issues over the next decade or so, and also has implications for research methods training in psychology.

Null hypothesis significance testing (NHST): a matter for confusion

The practice of NHST dates back to the work of Ronald Fisher, the creator of ANOVA (see Chapter 1), and has been adopted wholesale by psychologists since the 1940s. A recent study by Hubbard *et al.* (1997) demonstrates how the use of significance testing in papers published in the *Journal of Applied Psychology* rose from around 23 per cent in the pre-war period to over 90 per cent in the 1990s. It is acknowledged by most (quantitative) researchers in psychology as the normal way to conduct statistical analysis; indeed, many might consider it the *only* way.

The training of psychology students has become fairly unequivocal on the matter. Introductory students, whether at A-level, or on the first year of a degree course, are told to *state the null hypothesis* at the outset of your study, then make a decision whether to *accept/retain* or *reject* the null hypothesis depending on the outcome of your statistical test. The null hypothesis is a statement about the population in which you are interested (for many psychologists, this is the world population). For example, 'smoking does not cause manic depression'. The accept/reject decision is based on the probability of obtaining your result if the null hypothesis is true. It is standard practice to accept a probability of 0.05 or lower as 'significant'. Therefore, if you obtain a *p* value of 0.05, this tells you that, *if the null hypothesis is true*, there is a 1 in 20 chance of such a result. This outcome is regarded as so unlikely as to lead to the rejection of the null hypothesis. Typically, an 'alternative' hypothesis, also stated in advance, is specified as the explanation for the finding.

You would think that a practice that has been universally adopted by psychology since the middle of the twentieth century would be clearly understood by all psychologists from level 1 upwards. However, this does not seem to be the case. In one study, 96 per cent of academic psychologists responding to a questionnaire claimed that a significance test indicated the probability that either the null hypothesis or the alternative hypothesis was 'true' (Oakes 1986). Such elementary mistakes abound in textbooks on introductory statistics (Dracup 1995) and in A-level statistics teaching (MacRae 1995).

Many methods teachers have tied themselves in knots trying to explain statistical significance to panic-stricken students. The students leave even more panic-stricken, and even those that grasp the basics of probability theory and its application to research fail to appreciate the precise meaning of *p* values and the role of the null hypothesis. The situation is not helped by the fact that methods teaching is seen as low-status fare by most academics, and is frequently left to postgraduates, who are almost as panic-stricken and confused as the undergraduates when it comes to statistical significance! The situation seems unlikely to improve in the future, with a move away from small group teaching and the increasing adoption of 'open learning' software packages for statistics teaching.

Various suggestions have been made to account for this degree of confusion. One argument is that the current situation arises from the 'hybridisation' of the Fisherian and Neyman-Pearson statistical traditions (Sedlmeier and Gigerenzer 1989). Whatever, the practice of NHST is commonly seen as counter-intuitive. Why test something you are not interested in? Most researchers set out to examine a particular effect or relationship, and they are interested in the size of that effect or relationship, not in a probability statistic relating to a supposedly uninteresting state of affairs as specified by a null hypothesis.

As a result of the confusion NHST has caused, some psychologists have gone so far as to claim that it should be abandoned in favour of alternative methods (Tryon 1998). Indeed in the late 1990s, a 'task force' was set up by the American Psychological Association (APA)'s Board of Scientific Affairs to examine the case for and against NHST. As a result, a new set of guidelines has been published which will have a substantial impact on reporting practices for psychology researchers (Wilkinson and the APA Task Force on Statistical Inference 1999)

PROBLEMS WITH NHST

In this section, I shall explore in more depth some frequently raised problems with, and objections to, NHST. I shall begin by considering some problems with the null hypothesis itself before moving on to issues concerning the nature of statistical significance and the use of probability.

What is the null hypothesis anyway?

Much of the confusion surrounding NHST lies in misunderstanding of the nature of the null hypothesis – what it refers to, what it means, and what we can say about it.

The null hypothesis is NOT a statement of 'no difference'

A common error is to assume that the word 'null' refers to 'nothing'. Although the etymological roots may be similar, null actually refers to the verb 'to nullify': therefore, the null hypothesis is the hypothesis to be nullified (Chow 1988). Rejecting the null hypothesis tells us nothing about an alternative hypothesis. We may specify an alternative hypothesis, but just because we have rejected the null, this does not mean that our alternative hypothesis is the one that best explains our results (although we would hope that our research design is sufficiently convincing for readers to draw that conclusion). This confusion is not helped by the use of the symbols H_0 and H_1, for null and alternative hypotheses respectively!

Nil or 'goodenough range' null hypotheses

If the null hypothesis is not a statement of 'no difference', how are we supposed to know when to reject it? This is the central concern of Cohen's now famous (1994) paper 'The earth is round ($p < 0.05$)'. Cohen argues that the specifications for the null hypothesis are sufficiently vague that statistical testing is meaningless. If the null hypothesis really does mean absolutely no difference whatsoever (i.e., that the difference between the lowest and highest means is zero), then it is almost certain to be rejected. Cohen assumes that researchers rarely mean, 'no difference whatsoever'. If they do, he suggests using the term *nil hypothesis*, which is more explicit.

It is more likely that a null hypothesis means 'no substantial difference', or 'no meaningful difference'. In which case, Cohen suggests the adoption of 'goodenough range' null hypotheses, where, on the basis of *a priori* power calculations, the researcher specifies precise limits for the null hypothesis. For example, 'the effect size is no greater than 8 raw score units, or $d = 0.5$'. The null hypothesis can then be rejected simply because the effect size is 9 units, or d is above 0.5.

What is the null hypothesis a statement about?

Some statisticians might balk at Cohen's suggestion of goodenough range hypotheses because it is too precise, and specifically concerned with the sample in the study. This relates to something of a debate-within-a-debate concerning the use of the null hypothesis – in particular, what rejection of the null hypothesis can tell us about our *population* of interest. Hagen (1997, 1998) points out that the null hypothesis is a statement about the population, not about the sample. This is not really in dispute. However, Thompson (1998), a fierce critic of NHST, argues that, while the *statement* may concern the population, the significance test can only tell us about the *sample*. Contrary to some claims, the p value tells us nothing about the likelihood of such results occurring in the rest of the population. Of course, as diligent researchers, we might like to think that our sampling procedure has been sufficiently thorough as to assemble a sample that is representative of the population. But significance tests cannot, by themselves, tell us the likelihood of replicating our finding with a different sample.

Use of *p* values

In psychological research over the last fifty years or so, rejection of the null hypothesis has been made solely on the basis of a probability statistic, or *p* value, calculated on the basis of an appropriate formula into which details of study design and observed values are entered, and the use of relevant tables which take sample size into account. A researcher obtained a test statistic, such as *F*, then looked this up against a critical value at a specified significance (alpha) level, typically $p = 0.05$. If the observed value was greater than the critical value (or lower, for ordinal tests), the researcher would claim the result as 'significant' and use this as the basis for rejecting the null hypothesis. It was then reported as $p < 0.05$.

Occasionally, an observed test statistic would be higher than the critical value at higher levels of significance, such as $p = 0.01$. For some time now, there has been a debate over whether to report such findings as $p < 0.01$, or $p < 0.05$. This may seem a point of pedantry, but it has notable implications for the use of statistical inference. In recent years, with the overwhelming popularity of statistical computer software, the situation has become more complex, with programs like SPSS producing precise *p* values at the click of a mouse. Contemporary journals are in a state of confusion over the issue.

The decision about using a preset alpha level is closely related to the other issues in NHST. Advocates of setting and referring to a preset cut-off point, such as 0.05, tend to be strong defenders of NHST, although even Fisher relented on this issue by the 1950s (Macdonald 1997). Most current authors recommend the reporting of precise *p*, so long as significance is not confused with statistics such as effect size. One way this happens is with the use of 'modifiers' – typically, 'highly/very significant' for *p* values below 0.01, and 'marginally significant' for those just below 0.05 (Harcum 1989). While probability is measured using an interval scale or continuum, whether or not a result is *significant* depends solely on the cut-off point. This is another argument against the use of NHST – as Rosnow and Rosenthal (1989: 1277) put it, 'surely God loves the 0.06 nearly as much as the 0.05'.

Alternatives to NHST

Given the increasingly stinging criticism of NHST, there have been major moves by the psychological establishment – in the US at least – to force journal editors to reconsider the emphasis placed on NHST in their papers. At least one journal (the *Journal of Applied Psychology*) now insists that its authors include measures of effect size 'unless there is a real impediment to doing so' (Murphy 1997).

Effect size, which I will consider in detail shortly, is not the only alternative to NHST, but it plays a crucial part in calculating the *power* of a study. Most critics of NHST regard power considerations as an essential element in a research report. Typically, power is portrayed as the reverse side of the coin, as featured in the classic 2×2 error type table often reproduced in textbooks (see Table 21.1).

Table 21.1 Typical 2 × 2 error type table

Decision	State of the world ('the truth')	
	Null is true	Null is false
Reject null	Type 1 error	Correct
'Accept' null	Correct	Type 2 error

A type 1 error is a rejection of a true null hypothesis. Obviously this is something we would want to avoid. Traditionally, measures such as the Bonferroni correction[1] are applied to avoid inflating the type 1 error rate when carrying out multiple comparisons, for example *post hoc* testing in ANOVA. A type 2 error is the failure to reject a false null hypothesis. This is sometimes regarded as a less serious error because it is portrayed as simply being over-cautious, depending of course on the nature of the null hypothesis.

Cohen (1992) and other writers have long railed against this view, urging journal editors and teachers of psychology to stress the importance of type 2 errors and the ways of avoiding them. This has led to the development of calculations of statistical power, where *power* is defined as the power of the study (or test) to detect a false null hypothesis. Its precise calculation is described in the next section, but essentially it is a combination of sample size, effect size, and level of significance.

Because power incorporates significance level, it is regarded as an all-encompassing alternative to NHST – as Cohen (1994) points out, it is not really an alternative to NHST but an *improvement*. However, it has taken a long time for it to make much impression on the psychology world as a whole. Cohen (1962) carried out a study of the *Journal of Abnormal Psychology* in 1960 and found that, for most studies, the likelihood of rejecting a false null hypothesis was less than 50 per cent – ironic given the emphasis on NHST. However, 24 years later, following many arguments for the consideration of power, and the development of calculations for this purpose, a follow-up study was conducted using the same journal by Sedlmeier and Gigerenzer (1989).

Remarkably, they found that the likelihood of rejecting a false null hypothesis was even *lower* in 1984. Where authors stated explicitly that they were testing a null hypothesis, it was estimated that, in 75 per cent of cases, a false null hypothesis would be accepted. Furthermore, in the 56 papers studied, there was hardly any mention of statistical power, and not a single calculation attempted. Nevertheless, 50 per cent of the papers adjusted the alpha level for the purpose of controlling type 1 errors in multiple significance tests (e.g. for a correlation matrix). The authors interpreted this finding as suggesting that researchers were 11–14 times more concerned with type 1 than with type 2 errors!

Cohen (1992) suggests the apparent reticence of editors and teachers to consider power is simply indicative of the slow pace of change in science, pointing out that it took Student's *t*-test 40 years to reach a textbook. Thompson (1999a) argues that the high rejection rate is a factor, and that until editors insist on power calculations, authors will continue to resist rocking the boat. He also argues that the adherence to NHST arises out of a misunderstanding of its application. Researchers behave as though a significant result indicates that the effect is present in the population (which it doesn't, it only refers to the sample), or at least that it tells us that a replication of the study would probably lead to similar results (again, this is not true).

These are plausible arguments for the neglect of power in psychological research. However, the most likely stumbling block concerns the teaching of power calculations as part of undergraduate training – or, more precisely, the lack of it. Typically students will be given a lecture on power, and some vague idea of its calculation, and that will be it. Ideally, power should not necessarily be allocated a slot by itself; it is either an essential part of the research design process, or not worth mentioning at all.[2] The point is illustrated by the result of a questionnaire study which found that, among a sample of postgraduates, most respondents recognised the relationship between power and sample size – but only one respondent (out of 52) understood the role of significance in power calculation (Wilkerson and Olson, 1997).

I will describe power analysis in more detail later in the chapter, but because there is still some uncertainty regarding the issue of effect size, I will discuss that statistic first, since it is an essential consideration for calculating power.

Effect size

The effect size (ES) of a study has been defined as the difference between the null hypothesis and the alternative hypothesis. To take a simple example, in an experiment with two groups of participants, with what Cohen describes as a 'nil' hypothesis (i.e., zero difference), then the ES is the difference between the treatment and control groups. Because we want to make inferences about the population, however, we do not simply use the difference in means; we need to adjust this according to the standard deviation of the population.[3] This would mean, in our experimental example, converting it to a different type of statistic. In regression-based studies, however, we can simply take R^2 as our effect size.

Thompson (1999b) identifies two classes of effect size statistics: *variance-accounted-for* statistics such as R^2 (and their corrected versions, i.e., adjusted R^2), and *standardised differences* such as Cohen's *d* and Hedges' *g*. Much of the time the nature of the statistical test will determine which class of statistic is more appropriate. For example, R^2 is produced by a typical regression study (and is often calculated by software programs along with an ANOVA table). For a t-test, though, a converted *d* score may be more appropriate.

The formulae for converting common test statistics to *d* are illustrated in Chapter 17. Essentially a *d* value is calculated by dividing the difference in raw scores by the standard deviation of the population (if known) or the sample. Cohen has proposed the following guide to interpreting *d* values (Table 21.2):

Table 21.2 Cohen's (1992) guide to interpreting the value of *d*

Effect	*d*
Small effect	0.2
Medium effect	0.5
Large effect	0.8

This is meant essentially as a *rough* guide, and some authors have warned against using these values as cut-off points, thereby repeating the fallacy of the 0.05 level in NHST.

There are some reservations about the use of ES as an abstract value (much the same as there are with *p*). We cannot necessarily use an ES derived from a controlled experiment as a measure of a real-world phenomenon in a population. As a remedy, Thompson (1999b) suggests that we try to make our ES meaningful – for example, the average number of years added to longevity through not smoking.

It is also important, for the same reasons, to treat ES as a descriptive statistic rather than a measure of significance *per se*. To cite Thompson (1999b) again, the *impact* of the effect is more important than its size; if smoking explains only 2 per cent of the variance in the incidence of lung cancer, this is nevertheless 'significant' in a real-world sense. The ES may be very small, and the *p* value well in excess of 0.05!

Incidentally, some software packages (notably SPSS) calculate a value known as η^2 (eta squared) as a measure of effect size. This belongs in Thompson's first class of ES statistics, so it is essentially a measure of 'variance accounted for'. It is important not to confuse this with Cohen's *d*, particularly when it comes to interpretation. Other authors recommend converting test statistics to *r* instead of *d*, and using this as a measure of effect (Howitt and Cramer 2000 illustrate the formulae for doing so). In these cases, you would need to interpret the statistic differently – Cohen suggests 0.10, 0.30 and 0.50 as low, medium and high effects respectively. There are a number of other plausible ES statistics – see Cohen (1988, 1992) for a full list.

Power calculations

As I indicated previously, the power of a study is a combination of sample size, effect size, and significance level. If we wish to calculate the power of a published study, these data are all we would need. However, there is a strong argument that power should not be used, like NHST, as part of a *post hoc* statistical analysis, but as a central feature of the study's design. It should be used before any data have been collected to inform researchers of the required sample size for a high power study.

Therefore, we can identify two types of power calculation: *prospective* power analysis and *retrospective* power analysis (from Sedlmeier and Gigerenzer 1989). Prospective power analysis is carried out at the end of the literature review, in the planning phase of a study, and relies on *estimates* of the relevant statistics. Retrospective power analysis is most useful for studies that have already been run, and is perhaps most appropriate for meta-analysis, or in studies where there are constraints on sample size, such as those using special populations.

Retrospective power analysis

Cohen (1988) contains a series of tables that can be used to calculate power retrospectively, if both *d* and sample size are known. The power statistic that results is a number between 0 and 1. Since the probability of making a type 2 error is symbolised by β (beta), power is $1 - \beta$, in other words the inverse of the probability of making a type 2 error. Therefore, if you have an extremely powerful study in which the probability of making a type 2 error is only 1 per cent, then power = 0.99. Cohen has recommended that 0.8 be regarded as a desirable power level; this is high enough to avoid a type 2 error with confidence, but not unrealistically high for most psychological studies.

Prospective power analysis

When planning a study, the calculation of power performs a different role, and makes quite a radical departure from the traditional research process of predicting some vague effects, and plucking a sample size out of thin air.

The goal of prospective power analysis is to identify the sample size you need to achieve a power of 0.8 in your study. In order to do this, you need to work backwards. You will require the following information:

- the test you will be using (t-test, ANOVA, chi square, etc.)
- a desired significance level (usually 0.05)
- a likely effect size (usually medium, but sometimes small or large; you estimate this on the basis of previous research in the area)

An example: you are using a t-test to compare two experimental groups, with a desired significance level of 0.05, and from the literature you would expect to obtain a medium ES; you will find that 64 participants are required for your experiment to obtain a power of 0.8.

Another example: you are planning to run a multiple regression analysis with four predictors from some survey data, with a desired significance level of 0.01 (recommended for multiple significance testing), and you are predicting a small effect size. You would need 841 respondents.

Generally speaking, power calculations are quite conservative when small effect sizes are predicted. Clearly, if we cannot demonstrate more than a small effect, we need to be certain that it is not a peculiarity of our sample, so the larger the sample, the more it informs us about the population. You might think that researchers could get away with predicting a medium effect each time and using fewer participants, even when the effect is never likely to be more than a small one. There is a case, therefore, for insisting that researchers provide evidence from the literature for the effects they are predicting. Where a study is purely exploratory, however, prospective power analysis would be less appropriate.

Some authors have suggested that the use of prospective power analysis points to a major shift in the way that research is evaluated. One went so far as to suggest that research articles should be submitted without results or discussion sections, so that editorial acceptance is guided by the power of the design rather than by the obtained results (Kupfersmid 1988).

Confidence intervals

Along with power calculations, many critics of NHST (notably Cohen 1994) encourage researchers to report confidence intervals (CIs) in the Results section of their reports. These have been available for some time on SPSS and other software packages, so their calculation poses little difficulty for a researcher. However it is important to be aware of what they refer to.

An experiment is conducted comparing performance in a driving simulation task between a sober group of students and a group whose members have consumed 4 units of alcohol (the groups have been matched on driving experience). The task resulted in two mean scores: 70/100 for the sober group and 45/100 for the drunk group. We find that the difference is significant at less than 0.05, which enables us to reject the null hypothesis that alcohol has no effect on driving performance. However, as has been argued earlier in this chapter, this does not tell us whether or not alcohol impairs driving performance for the *population* (i.e., all drivers). Perhaps students are less resistant to alcohol's effects!

In relation to the population, the means in a study of this type are referred to as 'parameter estimates'. They estimate the value we would expect any driver chosen at random from the population to obtain on the driving task. However, unless there is a standard deviation of practically zero in our study, it would be unlikely that that individual happened to score 70 when sober (or 45 when drunk). Therefore we need to be a bit more generous in our predictions, and specify a range, or interval, into which we can be expect their score to fall. This range is known as the *confidence interval*.

The confidence interval is important in terms of inference, because we assume that it contains the true mean for the population. If we set a range of 40–50 for drunk drivers, and 65–75 for sober drivers, then our study is more informative regarding the population we are interested in. If we make the intervals even larger, we are even more confident that they contain the population mean. We can use the standard deviation and sample size to calculate the probability of the population mean falling into the interval. In line with NHST, a value of 95 per cent is generally set as the minimum confidence level for these intervals; therefore, the intervals produced by SPSS and other programs are those where we can be 95 per cent confident that they contain the population mean. The top and bottom values in each interval are referred to as *confidence limits*.

Confidence intervals are popular because they are more informative than a bald statement of significance. In relation to NHST, all a *p* value does is offer the best guess about whether or not an effect equals zero; confidence intervals offer the best guess about the *value* of that effect (McGrath 1998).

Arguments against alternatives to NHST

Not surprisingly, given the slow response to their suggestions, the critics of NHST have themselves come in for some harsh criticism. Needless to say, the most resilient defenders of NHST are those who continue to ignore the criticisms, perhaps hoping that they will go away in time. Nevertheless, a few arguments have been made against the proposals of Cohen and others.

The most frequently voiced criticism of power analysis and confidence intervals is that they are essentially based on the same flawed logic as NHST (Frick 1995; Hagen 1997). Given that CIs are calculated using probability theory, and alpha level plays an important role in calculating power, this would seem a valid point – but only if power is treated as an *alternative* to NHST rather than a supplement (as in Cohen's argument). In the same way, criticisms that CIs and effect size tell us nothing about the *direction* of effect are valid only if they are to be used instead of NHST.

A more pertinent criticism of CIs and ES is one that has been touched on earlier, namely that they are somewhat bound to the particular idiosyncrasies of the study. To return to the driving simulation study example above, the CIs would only be relevant for the materials used in that particular study. Should the driving simulator be altered in any way, or damaged, so that it was impossible to replicate the study, the values would become meaningless. Parker (1995) argues that this argument can be extended to all kinds of psychological data, such as rating scales, and that even CIs determined from interval data are related to the number of items and are therefore of little use. While this criticism may seem to have some validity, it has to be said that it could be applied to most quantitative analyses of psychological data. Essentially, what we take from a study must be interpreted in the context of that study, and we should exercise caution when inferring from sample to population.

Perhaps the most inevitable source of resistance to the criticisms of NHST will be the teachers of statistics to psychology students. Given Cohen's insistence that power calculations and confidence intervals are supplementary to NHST rather than a replacement, this is understandable. Many of us have experienced headaches trying to explain the logic of statistical significance to undergraduates; now we will have to devote more precious timetable space to teaching power to a level that enables students to use it for all their practical exercises! In some respects, this is a good thing: it guards against the unthinking use of inferential statistics in research, a bad habit that is probably acquired during undergraduate training. If nothing else, the criticisms of NHST force us to rethink the way we do, and interpret, quantitative research.

Guidelines proposed by the APA Task Force on Statistical Inference

A set of guidelines drawn up by the APA were published in the *American Psychologist* in 1999 (Wilkinson and the APA Task Force on Statistical Inference 1999). These are aimed primarily at the editors of psychology journals, particularly those published by the APA, with regard to the kind of information they should demand from their authors, and were devised by a large panel of experts (such esteemed figures as Cronbach and Tukey acted as consultants). APA journals are generally regarded as the most prestigious in the psychology world at present, and include such titles as *Psychological Bulletin*, *Psychological Review*, *Developmental Psychology*, *Journal of Experimental Psychology* and *Journal of Personality and Social Psychology*. Any advice adopted by these journals is likely to lead the rest of the field in effecting change over the next few years, so it is worth taking note of the suggestions.

Some of the guidelines address directly the criticisms of NHST outlined in this chapter; others concern unrelated or indirectly related matters. What follows is a potted summary of these guidelines, or at least those guidelines that indicate a shift away from earlier conventions.

Use of 'control groups'

This is partly a matter of experimental design, and partly a matter of terminology. The task force points out that, for a no-treatment group to be called a 'control' group, its members should be assigned on a truly random basis, either using a computer program or random number tables. If your group is a no-treatment group, or another sort of comparison group, the task force recommends 'contrast' group as the appropriate term.

Numbers of participants

This is a direct result of power considerations: in addition to stating the size of the sample in a study, the author must justify the use of that sample size. In other words, you should describe the power calculations that were used to arrive at that figure, along with (where appropriate) the effect size estimates derived from the research literature. This is intended to prevent researchers opting for the smallest possible N when they have no reason to expect more than a small effect.

Report complications in the data

As much as anything, this recommendation is intended for the benefit of the reader who might be considering following up the research. Any complications, such as missing data, or nonresponse, should be reported, and also the means for dealing with these. In particular, authors are advised against pairwise and listwise deletion (often offered by statistical packages).

Use minimal methods

'Do not choose an analytic method to impress your readers or to deflect criticism' (Wilkinson and the APA Task Force on Statistical Inference 1999: 598).
If a t-test will suffice, there is no need for a $3 \times 4 \times 3$ ANOVA.

Null hypothesis significance testing

'It is hard to imagine a situation in which a dichotomous accept–reject decision is better than reporting an actual p value, or, better still, a confidence interval. Never use the unfortunate expression "accept the null hypothesis". Always provide some effect size estimate when reporting a p value' (ibid. 1999: 599). Authors are encouraged to check out Cohen's (1994) article, which recommends 'goodenough' range hypotheses, although these are not explicitly referred to in the guidelines.

Avoid multiple effects testing

This is perhaps the most controversial guideline in the paper, if only because it has repercussions for a substantial number of studies (perhaps the majority of psychology studies). It is therefore the least likely to be taken into account. The task force is highly critical of studies that display a correlation matrix spattered with asterisks indicating significant r values. 'If a specific contrast interests you, examine it. If all interest you, ask yourself why' (ibid. 1999: 599). The suggestion is that authors use this device in order to 'fish' for significant results to discuss. I would argue that the principal reason for this is fear of rejection. Therefore, if editors are asked to refrain from their bias towards significant results, then there will be less use of indiscriminate significance testing!

Greater use of graphics

The task force encourages authors to make more use of graphical information, particularly displays of interval estimates using meaningful scales (e.g., boxplots).

Effect size comparison

Where appropriate, compare the effect size of your study with those obtained in previous research as part of the Discussion.

Summary

The NHST/power debate will run and run. Cohen's first power analysis of the psychological literature was conducted at the beginning of the 1960s, yet its implications have only recently begun to be appreciated by most psychologists. I could have included large chunks of this chapter in Part IV of the book, as good reasons for conducting qualitative research. It certainly seems that the criticisms of NHST are more convincing than the remedies, which appear somewhat cumbersome, as if in these days of structural equations, log-linear modelling and factor analysis we are not churning out enough statistics. One of the best arguments against padding out research articles with confidence intervals and the like is that applied psychologists have enough trouble explaining significance to the users of their research, without piling more numbers on top. There is a real danger that overegging the pudding with stats pushes psychology further up the ivory tower; the opposite of the 'dumbing down' that we try so desperately to avoid. However, if focusing on power issues forces psychologists to think harder about the real meaning of significance testing and the routine use of inferential statistics, perhaps it is for the best.

Notes

1 To apply the Bonferroni correction, you need to divide alpha (usually 0.05) by the number of comparisons in the study. For example, if you have a one-way ANOVA with four levels, and you wish to compare (level 1 vs. level 2) and (level 1 vs. level 4), then you should raise alpha to 0.025. This is based on probabilistic assumptions concerning the likelihood of obtaining a significant result by chance.
2 An eagle-eyed (pedantic) reader might observe that, inserting a chapter on significance and power at the back of the book is committing the same error as I am presently criticising psychology teachers for. The same argument could be applied to the chapter on ethics. All I can say in my defence is that the book is intended to

be helpful and accessible, not groundbreaking. Throughout, this book is intended to reflect the state of research methods teaching and thinking as it is, not as it ought to be (although I allow myself a spot of didacticism from time to time . . .).

3 Statisticians often talk about obtaining 'population' information as though this were a simple matter of consulting the research literature, or a special data base. In psychological research, this information is rarely available, so we can only use the data available in our study. In this case, the nearest estimate we would have to the population is the standard deviation of the sample as a whole (i.e., regardless of whether the participants are in the control or treatment groups).

22 Writing for publication

Introduction

The final two chapters in the book concern the scholarly activities that academic staff find themselves engaged in much of the time when they are not actively carrying out teaching and research. It is not enough simply to conduct research in a vacuum; if you have found anything interesting at all, it needs to be reported and disseminated to the outside world. Naturally, the most obvious way of doing this would be to contact a national newspaper and sell them a story, but journalists are unlikely to be impressed by a single researcher's claim. Your claim needs rubber-stamping, and the most impressive way of doing this is to publish your findings in an academic journal.

Writing research papers for journals is a daunting task for all but the most successful and experienced researchers. The world is full of research psychologists who want to further their reputations, and there is only so much paper to go round. There are literally hundreds of academic journals which publish articles by psychologists, and it is still not enough. As a result, each submitted paper is more likely to be rejected than accepted. Most that are accepted are only accepted after substantial revision. Getting published involves a lot of hard work, and, worst of all, there is no material benefit to the author whatsoever. Increasingly, however, academics are evaluated by their lists of publications, and the quality of the list may make all the difference between success and failure in future job applications. Learning the skills of successful publishing early on in your career can do you no harm.

The review process

As I have said, there are hundreds of academic journals out there, but none is itching to publish your research. Their offices are all groaning under the weight of submitted papers, most of which will be returned to the authors with 'Dear John' letters attached. What makes an editor reject a paper? How do they decide which ones to accept? These questions have vexed academics for years.

I shall start off by saying a little about the review process itself, since it helps to be familiar with the procedure. Imagine you have written a report of your most recent study and decided to send it to a moderately prestigious journal (more on prestige later) – let's call it the *Bognor Regis Journal of Psychology*. The inside cover of the journal contains all the submission information you need, including the presentation details (how many copies you need to send, whether to include a title page, whether to put tables and figures on separate pages, etc.), the name of the editor, and the address.

Since the editor is almost certain to be a tenured academic (i.e., working for a university somewhere), there will be a delay between your paper arriving at the address and the editor opening the package. If the address is a special office at a publishing company, or at the APA or BPS, it will sit there until the editor calls in, or (more likely) an assistant decides that it's time s/he bundled up the last 50 papers that have arrived and sends them to the editor in the post. In some cases the address is the editor's institution, in which case it will be dealt with more speedily.

The editor will probably set aside one day each month to go through the last batch of submitted papers, and will spend that day allocating the papers to the various subeditors listed on the masthead of the journal. Big journals, such as *Psychological Bulletin*, who have hundreds of submissions each month, have a long list of subeditors, because one person alone could not hope to deal with all those papers. Your paper will be allocated to the subeditor who is the closest person on that list who is a specialist in your field. Imagine your paper is an observation of children fighting in the school playground. There may not be anyone specialising in children and aggression, but on a general psychology journal, there is almost certain to be someone with a broad knowledge of developmental psychology. Your paper will be sent to that person in due course.

The next step in the process involves the subeditor skim-reading your paper to see, first of all, whether it is worth putting through the review process. Often, papers get sent back to authors without any peer review at all, because it is plain at first sight that the paper is unsuited to the journal. This may be because the content is inappropriate (more likely with specialist journals with well-defined fields), or because the presentation is inadequate (sections missing, inappropriate writing style, only one copy, wrong sort of article). Indeed many such papers would be returned by the editor at the first hurdle. The next task for the subeditor is to select appropriate referees for your paper. These are academics with expertise in your area (or as close as possible) who will give your paper a thorough review and make suggestions as to whether the paper should be published or not, and if so, whether there are any revisions or additions to be made.

Next, the subeditor then sends the copies of your paper (which is why you have to produce all those extra copies) out to two or three referees, who are asked to review the paper as quickly as possible. Given the number of hoops your paper has had to jump through, and that all the people involved are academics who are ferociously busy with teaching and research of their own, this process takes a long time. It may be six months before you hear anything, by which time you have probably forgotten you ever wrote the thing. Or you have found another study that completely invalidates your findings. What you should not do, in this period, is wait and wait for the outcome before moving on to the next stage of your research. You should not plan a research career one study at a time, because the academic world does not move quickly enough! The outcome of the review process should be little more than icing on the cake, and ideally, you should never have fewer than two papers under review at any given time. That way, each rejection is buffered by the knowledge that there is still another paper that might be accepted.

Eventually, one day when you least expect it, a letter lands in your pigeon-hole in an envelope headed *The Bognor Regis Journal of Psychology*. It contains a covering letter from the subeditor that describes the outcome of the review process, followed by a number of observations or recommendations. These letters are fairly formulaic, so after a while you get used to scanning them quickly for the important news. Typically, they begin with a certain amount of puffery about the review process (e.g. 'Three excellent reviews of your paper are enclosed . . . from experienced researchers with a great deal of expertise in the field'), and your eyes skip this to the important announcement in the second paragraph. This is indicated by one of two words. These words are 'sorry' and 'delighted'.

> I am sorry to say that, in the light of the reviewers' comments, this paper is not suitable for publication in *The Bognor Regis Journal of Psychology*.

> I am delighted to tell you that your paper is accepted for publication in *The Bognor Regis Journal of Psychology*.

Accompanying this letter will be copies of the referees' comments. These are usually anonymous, especially if the referee has recommended rejecting the paper. Receiving negative anonymous reviews makes for the lowest points of an academic career. Some reviewers can be unbelievably petty or pedantic, and occasionally quite insulting, and you don't even have a picture to place on your dartboard. Even positive reviews can contain gripes and patronising remarks. Take comfort from the thought that referees often treat manuscripts as the work of a novice, no matter how experienced the researcher. They are given no information about the author (this is referred to as a *blind* refereeing procedure), so the remarks are not personal – even though we always take them that way!

The best way to read these reviews is as constructive criticism. This is usually how the reviewers intend their remarks to be taken. Even if rejection is recommended, they try to be positive ('You have identified an important research question', 'I look forward to reading a resubmitted article', etc.), and sometimes even say things like 'I regret that I cannot recommend this paper'. Often the reviewer is very interested in your research but realises that, for whatever reason, it is not appropriate for the journal in its present state. I recently received, from the editor of a major journal, no fewer than four pages of suggestions of how to improve a (rejected) study. These involved writing a completely different paper, as it happens, but at least it demonstrated an interest from this journal in publishing my research! Generally, supportive referees *will* disclose their identity: this is a way of saying to the author that they are prepared to offer advice if s/he wishes to get in touch. Indeed, such communication has been known to lead to research collaboration!

Occasionally, things are a little more complicated. The editor is neither sorry nor delighted, but remains to be convinced: the paper is suitable for the journal, but needs substantial revision before it can be published. Sometimes this is expressed in the form of an invitation to *resubmit*, in which case the whole paper needs to be rehashed and submitted again as though it were the first time (except that you should include a covering letter explaining that it is a resubmission, and a detailed description of how you have addressed the referees' criticisms). It will be sent out again to at least one of the original referees, but also to at least one new referee.

An invitation to resubmit is, in some ways, the biggest headache for an author. Although it gives you hope, and is more positive than outright rejection, it means six months or more agonising over the rewrite, sending it off again and awaiting the outcome, which may yet result in outright rejection. Usually, resubmissions are invited because there is mixed opinion among the referees – you would not be asked to resubmit if all the reviews were negative or overwhelmingly positive. Alternatively, all the referees have identified the same flaw, and they have all recommended publication if that flaw is ironed out.

The best outcome – short of outright acceptance, which is very unusual in high-quality journals – is that you are asked to revise part of the manuscript. This may be something fairly cosmetic, like the design of a table or illustration. Or it may be more substantial, like adding a new section to the literature review, or carrying out additional statistical analyses. Sometimes you may be asked to integrate a particular theory into the paper in a way that affects all the different sections. Some of the most prestigious journals ask their authors to resubmit such papers. (This procedure holds things up a bit, and stops a popular journal from being overburdened with 'in press' material.)

Never mind – you are almost there. The editor will just check your revision, and then ask for a computer disk of the paper, which will be sent off to the production team. Then comes another long wait. It takes a surprisingly long time for journals (and books, for that matter) to be printed, so be patient, or, better still, forget about it completely for the meantime. Usually, you will have to wait at least a year to see the fruits of your labour. Notice how many journal articles end with a short statement like: 'Manuscript received 14 July 1997, accepted 28 March 1998'. You will find that the date of that journal itself will be 1999 (if not later).

While you are waiting, you can at least add a new entry to your publications list:

> Bloggs, J. (in press). Children fighting in the playground. *Bognor Regis Journal of Psychology*.

Selecting an appropriate outlet

As suggested in the previous section, a very common reason for rejection is that the author has sent the paper to the wrong journal. It is easy as a novice researcher to treat all journals as equivalent founts of knowledge, or variants on a general theme. In fact, each journal has its own history, its own readership, and its own editorial agenda. A paper may be rejected simply because it doesn't fit in with current editorial policy.

Therefore it is essential that you are familiar with any journal you would like to publish your research in. Read the contents of the most recent issues carefully. The masthead of the journal will include a brief description of the sort of articles it accepts – whether it will consider reviews of the literature, or short research reports, or qualitative studies. Often it states word limits for certain types of article, which gives you some idea of the types of paper the journal likes to accept. Some journals insist that articles report empirical research, which rules out theoretical papers and literature reviews. A number of journals, such as *Cognitive Psychology*, only accept papers that knit together the results of several studies – so clearly a short report of a single study would not be acceptable. The best way of testing the water is to send the editor a brief e-mail describing your paper and ask whether it is likely to be appropriate for the journal.

Although research assessors frequently deny it, there is undoubtedly a *hierarchy* of academic journals, with which it is important to be familiar at the outset of an academic career. Some journals are, indisputably, less prestigious than others, and some journals are so prestigious that a single publication in one of them is worth any number of publications in lesser outlets. Top of the psychology tree are the APA journals *Psychological Bulletin* and *Psychological Review*. Most research psychologists will privately admit that it is their career objective to publish in either of these. Most of us never will, so we may try to aim for the most prestigious journal in our field. For example, developmental psychologists might hope to publish in *Developmental Psychology* or *Child Development*, probably the leading journals in that general field. Or they may narrow the field further and aim for something like the *Journal of Adolescent Health*, or *Journal of Experimental Child Psychology*.

The situation becomes more complicated when we consider publishing in interdisciplinary outlets. These are often hard to evaluate by psychologists unless they are experts in a particular area, especially if they are new journals that have yet to become established. It is very easy to be fooled by journal titles that are familiar, or sound prestigious. With all due respect to the editors and authors (and I have published there myself), the *Journal of Psychology* is not quite as prestigious as it sounds. It is long established (founded in 1935), but as the discipline has become more established, it has taken a back seat to weightier journals such as *Psychological Bulletin* and more specialised journals. Nevertheless, it still publishes some useful short reports. On the other hand, a brand new journal, staffed by leading experts in a specialist field, may struggle initially to establish a reputation.

The question, then, becomes: where should you target your paper? You could decide to be realistic, and opt for a safe bet. If you have a bit of money knocking around, you could play really safe and send your paper to a journal like *Perceptual and Motor Skills* or *Psychological Reports*, long-established publications that accept many articles, and charge authors for the privilege. These may be quite high figures, such as $300 for a shortish report, especially if figures need to be prepared. The costs are often explained to the author as covering 'fifty reprints' or whatever, although if you decide to waive the reprints (and the payment), you will find your paper heading swiftly for the bin. Nonetheless, many researchers cough up and publish quite happily in these journals – and, again, you often find useful material in them.

The opposite approach is to aim high, cross your fingers tightly, and see what happens. One argument in favour of this approach is that, whatever feedback you get, it will come from a lofty source. Bearing this in mind, though, you need to be very confident that your paper is worthy of consideration at this level, otherwise it will be returned unreviewed and you have wasted a month or two. Your best bet, at the start of your career, is to compare your paper to others, perhaps those covered in your literature review, and send it to one of the journals that have published those papers. This is a particularly sensible option if your research follows in a particular research tradition, or employs a particular methodology or theoretical approach that is being encouraged by a specific journal.

In practice, your choice of outlet is likely to be made long before you complete the paper. Ideally, you should select your outlet before you start writing, because it is more efficient to tailor your paper to a specific audience. That audience includes a wide range of readers, from undergraduate students to leading world experts in your specialist field. Most importantly, you may well find your eventual referees among those readers. It is worth second-guessing who your referees are likely to be, and keep them in mind while writing your paper. This is especially important if you are preparing to aim some stinging criticism in the direction of a leading researcher in the field. Remember, that researcher may be approached for a review, and could have steam emerging from their ears by the end of the first page!

Preparing the manuscript

Once your paper has entered the review process, it is highly unlikely that it would be rejected on the grounds of poor presentation. (If the presentation is so bad that the paper is unacceptable to the journal, it will have been returned unreviewed by the editor along with an explanatory covering letter.) All the same, a shoddily or inappropriately presented paper is unlikely to do you any favours with the referees. As much as anything, it suggests a lack of publishing experience and creates the (possibly false) impression that the reviewer is dealing with a beginner, and this may exaggerate any flaws that the referee has identified in the paper. So it is important to get it right from the start.

Journals vary in the amount of presentation detail contained on the inside cover. Many American journals simply state 'the manuscript should be prepared according to the publication manual of the American Psychological Association'. Non-APA journals will, of course, have their own guidelines. BPS journals, for example, have a similar set of guidelines, though these are usually reproduced in full in their journals. By and large, leading journals vary little in their basic presentation criteria. The things to watch out for tend to be the number of hard copies to send (varies anything from three to five, depending on the number of referees a journal likes to call on), and the referencing format (though seemingly trivial, there are some quite wide variations here).

In addition to these presentation guidelines, there are often extra criteria to observe; for example, journals sometimes ask that the data be 'made available' during the review process. These requests are intended to deal with the ethical issues surrounding publication that were outlined in Chapter 20, but are very rarely taken up.

Journals usually warn authors against submitting their work to more than one outlet. Indeed, in the covering letter with your submitted article you are encouraged to make a statement to the effect that the research reported in the paper is not under review for any other publications. Most new researchers find this rather irksome. Given the time journals take to review a paper, and the high rejection rates, it seems rather unfair that you are not able to hedge your bets and try every outlet you can find. However, imagine you have carried out a blinding piece of research with great scientific importance, and reported this immaculately. You submit this to ten journals, and they all publish it within several weeks of each other. *You* would get fantastic publicity – yet nine journals will have infringed the copyright laws, been hit by hefty fines, and the next time you send off a paper, an editor will be very cautious about sending it out for review!

Tips and hints

Sternberg (1993) is pretty much the definitive guide, along with the APA Publications Manual (APA 2001), to writing for publication. He lists 21 tips

for gaining acceptance from journals, which I have condensed here to ten.
Bear in mind that Sternberg is a vastly experienced author with hundreds of
publications on his CV. To him, an article that is published, but with little
impact, is as much a failure as an article that is rejected outright. In a purely
academic sense, this may be true, but your concerns may well be more
materialistic, and getting your career off the ground is often simply a case of
jumping through hoops. However, the points made here apply to pretty
much any submitted piece of research.

- *Grab the reader's attention*   The article should open with a clear declaration of intent that you follow through as the paper progresses. You
should make the opening as interesting as possible, so that a reader will
persist beyond the first paragraph, and make the paper as a whole
relevant to your target audience. (In many respects, this last point is
similar to those made about qualitative research in Chapter 11). Be
interesting throughout, and at no point allow the argument to sag: this
is particularly true of the final paragraph, which should send the reader
off with a 'clear take-home message' (Sternberg 1993: 176).
- *Ensure a balanced, comprehensive literature review*   One of the most frequent criticisms voiced by PhD examiners and journal reviewers is that
students, or authors, have not done their homework properly. If there
are gaping holes in a literature review, the outcome of the research may
lack a theoretical link with previous studies; worse still, those previous
studies, if reviewed, may well have led the author to abandon the present
line of enquiry! Almost as bad as an incomplete literature review is
a biased one, in which counter-arguments are brushed under the carpet
or simply dismissed. Remember, that person whose research you are
rubbishing could well be asked to review your paper.
- *Interpret your results – but leave the readers' options open*   Results
sections are hard to follow at the best of times. Don't leave your interpretation until the Discussion section. However, allow for alternative
interpretations of the data. Again, this relates back to guidelines for
reporting qualitative research, where issues around subjectivity are
brought to the fore. Just because you have numerical data, and inferential statistics, you cannot afford to be smug or over-confident.
- *Clear sentences and a coherent argument*   These are obvious points that
your lecturers should have rammed home repeatedly throughout your
higher education, but they still apply to scientific writing. They are
especially important when you are trying to communicate complex ideas
or data. Your argument can be made more coherent if you engage the
reader directly at regular points: in Sternberg's words, 'explain what
you're going to say, say it, and then restate what you've said' (1993:
176). The trick here is to avoid pedantry in the process.
- *Ground your arguments in concrete examples*   I have tried to do that
throughout this book, to the point where 'for example' has started to

sound like a cliché. Nevertheless, the worst academic writing is full of theories, concepts and arguments that fly over the readers' heads, to be reproduced later by students and other academics who are still not entirely sure what the original author meant. In the context of a journal article, reviewers do not have the patience (or the reverence) to try to demystify obtuse ideas: they want a clear explication of those ideas, with a concrete example that will make sense to all readers. And avoid specialist jargon or abbreviations too. If 5 per cent of the readers understand a term you've used, this is 95 per cent too few.

- *Avoid typos*   An obvious point, surely, but it is amazing how many typos creep into the work of otherwise esteemed academics. The use of word processing packages is a major factor: spellcheckers pick up some gaffes but not others: for instance, you often find the 'r' missing from 'your', a mistake that is not identified by spelling (or even grammar) checkers.
- *Meet the journal guidelines and subject matter*   See the previous section for more details.
- *Read over your work*!   Again, fundamental student advice, but with word processing speeding everything up, it is often ignored in the desperate scramble to get your work printed out and sent off to the editor as soon as possible. It is important to remember how different from the computer screen your work may look on the printed page.
- *Don't take reviews too seriously or personally*   These points have been made earlier in this chapter. Sternberg reiterates the point about reviewers being drawn from the same 'pool' as authors, and that, after a few years, you could easily find yourself sitting on the other side of the fence.
- *Don't give up*   Again, this reinforces points made earlier. Sternberg makes the very good point that articles are often rejected because 'people are not yet ready to hear the message' (1993: 180). This depends on how creative you are trying to be; see the next section for a slightly more cynical view of the situation.

Books

Of course, journals are not the only outlets for reporting research. I ought to include a word about academic book publishing, because very often research in journal form fails to make an impact until packaged together in book form. Alternatively, for various reasons, some academics avoid journals as far as possible and aim straight for the book market.

When considering books, publishers exercise very different acceptance criteria to those governing journal articles. At journal article level, the acceptance process is placed entirely in the hands of the (unpaid) academic editors. Accepting a book is the equivalent to accepting a whole journal, and so it is a decision that is made by the publishers themselves, and is based largely on financial criteria rather than academic quality.

There is a huge variety of academic books: some are basic textbooks, aimed solely at students; some are specialist books on a particular topic that will sell to students but also to other academics; occasionally publishers will consider 'research monographs' which are extended journal papers covering a long series of studies. Alternatively, you might prefer to write for a lay audience on a psychological topic. Here, marketability is the key criterion for acceptance, and you may be better off submitting your proposal to a general non-fiction publisher rather than an academic publisher, whose target is the student market.

Generally, there are three reasons why you should consider a book rather than a journal as the outlet for your research.

- *There is too much to fit in a single paper* If you have been publishing journal articles for a few years on a related topic, you may find that you have amassed a body of work that merits a wider audience. Or you may consider yourself a leading expert in a field that requires a fresh theoretical perspective, supported by the research you have conducted. The time may be ripe for a specialist text that takes a new, or updated, look at a particular topic, in which you can refer liberally to your own academic publications.

- *Journals have been unsympathetic to your research* Continuous rejection by academic journals is not always a reflection of poor research or writing. As Sternberg (1993) points out, people are often not ready for your message. Journals are often fussy about methodology (qualitative researchers in psychology have long preferred books to journals for these reasons). Sometimes research is simply not suited to journal article format – a single paper will fail to do justice to an ethnographic study that has occupied two or three years. Alternatively, you may want to use book form to express a critical position on some aspect of psychology. There is debate over whether such work constitutes 'research' as such, but such books have a ready audience in undergraduate psychology.[1]

- *You have spotted a gap in the market* Finally, you can publish a book that contains no empirical research of your own: this can be a textbook that you feel there is a demand for, or a theme in psychology that has not been explored. My first book (Giles 2000), on the psychology of fame and celebrity, contained very little of my own research, simply because it was a difficult topic to research empirically, and I had to knit together different literatures from outside psychology and draw my examples from the media. I knew that, because of the subject matter, it would be popular with students and nonacademics, but that it would get a rough ride from academics themselves. So far they have been mostly kind . . .

The process of writing a book begins differently from a journal article. Some publishers like to see a draft chapter or two in advance, which is not a bad idea for a previously unpublished author. Even if you have dozens of journal articles under your belt, you may take a while to perfect the writing style for a wider audience that publishers would expect from a book. However, your publishers may be so taken with your idea that they are happy just to see a proposal. Book proposals follow a more or less standard format. You should include:

- A brief overview of the book
- A description of the target audience
- Reasons why the book will sell
- Why you are the best person to write it
- A chapter-by-chapter synopsis (a short paragraph summarising each chapter)
- Some idea of the time scale, and the eventual length of the book
- A summary of competing titles (i.e., other books on the market)

The proposal is then refereed in the same way as a journal article. The referees are chosen, as for journal articles, on the basis of their expertise in the area. Ultimately, however, publishers are looking for an indication that the book will *sell*, so they are less bothered than journal editors about theoretical and methodological issues. However, if referees consider the proposal to be of no academic merit whatsoever, the publisher may well ask the author to revise the proposal substantially or seek another outlet. Academic publishers are not, on the whole, geared up to selling books to the general public, and if there is no way lecturers are ever likely to recommend your book to their students, they will suggest that you seek a more commercial outlet. The only problem then is that general non-fiction publishers are less willing to take a risk on an unknown author.

It is very rare that a book ends up in exactly the same format as its proposed chapter-by-chapter synopsis. Referees almost always suggest some changes, and once the writing gets underway, many changes suggest themselves; often these are fairly cosmetic, such as collapsing together chapters that are less substantial than you expected, or expanding other sections as more material comes to light. Sometimes a whole section goes by the way because it simply hasn't worked in book form. However, the review process often continues while the book is being written, and the publisher will almost certainly require a number of critical reviews of the draft manuscript.

As with journal articles, there are invariably a few corrections or revisions to be made to the final manuscript before you engage in the tedious process of printing the whole thing out. It is then sent off to proofreaders, in the same way as a journal article, who then return the copy to you for further minor corrections before it goes to the typesetters. Bearing in mind the relative size of a book, this process is even more long-winded than for journal articles. At the end of the day, however, there is nothing more satisfying for an academic than seeing a book in its eventual cover (which you will have had some input in choosing), and on the bookshelves! Best of all, you may even make some money out of it – though this is rarely more than a small top-up to your annual income.

Some thoughts on the review process

I have tried so far to be positive about publishing research. It really is best to be positive about it, even through the bad times, because many academic careers fall by the wayside as a result of the knockbacks that young researchers have received from early submissions. Once you are in a tenured academic position it is all too easy to relax, and fulfil the minimum requirements of your employment contract (i.e., teaching and administration – 'scholarly activity' is rarely defined, and could be interpreted as striding around the campus in a gown pretending to be an Oxbridge don). Such figures often find themselves stuck in the same institution for the rest of their careers. That may be fine if the institution is Oxford or Harvard, but it is unlikely that those universities would retain a non-active researcher unless they did something spectacularly innovative on the teaching front. However if you are lumbered at an early stage in your career with a heavy teaching and admin load, and research has to be conducted and written up in evenings and at weekends, it is very easy to let it fall by the wayside.

All the same, I shall end this chapter with some barbed cynicism (novice researchers of a nervous disposition may prefer to skip to the next chapter). Some years ago an ingenious study was carried out to investigate the reliability of the peer review process in psychology. Peters and Ceci (1982) selected twelve papers that had been published in high-quality journals in the same year. They rewrote those papers in submission format, changing only the names of the researchers and the institutions (to the same fictitious names and titles). They then submitted the papers to the same journals in which they had been published previously. Of the 38 editors (including sub-editors) and reviewers that eventually read the resubmitted papers, only *three* identified the papers as identical to ones they had already published. This happened despite the fact that they had only been published in the previous 18–32 months. Worse still for reliability, of the nine papers that went through the review process, all but one were eventually rejected, with sixteen of the eighteen referees recommending against publication, in several cases, on grounds of 'serious methodological flaws'.

This study sparked off a furious debate among academics about the virtues of peer review (see the papers published in the same issue of the journal), not least because the journals selected had a nonblind reviewing policy (i.e., the referees could see the names of the authors and their institution). It was argued that the referees were biased against an unknown research centre and unknown authors. Happily this situation has since been rectified, with most journals doing their best to operate blind reviewing, although citations often give the game away (it is part of the fun to try to guess the authors' identities!).

However, much of the criticism levelled at the journals involved is still relevant today. Because of the intense competition (and the glamour associated with high rejection rates), there is a kind of type 1 error made by journals in that editors (and referees) tend to search for reasons to reject rather than reasons to publish. This works against articles that are innovative and challenging and in favour of bland, unadventurous reports of studies that simply tweak aspects of previous research. In response to the Peters and Ceci article, Armstrong (1982) outlined an alternative set of tips for successful submissions to journals:

- Don't pick an important problem
- Don't challenge existing beliefs
- Don't obtain surprising results
- Don't use simple methods
- Don't provide full disclosure
- Don't write clearly

This advice is clearly tongue-in-cheek, but contains a germ of truth!

On a more serious note, there are a number of aspects of the review process that could be substantially improved. To begin with, editors' choice of referees sometimes leaves a lot to be desired. I recently submitted a qualitative study of parasocial relationships to a general psychology journal – probably not the best outlet, but I wanted as wide an audience as possible – and unwisely included the word 'bereavement' in the title. The editor, who clearly had some knowledge of the literature on bereavement, but no knowledge or interest in media psychology, sent the paper to three experts on bereavement, all hard-line quantitative researchers who were highly critical of the methodology and of the literature review, which they regarded, understandably, as inappropriate for a study of bereavement! A more sympathetic editor would have looked through the reference section to get a clearer idea of the precise field that the research had taken place in, or would have selected reviewers with some understanding of qualitative methods.

Another problem is the confidential nature of the refereeing process. Some reviewers blatantly hide behind the mask of anonymity and treat it as an opportunity to attack other researchers or perspectives. Forcing referees to disclose their identity may cause the occasional problem when the referee has some kind of personal relationship with the author, but this should not really be a concern for psychology as a discipline, just something that individuals deal with on the occasions it arises. In most cases, the obligation of referees to sign reviews is likely to result in more balanced assessments, and a greater degree of respect towards submitting authors.

Finally, editors should perhaps be more scrupulous in deciding whether to proceed with the review process. Often, papers are handled by subeditors who are clearly unsympathetic to the topic or its treatment, who choose deliberately negative referees, and waste everyone's time. Similarly, invitations to resubmit should only be based on very tangible criteria. Sometimes, authors are asked to revise the manuscript in such a way that effectively involves writing a different paper (perhaps one that the editor has designed to suit his or her preferences). In such cases, I would recommend that the author tries a different outlet.

Summary

I have tried where possible to be positive in writing this chapter. Publishing research is a lifelong learning experience, and getting rejected becomes a familiar fact of life after a while. Developing a thick skin is essential for one's psychological survival. My goal here is to pass on all the advice I wish I had received when a postgraduate and a fledgling academic, and hope that readers who fall into either category will find it useful and encouraging. Ultimately, research is pointless without publication at the other end, so you should report your data as soon as you have worked out the story they tell. Selecting the appropriate publication is then the most important consideration, and doing a bit of research here is essential. I was interested to hear, at a recent symposium presented by several journal editors, that most of them encouraged authors to contact them personally before sending in papers, to save them the effort of having to reject something that is entirely inappropriate. This seems like very sensible advice for an author.

Note

1 There is a more general debate on the status of book publishing in academic psychology that has been thrown up by the Research Assessment Exercise (RAE) in the UK. The RAE assessors draw a distinction between books which are intended for use as teaching materials, and books which report original research, or collections of an author's research. (Articles in leading journals receive higher kudos in this exercise than either, but that is another debate.) However, many books written by academics fall somewhere in between. This book, for instance, has involved years of painstaking research, but I am prepared to bet a tidy amount on it not being included in the next RAE! This may reflect something of an empiricist bias within psychology as a discipline, where 'research' is still seen as something involving data collection, preferably in numerical form. Archival ('library') research is not generally given anything like the same status as in other disciplines, where professorial status and standing within the discipline are often measured by the number of *books* (rather than papers) that an individual has published.

23 Writing research grant proposals

Introduction

There are times in Chapter 22 when I refer, perhaps with a touch of irony, to academics building up their lists of publications and enlarging their CVs. It may create the impression in places that a successful academic career is based around simply churning out journal article after journal article, plus the occasional book. I am certain many academics would be only too happy if this were the case. However, those academics need to get the material for their papers from somewhere, and for better or for worse, in reality, much of their time will be spent filling out forms in order to apply for grants from various funding bodies. In this chapter I will go through the process of applying for research funding and make some suggestions that might improve your chances of success.

It is possible to conduct research without the aid of external funding organisations. Most institutions have a limited amount of money that is put aside to support internal research projects. However, this money is usually offered on a competitive basis only, so that you would still need to enter into the proposal-writing process. This can be good practice for applying externally, although the amounts are usually small, and are often used for little more than 'buying out' of teaching time. Unless your teaching load is crippling, this is really an opportunity squandered, since cash-strapped departments will usually get their pound of flesh some way, and the funding is much better spent on research assistance, or investment in equipment or developing research materials.

Where internal money is hard to come by, many academics prefer to get on with research in their own time. This is not an option if you require expensive equipment to conduct research, but qualitative research and limited questionnaire or scale-based studies can be carried out without incurring any expense to the researcher (although the departmental photocopying bill could be suspiciously high if the sample is going to reach publishable proportions). If you have external contacts you may even be able to access specialist populations. Occasionally final year undergraduates produce publishable project work. Increasingly, though, academics are evaluated on the amount of money they bring into the department. In some research institutions, particularly where a centre is established that attracts little money from teaching, the ability to attract research money is prized more highly than evidence of research output. This is an unfortunate position for an academic institution to be in, but it underlines the importance of developing an expertise for writing grant proposals.

What funds, where?

One of the hardest tasks in publishing research is deciding to which of the many possible outlets you should send your paper. The situation is rather different when it comes to applying for funding: alas, there is not a bottomless pool of research money with a hundred different institutions throwing it about. On the contrary, you may be stuck with a mere handful of appropriate funding sources, and some of those bodies may have irksome stipulations that prevent you from using the money as you wish. However, psychologists are in a relatively fortunate position in that their research often touches a number of disciplinary boundaries, and there are usually a number of profitable avenues that are worth exploring.

Types of funding

Research grants

By far the most typical form of award in psychology is a standard research grant that is paid directly to an institution via the finance department. It is applied for either by a single academic or by a small team of two or three collaborating researchers. Once the money arrives at the institution, it can only be used by those individuals for the purposes described in the proposal. It can be any amount from a few hundred pounds to over £100,000. Some funding bodies require slightly different applications according to the amount that is requested. Clearly you will not need to provide as much information for a small material grant than for a three-year research assistant post.

Project grants

These are large sums, over £100,000 and as much as £500,000, that are usually bid for by a number of academics, often at a range of institutions. They may be spent on salaries for a number of research staff, or for expensive equipment, possibly even the establishment of a research centre that requires accommodation and computing facilities.

Contracts

These are agreements between two institutions to collaborate on a research project. Typically, a major institution, such as a regional health authority, puts out an invitation for applicants to 'tender' for a large sum of money. The resulting contract may involve many individuals, and ensures that a steady flow of income is maintained for the successful institution over a number of years. Such contracts are highly prized by universities because they promote research growth in that particular department and haven't cost the institution a penny! However, this type of arrangement places a lot of restriction on the type of research carried out, and tends to focus research in a specific direction that may only suit a handful of academics in the department. Often such contracts are interdisciplinary, so a whole school may reap the benefits. Generally speaking, new researchers are only involved on the periphery of such projects, so I will not discuss this type of funding in the remainder of the chapter.

Career development grants to individuals

A lot of different funding schemes may be lumped together under this particular heading, but their basic similarity is that they provide money for a single individual to further his or her research career. The highest prizes on offer tend to be research *fellowships* which may cover a number of years. During this time, the successful applicant's institution will be paid the equivalent of a lecturing salary to enable him or her to concentrate on research. However the institution is usually expected to provide basic accommodation and facilities for the research. Smaller amounts of money may be offered to individuals for basic expenses, or to assist with overseas conference attendance. Sometimes money is offered to help develop international research links by supporting an overseas academic to spend time in the host country, or to organise conferences or workshops.

Funding bodies

The awards described above are usually offered by major funding bodies, although contract-type funding is normally offered by institutions that already carry out research themselves. These organisations usually support research that is being carried out in their country. The most common source of research funding is usually the government. In the UK, there are a number of state-funded research councils who offer grants and fellowships to institutions and individuals. The ones which most regularly fund proposals in psychology are the ESRC (Economic and Social Research Council) in the UK and the National Science Foundation in the US.

There are usually a number of charitable institutions in a given country that fund psychological research. In the UK, the Leverhulme Trust was set up in the 1920s specifically for the support of original research, and offers a variety of grants covering a wide range of academic disciplines. Other organisations offer research funding on a more restricted basis. For instance, the Nuffield Foundation and the Joseph Rowntree Foundation support applied research projects which directly contribute to social welfare. Alternatively, there are many charitable sources of funding for applied research in specific areas, largely health-based, such as drug and alcohol use.

Other sources of funding include private, profit-making organisations such as businesses, industries and other institutions. These organisations do not advertise funding opportunities in the style of research councils and charities. Nevertheless, they often have more money available for research than these bodies, and they have different concepts of research income; they are often stunned by the comparatively modest requests made by academics! The downside is that, in the absence of competitive bidding, you will need to approach the organisation directly, and sell your research proposal to them (some companies expect you to go and impress them with your presentation skills before parting with any money!).

Applying for funding

Unlike writing a journal article, which in theory can be done before you have even decided where to send it, grant proposals need to be targeted specifically from the outset. Very often you will need to tailor your proposal to the interests of the funding organisation – this is particularly important where the organisation has a clear agenda for funding research, such as a limited range of themes which it would like to concentrate on (these are usually clearly stated in application booklets).

Once you have completed your research into the funds available, contact the relevant organisation for a copy of their application guidelines and a copy of the application form. These days, most of this information can be downloaded from the organisation's website; a number of bodies have created electronic application forms which can be downloaded (although they are not always compatible with the vagaries of your institution's computing facilities!).

A typical grant application form requires the following information:

- Details about the applicant(s): contact information and short CVs
- Descriptions of the research itself, some brief, others more detailed, for various uses (putting on databases, etc.)
- Full breakdown of costings (i.e., what you plan to spend the money on)
- Details of time management for the applicant(s) and a rough schedule for completing the research
- Nominated reviewers (applicants may select a couple of referees to review the proposal)
- Details of collaboration or co-funding
- The research proposal

Most universities have a support system for research funding that will enable you to put a bid together without too much trouble. For example, the costings will usually be calculated by a research officer who has a wide knowledge of the systems within the institution and who is familiar with the kind of information that funding organisations require. Often, very detailed information is required; if you request money for a piece of equipment, even if it is just a dictaphone, the form might ask you to specify the model, its serial number, and its current value. Your technicians should be able to provide you with this information.

Some of the detail requested on the application form will be pure guess-work. Some organisations want to have a rough idea of your commitment (and that of other applicants) to the project. After all, you might hire an inexperienced research assistant who is then expected to run the whole project single-handedly. Or it might be clear from your other commitments that you simply don't have the time to devote much effort to the research. If you are the principal applicant you will be expected to set aside several hours a week. Of course, it is tempting to lie on this part of the form. However, it is important to be realistic; if you are expected to contribute simultaneously to a number of research projects, will you really be able to fit in your own alongside any extra teaching and admin work? These considerations may well determine what you spend the money on. If most of it is going on research assistance, you can afford to devote less time to the project than if you are planning to spend it on expensive equipment that will lie idle while you are running around fulfilling other commitments.

Unlike writing for publication, funding application forms usually ask you to nominate the referees who will be consulted about the project. This gives you something of an advantage when it comes to writing the proposal, since you can slant it towards the interests of a known referee, rather than trying to guess who will be asked to comment on your work. Bear in mind, though, that *all* applicants will benefit from this!

Some funding organisations operate a two-stage procedure for applications. You will be asked to provide rough outlines of the above information, and a shorter proposal, for an initial outline application. This is reviewed more speedily than a full application, because the organisation wants to see if it is worth your while putting together a full application, thus saving a lot of time all round.

The review process

Before I discuss the proposal itself, I ought to describe in brief the procedure once the application is completed and sent off to the organisation. (The application usually needs to be rubber-stamped by the administering institution first, so your research office will deal with the submission itself.)

Your application will be sent out to your nominated referees as soon as it is processed, and these people are normally given a month or so to respond. The reviews will determine whether the proposal is taken forward to a panel review, or whether it should simply be placed in a pile under the heading 'must try harder'. Some organisations will give you a certain amount of feedback on unsuccessful proposals – the ESRC in the UK gives each proposal a grade which is a rough indication of its quality, although many top grade proposals fail at the final hurdle, so it's not always clear why.

The review panel of a major funding organisation will usually sit four times a year, and you may well be asked to time your application so as to meet reasonable deadlines for these meetings. The panel consists of a number of leading academics in a variety of disciplines, who will each have some broad knowledge of the major fields in their discipline (this is another reason why funding policy tends to the conservative). Each panellist then sifts through the relevant proposals, and their reviews, to decide which are worthy of the small allocation of funds made for his or her area.

Eventually, the good proposals are whittled down to a small number that are vociferously defended by their respective panellists, and the applicants are all sent letters of the variety described in Chapter 22 (the key words again being 'delighted' and 'sorry'). It usually takes a short while for the money to be transferred into the institutional coffers, so in the meantime you may need to owe personnel a certain amount while you advertise for your research posts. Best of all, though, you are ready to start planning a properly supported research project!

Writing the grant proposal

The next step involves writing the proposal itself, which you are normally asked to provide separately from, although in the same package with, your application form. A grant proposal can be over 5000 words, although for smaller sums, 1000 words may suffice. The main purpose of the grant proposal is for referees to decide whether the proposed research is worthy of the organisation's money – therefore, they are evaluating your proposal in terms of the following features.

Why the research needs to be done

The first of these points will be determined by your literature review, and any proposed applications of the research. These will depend very much on the interests of the funding body. If it is a charitable institution that seeks to fund philanthropic projects, it is no use relying on the theoretical literature to support your bid. You will need to think of ways in which the research has a direct impact on the welfare of the participants. Often such proposals are strengthened by the involvement of nonacademic bodies, such as youth organisations or other charitable bodies.

However, since you are an academic, and your referees will also be academics, your proposal should contain sufficient reference to the appropriate literature. You need to ensure that the project is timely, in that it builds on previous research in the area, rather than simply repeating previous research, and also that it is linked to existing theory and research. Some proposals are rejected because they are too speculative, relying on media interest or popular lore for their impact. Your proposal needs to be rooted in the academic literature, but its real-world value should be brought to the fore.

Why you are the best person to supervise the project

The suitability of the applicants for the proposed research is the trickiest aspect of funding applications for the organisations concerned. Ultimately, the applicants are the best people to conduct the project simply because they thought of it first and had the initiative to put the proposal together! However, referees (and the organisation's review panel) need a bit more to go on. Suitability is normally determined by your research record to date – this is where the CV comes in, so make sure that the publications you list on it, and the other information you provide, are relevant to the research you are proposing.

Then there are a number of other considerations that may enhance your chances of success. Unfortunately, research is sometimes rejected because the host institution is not capable of supporting the proposal (although this is more true of large project grants, where the funding body may actually arrange an on-site visit to check the facilities for themselves). For a long time, there have been accusations of bias on the part of funding bodies towards applications from more prestigious institutions. It isn't hard to see why – the best institutions should recruit the best researchers, and have the best facilities, so the funding body should enjoy the best outcome from the proposed research. This is not a desirable outcome for the academic research community because it serves to sharpen the division between research-oriented and teaching-oriented universities, a division that does nobody any good.

There is also a perceived bias that successful funding is dependent on previously successful funding. This often leaves novice researchers in the same position as school leavers who are desperately trying to find work, only to discover that every job advertisement states 'previous experience required'. Indeed, some researchers spend their whole careers tagging on to large research projects so that they can build up a long list of grants on their CV. This is particularly true in areas like health research, where it is not uncommon to find more than a dozen individuals named on the same proposal. However, in much psychological research, there are only two or three named applicants, and previous experience of grant-holding may not be regarded as the sole evidence of their ability to conduct the proposed research.

Given these potential stumbling blocks, you may impress the review panel more if your referees are pulled from the top drawer. This increases your risk of getting a poor review, especially if the referee has never heard of you before, but if your proposal is good (and especially if it flatters the referee!) a recommendation from a major figure in psychology will make a big impression on a review panellist.

Whether or not the requested funding is appropriate for the proposed research

If your institution's research office has done its job properly, there should be no problems with this aspect of the proposal. Where the referee is concerned, however, there may be practical considerations too. For example, one project of mine foundered slightly because I was unable to recruit participants in the anticipated way, and the grant money was all but gone by the time I had negotiated access. The referees on that occasion did not address the issue of recruitment, but someone who has worked on a similar project may have identified this as a potential problem, and recommended less ambitious targets for the research (or alternative methodologies). Unfortunately, such concerns are more likely to lead to a proposal being rejected than to an acceptance on the basis that changes are made. Unlike with journal articles, there are no invitations to revise or resubmit research proposals – queries like these are ready-made reasons for a panellist to favour someone else's application. It's better to get it right first time.

What output will arise from the proposed research

Finally, you should always include a brief statement about the likely output that you expect from the research. By 'output' I am referring to journal articles, books, and conference papers. More applied projects may result in nonacademic literature – for example, a report to a government agency or health authority. Be realistic about the sort of output you can expect to produce given your research track record, the nature of the research, and the duration of the project. A three-year project may yield a dozen or so publications, while a small grant for £2000 is unlikely to result in more than one or two – and that's if the research goes well!

Some tips on writing grant proposals

Sternberg (1993) has some useful advice on writing successful research proposals, which I will summarise here. I have condensed his eighteen tips to ten, adding some extra suggestions along the way.

- *State your 'big question' clearly and emphasise its importance* Try to focus your proposal on a single question that is relatively simple to grasp, and explain why it is important. There may be a point in the review process where a non-specialist has to make a key decision whether to fund your project or a project from another discipline, and if the purpose of your research is obvious to any intelligent reader, this could swing the decision in your favour.

- *Root your proposal in the research literature*   You should present sufficient evidence from the literature to support the proposal on theoretical grounds, although, as I have suggested earlier, the extent to which you do this is determined by the agenda of the funding organisation. Clearly proposals will be preferred if they advance theory and build on previous research rather than simply repeating previous findings.

- *Present pilot data*   Very often, projects are already partially underway when a formal application for funding is made. While nobody wants to fund research that has already been completed, it may enhance the credibility of your proposal if you have carried out some exploratory studies. It may be that you have piloted a new measure, or collected a small amount of data, or that you have supervised a student project on a related issue. All this information will indicate to a referee that you are not about to enter into uncharted territory.

- *Write clearly and concisely*   Even more so than writing journal articles, you need to grip the reader's attention. The keen word limit means that you have less opportunity to weave complex arguments, so you really need to try to focus your proposal and make it comprehensible. You should also write in as direct and uncomplicated a fashion as possible. Be very positive about what you are proposing; remove any perhaps, possiblies, maybes, and mights, and state that you *will* do what you suggest, not that you merely plan or intend to.

- *Make your proposed data analysis clear*   It is very important that you are thinking ahead. A project might look good if the 'big question' is relevant and important, access to participants is guaranteed, and ingenious research materials have been designed, but may falter if the applicant has not said anything about how the data will be analysed. You don't necessarily need to state every statistical test that you plan to run, but referees need some basic idea of how the analysis will match the design. For instance, if you are proposing a survey with a number of scales and questionnaires, you could explain that you will analyse the data using structural equation modelling (you might even specify appropriate software in the expenses).

- *Predict the outcome of your research*   Research that is purely exploratory may be supported in some cases, but most of the time a funding organisation would expect to have some idea of the eventual outcome. Furthermore, you should be able to explain the implications of this outcome, and those of any alternative outcomes.

- *Focus your CV on the important points*   Don't simply reproduce the CV that got you your current academic post, which needs to include all manner of peripheral information such as temporary bar jobs. Ideally you should be able to condense it to a single sheet or two.

- *Do not request more money than you need*   One of the reasons finance departments get involved at the costings stage of the proposal is to ensure that you are not requesting funds for facilities that already exist, or that you are planning to overpay your research staff. The whole procedure is very much above board.
- *Observe the formalities of the guidelines*   The formal requirements are important. Your application should have a professional air, since you want to create the impression that you are a high quality act. Part of this impression lies in strict adherence to the guidelines that the organisation has set, even down to putting the right information in the right box on the form. Sloppy forms, or poorly organised proposals, will not cut much ice with a review panel.
- *Be persuasive*   Applying for funding is like applying for a job (except that you specify the work). You need to sell yourself as you would at an interview or on a job application form. So don't be afraid to 'embroider' from time to time, but only as far as you can get away with it . . .

Summary

The business of applying for research money can be as dispiriting for a novice researcher as his or her efforts at publishing. My only advice is to keep going! Start off by requesting small amounts, ideally for pilot projects, and when you have demonstrated the ability to spend the funding body's money wisely, submit a more ambitious proposal. Alternatively, shop around; look for opportunities in the private sector where you can sell your research. Perhaps the best thing about applying for research money is that it focuses our attention on the usefulness of the research we do. At the same time, it is a shame that less and less value is being placed on purely theoretical research and academic scholarship, and more emphasis on finding universities alternative means of income. This is a political issue which ultimately threatens the future of the university system, and is best saved for another book.

Appendix 1

Additional data

Table A1 Full set of data for logistic regression example

Group	Salary	Promos	PhD	London	NY	Hawaii	Location
1	20,000	2	0	1	0	0	1
0	15,000	0	0	0	1	0	2
1	25,000	4	0	0	0	1	3
0	27,000	4	1	0	1	0	2
1	24,000	1	1	0	0	1	3
0	19,000	2	0	1	0	0	1
1	17,000	1	1	0	0	1	3
0	16,000	0	1	0	1	0	2
1	19,000	2	1	1	0	0	1
0	22,000	2	0	0	0	1	3
1	26,000	7	0	0	1	0	2
0	19,000	2	1	0	1	0	2
1	35,000	6	1	0	0	1	3
0	24,000	3	0	1	0	0	1
1	25,000	6	1	0	0	1	3
0	16,000	0	1	0	1	0	2
1	18,000	1	0	1	0	0	1
0	21,000	2	0	1	0	0	1
1	24,000	3	0	0	0	1	3
0	22,000	1	0	1	0	0	1
1	36,000	10	0	1	0	0	1
0	17,000	1	1	0	1	0	2
1	21,000	3	0	0	1	0	2
0	22,000	1	1	0	1	0	2
1	15,000	0	0	1	0	0	1
0	14,000	0	1	0	1	0	2
1	25,000	5	0	0	0	1	3
0	19,000	2	0	0	1	0	2
1	30,000	11	1	0	0	1	3
0	25,000	4	1	1	0	0	1
1	26,000	6	0	0	1	0	2
0	21,000	3	1	0	0	1	3
1	40,000	8	1	0	1	0	2

Table A1 (cont'd)

Group	Salary	Promos	PhD	London	NY	Hawaii	Location
0	30,000	3	0	1	0	0	1
1	19,000	1	1	0	0	1	3
0	13,000	0	0	0	1	0	2

Appendix 2

Additional transcription symbols (for use in discourse and conversation analysis)

:::	a row of colons are sometimes used to indicate drawn-out speech; for example, 'hanging around and a:::h just start drinking'
hhh	a noticeable exhalation of breath, for example a sigh.
.hhh	a noticeable inhalation of breath
\<faster\>	a notably speeded up section of speech
\>slower\<	a notably slower section of speech
=	used to indicate where two speakers exchange turns without pause, for example:

Dan (to Sven): <u>You</u>'ve surely got some good stories of blackouts haven't you=

Sven: =yeah

(...)	Indicates omitted material. When you carry out your initial transcription, you should commit everything to print; however, when reporting or analysing extracts from the transcript, you can use this symbol to jump from one bit to the next.
(unclear)	very often a word or whole utterance may be impossible to decipher from the tape. In this case you need to indicate where something was said, even if you can only mark it 'unclear' or 'inaudible'. Sod's law dictates that the unclear word will be in a key utterance – if this happens, you can make a logical guess at the word, but again this should be indicated in the transcript.
?,.	Ordinary punctuation may be used to help the reader 'parse' the speech into standard sentences.

References

Abell, J. and Stokoe, E. (1999) '"I take full responsibility, I take some responsibility, I'll take half of it but no more": Princess Diana and the negotiation of blame in the Panorama interview', *Discourse and Society* 10: 297–319.

Adair, J.G., Dushenko, T.W. and Lindsay, R.C. (1985) 'Ethical regulations and their impact on research practice', *American Psychologist* 40: 59–72.

Aiken, L.S. and West, S.G. (1996) *Multiple Regression: Testing and Interpreting Interactions*, Thousand Oaks, CA: Sage.

American Psychological Association (APA) (1973) *Ethical Principles in the Conduct of Research with Human Participants*, Washington, DC: American Psychological Association.

American Psychological Association (APA) (2001) *Publication Manual of the American Psychological Association* (5th edn), Washington, DC: American Psychological Association.

Anastasi, A. and Urbina, S. (1997) *Psychological Testing* (7th edn), Upper Saddle River, NJ: Prentice Hall.

Antaki, C., Condor, S. and Levine, M. (1996) 'Social identities in talk: Speakers' own orientations', *British Journal of Social Psychology* 35: 173–92.

Antaki, C. and Widdicombe, S. (eds) (1998) *Identities in Talk*, London: Sage.

Anthony, J.L., Lonigan, C.J. and Hecht, S.A. (1999) 'Dimensionality of posttraumatic stress disorder symptoms in children exposed to disaster: Results from confirmatory factor analyses', *Journal of Abnormal Psychology* 108: 326–36.

Antrop, I., Roeyers, H., Van Oost, P. and Buysse, A. (2000) 'Stimulation seeking and hyperactivity in children with ADHD', *Journal of Child Psychology and Psychiatry* 41: 225–31.

Archer, J. and Winchester, G. (1994) 'Bereavement following death of a pet', *British Journal of Psychology* 85: 259–72.

Arminger, G., Clogg, C.C. and Sobel, M.E. (eds) (1995) *Handbook of Statistical Modelling for the Social and Behavioral Sciences*, New York: Plenum.

Armstrong, J.S. (1982) 'Barriers to scientific contributions: The author's formula', *Behavioral and Brain Sciences* 5: 197–9.

Atkinson, J.M. and Heritage, J.C. (eds) (1984) *Structures of Social Action: Studies in Conversation Analysis*, Cambridge: Cambridge University Press.

Auburn, T., Drake, S. and Willig, C. (1995) '"You punched him, didn't you?": Versions of violence in accusatory interviews', *Discourse and Society* 6: 353–86.

Baker, F.B. (1992) *Item Response Theory: Parameter Estimation Techniques*, New York: Marcel Dekker.

Bem, S.L. (1981) *Bem Sex Role Inventory Professional Manual*, Palo Alto, CA: Consulting Psychologists Press.

Bentler, P.M. and Weeks, D.G. (1980) 'Linear structural equation with latent variables', *Psychometrika* 45: 289–308.

Berelson, B. (1952) *Content Analysis in Communication Research*, New York: Free Press.

Berg, B.L. (1995) *Qualitative Research Methods for the Social Sciences*, New York: Allyn & Bacon.

Billig, M. (1987) *Arguing and Thinking: A Rhetorical Approach to Social Psychology*, Cambridge: Cambridge University Press.

Billig, M. (1991) *Ideology and Opinions: Attitudes in Rhetorical Psychology*, London: Sage.

Billig, M. (1999) 'Whose terms? Whose ordinariness? Rhetoric and ideology in conversation analysis', *Discourse & Society* 10: 543–58.

Block, J. (1978) *The Q-sort Method in Personality Assessment and Psychiatric Research*, Palo Alto, CA: Consulting Psychologists Press.

Bond, R. and Smith, P.B. (1996) 'Culture and conformity: A meta-analysis of studies using Asch's (1952b, 1956) line judgment task', *Psychological Bulletin* 119: 111–37.

Bookstein, F.L., Sampson, P.D., Streissguth, A.P. and Barr, H.M. (1996) 'Exploiting redundant measurement of dose and developmental outcome: New methods from the behavioral teratology of alcohol', *Developmental Psychology* 32: 404–15.

Borg, I. and Lingoes, J. (1987) *Multidimensional Similarity Structure Analysis*, New York: Springer Verlag.

Breckler, S.J. (1990) 'Applications of covariance structure modeling in psychology: Cause for concern?', *Psychological Bulletin* 107: 260–73.

Bretherton, I. and Beeghly, M. (1982) 'Talking about internal states: The acquisition of an explicit theory of mind', *Developmental Psychology* 18: 906–21.

Brewer, N., Socha, L. and Potter, R. (1996) 'Gender differences in supervisors' use of performance feedback', *Journal of Applied Social Psychology* 26: 786–803.

Brown, S.D. (1999) 'Stress as regimen: Critical readings of self-help literature', in C. Willig (ed.) *Applied Discourse Analysis: Social and Psychological Interventions*, Chichester: Wiley.

Bryman, A. (1988) *Quantity and Quality in Social Research*, London: Unwin Hyman.

Bulmer, M. (1982) *Social Research Ethics: An Examination of the Merits of Covert Participant Observation*, London: Macmillan.

Burgoyne, C.B. (1997) 'Distributive justice and rationing in the NHS: Framing effects in press coverage of a controversial decision', *Journal of Community and Applied Social Psychology* 7: 119–36.

Burman, E. (1994a) *Deconstructing Developmental Psychology*, London: Routledge.

Burman, E. (1994b) 'Feminist research', in P. Banister, E. Burman, I. Parker, M. Taylor and C. Tindall (eds) *Qualitative Methods in Psychology: A Research Guide*, Buckingham: Open University Press.

Burman, E. and Parker, I. (eds) (1993) *Discourse Analytic Research: Repertoires and Readings of Texts in Action*, London: Routledge.

Burr, V. (1995) *An Introduction to Social Constructionism*, London: Routledge.

Cattell, R.B. (1966) 'The meaning and strategic use of factor analysis', in R.B. Cattell (ed.) *Handbook of Multivariate Experimental Psychology*, Chicago: Rand McNally.

Chamberlain, K. (1999) 'Using grounded theory in health psychology', in M. Murray and K. Chamberlain (eds) *Qualitative Health Psychology: Theories and Methods*, London: Sage.

Chang, L. (1994) 'A psychometric evaluation of 4-point and 6-point Likert-type scales in relation to reliability and validity', *Applied Psychological Measurement* 18: 205–15.

Charmaz, K. (1995) 'Grounded theory', in J.A. Smith, R. Harré and L. Van Langenhove (eds) *Rethinking Methods in Psychology*, London: Sage.

Chatham-Carpenter, A. and DeFrancisco, V. (1998) 'Women construct self-esteem in their own terms: A feminist qualitative study', *Feminism and Psychology* 8: 467–89.

Chow, S.L. (1988) 'Significance test or effect size?', *Psychological Bulletin* 103: 105–10.

Clarkson-Smith, L. and Hartley, A.A. (1990) 'The game of bridge as an exercise in working memory and reasoning', *Journal of Gerontology* 45: 233–8.

Clegg, J.A., Standen, P.J. and Jones, G. (1996) 'Striking the balance: A grounded theory analysis of staff perspectives', *British Journal of Clinical Psychology* 35: 249–64.

Cliff, N. (1983) 'Some cautions concerning the application of causal modeling methods', *Multivariate Behavioral Research* 18: 147–67.

Cloninger, C.R. (1994) 'The genetic structure of personality and learning: a phylo-genetic model', *Clinical Genetics* 46: 124–37.

Cohen, J. (1962) 'The statistical power of abnormal-social psychological research: A review', *Journal of Abnormal and Social Psychology* 65: 145–53.

Cohen, J. (1968) 'Multiple regression as a general data-analytic system', *Psychological Bulletin* 70: 426–43.

Cohen, J. (1988) *Statistical Power Analysis for the Behavioral Sciences* (2nd edn), Hillsdale, NJ: Erlbaum.

Cohen, J. (1992) 'A power primer', *Psychological Bulletin* 112: 155–9.

Cohen, J. (1994) 'The earth is round ($p < 0.05$)', *American Psychologist* 49: 997–1003.

Cole, T. and Bradac, J.J. (1996) 'A lay theory of relational satisfaction with best friends', *Journal of Social and Personal Relationships* 13: 57–83.

Condor, S. (1997) 'And so say all of us? Some thoughts on "experiential democrat-isation" as an aim for critical social psychologists', in T. Ibáñez and L. Iñiguez (eds) *Critical Social Psychology*, London: Sage.

Conner, M., Fitter, M. and Fletcher, W. (1999) 'Stress and snacking: A diary study of daily hassles and between-meal snacking', *Psychology and Health* 14: 51–63.

Cook, G. (1992) *The Discourse of Advertising*, London: Routledge.

Cortina, J.M. (1993) 'What is coefficient alpha? An examination of theory and applications', *Journal of Applied Psychology* 78: 98–104.

Costa, P.T. and McCrae, R.R. (1992) *Revised NEO Personality Inventory (NEO-PI-R) and NEO Five-factor Inventory (NEO-FFI): Professional Manual*, Odessa, FL: Psychological Assessment Resources.

Costain Schou, K. and Hewison, J. (1998) 'Health psychology and discourse: Per-sonal accounts as social texts in grounded theory', *Journal of Health Psychology* 3: 297–311.

Coxon, T. (1988) '"Something sensational . . ." The sexual diary as a tool for mapping detailed sexual behaviour', *Sociological Review* 36: 353–67.

Coyle, A. (2000) 'Discourse analysis', in G. Breakwell, S. Hammond and C. Fife-Schaw (eds) *Research Methods in Psychology* (2nd edn), London: Sage.

334   *References*

Creed, A.T. and Funder, D.C. (1998) 'Social anxiety: from the inside and outside', *Personality and Individual Differences* 25: 19–33.

Crossley, M. (2000) 'Narrative psychology, trauma and the study of self/identity', *Theory & Psychology* 10: 527–46.

Curtis, S., Bryce, H. and Treloar, C. (1999) 'Action research', in M. Murray and K. Chamberlain (eds) *Qualitative Health Psychology: Theories and Methods*, London: Sage.

Danziger, K. (1990) *Constructing the Subject: Historical Origins of Psychological Research*, Cambridge: Cambridge University Press.

Davies, B. and Harré, R. (1990) 'Positioning: The discursive production of selves', *Journal for the Theory of Social Behaviour* 20: 43–63.

Denzin, N.K. and Lincoln, Y.S. (eds) (2000) *Handbook of Qualitative Research* (2nd edn), Thousand Oaks, CA: Sage.

Derrida, J. (1976) *Of Grammatology*, Baltimore: Johns Hopkins University Press.

Diamantopoulos, A. and Siguaw, J.A. (2000) *Introducing LISREL: A Guide for the Uninitiated*, London: Sage.

Dollinger, S.J. and Clancy, S.M. (1993) 'Identity, self and personality: II. Glimpses through the autophotographic eye', *Journal of Personality and Social Psychology* 64: 1064–71.

Dracup, C. (1995) 'Hypothesis testing – what it really is', *The Psychologist* 8: 359–62.

Drew, P. and Heritage, J.C. (eds) (1992) *Talk at Work: Interaction in Institutional Settings*, Cambridge: Cambridge University Press.

Edwards, D. (1997) *Discourse and Cognition*, London: Sage.

Edwards, D. and Potter, J. (1992) *Discursive Psychology*, London: Sage.

Eiser, R.J. (1994) *Attitudes, Chaos and the Connectionist Mind*, Oxford: Blackwell.

Ekman, P. (1993) 'Facial expression and emotion', *American Psychologist* 48: 384–92.

Elliott, C.D. (1983) *The British Ability Scales: Handbook and Technical Manual*, Windsor: NFER-Nelson.

Elliott, R., Fischer, C.T. and Rennie, D.L. (1999) 'Evolving guidelines for publication of qualitative research studies in psychology and related fields', *British Journal of Clinical Psychology* 38: 215–29.

Everitt, B.S. (1998) 'Analysis of longitudinal data: Beyond MANOVA', *British Journal of Psychiatry* 172: 7–10.

Eysenck, H.J. and Eysenck, M.W. (1975) *Manual of the Eysenck Personality Questionnaire*, San Diego: Educational and Industrial Testing Service.

Fairclough, N. (1995) *Media Discourse*, London: Arnold.

Fenigstein, A., Scheier, M.F. and Buss, A.H. (1975) 'Public and private self-consciousness: Assessment and theory', *Journal of Consulting and Clinical Psychology* 43: 522–7.

Fetterman, D.M. (1989) *Ethnography Step by Step*, London: Sage.

Finn, S. (1997) 'Origins of media exposure: Linking personality traits to TV, radio, print and film use', *Communication Research* 24: 507–29.

Fischer, C. (1999) 'Designing qualitative research reports for publication', in M. Kopala and L.A. Suzuki (eds) *Using Qualitative Methods in Psychology*, Thousand Oaks, CA: Sage.

Fisher, R.A. (1935) *The Design of Experiments*, London: Oliver and Boyd.

Foucault, M. (1972) *The Archaeology of Knowledge*, London: Tavistock.

Fox, D. and Prillitensky, I. (eds) (1997) *Critical Psychology: An Introduction*, London: Sage.

Francis, B. (1999) 'An investigation of the discourses children draw on [*sic*] their constructions of gender', *Journal of Applied Social Psychology* 29: 300–16.

Frick, R.W. (1995) 'A problem with confidence intervals', *American Psychologist* 50: 1102–3.

Gahan, C. and Hannibal, M. (1998) *Doing Qualitative Research Using QSR NUD•IST*, London: Sage.

Gatton, D.S., DuBois, C.L.Z. and Faley, R.H. (1999) 'The effects of organizational context on occupational gender stereotyping', *Sex Roles* 7/8: 567–82.

Geertz, C. (1973) *The Interpretation of Cultures*, New York: Basic Books.

Gergen, K.J. (1985) 'The social constructionist movement in modern psychology', *American Psychologist* 40: 266–75.

Gigerenzer, G. and Murray, D.J. (1987) *Cognition as Intuitive Statistics*, Hillsdale, NJ: Erlbaum.

Gilbert, G.N. and Mulkay, M.J. (1984) *Opening Pandora's Box: A Sociological Analysis of Scientists' Discourse*, Cambridge: Cambridge University Press.

Giles, D.C. (1999) 'Retrospective accounts of drunken behaviour: Implications for theories of self, memory, and the discursive construction of identity', *Discourse Studies* 1: 387–404.

Giles, D.C. (2000) *Illusions of Immortality: A Psychology of Fame and Celebrity*, Basingstoke: Macmillan.

Giles, D.C. (in press) *Media Psychology*, Mahwah, NJ: Lawrence Erlbaum Associates.

Giles, D.C. and Terrell, C.D. (1997) 'Visual sequential memory and spelling ability', *Educational Psychology* 17: 245–54.

Gill, R. (1996) 'Discourse analysis: practical implementation', in J. Richardson (ed.) *Handbook of Qualitative Research Methods for Psychology and the Social Sciences*, Leicester: BPS Books.

Gillies, V. (1999) 'An analysis of the discursive positions of women smokers: Implications for practical interventions', in C. Willig (ed.) *Applied Discourse Analysis: Social and Psychological Interventions*, Chichester: Wiley.

Glaser, B.G. (1978) *Theoretical Sensitivity: Advances in the Methodology of Grounded Theory*, Mill Valley, CA: Sociology Press.

Glaser, B.G. (1992) *Emergence vs. Forcing: Basics of Grounded Theory Analysis*, Mill Valley, CA: Sociology Press.

Glaser, B.G. and Strauss, A.L. (1965) *Awareness of Dying*, Chicago: Aldine.

Glaser, B.G. and Strauss, A.L. (1967) *The Discovery of Grounded Theory: Strategies for Qualitative Research*, Chicago: Aldine.

Gone, J.P., Miller, P.J. and Rappaport, J. (1999) 'Conceptual self as normatively oriented: The suitability of past personal narrative for the study of cultural identity', *Culture & Psychology* 5: 371–98.

Gordo-Lopez, A.J. and Parker, I. (1999) *Cyberpsychology*, Basingstoke: Macmillan.

Gorsuch, R.L. and Venable, G.D. (1983) 'Development of an "age universal" I-E scale', *Journal for the Scientific Study of Religion* 22: 181–7.

Green, J.A. (1988) 'Loglinear analysis of cross-classified ordinal data: Applications in developmental research', *Child Development* 59: 1–25.

Gross, A.E. and Fleming, I. (1982) 'Twenty years of deception in social psychology', *Personality and Social Psychology Bulletin* 8: 402–8.

Guttman, L. (1944) 'A basis for scaling quantitative data', *American Sociological Review* 9: 139–50.

Hagen, R.L. (1997) 'In praise of the null hypothesis significance test', *American Psychologist* 52: 15–24.

Hagen, R.L. (1998) 'A further look at wrong reasons to abandon statistical testing', *American Psychologist* 53: 801–2.

Hammersley, M. and Atkinson, P. (1983) *Ethnography: Principles in Practice*, London: Routledge.

Haney, C., Banks, W.C. and Zimbardo, P.G. (1973) 'Interpersonal dynamics in a simulated prison', *International Journal of Criminology and Penology* 1: 69–97.

Harcum, E.R. (1989) 'The highly inappropriate calibrations of statistical significance', *American Psychologist* 44: 964.

Harding, S. (ed.) (1987) *Feminism and Methodology*, Indianapolis: Indiana University Press.

Harré, R. (1993) *Social Being* (2nd edn), Oxford: Blackwell.

Harré, R. and Secord, P.F. (1972) *The Explanation of Social Behaviour*, Oxford: Blackwell.

Harris, R.J. (1985) *A Primer of Multivariate Statistics* (2nd edn), New York: Academic Press.

Heath, C. (1997) 'The analysis of activities in face to face interaction using video', in D. Silverman (ed.) *Qualitative Research: Theory, Method, and Practice*, London: Sage.

Hedges, L.V. and Olkin, I. (1985) *Statistical Methods for Meta-analysis*, Orlando, FL: Academic Press.

Hendrix, L.J., Carter, M.W. and Scott, D.T. (1982) 'Covariance analyses with heterogeneity of slopes in fixed models', *Biometrics* 38: 641–50.

Henwood, K. (1996) 'Qualitative inquiry: perspectives, methods and psychology', in J.T.E. Richardson (ed.) *Handbook of Qualitative Research Methods for Psychology and the Social Sciences*, Leicester: BPS Books.

Henwood, K. and Nicolson, P. (1995) 'Qualitative research', *The Psychologist* 8: 109–10.

Henwood, K.L. and Pidgeon, N.F. (1992) 'Qualitative research and psychological theorizing', *British Journal of Psychology* 83: 97–111.

Hinkle, D. (1965) 'The change of personal constructs from the view point of a theory of construct implications', unpublished PhD thesis, Ohio State University.

Hobbs, D. and May, T. (1993) *Interpreting the Field: Accounts of Ethnography*, Oxford: Clarendon Press.

Hofstede, G. (1980) *Culture's Consequences: International Differences in Work-related Values*, Beverly Hills, CA: Sage.

Hood, N. (2000) 'Constructing phobia', unpublished BSc Dissertation, Sheffield Hallam University.

Howitt, D. and Cramer, D. (2000) *An Introduction to Statistics in Psychology: A Complete Guide for Students* (2nd edn), Harlow: Prentice Hall.

Hoyle, R.H. (ed.) (1995) *Structural Equation Modeling: Concepts, Issues, and Applications*, Thousand Oaks, CA: Sage.

Hubbard, R., Parsa, R.A. and Luthy, M.R. (1997) 'The spread of statistical significance testing in psychology: The case of the *Journal of Applied Psychology*, 1917–1994', *Theory and Psychology* 7: 545–54.

Huberty, C.J. (1984) 'Issues in the use and interpretation of discriminant analysis', *Psychological Bulletin* 95: 156–71.

Huberty, C.J. and Morris, J.D. (1989) 'Multivariate analysis versus multiple univariate analyses', *Psychological Bulletin* 105: 302–8.

Huitema, B.E. (1980) *The Analysis of Covariance and Alternatives*, New York: Wiley.

Hunter, J.E. and Schmidt, F.L. (1990) *Methods of Meta-analysis: Correcting Error and Bias in Research Findings*, Newbury Park, CA: Sage.

Ibáñez, T. and Iñiguez, L. (eds) (1997) *Critical Social Psychology*, London: Sage.

Jenkins, G.D., Mitra, A., Gupta, N. and Shaw, J.D. (1998) 'Are financial incentives related to performance? A meta-analytic review of empirical research', *Journal of Applied Psychology* 83: 777–87.

Jenkins, J.M. and Buccioni, J.M. (2000) 'Children's understanding of marital conflict and the marital relationship', *Journal of Child Psychology and Psychiatry* 41: 161–8.

Kaiser, H.F. (1960) 'The application of electronic computers to factor analysis', *Educational and Psychological Measurement* 20: 141–51.

Kamin, L.J. (1977) *The Science and Politics of I.Q.*, Harmondsworth, Middlesex: Penguin.

Kashima, Y., Yamaguchi, S., Kim, U., Choi, S., Gelfand, M.J. and Yuki, M. (1995) 'Culture, gender and self: A perspective from individualism-collectivism research', *Journal of Personality and Social Psychology* 69: 925–37.

Katsikitis, M. (1997) 'The classification of facial expressions of emotion: A multidimensional-scaling approach', *Perception* 26: 613–26.

Kaufman, G. (1999) 'The portrayal of men's family roles in television commercials', *Sex Roles* 41: 439–58.

Kelly, G. (1955) *The Psychology of Personal Constructs*, Norton: New York.

Kimmel, A.J. (1996) *Ethical Issues in Behavioural Research: A Survey*, Cambridge, MA: Blackwell.

Kline, P. (1994) *An Easy Guide to Factor Analysis*, London: Routledge.

Knight, G.P., Fabes, R.A. and Higgins, D.A. (1996) 'Concerns about drawing causal inferences from meta-analyses: An example in the study of gender differences in aggression', *Psychological Bulletin* 119: 410–21.

Kools, S., McCarthy, M., Durham, R. and Robrecht, L. (1996) 'Dimensional analysis: Broadening the conception of grounded theory', *Qualitative Health Research* 6: 312–30.

Kruskal, J.B. and Wish, M. (1978) *Multidimensional Scaling*, Beverly Hills, CA: Sage.

Kupfersmid, J. (1988) 'Improving what is published: A model in search of an editor', *American Psychologist* 43: 635–42.

Kvale, S. (ed.) (1992) *Psychology and Postmodernism*, London: Sage.

Lawes, R. (1999) 'Marriage: An analysis of discourse', *British Journal of Social Psychology* 38: 1–20.

Lazar, A. and Torney-Purta, J. (1991) 'The development of the subconcepts of death in young children: A short-term longitudinal study', *Child Development* 62: 1321–33.

Levine, J. (1975) 'The nature and definition of informed consent in various research settings', paper prepared for the National Commission for the Protection of Human Subjects of Biomedical and Behavioural Research. Bethesda, MD: US Department of Health, Education and Welfare. Reprinted in Kimmel (1996), *op. cit.*

Levine, M.S. (1977) *Canonical Analysis and Factor Comparison. Series: Quantitative Applications in the Social Sciences*, Beverly Hills, CA: Sage Publications.

Likert, R. (1932) 'A technique for the measurement of attitudes', *Archives of Psychology* 140.

Lingoes, J. and Borg, I. (1976) 'PINDIS: procrustean individual differences scaling', *Journal of Marketing Research* 13: 406–7.

338   *References*

Lippa, R. (1997) 'The display of masculinity, femininity, and gender diagnosticity in self-descriptive photo essays', *Journal of Personality* 65: 137–69.

Livingstone, S. and Green, G. (1986) 'Television advertisements and the portrayal of gender', *British Journal of Social Psychology* 25: 149–54.

Loehlin, J.C. (1992) *Latent Variable Models: An Introduction to Factor, Path, and Structural Analysis* (2nd edn), Hillsdale, NJ: Lawrence Erlbaum.

Macdonald, R.R. (1993) 'Qualitative generalisations from quantitative analyses', *British Journal of Mathematical and Statistical Psychology* 46: 49–62.

Macdonald, R.R. (1997) 'On statistical testing in psychology', *British Journal of Psychology* 88: 333–47.

MacRae, A.W. (1995) 'Statistics in A-level psychology: A suitable case for treatment?', *The Psychologist* 8: 363–6.

McCallum, R.C., Roznowski, M. and Necowitz, L.B. (1992) 'Model modifications in covariance structure analysis: The problem of capitalization on chance', *Psychological Bulletin* 111: 490–504.

McGrath, R.E. (1998) 'Significance testing: Is there something better?', *American Psychologist* 53: 796–7.

McGue, M., Slutske, W. and Iacano, W.G. (1999) 'Personality and substance abuse disorders: II. Alcoholism versus drug use disorders', *Journal of Consulting and Clinical Psychology* 67: 394–404.

Madill, A. and Doherty, K. (1994) '"So you did what you wanted then": Discourse analysis, personal agency, and psychotherapy', *Journal of Community and Applied Social Psychology* 4: 261–73.

Madill, A., Jordan, A. and Shirley, C. (2000) 'Objectivity and reliability in qualitative analysis: Realist, contextualist and radical contructionist epistemologies', *British Journal of Psychology* 91: 1–20.

Maltby, J. (1999) 'Personality dimensions of religious orientation', *Journal of Psychology* 133: 631–40.

Maltby, J., Lewis, C.A. and Hill, A. (eds) (2000) *Commissioned Reviews of 250 Psychological Tests* (vols 1 & 2), Lampeter, Wales: Edwin Mellen Press.

Marcovitch, S. and Zelazo, P.D. (1999) 'The A-not-B error: Results from a logistic meta-analysis', *Child Development* 70: 1297–313.

Marsh, P., Rosser, E. and Harré, R. (1978) *The Rules of Disorder*, London: Routledge and Kegan Paul.

May, R.A.B. (1999) 'Tavern culture and local television viewing: The influence of local viewing culture on patrons' reception of television programs', *Journal of Contemporary Ethnography* 28: 69–99.

Middleton, D. and Edwards, D. (eds) (1990) *Collective Remembering*, London: Sage.

Miles, M.B. and Huberman, A.M. (1994) *Qualitative Data Analysis: An Expanded Sourcebook*, Thousand Oaks, CA: Sage.

Milgram, S. (1974) *Obedience to Authority*, New York: Harper and Row.

Miller, N.B., Cowan, P.A., Cowan, C.P. and Hetherington, E.M. (1993) 'Externalising in preschoolers and early adolescents: A cross-study replication of a family model', *Developmental Psychology* 29: 3–18.

Moore, M., Beazley, S. and Maelzer, J. (1998) *Researching Disability Issues*, Buckingham: Open University Press.

Moran, J. (1998) 'Cultural studies and academic stardom', *International Journal of Cultural Studies*, 1: 67–82.

Morgan, M. (1996) 'Qualitative research: A package deal?', *The Psychologist* 9: 31–2.

Morgan, M. (1998) 'Qualitative research . . . Science or pseudo-science?', *The Psychologist* 11: 481–3.

Moustakas, C. (1994) *Phenomenological Research Methods*, Thousand Oaks, CA: Sage.

Mulry, G., Kalichman, S.C., Kelly, J.A., Ostrow, D.G. and Heckman, T.G. (1997) 'Grouping gay men on dimensions reflecting sexual behaviour preferences: Implication for HIV-AIDS prevention', *Psychology and Health* 12: 405–15.

Murphy, K.R. (1997) 'Editorial', *Journal of Applied Psychology* 82: 3–5.

Murray, K.D. (1995) 'Narratology', in J.A. Smith, R. Harré, and L. Van Langenhove (eds) *Rethinking Psychology*, London: Sage.

Murray, M. and Chamberlain, K. (eds) (1999) *Qualitative Health Psychology: Theories and Methods*, London: Sage.

Neighbors, C.J., O'Leary, A. and Labouvie, E. (1999) 'Domestically violent and nonviolent male inmates' responses to their partners' requests for condom use: Testing a social-information processing model', *Health Psychology* 18: 427–31.

Nicolson, P. (1995) 'Feminism and psychology', in J.A. Smith, R. Harré, and L. Van Langenhove (eds) *Rethinking Psychology*, London: Sage.

Oakes, M. (1986) *Statistical Inference: A Commentary for the Social and Behavioral Sciences*, New York: Wiley.

Orona, C.J. (1997) 'Temporality and identity loss due to Alzheimer's disease', in A.L. Strauss and J. Corbin (eds) *Grounded Theory in Practice*, Thousand Oaks, CA: Sage.

Osgood, C.E., Suci, C.J. and Tannenbaum, P.H. (1957) *The Measurement of Meaning*, Urbana, IL: University of Illinois Press.

Parker, I. (1992) *Discourse Dynamics: Critical Analysis for Social and Individual Psychology*, London: Routledge.

Parker, I. (1994) 'Discourse analysis', in P. Banister, E. Burman, I. Parker, M. Taylor and C. Tindall, *Qualitative Methods in Psychology: A Research Guide*, Buckingham: Open University Press.

Parker, I., Georgaca, E., Harper, D., McLaughlin, T. and Stowell-Smith, M. (1995) *Deconstructing Psychopathology*, London: Sage.

Parker, S. (1995) 'The "difference of means" may not be the "effect size"', *American Psychologist* 50: 1101–02.

Peters, P.D. and Ceci, S.J. (1982) 'Peer-review practices of psychological journals: The fate of published articles, submitted again', *Behavioral and Brain Sciences* 5: 187–255.

Pidgeon, N. (1996) 'Grounded theory: theoretical background', in J.T.E. Richardson (ed.) *Handbook of Qualitative Research Methods for Psychology and the Social Sciences*, Leicester: BPS Books.

Pidgeon, N. and Henwood, K. (1996) 'Grounded theory: practical implementation', in J.T.E. Richardson (ed.) *Handbook of Qualitative Research Methods for Psychology and the Social Sciences*, Leicester: BPS Books.

Pidgeon, N. and Henwood, K. (1997) 'Using grounded theory in psychological research', in N. Hayes (ed.) *Doing Qualitative Analysis in Psychology*, Hove: Psychology Press.

Pollock, P.H. and Kear-Colwell, J.J. (1994) 'Women who stab: A personal construct analysis of sexual victimisation and offending behaviour', *British Journal of Medical Psychology* 67: 13–22.

Potter, J. (1996) 'Discourse analysis and constructionist approaches: Theoretical background', in J.T.E. Richardson (ed.) *Handbook of Qualitative Research Methods for Psychology and the Social Sciences*, Leicester: BPS Books.

Potter, J. (1997) 'Discourse analysis as a way of analysing naturally occurring talk', in D. Silverman (ed.) *Qualitative Research: Theory, Method and Practice*, London: Sage.

Potter, J. and Wetherell, M. (1987) *Discourse and Social Psychology: Beyond Attitudes and Behaviour*, London: Sage.

Price, B. (1977) 'Ridge regression: Application to nonexperimental data', *Psychological Bulletin* 82: 759–66.

Rasch, G. (1960) *Probabilistic Models for Some Intelligence and Attainment Tests*, Chicago, IL: MESA Press.

Reicher, S. (1997) 'Laying the ground for a common critical psychology', in T. Ibáñez and L. Iñiguez (eds) *Critical Social Psychology*, London: Sage.

Reicher, S. (2000) 'Against methodolatry: Some comments on Elliott, Fischer and Rennie', *British Journal of Clinical Psychology* 39: 1–6.

Reinharz, S. (1992) *Feminist Methods in Social Research*, New York: Oxford University Press.

Rennie, D.L. (1998a) 'Grounded theory methodology: The pressing need for a coherent logic of justification', *Theory & Psychology* 8: 101–19.

Rennie, D.L. (1998b) 'Reply to Corbin: From one interpreter to another', *Theory & Psychology* 8: 129–35.

Rennie, D.L. (2000) 'Grounded theory methodology as methodical hermeneutics: Reconciling realism and relativism', *Theory & Psychology* 10: 481–502.

Rhodes, J.E. and Jakes, S. (2000) 'Correspondence between delusions and personal goals: A qualitative analysis', *British Journal of Medical Psychology* 73: 211–25.

Rini, C.K., Dunkel-Schetter, C., Wadhwa, P.D. and Sandman, C.A. (1999) 'Psychological adaptation and birth outcomes: The role of personal resources, stress and sociocultural context in pregnancy', *Health Psychology* 18: 333–45.

Robson, C. (1993) *Real World Research: A Resource for Social Scientists and Practitioner-researchers*, Oxford: Blackwell.

Rose, J.S., Chassin, L., Presson, C.C. and Sherman, S.J. (1996) 'Prospective predictors of quit attempts and smoking cessation in young adults', *Health Psychology* 15: 261–8.

Rose, N. (1990) *Governing the Soul: The Shaping of the Private Self*, London: Routledge.

Rosenthal, R. (1995) 'Writing meta-analytic reviews', *Psychological Bulletin* 118: 183–92.

Rosenthal, R. and Rosnow, R.L. (eds) (1991) *Essentials of Behavioural Research: Methods and Data Analysis* (2nd edn), New York: McGraw-Hill.

Rosenthal, R. and Rubin, D.B. (1994) 'The counternull value of an effect size: A new statistic', *Psychological Science* 5: 329–34.

Rosnow, R.L. and Rosenthal, R. (1989) 'Statistical procedures and the justification of knowledge in psychological science', *American Psychologist* 44: 1276–84.

Rothstein, H.R. and McDaniel, M.A. (1989) 'Guidelines for conducting and reporting meta-analyses', *Psychological Reports* 65: 759–70.

Rozeboom, W.W. (1979) 'Ridge regression: Bonanza or beguilement?', *Psychological Bulletin* 86: 242–9.

Rust, J. and Golombok, S. (1999) *Modern Psychometrics: The Science of Psychological Assessment* (2nd edn), London: Routledge.

Rutherford, A. (1992) 'Alternatives to traditional analysis of covariance', *British Journal of Mathematical and Statistical Psychology* 83: 197–223.

Rutherford, A. (2000) *Introducing ANOVA and ANCOVA: A GLM Approach*, London: Sage.

Sacks, H. (1992) *Lectures on Conversation* (vol. 1 and vol. 2), Oxford: Blackwell.

Sapsford, R. (1999) *Survey Research*, London: Sage.

Schatzman, L. (1991) 'Dimensional analysis: Notes on an alternative approach to the grounding of theory in qualitative research', in D.R. Maines (ed.) *Social Organisation and Social Process*, New York: Aldine.

Schegloff, E.A. (1999) ' "Schegloff's texts" as "Billig's data": A critical reply', *Discourse & Society* 10: 558–72.

Scheidt, D.M. and Windle, M. (1996) 'Individual and situational markers of condom use and sex with nonprimary partners among alcoholic inpatients: Findings from the ATRISK study', *Health Psychology* 15: 185–92.

Seale, C. (2000) 'Using computers to analyse qualitative data', in D. Silverman *Doing Qualitative Research: A Practical Handbook*, London: Sage.

Sedlmeier, P. and Gigerenzer, G. (1989) 'Do studies of statistical power have an effect on the power of studies?', *Psychological Bulletin* 105: 309–16.

Seibert, S.E., Crant, J.M. and Kraimer, M.L. (1999) 'Proactive personality and career success', *Journal of Applied Psychology* 84: 416–27.

Silverman, D. (2000) *Doing Qualitative Research: A Practical Handbook*, London: Sage.

Sloan, T. (ed.) (2000) *Critical Psychology: Voices for Change*, Basingstoke: Macmillan.

Smith, J.A. (1995) 'Idiography and the case study', in J.A. Smith, R. Harré and L. Van Langenhove (eds) *Rethinking Psychology*, London: Sage.

Smith, J.A. (1996a) 'Evolving issues for qualitative psychology', in J.T.E. Richardson (ed.) *Handbook of Qualitative Research Methods for Psychology and the Social Sciences*, Leicester: BPS Books.

Smith, J.A. (1996b) 'Beyond the divide between cognition and discourse: Using interpretative phenomenological analysis in health psychology', *Psychology and Health* 11: 261–71.

Smith, J.A., Jarman, M. and Osborn, M. (1999) 'Doing interpretative phenomenological analysis', in M. Murray and K. Chamberlain (eds) *Qualitative Health Psychology: Theories and Methods*, London: Sage.

Smith, S.G. (1994) 'The psychological construction of home life', *Journal of Environmental Psychology* 14: 125–36.

Sommer, B. (1992) 'Menstruation and performance', in J.T.E. Richardson (ed.) *Cognition and the Menstrual Cycle*, London: Lawrence Erlbaum Associates.

Stainton Rogers, R. (1995) 'Q methodology', in J.A. Smith, R. Harré and L. Van Langenhove (eds) *Rethinking Methods in Psychology*, London: Sage.

Steinberg, L. and Thissen, D. (1996) 'Uses of item response theory and the testlet concept in the measurement of psychopathology', *Psychological Methods* 1: 81–97.

Stenner, P. and Stainton Rogers, R. (1998) 'Jealousy as a manifold of divergent understandings: a Q methodological investigation', *European Journal of Social Psychology* 28: 71–94.

Stenner, P. and Stainton Rogers, R. (in press) 'Q methodology and qualiquantology: The example of discriminating between emotions'.

Stephenson, W. (1935) 'Technique of factor analysis', *Nature* 136: 297.

Steptoe, A. and Wardle, J. (1992) 'Cognitive predictors of health behaviour in contrasting regions of Europe', *British Journal of Clinical Psychology* 31: 485–502.

Sternberg, R.J. (1993) *The Psychologist's Companion: A Guide to Scientific Writing for Students and Researchers* (3rd edn), Cambridge: Cambridge University Press.

Stevens, J. (1996) *Applied Multivariate Statistics for the Social Sciences* (3rd edn), Hillsdale, NJ: Lawrence Erlbaum Associates.

Strauss, A.L. and Corbin, J. (1990/1998) *Basics of Qualitative Research: Techniques and Procedures for Developing Grounded Theory*, Newbury Park, CA: Sage.

Strauss, A.L. and Corbin, J. (eds) (1997) *Grounded Theory in Practice*, Thousand Oaks, CA: Sage.

Stringer, E.T. (1996) *Action Research: A Handbook for Practitioners*, London: Sage.

Stroebe, W., Stroebe, M.S. and Abakoumkin, G. (1999) 'Does differential social support cause sex differences in bereavement outcome?', *Journal of Community and Applied Psychology* 9: 1–12.

Sunderland, J. (2000) 'Baby entertainer, bumbling assistant and line manager: Discourses of fatherhood in parentcraft texts', *Discourse and Society* 11: 249–74.

Tabachnick, B.G. and Fidell, L.S. (2001) *Using Multivariate Statistics* (4th edn), New York: HarperCollins.

Tanaka, J.S. (1987) '"How big is big enough?": Sample size and goodness of fit in structural equation models with latent variables', *Child Development* 58: 134–46.

Taylor, L. (1984) *In the Underworld*, London: Unwin.

Taylor, M. (1994) 'Action research', in P. Banister, E. Burman, I. Parker, M. Taylor and C. Tindall (eds) *Qualitative Methods in Psychology: A Research Guide*, Buckingham: Open University Press.

ten Have, P. (1999) *Doing Conversation Analysis: A Practical Guide*, London: Sage.

Thomas, S. (1994) 'Artifactual study in the analysis of culture: A defense of content analysis in a postmodern age', *Communication Research* 21: 683–97.

Thompson, B. (1998) 'In praise of brilliance: Where that praise really belongs', *American Psychologist* 53: 799–800.

Thompson, B. (1999a) 'Why "encouraging" effect size reporting is not working: The etiology of researcher resistance to changing practices', *Journal of Psychology* 133: 133–40.

Thompson, B. (1999b) 'If statistical significance tests are broken/misused, what practices should supplement or replace them?', *Theory and Psychology* 6: 165–81.

Thurstone, L.L. (1947) *Multiple Factor Analysis: A Development and Expansion of Vectors of the Mind*, Chicago: University of Chicago Press.

Thurstone, L.L. and Chave, E.J. (1929) *The Measurement of Attitude*, Chicago: University of Chicago Press.

Tidwell, M.O., Reis, H.T. and Shaver, P.R. (1996) 'Attachment, attractiveness and social interaction: A diary study', *Journal of Personality and Social Psychology* 71: 729–45.

Tindall, C. (1994) 'Issues of evaluation', in P. Banister, E. Burman, I. Parker, M. Taylor and C. Tindall (eds) *Qualitative Methods in Psychology: A Research Guide*, Buckingham: Open University Press.

Torsch, V.L. and Xueqin-Ma, G. (2000) 'Cross-cultural comparison of health perceptions, concerns, and coping strategies among Asian and Pacific Islander American elders', *Qualitative Health Research* 10: 471–89.

Tryon, W.W. (1998) 'The inscrutable null hypothesis', *American Psychologist* 53: 796–807.

Tweed, A.E. and Salter, D.P. (2000) 'A conflict of responsibilities: A grounded theory study of clinical psychologists' experiences of client non-attendance within the British National Health Service', *British Journal of Medical Psychology* 73: 465–81.

Ullman, J.B. (2001) 'Structural equation modeling', In B.G. Tabachnick and L.S. Fidell, *Using Multivariate Statistics* (3rd edn), New York: HarperCollins.

Ussher, J.M. (1999) 'Feminist approaches to qualitative health research', in M. Murray and K. Chamberlain (eds) *Qualitative Health Psychology: Theories and Methods*, London: Sage.

Uzzell, D. (2000) 'Ethnographic and action research', in G.M. Breakwell, S. Hammond and C. Fife-Schaw (eds) *Research Methods in Psychology* (2nd edn), London: Sage.

van Dijk, T.A. (1993) 'Principles of critical discourse analysis', *Discourse and Society* 4: 249–83.

Vangelisti, A.L., Crumley, L.P. and Baker, J.L. (1999) 'Family portraits: Stories as standards for family relationships', *Journal of Social and Personal Relationships* 16: 335–68.

Vaughn, C.E. and Leff, J.P. (1976) 'The measurement of expressed emotion in the families of psychiatric patients', *British Journal of Social and Clinical Psychology* 15: 157–65.

Weisman, A.G., Nuechterlein, K.H., Goldstein, M.J. and Snyder, K.S. (1998) 'Expressed emotion, attributions, and schizophrenia symptom dimensions', *Journal of Abnormal Psychology* 107: 355–9.

Wellman, H.M., Cross, D. and Bartsch, K. (1986) 'Infant search and object permanence: A meta-analysis of the A-not-B error', *Monographs of the Society for Research in Child Development* 51: 1–51, 62–7.

Westen, D., Murderrisoglu, S., Fowler, C., Shedler, J. and Koren, D. (1997) 'Affect regulation and affective experience: Individual differences, group differences, and measurement using a Q-sort procedure', *Journal of Consulting and Clinical Psychology* 65: 429–39.

Wetherell, M. and Potter, J. (1992) *Mapping the Language of Racism*, Hemel Hempstead: Harvester Wheatsheaf.

Wetherell, M., Taylor, S. and Yates, S.J. (eds) (2001a) *Discourse Theory and Practice: A Reader*. London: Sage.

Wetherell, M., Taylor, S. and Yates, S.J. (eds) (2001b) *Discourse as Data: A Guide for Analysis*, London: Sage.

Whyte, W.F. (1991) *Participatory Action Research*, London: Sage.

Wilkerson, M. and Olson, M.R. (1997) 'Misconceptions about sample size, statistical significance, and treatment effect', *Journal of Psychology* 131: 627–31.

Wilkinson, L. and the APA Task Force on Statistical Inference (1999) 'Statistical methods in psychology journals: Guidelines and explanations', *American Psychologist* 54: 594–604.

Wilkinson, S. (1988) 'The role of reflexivity in feminist research', *Women's Studies International Forum* 11: 493–502.

Wilkinson, S. (ed.) (1996) *Feminist Social Psychologies: International Perspectives*, Buckingham: Open University Press.

Wilkinson, S. (2000) 'Women with breast cancer talking causes: Comparing, content, biographical and discursive analyses', *Feminism & Psychology* 10: 431–60.

Wilkinson, S. and Kitzinger, C. (eds) (1996) *Representing the Other: A 'Feminism & Psychology' Reader*, London: Sage.

Willig, C. (ed.) (1999) *Applied Discourse Analysis: Social and Psychological Interventions*, Chichester: Wiley.

Willott, S. and Griffin, C. (1997) '"Wham Bam, am I a Man?": Unemployed men talk about masculinities', *Feminism & Psychology* 7: 107–28.

Wold, H. (1985) 'Partial least squares', in S. Kotz and N.L. Johnson (eds) *Encyclopaedia of Statistical Sciences* (vol. 6), New York: Wiley.

Woolgar, S. (1988) *Science: The Very Idea*, Chichester: Ellis Horwood.

Yardley, L. (2000) 'Dilemmas in qualitative health research', *Psychology and Health* 15: 215–28.

Yardley, L. and Beech, S. (1998) '"I'm not a doctor": Deconstructing accounts of coping, causes and control of dizziness', *Journal of Health Psychology* 3: 313–27.

Zakzanis, K.K. (1998) 'The reliability of meta-analytic review', *Psychological Reports* 83: 215–22.

Ziller, R.C. (1990) *Photographing the Self*, Newbury Park, CA: Sage.

Index

DATE DUE

2013 -09- 18			